The U.S. Banking System

THIRD EDITION

Center for Financial Training

SOUTH-WESTERN
CENGAGE Learning™

Australia • Brazil • Mexico • Singapore • United Kingdom • United States

SOUTH-WESTERN
CENGAGE Learning™

The U. S. Banking System, **Third edition**
Center For Financial Training

SVP, GM Skills & Global Product Management: Dawn Gerrain

Product Director: Matthew Seeley

Product Manager: Nicole Robinson

Senior Content Developer: Karen Caldwell

Consulting Editor: Hyde Park Publishing Services

Product Assistant: Deborah Handy

Product Marketing Manager: Kelsey Hagan

Art and Cover Direction, Production Management, and Composition: Lumina Datamatics Inc.

Intellectual Property Analyst: Ashley Maynard

Intellectual Property Project Manager: Carissa Poweleit

Manufacturing Planner: Kevin Kluck

Photo Researcher: Darren Wright

Cover Image: iStockphoto.com/konstantin32

Design Images:
Image of gold currency symbols around a globe: Michelangelus/Shutterstock.com,
Calculator and pen on bank account passbook: punsayaporn/Shutterstock.com,
Climbing the Ladder: iStockphoto.com/skodonnell,
Respect Ethics Honest Integrity Signpost: Stuart Miles/Shutterstock.com,
Green plant growing on money coins over: TZIDO SUN/Shutterstock.com,
A key with a dollar-sign: James Steidl/Shutterstock.com,
Laptop, mobile and tab: Daboost/Shutterstock.com,

For product information and technology assistance, contact us at
Cengage Learning Customer & Sales Support, 1-800-354-9706

For permission to use material from this text or product, submit all requests online at **cengage.com/permissions**.
Further permissions questions can be e-mailed to
permissionrequest@cengage.com

Student Edition:
ISBN: 978-1-285-09089-4

Cengage Learning
20 Channel Center Street
Boston, MA 02210
USA

Cengage Learning is a leading provider of customized learning solutions with employees residing in nearly 40 different countries and sales in more than 125 countries around the world. Find your local representative at **www.cengage.com**.

Cengage Learning products are represented in Canada by Nelson Education, Ltd.

For your course and learning solutions, visit **ngl.cengage.com**.
Visit our company website at **www.cengage.com**.

Printed in the United States of America
Print Number: 01 Print Year: 2016

Banking Consultants

Christine Bumgardner
President & CEO
Center for Financial Training
Western States
Denver, Colorado

Marta W. Carey
VP, Distance Learning
Center for Financial Training
Chesterfield, Massachusetts

Loyd Hoskins
Educational Consultant
Loyd Hoskins and Associates
Lakewood, Colorado

Michael Mackay
Senior Vice President, Retired
First Niagara Bank
Albany, New York

Michael Meakem
President
Center for Financial Training
Atlantic & Central States
Norwich, Connecticut

Rita Maria A. St. John
VP/Banking Information Center Manager
Home State Bank
Loveland, Colorado

Michael Phillips
Executive Vice President and
Director of Corporate Administration
State Bank Financial Corporation
Atlanta, Georgia

Jeffrey M. Smith
VP/Chief Lending Officer
Freedom Credit Union
Springfield, Massachusetts

About Center for Financial Training

The Center for Financial Training (CFT) is a network of centers throughout the country that provides career enhancing training solutions to the financial services industry. Through innovative educational formats, CFT is the training partner for financial institutions that helps improve performance to meet the needs of tomorrow's challenging business environment. Visit CFT at www.cftnow.org or call us at 800-795-5242.

Contents

CHAPTER 13

INSIDE THE STUDENT EDITION

climbing the ladder

From Web Content Consultant to Documentation Manager

While his children slept on the flight home from a hectic week at a Florida amusement park, Reza reflected on his career. After college, he had accepted a position at a diversified financial institution. Working as a web marketing consultant for the annuity and mutual funds division, his job involved developing and executing online marketing initiatives. Reza supported multiple products that were advertised on a variety of websites. He developed web content and designed site layouts. Ensuring that the written and visual elements complemented each other and functioned smoothly were a critical part of this position.

Reza had realized he could enhance his job security by working in a variety of areas. Having a broader base of experience also would allow him to expand his personal network.

Next Reza had accepted a job as an implementation technical consultant in the company's credit card division. Reza was responsible for assessing data technology needs, file specifications, and delivery methods. He streamlined processes and met with internal customers to determine electronic reporting formats for products.

Realizing he wanted to move higher in the organization, Reza routinely reviewed internal job postings for supervisory positions. He had been delighted to pass the rigorous interview process for a job as a business technology supervisor in his company's trust division. In this role, Reza was responsible for application systems analysis and programming activities. After leading teams to conduct feasibility studies and time and cost estimates, Reza assigned members of his group to complete various components of the projects.

Reza's stellar reputation as an effective supervisor had led to a job offer as a network security manager. His team was responsible for developing systems and procedures that protected host and network systems from unauthorized access. He managed the creation of firewall security standards and intrusion detection procedures. The team perpetually evaluated the information technology (IT) infrastructure to identify new areas of risk.

After the birth of his twins, Reza had decided to scale back on his hours at the office. By working in his current position as an online training documentation manager, Reza was able to work from home three days a week. The flexibility in his schedule helped him and his wife manage childcare needs. In this position, Reza is responsible for overseeing the content development of online training courses, updating existing online courses, and writing and maintaining operational procedures.

Upper Rungs to Consider

Now that his children were older, Reza realized it was time to find a challenging onsite position. Management positions that Reza planned to look for included technology integration, IT project management, and network operations.

Preparing for the Climb

Over the course of a long career, are there ways to occasionally scale back to handle temporarily demanding life needs? What is the best way to stay involved in your field to make it easy to reenter the field?

1.1   Introduction to Banking

Learning Objectives

1.1.1 Define the business of banking.

1.1.2 Identify trends in modern banking.

Key Terms

- medium of exchange
- financial intermediary
- commercial bank
- retail bank
- central banks

Banking Scene

Edouard Ramirez has taken his first full-time job working as a lifeguard at a local pool. After receiving his first paycheck, Edouard has decisions to make about how to handle his money. Along with choices about budgeting and spending, Edouard must decide what to do with his check, such as how to cash it, where to put his money, how to gain access to it, how to use it effectively, and how to take advantage of the range of financial services available to consumers. Writing checks, using ATMs, learning about debit and credit cards, and investigating forms of saving and investment are all things Edouard wants to consider. How can he get this information?

1.1.1 WHAT IS A BANK?

When you think of a bank, what image comes to mind? Do you see a

FEATURES YOU CAN BANK ON

One World

U.S. Currency Abroad

Of the $1.39 trillion worth of Federal Reserve notes estimated to be in circulation during 2015, at least two-thirds were held by people from abroad. Though their governments have their own money and may not be part of our fiat system, many people around the world use U.S. Federal Reserve notes and coins as a medium of exchange for both local and international business.

Think Critically Why might U.S. currency be seen as valuable in other countries? Why might people who have no direct business with anyone in the United States value U.S. currency?

> **ONE WORLD** addresses relevant international banking topics.

Tech Talk

Measuring Nontraditional Forms of Money

How do "electronic money" and automated payment systems affect the money supply and monetary policies? These nontraditional forms can alter the measurement of the money supply, which in turn could shift the way monetary policy is implemented. Most consumer electronic money falls easily into the M1 demand-deposit category, and it has already begun to be measured as such. But as these services grow, they may alter the definition of certain monetary instruments. Economists rely less on the M1 and M2 measures than they once did, and some think they are relatively unimportant.

Think Critically Why are the M1 and M2 measures becoming less important? How does changing technology also alter the Federal Reserve's supervisory task?

> **TECH TALK** discusses the use of technology and its impact on the banking industry.

Ethics in Action

Banks are required by law to offer their products and services on an equal opportunity basis. According to the Federal Trade Commission, the Equal Credit Opportunity Act (ECOA), and the Consumer Financial Protection Bureau ensures that all consumers are given an equal chance to obtain credit. This doesn't mean all consumers who apply for credit get it. Factors such as income, expenses, debt, and credit history are considerations for creditworthiness.

What the law guarantees is that all applicants be treated fairly. Applications for credit cannot be evaluated on the basis of gender, race, marital status, national origin, or religion.

Think Critically

Banks want to attract and keep customers. Why do you think a law like ECOA might have become necessary?

> **ETHICS IN ACTION** challenges students to think about legal and ethical issues related to banking.

branching out

Walmart

Realizing that a substantial number of its customers do not have traditional bank accounts, Walmart developed creative ways of providing financial services. Walmart partnered with a variety of third parties to provide bank-like services to its customers. By developing these partnerships, Walmart was not required to go through the regulatory processes and approvals required of banks. The Walmart MoneyCard is one example of a product developed as a result of a partnership. The MoneyCard allows customers to set up direct deposit of their payroll checks onto their Walmart MoneyCard. When the MoneyCard is used for a transaction, the stored value of the money on the card is used. The MoneyCard is not a credit card. No credit check or bank account is required. There can be fees for reloading the card, for monthly card maintenance, and for assorted administrative costs that a customer may elect to use. Under certain circumstances, specific fees may be waived.

Think Critically How does the entry of a retail outlet with the consumer reach of Walmart affect competition within the banking industry?

> **BRANCHING OUT** presents interesting and unique ways banks and other companies provide banking services.

skills that pay dividends

Quantitative Skills

The choice of computing methods—from calculators, to cell phones, to spreadsheets, to online services—has made it extraordinarily easy for you to enter data into a computing device and get an answer. Whether doing multiplication to calculate the cost of buying enough pizzas for a Little League team or performing complex analytical functions to determine the economic performance of a business, you can get a machine to provide an answer.

Do people using electronic calculators understand the concepts behind the computations? If electricity failed and batteries were not available, could most people manually calculate the answers? Maybe not, given the scores from U.S. students during a recent International Student Assessment that indicated 15-year-old U.S. students performed less well on math than peers from 23 other countries.

The ability to mentally perform a "ballpark" calculation for financial transactions enables you to think on your feet. You will be able to quickly assess the reasonableness of the results you see on your screen. By having a rough idea of what an answer should be, you can catch errors early on.

In the banking industry, percentages are used in a variety of ways. Calculations that use percentages include simple interest and mutual fund performance.

Simple interest is calculated by multiplying the beginning amount, or principal, by the interest rate and by the duration of the investment. The interest rate is expressed as a percentage. The duration of the investment is expressed, in decimal form, in relation to a year. A three-month investment is 25 percent of a year, or 0.25 years. A 21-month investment is 1.75 years.

Mutual funds are comprised of a variety of distinct investments that have various degrees of risk and varying maturity dates. Typically the investments are diversified across a number of different industries to minimize the exposure caused by a downturn in any specific industry. The performance of each investment in each industry contributes to the performance of the fund as a whole.

Mutual fund returns are expressed based on the performance of each industry in the fund. For example, the fund may state that 50 percent of its results are based on performance of the airline industry, 30 percent on the performance of the pharmaceutical industry, and 20 percent on the performance of the software industry. Stated another way, half of the fund is invested in the airline industry, a bit less than a third is invested in the pharmaceutical industry, and one fifth of it is invested in the software industry.

Develop Your Skill

Create a quiz on percentages that has 10 values and 10 percentages to calculate. Exchange papers with classmates and complete the quizzes. Grade the quizzes and see who had the greatest percentage of correct answers.

> **SKILLS THAT PAY DIVIDENDS** focuses on the necessary skills required for success in the banking industry.

SPECIAL FEATURES ENHANCE LEARNING

NET KNOWLEDGE

NET KNOWLEDGE incorporates Internet-based research activities into every chapter.

Tax incentives influence consumer behavior in support of government objectives. Visit the IRS website to learn about hybrid cars and alternative fuel vehicles. Review the current status of hybrid vehicle tax credits. Would the stated tax credit influence your decision about what type of car to purchase? Why or why not?

Banking Math *Connection*

Calculate the one-year spread for a bank that receives a deposit of $10,000 from a customer and lends it out to a homeowner who needs to make some repairs. Assume the bank pays a straight 6 percent per year interest to the customer and charges 12 percent per year for the loan.

Solution

The formula for calculating the spread is

Income from interest − Interest paid to depositors = Spread
Income from interest: 12% × $10,000 = $1,200
Interest to depositor: 6% × $10,000 = $\underline{\ \ \ 600}$
                                                Spread = $600

The spread is $600. This is a simplified example and does not take into account compounding, declining balances, or other factors that affect deposits and loans in the real world.

BANKING MATH CONNECTION provides worked examples that reinforce and review math concepts used in the banking world.

interesting *facts*

The word *bank* comes from the Italian word *banco*, or bench, from which money changers in medieval Italy carried on their business in the marketplace. ▪

INTERESTING FACTS offers additional information about the topic at hand.

"**communicate**"

Interview someone who experienced either the Great Depression firsthand or a recent FDIC takeover of a financial institution. Find out ways that people coped with the economic crisis. Write a short report on what you learn and what your interviewee thinks should be learned from bank failures.

COMMUNICATE provides activities to reinforce, review, and practice communication skills.

ONGOING ASSESSMENT

✓checkpoint

List four functions that define a bank.

_____

_____

CHECKPOINT   allows students to assess their understanding at key points in each lesson.

assessment 1.1

Think Critically

1. What are ways a bank is like any other business? What are ways it is different from other businesses?

2. Name three ways you interact with your own bank. For each, explain how technology has changed the interaction between the bank and the customer.

3. Why do governments regulate banks?

4. What challenges do you think the trend toward mergers poses to banks? What skills will these challenges require of those making careers in banking?

Make Academic Connections

5. **COMMUNICATION**   Banking has changed over the years. Interview a member of a previous generation to find out more. Prepare a list of questions that will generate memories about banking in earlier days. What were banks and banking like? In what specific ways have banks changed? Which of those changes were for the better? Which, in the opinion of your interviewee, were for the worse? Compare the results of your interview with those of classmates. Compile a class list or table showing the composite results.

6. **MATH**   In international banking, exchange rates are used to compute the value of currencies between different countries. Locate the current exchange rates in a newspaper or on the Internet. Using these exchange rates, compute the value of $20,000 $US expressed in Canadian dollars, Mexican pesos, and Japanese yen.

THINK CRITICALLY   provides opportunities to apply concepts.

MAKE ACADEMIC CONNECTIONS   offers integrated curriculum activities that show how banking concepts relate to other courses of study.

CHAPTER ASSESSMENT   includes a summary of concepts and a variety of review questions and activities that apply and test student knowledge.

---

chapter 1 assessment

Chapter Summary

1.1 Introduction to Banking
A. Banks are financial intermediaries that safeguard, transfer, exchange, and lend money. Commercial, retail, and central banks are three main types.
B. Mergers, technology, and competition have reshaped banking.

1.2 Role of Banks in the Economy
A. Banks safeguard our money through various business practices that protect, record, and evaluate banking transactions and businesses.
B. Banks expand the economy by transferring and lending funds to creditworthy borrowers, thus supporting markets and providing economic stimulus for jobs.

1.3 How the Banking System Works
A. Banks make money on the spread between interest paid and received. Bank assets include earnings and investments. Deposits are liabilities. ROA and ROE are two ratios used to measure a bank's profitability.
B. Bank deregulation brought expansion of customer services. New services banks offer to stay competitive involve credit cards, new types of loans, smart cards, online banking, and mobile banking.

1.4 Other Financial Institutions
A. Depository intermediaries include banks, savings and loan associations, mutual savings banks, and credit unions. Most of these are backed by the government.
B. Nondepository institutions include insurance companies, trust companies, brokerage houses, loan companies, and currency exchanges. Most of these are private firms not part of the national banking system.

Vocabulary Builder

a. asset
b. central banks
c. commercial bank
d. creditworthy
e. depositor
f. depository intermediary
g. deregulation
h. equity
i. financial intermediary
j. identity theft
k. liability
l. liquid asset
m. medium of exchange
n. niche market
o. nondepository intermediary
p. profit
q. retail bank
r. return on assets (ROA)
s. return on equity (ROE)
t. spread
u. wholesale bank

Choose the term that best fits the definition. Write the letter of the answer in the space provided. Some terms may not be used.

___ 1. The difference between interest paid and interest received
___ 2. A private company that does not receive deposits but sells financial services
___ 3. Government banks that regulate and manage money supply
___ 4. The ratio of net income to total assets
___ 5. Most common form of government-backed corporate bank
___ 6. To banks, deposits represent this type of obligation
___ 7. The loosening of government control
___ 8. Anything of value that can be readily exchanged
___ 9. Revenue minus cost
___ 10. An agreed-upon system for measuring value of goods and services
___ 11. Net income ÷ Total equity
___ 12. Total assets − Total liabilities

Review Concepts

13. Why are banks called financial intermediaries?

14. List four functions that banks perform.

Apply What You Learned

26. How did deregulation ultimately result in more banking services for consumers?

27. Would consumers be better off if all public utilities, including electric and gas companies, were deregulated so that the marketplace could set prices?

Make Academic Connections

31. **CRITICAL THINKING**   Most insurance is bought to protect against the possibility of loss, except life insurance. Everybody who buys life insurance eventually dies. Explain how life insurance works.

32. **ADVERTISING**   Analyze five bank advertisements from a variety of media, such as newspapers, magazines, radio, television, billboards, and the Internet. What do banks do to get your business? Keep a journal for one week, noting each advertiser, the services being advertised, and a basic description of each ad. Make a chart that shows your analysis.

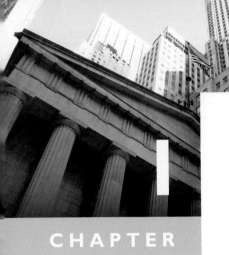

CHAPTER

1

The Business of Banking

iStockphoto.com/istockshares

2

climbing the ladder

From Human Resources Assistant to Human Resources Specialist

Leya, a banking human resources specialist, finished giving a brief welcoming speech to a group of administrative assistants recently hired. Their eager faces and attentive manner prompted her to reflect fondly on the beginning of her career.

Leya began her banking career as a human resources administrative assistant. This entry-level position provided Leya the opportunity to demonstrate her project management skills. By effectively processing job applications, co-coordinating new employee orientation, administrating employee training schedules, and handling travel schedules and expense reports for managers, she had proven herself as a reliable employee.

Leya's experience with new employees helped her earn an entry-level corporate recruiter position. Conducting reference checks, overseeing background investigations, and arranging pre-employment drug screening were among her routine duties. Leya also enjoyed publicizing job postings, following up on employee referrals, representing her bank at career fairs, and traveling to colleges for campus recruitment.

As Leya had a knack for recognizing talent and sending viable candidates forward for additional interviews, she was tapped for a position as a corporate recruiter. To ensure she carried out her duties effectively, and in compliance with the law, Leya obtained training in employment law as well as wage and hour regulations. She also received training regarding how to avoid discrimination in the hiring process.

Her duties as a corporate recruiter varied. She updated and maintained her bank's Open Requisition Report that contained job postings for all open positions. Leya managed the bank's New Hire Orientation Program. She also participated in final hiring interviews for management level employees. Developing employment agreements was another part of her job.

As a corporate recruiter, Leya conducted exit interviews for employees. She developed a continuous improvement program, which incorporated comments of exiting employees to develop strategies for reducing turnover.

With the breadth of her prior experience to support her, Leya applied for and obtained her current position as a human resources specialist. Leya enjoys her current duties, which include staying current on banking salary trends to ensure her company offered competitive salaries, developing best practices for employee career development, and facilitating smooth transitions of employees from acquired banks into her bank's organization.

Upper Rungs to Consider

Leya finds her current position challenging and gratifying. In order to prepare for future job opportunities, she plans to investigate the job responsibilities for a human resources manager and for a corporate training manager.

Preparing for the Climb

Career manuals often suggest taking on pieces of jobs that you would like to have while you are still in your current role. Are there responsibilities or projects you could ask for, in your current job, that would give you experience in a job you would like to have?

What are those projects? What areas of banking interest you the most? If they are outside of your current position, how can you gain experience in those areas so you are prepared when there is an opening? Have you discussed your career goals with your supervisor or manager?

1.1

Introduction to Banking

Learning Objectives

1.1.1 Define the business of banking.

1.1.2 Identify trends in modern banking.

Key Terms

- medium of exchange
- financial intermediary
- commercial bank
- retail bank
- central banks

Banking Scene

Edouard Ramirez has taken his first full-time job working as a lifeguard at a local pool. After receiving his first paycheck, Edouard has decisions to make about how to handle his money. Along with choices about budgeting and spending, Edouard must decide what to do with his check, such as how to cash it, where to put his money, how to gain access to it, how to use it effectively, and how to take advantage of the range of financial services available to consumers. Writing checks, using ATMs, learning about debit and credit cards, and investigating forms of saving and investment are all things Edouard wants to consider. How can he get this information?

1.1.1 WHAT IS A BANK?

When you think of a bank, what image comes to mind? Do you see a nearby building where people deposit their paychecks? Maybe you visualize the automated teller machine (ATM) where people use a card to get cash fast, or you recall the bank statements that some people still get in the mail. Perhaps you see a tall tower with a logo or a name you recognize. Maybe you think of managing all of your accounts from the convenience of your home computer or laptop. Performing account management functions from your cell phone is another option.

However you think of banks, and they include all these ideas and more, don't lose track of one basic idea. A bank is a business. Banks sell their services to earn money, and they market and manage those services in a competitive field. In many ways, banks are like other businesses that must earn a profit to survive. Understanding this fundamental idea helps explain how banks work, and helps you understand many modern trends in banking and finance.

A Unique Business

Banks, of course, don't manufacture cell phones or repair automobiles. The services banks offer to customers have to do almost entirely with handling money for other people. Money is a medium of exchange, an agreed-upon system for measuring the value of goods and services. Once, and still in some places today, precious stones, animal products, or other goods of value might be used as a medium of exchange. Roman soldiers were sometimes paid in

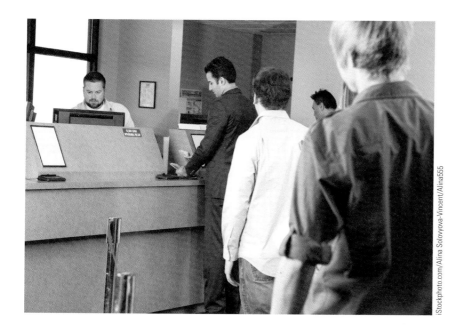

iStockphoto.com/Alina Solovyova-Vincent/Alina555

salt, because it was critical to life and not easy to get. The word *salary* and the expression *not worth his salt* come from that practice. Anything with an agreed-upon value might be a medium of exchange. Today, many forms of money are used. Money simply shows how much something is worth, whether it is a new stereo or two hours of your labor. When you have money, a bank can act as your agent for using or protecting that money. A bank is a financial intermediary for the safeguarding, transferring, exchanging, or lending of money. Banks distribute the medium of exchange.

Because banks and money are essential to maintaining not only economies but entire societies, they are closely regulated and must operate by strict procedures and principles. In the United States, banks may be chartered by federal or state governments. Banks are usually corporations and may be owned by groups of individuals, corporations, or some combination of the two. In the United States, all federally chartered banks have been required to be corporations since 1863. A few states permit noncorporate banks, which are owned by partnerships or individuals. Around the world, however, banks are supervised by governments to guarantee the safety and stability of the money supply and of the country.

Types of Banks

Many businesses are involved in financial services. If you consider the definition of a bank to be a business that safeguards, transfers, exchanges, and lends money, many firms might qualify. Certainly banks perform these roles, but so do trust companies, insurance companies, stockbrokers, investment bankers, and other companies. Since the deregulation of banks in in the 1980s, there has been a blurring of the line between "pure" banking and other providers of financial and investment services. Banks provide a multitude of financial services beyond the traditional practices of holding deposits and lending money. Consequently, not only has banking changed considerably, so have the people who work in the banking world.

iStockphoto.com/andresr

- **Commercial banks** are the institutions commonly thought of as banks. Commercial banks provide familiar services such as checking and savings accounts, credit cards, investment services, and others. Historically, commercial banks offered their services only to businesses. Today, commercial banks seek the business of any worthy customer.

- **Retail banks** and other thrift institutions such as mutual savings banks, savings and loans, and credit unions, developed to help individuals not served by commercial banks. These institutions help customers save money, acquire loans, and invest. They also offer a wide range of financial services to a broad customer base.

- **Central banks** are the government banks that manage, regulate, and protect both the money supply and the banks themselves. Central banks serve as the government's banker. Central banks issue currency and conduct monetary policy. In the United States, the Federal Reserve System performs the central banking function. Although the Federal Reserve is technically owned by the banks themselves, the Board of Governors is appointed by the President with the consent of the Senate. The President also selects the powerful chair of the Federal Reserve.

Edouard Ramirez has a number of options for what he might do with his paycheck. He'll need to know more about banking to make wise decisions that fit his needs.

✔checkpoint

List four functions that define a bank.

1.1.2 Banking Today ●

Banking used to be thought of as a solid and slow-moving industry. Banking today is an exciting, fast-moving, around-the-clock, global activity. Changes in regulation, changes in technology, and changes in competition have pushed banking, like most other businesses, to become organizations that must respond rapidly to changing business conditions in order to survive.

Mergers

One of the most significant changes in banking in the last 20 years has been the number of mergers. A *merger* occurs when one or more banks join or acquire another bank or banks. Mergers increase the size of banks, giving them more resources. Mergers also decrease the number of banks.

The effects of mergers have been mixed. Banks are larger and ownership is concentrated. Fewer banks control more and more of the nation's money. The six largest banks in the United States now have 67% of the total assets in the U.S. financial system. That is up 37% from 2008. This is not only due to mergers but to bank failings as well. More than 500 banking institutions have failed since the banking crisis of 2007. Another 900 banking institutions have disappeared due to mergers creating a lot less competition for those assets.

The top ten largest banks in the world in 2015 include two banks from the United States. The U.S. uses a different accounting method than the rest of the world for total assets. The Unites States uses GAAP (generally accepted accounting principles), which reports only net derivative positions, while the rest of the world uses IFRS (international financial reporting standards), which reports gross derivatives.

Top Ten Largest Banks Worldwide

(Ranked by size of assets)

Rank	Bank	Country	Total Assets (US$ Billion)
1	Industrial and Commercial Bank of China	China	3,616.39
2	China Construction Bank Corp	China	2,939.15
3	Agricultural Bank of China	China	2,816.60
4	Bank of China	China	2,629.31
5	HSBC Holdings	U.K.	2,571.71
6	JPMorgan Chase & Co	U.S.	2,449.60
7	BNP Paribas	France	2,400.04
8	Mitsubishi UFJ Financial Group	Japan	2,323.24
9	Bank of America	U.S.	2,149.03
10	Credit Agricole Group	France	1,911.27

RELBANKS 2015 STATISTICS

After a merger, some consumers face higher fees and find less community involvement and lending in local areas. People like to feel that their money is staying home. Mergers also created an opening, though, for a new wave of small local banks. Small banks have doubled the amount loaned to businesses in the last decade.

Banking is an international business as well, and it is becoming more so all the time. Technology has allowed instant communication as well as transfer of funds, so barriers of geography apply less than ever. U.S. commercial banks actively seek international business, putting together huge investment transactions overseas and engaging in investment banking prohibited in the United States.

Technology

As with many industries, technology has changed everything. Perhaps no business has been more affected by the growth of computers and telecommunications than banking. Not only have accounting, auditing, and

Rafael Ramirez Lee/Shutterstock.com

examining functions been taken over by fast and efficient technology, funds transfer, record keeping, and financial analyses have become instantaneous because of the powerful tools now available.

Technology's changes are not limited to bankers, either. Consumers' relationships with their banks have changed also. Gone are the banker's hours of 9:00 a.m. to 3:00 p.m. Today's consumers want instantaneous access to banking services just as they do from other businesses. They want access to their money and account information at any time. Automated teller machines (ATMs), networked computers that allow access from around the world, "smart" cards with embedded microchips, online and mobile banking via the Internet and cell phone, and the ability to deposit a check remotely (remote deposit) are some of the technological innovations changing the face of banking.

Banks have, in essence, revolutionized their own industry. In the last 20 years, banks have successfully implemented technology that will forever change the day-to-day business of banking. Everything from instant-issue debit card machines, more sophisticated online platforms, mobile banking, and Remote Deposit Capture machines, to name a few. The *brick and mortar* banking model, while certainly valuable, is being complemented by serious advancements in technology.

Competition

Banking is a business, and as with any business, competition is an ongoing challenge. As government regulations have loosened, competition between banks has become fiercer. This fact has resulted in mergers and decreasing numbers of banks, but it has also made more services available to consumers, as banks compete to earn customers' financial business. Banks compete not only with other banks, but also with other businesses that sell financial services, such as credit unions. Banks are more sales oriented than ever, with an emphasis on service, innovation, and marketing that could scarcely have been imagined 30 years ago.

"communicate"

Interview someone from a local bank and learn more about its history. Find out when and where it was founded and how it has changed over the years. Prepare a brief PowerPoint presentation for the class. Be sure to identify your sources.

✔checkpoint

What three factors in modern banking have changed the industry?

assessment 1.1

Think Critically

1. What are ways a bank is like any other business? What are ways it is different from other businesses?

2. Name three ways you interact with your own bank. For each, explain how technology has changed the interaction between the bank and the customer.

3. Why do governments regulate banks?

4. What challenges do you think the trend toward mergers poses to banks? What skills will these challenges require of those making careers in banking?

Make Academic Connections

5. **COMMUNICATION** Banking has changed over the years. Interview a member of a previous generation to find out more. Prepare a list of questions that will generate memories about banking in earlier days. What were banks and banking like? In what specific ways have banks changed? Which of those changes were for the better? Which, in the opinion of your interviewee, were for the worse? Compare the results of your interview with those of classmates. Compile a class list or table showing the composite results.

6. **MATH** In international banking, exchange rates are used to compute the value of currencies between different countries. Locate the current exchange rates in a newspaper or on the Internet. Using these exchange rates, compute the value of $20,000 $US expressed in Canadian dollars, Mexican pesos, and Japanese yen.

1.2

Role of Banks in the Economy

Learning Objectives

1.2.1 List banking activities that contribute to economic stability.

1.2.2 Explain how banking expands the economy.

Key Terms

- identity theft
- creditworthy

Banking Scene

As Edouard Ramirez thinks about how to use his paycheck, he begins to notice money and banking in the world around him. On the radio and television, he hears ads about buying new cars with low interest rates and financing or refinancing plans for houses. He sees people using checks, debit cards, and credit cards as well as cash at the grocery store. Some even use an ATM in the store. When Edouard notices a clerk examining a 20-dollar bill at a fast-food restaurant, he begins to wonder about the nature of money itself. What other ways do banking functions play a role in Edouard's life?

1.2.1 BANKS AND ECONOMICS ● ● ● ● ● ● ● ● ● ● ● ● ● ● ● ● ● ●

Money is a medium of exchange and the basis of the modern economy. Banks play a huge role in the distribution of funds throughout society. Although there are many institutions involved in the movement of money today, banks remain fundamental to the flow of money that maintains local, national, and global economies.

Banks and other institutions play this critical role by performing services essential to the functioning of an economy. Safeguarding, transferring, lending, and exchanging money in various forms, along with evaluating creditworthiness of customers, are the main functions that banks perform. Each of these roles has a ripple effect in the economy that helps keep money moving.

Keeping Your Money Safe

Safeguarding the holdings of people may be the oldest bank function. Long before banks existed, people looked for ways to secure their valuables, whatever the medium of exchange. Many of these you may easily imagine. In some societies, such as Babylonia about 2000 b.c., people began to store money in temples, perhaps because they thought others would be less likely to steal from houses of gods. Ancient records indicate that about 4,000 years ago temples were in the business of lending and exchanging money. At that time, temples were acting as banks.

You may think of a bank vault or a safe deposit box when you think of safeguarding money, and those on-site measures are certainly ways of protecting valuable assets. Yet there is much more to safeguarding money than simply storing it in a secure place.

Stockbyte/Getty Images

- **Record keeping is an important part of securing your money.** Banks devote much time and attention to both the practice and technology of maintaining and storing accurate records. If banks expect you to let them hold and use your money, they know you expect them to keep careful track of it. The same principle applies to large transactions between banks and industry and between banking institutions and the government.

- **Identification is an important security function of banking.** Obviously, you don't want unauthorized people walking in and taking money from your account, but the issue of security and identification goes far beyond the local branch. Identity theft is a growing concern in the economy, and bank officials work closely with technology experts and law-enforcement agencies to prevent various forms of it. Identity theft occurs when someone achieves financial gain by using another person's personal information to unlawfully assume the identity of the other person. An identity thief conducts transactions illegally for personal gain. With the increased reliance on the Internet for financial transactions, identity theft protections extend beyond conventional checking accounts to include online banking, automatic bill pay, and online shopping.

  Financial institutions are required by the U.S. government to know their customer. The Customer Identification Program (CIP) was implemented in 2003 as part of the USA Patriot Act. Institutions are required to develop a CIP process that is appropriate to their size and incorporate it with the institution's Bank Secrecy Act/Anti-money laundering compliance program. Whether customers are new to the institution or currently existing, the bank employee must verify their true identity when the customer is opening a deposit account or applying for a loan.

- **Enforcement is a part of safeguarding money that involves catching those who attempt to take it.** Not only does this function involve physical security, but it also includes tracking down fraud, making collections, and pursuing legal actions against those who inflict losses on the bank. Robbers, white-collar embezzlers, or people who default on loans are all included in the group targeted by enforcement efforts.

- **Transfer security is important to banks.** Although cash is still an important part of bank transactions, most money moves electronically. High-tech security measures are increasingly more critical to banking operations between banks and customers, between banks and banks, and between banks and the government. As all financial intermediaries become more dependent on electronic banking, technological security takes a on a more significant role.

- **Sound business practices also safeguard your money.** Most of these involve good judgment and management of daily bank operations. Banks invest time and money to train employees in procedures and practices. Training goals include ensuring accuracy, encouraging good decision-making regarding creditworthiness of perspective customers, and teaching how to make sound financial decisions.

- **Federal and/or state bank examiners closely review the records of banks to protect consumers.** Their examinations include not only the accuracy of records but also the prudence of banks' policies. These thorough examinations may take a week or more for a small bank, and a much longer time for a larger institution.

The Dodd-Frank Wall Street Reform and Consumer Protection Act of 2010 established the Consumer Financial Protection Bureau which has taken primary jurisdiction for consumer protection. You can see how these various ways of safeguarding your money work together within the local bank and the banking community at large to create a more secure financial environment. This system of checks and balances is important to the economy and to society.

 checkpoint

Name six ways banks safeguard your money.

1.2.2 SPREADING THE WEALTH

Banks are critical to the economy. Although there are many ways that money moves around the economy, banks play a central role in establishing the financial environment. Transferring money to provide growth and stabilizing the monetary supply are important functions performed by banks. Lending by banks makes money available to consumers and businesses to make purchases they might not otherwise be able to make, or at least not for a very long time. Banks also help determine the creditworthiness of prospective customers so that good money is not lost on bad loans.

Transferring

Banks move money. They move it between banks, between banks and individual customers, between banks and industry, between banks and governments, and sometimes between governments. Sometimes the sums involved are

Photodisc/Getty Images

huge. This motion of money throughout the nation and the world allows businesses to have access to capital. With capital to invest, businesses expand, job creation occurs, products get manufactured, services are performed, and the economy grows. This large-scale transfer of assets is a feature of the modern economy particularly in an age of fierce competition and globalization. Industries seek out financing wherever they can find it, and banks seek out investment opportunities wherever they may be.

In international banking, exchange rates measure the relative strength of one form of currency against another. These variable rates are often indications of the strength of a nation's economic position.

The ability to transfer sums of money between financial institutions safely and effectively depends on the stability of the institutions, the stability of the countries where the banks reside, and the security of the money supply itself.

Lending

Need a new car? Reach into your wallet and pull out $28,000. How about a new home? Do you have $246,000 in your piggy bank? Most people don't, of course, and bank lending is the main reason that people are able to own

One World

The European Union and the Euro

In Europe, banking has changed dramatically in the past decade. European nations have been working since 1958 to provide a single market and single banking structure. The European Union (EU) currently consists of 28 nations. On January 4, 1999, these nations began using the euro, an agreed-upon currency with stable values among the nations. For example, a euro is always worth 6.55957 French francs, the same way a dollar is always worth ten dimes, regardless of the overseas value of a dollar.

Nineteen EU member countries use the euro. A few nonmember nations also use the euro.

The implications for banking were huge. Although recognizing the primacy of a host country's banking laws, member nations accepted common rules and a common central bank, the European Central Bank (ECB), for the euro. All government debt, stock quotes, prices, and monetary policies were referenced in euros. Results have been mixed so far, as differing laws in countries have affected the flow of capital. However, with the pressures of technology and globalization increasing, the EU may eventually bring about price stability, increased banking efficiency, and more services for member nations and their neighbors.

Photodisc/Getty Images

Think Critically
What are the advantages of using a common currency for member nations? Why might some nations be reluctant to do so? Do you think there will ever be a world currency? Why or why not?

homes and cars without needing all the cash on hand.

Lending makes up most of a bank's business. Many bank deals are more complex than automobile or home loans. In fact, banks lend money to businesses and governments in a wide variety of ways, with loan duration ranging from a single day to decades. A variety of loan products provide many choices for banks to transfer money in the economy. In the far-ranging and fast-moving world of banking, strong management skills and a thorough understanding of finance are required.

Credit cards issued by banks are another form of lending, and they are not only good business for the bank, but they also help the economy. People buy goods and services with credit. This keeps merchandise moving and manufacturing producing at a more rapid rate than if transactions had to take place in cash. Although there is risk in the unwise use of credit cards by consumers, the judicious use of credit stimulates the economy.

Home loans are an important part of the banking business, too. Loan decisions need to be made in a healthy, rational way to borrowers who are qualified for the loans they obtain. The mortgage loan crisis that began escalating in the summer of 2007 illustrates the fundamental importance of a healthy, stable mortgage market in the U.S. economy. As the mortgage crisis escalated, the ripple effect of loan defaults were seen in all areas of the economy—from the impact on the personal lives of individual homeowners, to businesses that did not get paid, to municipalities that were faced with bearing the costs of maintaining the safety of abandoned properties.

People want to own their own homes and will work hard to do so. Matching appropriate loans to qualified buyers facilitates long-term home ownership. A healthy housing economy provides jobs for people who construct, furnish, and repair homes. Workers in construction industries want homes built, furnished, and repaired for themselves, and so the cycle of economic activity expands. Without bank lending, the cycle would be far smaller and slower. The automobile and housing industries have grown hand in hand with a solid banking industry, and the American economy has grown with it.

Creditworthiness

A creditworthy customer has a good credit rating, sufficient collateral for loans, and an ongoing income source sufficient to make timely loan payments. Evaluating the creditworthiness of customers, whether they are large industries, governments, or individual consumers, is a critical banking function that affects the economy. It is a good business practice for banks to evaluate loan applications carefully because their profits, and in some cases their survival, depend upon being repaid the principal and the interest from loans. If banks were to overextend themselves with uncollected loans, they could begin to fail, and if they fail, the economy is at risk. Bank failures played a role in the Great Depression. The mortgage loan crisis, which began in the summer of 2007, pushed the American economy into a recession. Banking policies and regulations regarding creditworthiness and the ratio of loans to deposits help guarantee a secure financial environment. These policies also assure that businesses get paid for the things that consumers buy with bank funds.

NET KNOWLEDGE

Compare interest rates offered at local banks. Find a website that compares mortgage rates and search for mortgage rates by selecting your state, nearest city, type of loan, and feature that is most important to you. Are you surprised at the amount of variation in interest rates? Is there any reason you might choose an account with lower interest?

Guaranteeing the Money

So what makes that piece of green paper that Edouard handed the cashier worth 20 dollars? The government guarantees the value of money, and the banks back up the guarantee. In the United States, banks and the government work together to form the banking system and to make sure the money supply is adequate, appropriate, and trustworthy. Much of this guarantee is backed through the central banking function of the Federal Reserve. Individual banks also work with the government to implement monetary policy, perform exchange functions for citizens, defeat counterfeiters of currency, and prevent identity theft.

If you write a check or schedule a payment from your account through online banking, you can be sure the recipient of the check or payment will get his or her money from your bank, provided you have sufficient funds in your account to cover the payment.

The Substance of Society

The functions that banking institutions perform do more than move money through the economy. They also provide a common system. A great part of an economic system is psychological. It is your belief and trust in the financial system that makes you willing to borrow and pay later for a car, to invest money in businesses you've never seen, to deposit money in banks that is in turn loaned to people you don't know, or to take on a 30-year mortgage. Banks are at the heart of this financial system, and their effect on your life cannot be calculated.

✔checkpoint

How does lending stimulate the economy?

assessment 1.2

Think Critically

1. How do banks contribute to the stability of the society at large while safeguarding the funds of their own customers?

2. Governments don't routinely examine the books of many businesses. Poor business practices just put them out of business. Why should banks be treated any differently?

3. In what ways have security issues for banks changed in the last 30 years?

Make Academic Connections

4. **TECHNOLOGY** Banks have been using computer networks to transfer funds for some time. Customers can now get in on the act with online banking. Use the Internet or other reference materials to learn about secure servers. Summarize ways that Internet providers attempt to guarantee security and privacy.

5. **HISTORY** One banking function is guaranteeing the worth of money. One big historical change was the growth of paper money, which depended upon people believing that the paper was worth something. Research the history of paper currency. Choose an interesting example, and write a one-page report explaining the case.

6. **COMMUNICATION** With a classmate, make a list of the most important services you want from a bank. Rank these services in order of importance. Compile a class list from the results of all pairs, and come to a consensus on the most important services wanted by customers.

How the Banking System Works

Banking Scene

As he considers places to deposit his paycheck, Edouard is confused about all the different offers from banks and other financial institutions. He recognizes that banks want his business, no differently from the electronics store where he bought an iPhone or the grocery where his family shops. Unlike those stores, however, banks are selling services. He knows that banks are big businesses, but he wonders where they get their funds. He knows they make money on services, but how exactly does the bank earn its profit? What sources of information might Edouard use to find answers to these questions?

1.3.1 MONEY AT WORK

Despite their central role in the economy at large, banks are businesses. For their services, banks earn money in various ways. Banks also have income from other sources, but most of their money comes from lending—or, to be more precise, the loan interest paid by borrowers.

When banks lend money, they put it to work. The money that people borrow goes to buy products or services, to manufacture goods, and to start businesses. In this way, the money that banks lend works to keep the economy going.

The Spread

A person who puts money into a bank is called a **depositor**. Banks encourage deposits by protecting the money and by paying the depositor *interest*, a percentage of revenue earned on the principal over a period of time. The depositor thus earns some money from the deposits. Using the accumulated funds of many depositors, the bank makes loans to customers who are likely to repay those loans. The bank charges more interest on the money it lends than it pays depositors, so when the money is repaid, more comes in than went out. The difference between what a bank pays in interest and what it receives in interest is the **spread**, or *net interest income*. The difference between profits and spread is cost.

The spread is not pure profit. The spread is income, or *revenue*, but costs have yet to be considered. Costs include maintaining the security of your

Revenue
− Cost
= **Profit**

money, personnel expenses, building maintenance costs, and so forth. Profit, or *net income*, is what's left of revenue after costs are deducted. What happens if a homeowner can't repay a loan? With the loss of these funds, the bank loses the ability to earn money on the loan.

What happens to your prior deposits if after two months a tree falls on your roof and you need to withdraw your $10,000 savings? The deposit you made created the liquidity and source of funds from which the bank uses to lend money. From this source of funds, the bank has loaned it to another homeowner, but it must have reserves to meet the obligation of your $10,000 withdrawal. It's not really the same money. The bank has other depositors, not all of whom, the bank hopes, need their money at the same time. Even if they did, the bank has a backup, the Federal Reserve System.

Other Funds

Banks have additional income sources. In addition to loan income, including credit-card interest, they also charge for various services. Charges include fees for rental of safe deposit boxes, checking account maintenance, online bill payment, and ATM transactions. It is important to note that banks do not earn interest on money kept on hand for services such as ATM transactions. Thus, banks charge fees to offset lost interest. To keep pace with the rising cost of servicing accounts, fees for services have increased significantly. These service fees provide substantial revenues for banks.

Banks, like people and other corporations, make money on investments. Especially since the early 1980s, banks have become large and careful investors in some types of securities and government bonds. Because banks can at times invest large amounts of money, they can do well, but they face the same risks as other investors. The speed of modern communication allows banks to move their investments quickly if

Banking Math *Connection*

Calculate the one-year spread for a bank that receives a deposit of $10,000 from a customer and lends it out to a homeowner who needs to make some repairs. Assume the bank pays a straight 6 percent per year interest to the customer and charges 12 percent per year for the loan.

Solution

The formula for calculating the spread is

Income from interest − Interest paid to depositors = Spread
Income from interest: 12% × $10,000 = $1,200
Interest to depositor: 6% × $10,000 =   600
                          Spread = $600

The spread is $600. This is a simplified example and does not take into account compounding, declining balances, or other factors that affect deposits and loans in the real world.

necessary. Even a day or two of a large investment can yield a good return. Professional investment staffs work hard to make every dollar return a profit in the financial market.

Because most banks are corporations, banks may have funds from stockholder investments to use. Stockholders buy bank shares, hoping to receive a return on them and get a say in how the bank does business.

Assets and Liabilities

Why aren't deposits themselves a form of bank income? The money in them doesn't really belong to the bank. You may not like to think of your savings account as a problem for the bank, but it is one in theory. If depositors simultaneously want all their money from all their accounts, banks would be in trouble.

An asset is anything of value. In financial terms, that usually means money. A liquid asset is anything that can readily be exchanged, like cash. A liability, in financial terms, is a cash obligation. If you borrowed $5 from a friend for lunch, you have a liability of $5 and your friend has an asset of $5. The asset's liquidity depends on how quickly you've agreed to repay the sum and how reliable you are.

For banks, deposits are liabilities. Depositors have the right to request their funds, and the bank must pay them. Money the bank borrowed is also a liability, a debt to be paid.

A bank's assets are its loans and investments, which may be less liquid by contract than deposits. Deposits may have to be returned any time, but assets can arrive in small amounts over a long period.

Because banks have more money out working than they keep on hand, two principles of the banking business come into play.

- **A bank's liabilities exceed its reserves.** The money is loaned out, and the reserves don't match the total of deposits (liabilities). However, the money is out working, financing businesses and expanding the economy.

- **A bank's liabilities are more liquid than its assets.** A bank must give depositors their money if they request it. The bank's assets, however, may be less liquid because they are tied up in longer-term loans, so the bank can't get them as quickly. If many depositors need their money at once, the bank must either break its promise to depositors or pay until its reserves are gone. If the bank fails, unpaid depositors lose their money. In the United States, deposit insurance, backed by the government since 1934, has kept people from fearing the loss of their deposits. A "run on the banks," when people call for their money all at once, is rare.

Faulty Investment Strategies

A problem for banks has been faulty investment strategies. Especially in international banking, some banks have invested substantial amounts of money in questionable businesses or complicated financial products. If those businesses fail, the banks don't get their assets. A crisis in the Asian economy in the late 1990s nearly destroyed the Asian banking system, which was neither carefully funded nor controlled. A crisis in the U.S. mortgage lending markets, which began in the summer of 2007, impacted foreign investors with investments in the mortgage market. In the first quarter of 2008, fraudulent investments by a trader at a French bank resulted in a massive sell-off of faulty investments that impacted international financial markets.

Banking today is not as simple as earning interest on the spread. Rapidly changing conditions, complex factors, a 24-hour-a-day global economy, and financial interdependency among nations set the banking climate.

Tests of Bank Profitability

Information from financial statements, which report a bank's assets, liabilities, and net income, can be used to determine its profitability—a necessary condition for survival. Of the various profitability tests, two commonly used are *return on assets* and *return on equity*.

Return on assets (ROA) is the ratio of net income to total assets. It indicates how well bank management used its total amount of assets (loans and investments) to earn income. ROA is also interpreted as the amount earned for each $1 in assets.

As an example, Hometown Bank (HB) has net income of $10,000 ($220,250 revenue − $210,250 in expenses). HB has total assets of $171,500 and total liabilities of $100,000. HB's ROA is calculated using net income from the financial statement as follows:

Net income ÷ Total assets = Return on assets
$10,000　　÷ $171,500　　= 0.058 or 5.8% ROA (5.8 cents on the dollar)

Another important ratio is **return on equity (ROE)**, which measures how well a bank is using its equity (also called stockholders' equity). **Equity** represents net assets, or total assets, minus total liabilities. HB's ROE is:

Net income ÷ Total equity = Return on equity
$10,000　　÷ $71,500　　= 0.139 or 13.9% ROE (13.9 cents on the dollar)

ROA and ROE are of particular interest to stockholders (investors). ROA measures how efficiently the bank is using its assets to generate revenue. ROE represents the amount or return earned on each dollar invested. Investors can compare a bank's ROA and ROE to those of other banks to see how it performed relative to the other banks. A bank's ratios for several years can be reviewed to determine whether they have remained the same, increased, or decreased. A bank's ratios that decrease or stay the same are cause for concern.

 ✔checkpoint

Name three sources of bank income. What is a bank's spread?

1.3.2 BANKS WORKING FOR YOU ● ● ● ● ● ● ● ● ● ● ● ● ● ●

Like any business, a bank must attract customers in order to make money. Banking has changed radically in the last 20 years, and it is now one of the most competitive businesses in the world. Today, large regional banks may have huge resources, and when these giants compete, consumers can sometimes be the winners. Smaller banks that target particular consumers work in a niche market, a specific customer base in a defined location that wants particular services. They use the flexibility that sometimes comes with smaller size to their advantage.

Although there are fewer commercial banks than there were 10 years ago, there is an ever-wider array of services. It was not always so. You'll learn more about the history of U.S. banking in Chapter 2, but one consequence of the Great Depression of the 1930s was heavy regulation of banking. Banks could earn high profits simply on the spread because there were fewer financial options for consumers.

High interest rates in the 1970s resulted in much "disintermediation." In the early 1980s, interest rates rose for all types of debts and investments. Banks were still paying only 5½ to 5¾ percent, as prescribed by law. Consumers, who could get 10 to 14 percent on other investments such as mutual funds, began removing their money from banks or depositing it elsewhere. Some banks (primarily savings and loans associations) had trouble, and with their problems the American economy was at risk. A series of laws passed in the early 1980s loosened the restrictions on bankers and let them compete in the open market like other financial businesses. This loosening of government control, called deregulation, changed the banking environment in the United States completely.

Changes in Traditional Services

One of the most obvious changes in banking was a new focus on consumers. Banks were not as customer-oriented as they are now and advertising was far different. They often kept the so-called "banker's hours" of 9:00 a.m. to 3:00 p.m., were closed on Saturdays and Sundays, and were sometimes closed Wednesdays. That way of doing business is a fading memory, as banks keep doors and windows open longer and have branches in more places than ever. Innovations such as drive-up windows with extended hours took on more importance as banks scrambled to attract customers. Many banks are now open six days a week, and bank operations at many locations run 24 hours a day, seven days a week. In addition, many banks have opened branches in retail stores and shopping centers, making it more convenient for consumers to access their services.

Changes in traditional services may help keep customers. These are the promotions you may often see in banking advertisements today. Several types of checking accounts, for example, are typically available at a single institution, as banks tailor their offerings to match consumer needs. No-cost checking above a minimum balance, overdraft protection, interest-bearing accounts, no-frills checking accounts, or a custom-tailored mix of features let customers pick an account to suit their wishes and balances.

Traditional savings accounts still exist too, but so do other savings options. A variety of ways to compound interest maximizes the money customers can earn, or they may place funds in special accounts, such as money-market accounts that may offer higher interest rates.

Marketing is an ever more important matter to banks in today's environment. Bank personnel often become experts in certain services, and selling is now a critical component of any banker's job. Sales is all about relationships. Product knowledge is key (after all, you can't sell what you don't know) but relationship-building is paramount. If you, as a banker, are not dedicated to building long-lasting relationships with your customers, then someone else will—and it's usually your competition.

New Services

One of the biggest effects of deregulation was that banks got into new areas of business. Banks began offering financial services such as innovative lending options and technology-related services.

Credit Cards Banks (or their holding companies) are facilitators in the credit card business in a big way. This profitable field is a form of lending that has greatly expanded in the last few years. Some economists worry that the growth in this business comes at the expense of saving, perhaps a recipe for long-term trouble. Still, banks compete fiercely for this business and offer varying forms and types of credit-card accounts. Many banks change or negotiate rates with consumers, and special low-rate promotions are offered daily.

Innovative Lending New types of lending are also made available to consumers. Home equity loans have become quite popular. Home equity loans are secured by the difference between the value of a home and the amount

Tech Talk

Intranet

You know about the Internet, of course, but do you know what an *intranet* is? An intranet is a private network that uses Internet software to store information for internal use by a company. Essentially, an intranet is a collection of websites to which only specified users can gain access. Passwords, software security measures, and data encryption protect the intranets from unauthorized use. Intranets make it possible for employees to use the resources on them with standard Internet browsers. Banks routinely use intranets to provide a centralized source for everything from updated forms to training materials to their recent financial performance.

Think Critically   In an industry that needs to keep current with changes ranging from legal requirements to fluctuating interest rates, how can the use of an intranet streamline the operating efficiency of a bank?

the homeowner still owes on it. The loans may take the form of a special credit card, a line of credit, or a single disbursement. They have become a popular form of credit because the interest on them is often tax-deductible for the consumer.

Reverse mortgages allow consumers age 62 or older to utilize the equity from their homes by receiving payments from a lender based on the value of the equity. These payments can be received either in monthly installments, in a lump sum, or as a line of credit. Typically the equity does not need to be paid back until the home is sold.

As financial institutions try to attract new customers, they continue to find ways to make their loan products more attractive. For example, 40-year fixed-rate mortgages and 15/15 adjustable rate mortgages (ARM) may be offered to customers. The 15/15 ARM has a fixed rate for the first 15 years, and then it adjusts once and is fixed for the remaining 15 years. This is a great product for someone who doesn't think they will be in a house for longer than 15 years.

Photodisc/Getty Images

Technology Tools   Probably the flashiest new services banks offer involve technology. The revolution in computers and telecommunications affected banks dramatically and helped drive a reliance on Internet-based transactions. New and expanded services based on a blend of technologies are now available.

- **Automated teller machines (ATMs)** were the first of the high-tech revolutions for consumers. First appearing as novelties in the late 1960s, ATMs have made "banker's hours" irrelevant. Customers can now perform almost any banking function from an ATM, and have access to their accounts day or night. Networked ATMs have made it possible to do business with one's bank at any time from almost anywhere in the world. ATMs reduce transaction costs, encourage the use of the bank, and earn income from fees. The reduced transaction costs apply to the bank and not necessarily to the customer. ATMs are available in a variety of venues, including shopping centers, amusement parks, universities, airports, sports arenas, and workplaces. Because ATMs are everywhere, using an ATM, which often intimidated early customers, is a common and casual act that most people take for granted today.

- **Smart cards** are credit, debit, or other types of cards that have embedded microchips. Smart cards are useful for a wide variety of "electronic purse" applications, which allow the card to store a value. When the card is used, the stored value decreases. You may have used these already in grocery or retail stores. Gift cards, security cards, and customer loyalty reward cards are also examples of smart cards. Consumers should use smart cards cautiously.

According to *The New York Times*, since 2005 $41 billion in money on gift cards has been lost or is likely never to be cashed in. The lion's share of money lost on gift cards from 2005 to 2009 came from fees and expiration dates. All that changed with the passage of the Credit Card Accountability Responsibility and Disclosure Act of 2009. The Act largely forbids fees on cards sold by retailers (cards given away as promotional items can still charge fees), and it prohibits expiration dates less than five years after the card is purchased.

- **Payroll cards** are a specific type of smart card. Banks can facilitate salary payments between employers and employees. By using a bank as an intermediary, payroll cards enable an employer to load salary payments onto an employee's smart card. Employees can then access their pay even if they do not have a bank account.

- **Online banking** takes advantage of growing Internet use. Whether called Internet banking, electronic banking, home banking, or PC banking, online banking allows customers to perform banking transactions from their home computers. Everything from balance inquiries to bill paying to applying for a loan may be available online at any time. Some banks use Internet technology in intranets, and others simply provide a dial-in service to their mainframe computer. Online services can be complicated and costly to set up, and some consumers are not comfortable using computers for private matters such as banking. The future is bright for online banking, though, as security systems improve, software applications become more sophisticated, and a new generation of customers comfortable with the technology matures.

- **Mobile banking** has grown in popularity as reliance on sophisticated cell phones and related technology has grown. Consumers can execute a variety of banking transactions on their mobile devices, such as check account balances, make requests for payments, deposit checks, and even receive updates regarding their accounts.

The new services and the new environment for banking offer both challenges and rewards to consumers and bankers alike. Opportunities to handle money more efficiently and effectively for both are increasing, and they offer possibilities unimagined just a few years ago. They also require a thorough understanding of how the system and its tools work, and how money moves in an increasingly complex economy.

 **checkpoint**

What changes have deregulation and competition brought to modern banking?

assessment 1.3

Think Critically

1. How does the fact that consumers have many choices for places to put their money affect the banking industry?

2. Savings deposits today are smaller by percentage than they once were. Why do you think some economists feel that this is a risk to the economy?

3. What reasons might some people have for not taking full advantage of today's banking services and technology?

4. How might smart-card technology reduce the number of cards in a consumer's wallet or purse?

Make Academic Connections

5. **MATH** If you had $8,400 placed in an account that earned 5½ percent interest, paid just once a year, how much money would be in the account at the end of four years, assuming you made no withdrawals of any kind from the account?

6. **TECHNOLOGY** Find out more about online and mobile banking. Visit the online site of three banks of your choice. Many online banking sites offer a demonstration of how the system works. List the services available on the sites, including whether mobile banking services are offered. Identify what is needed to enroll in online and mobile banking.

1.4

Other Financial Institutions

Learning Objectives

1.4.1 Define depository financial institutions.

1.4.2 Explain nondepository financial institutions.

Key Terms

- depository intermediaries
- nondepository intermediaries
- wholesale bank

Banking Scene

While deciding how to manage his earnings, Edouard investigated various local banks and learned about their services. His uncle, who works at a nearby college and is a member of the college's credit union, mentioned to Edouard that credit unions can perform many of the same functions of a bank, although some of the terms may be different. Edouard wants to learn more about credit unions. What other types of financial institutions act as intermediaries to help people handle money?

1.4.1 DEPOSITORY INTERMEDIARIES

A bank is a financial intermediary for the safeguarding, transferring, exchanging, or lending of money. There are two primary types of financial institutions. Depository intermediaries are those that get funds from the public and use them to finance their business. Nondepository intermediaries are those that do not take or hold deposits. They earn their money selling specific services or policies.

Depository intermediaries receive deposits from customers and use the money to run their businesses. These institutions may have other sources of income, but the bread and butter of their business is handling deposits, paying interest on them, and lending money based on those deposits. There are four main types of depository institutions. Although there are fewer differences today than in the past, some important distinctions remain.

Commercial Banks

You have been working with concepts and services based mostly on commercial banks throughout this chapter. One of the big distinctions between commercial banks and other depository institutions is that commercial banks are owned by stockholders who expect a profit on their investments. Today commercial banks may work with both businesses and individuals. A commercial bank that specializes only in business banking is sometimes called a wholesale bank.

Savings and Loan Associations

Savings and loan associations (S&Ls) may go by various names. Building and loan associations, homestead banks, and cooperative banks are all names for savings and loan associations. Savings and loan associations receive most of their deposits from individuals. Chartered by either state or federal governments, these institutions grew by focusing on real-estate lending for people. Today they offer most of the same services as commercial banks. Savings and loan associations are owned not by outside investors, but by depositors themselves, who receive shares of the company.

Mutual Savings Banks

Mutual savings banks are similar to savings and loan associations. They receive deposits primarily from individuals and concentrate also on private real-estate mortgages. Mutual savings banks are owned by depositors as well. These state-chartered banks are sometimes granted greater powers with regard to assets and liabilities than S&Ls, but usually not as much as those of commercial banks.

Mutual savings banks and savings and loan associations are sometimes called *thrift institutions*. Few remain as a result of a crisis in the industry in the 1980s. These institutions are regulated and protected by the state or federal government, which is not necessarily true of nondepository intermediaries.

Credit Unions

Credit unions also are owned by depositors, but there are a couple of key differences. First, users of credit unions must be members. Membership is usually based on some type of association, such as a common employer, a certain line of work, a geographical region, or even a social or religious

iStockphoto.com/Deborah Cheramie

affiliation. Second, credit unions are *not-for-profit* financial institutions that exist to benefit the members. Any money beyond costs is returned to the members in the form of dividends on savings, reduced fees for services, or lower rates for loans.

✔ checkpoint

What is a wholesale bank? What is the primary difference between credit unions and other depositor-owned financial institutions?

1.4.2 NONDEPOSITORY INTERMEDIARIES

As the name suggests, nondepository intermediaries don't take deposits. Instead, they perform other financial services and collect fees for them as their primary means of business. In many cases, these institutions are private companies. Although they may be regulated by the government, they are usually not backed or protected by the government.

Insurance Companies

You might not think of insurance companies as financial institutions, but they are. Insurance companies make money on the policies they sell, which protect against financial loss and/or build income for later use. The policies are not tangible and the protection they offer is financial, so the companies are performing a financial service. Some types of insurance policies have a cash value that can be redeemed at any time, and some policies let customers remove cash gradually. Although insurance companies do not typically make loans, in some cases the cash value of a policy may be used to secure a loan from elsewhere. Insurance premiums (costs) are not deposits. Private insurance companies try to earn a profit from the premiums beyond the cost of insurance payouts. Many professional money managers regard insurance as essential financial protection, but not a good investment.

iStockphoto.com/DNY59

Trust Companies/ Pension Funds

Companies that administer pension or retirement funds also perform financial services. These companies manage money for a fee and promise in return to provide future income. Some pension funds are closely regulated, but others may not be. Growth for the contributor comes not from interest on deposits, but investments made by the administrator. These investments may yield a profit, but there is a risk of loss as well.

Brokerage Houses

Brokers are people who execute orders to buy and sell stocks and other securities. They are paid commissions. Their service is to help investors do as well as possible with their investments. Brokerage houses may offer advice or guidance, but are private companies who make a profit on the transactions.

Loan Companies

Loan companies, sometimes called finance companies, are not banks. They do not receive deposits, and they should not be confused with banks, savings and loan associations, or credit unions. They are private companies who lend money and make a profit on the interest. Loan companies sometimes make loans to customers when other institutions will not, but they charge higher interest rates to offset the risk.

Payday Loans

A specific form of loan company focuses on payday loans. These companies offer extremely short-term loans against an expected paycheck or other check with high interest rates and fees. Other names for these loans include deferred deposit check loans, check advance loans, or post-dated check loans.

Ethics in Action

Banks are required by law to offer their products and services on an equal opportunity basis. According to the Federal Trade Commission, the Equal Credit Opportunity Act (ECOA), and the Consumer Financial Protection Bureau ensures that all consumers are given an equal chance to obtain credit. This doesn't mean all consumers who apply for credit get it. Factors such as income, expenses, debt, and credit history are considerations for creditworthiness.

What the law guarantees is that all applicants be treated fairly. Applications for credit cannot be evaluated on the basis of gender, race, marital status, national origin, or religion.

Think Critically

Banks want to attract and keep customers. Why do you think a law like ECOA might have become necessary?

Payday loans usually require an upfront fee that is immediately deducted from the loan amount. Exorbitantly high interest rates are common for payday loans. Although disclosure of the effective annual percentage rate (APR) is required by law, consumers who utilize this type of loan may not fully understand the financial consequences of using this type of financing.

Many online sites are available to facilitate obtaining payday loans. Many even sweeten the offer by providing direct deposit of the loan to a consumer's banking account. However, these same loan providers often require authorization for automatic withdrawal of the funds from the consumer's bank account on a predesignated date. These companies also may perform some of the same services as currency exchanges.

Currency Exchanges

Currency exchanges do not make loans or receive deposits. Currency exchanges are private companies that cash checks, sell money orders, or perform other exchange services. They charge a fee, usually a percentage of the amount exchanged. Because their business depends on these fees, interest rates are usually higher than at banks or other financial institutions. Currency exchanges often locate in areas where no other financial intermediaries exist, and they offer the only financial services available to people in those areas.

A wide range of financial services is available from both depository and nondepository intermediaries. Most of the nondepository institutions are private companies earning money by performing specific services. You don't make deposits, earn interest, or have checking or savings accounts with them. Nondepository institutions are a part of the financial world and help move money through the economy. However, they are not part of the banking system and may not really be considered to be in the business of banking.

✔ checkpoint

Why is an insurance company considered a financial intermediary? What is the primary difference between depository institutions and most nondepository institutions?

assessment 1.4

Think Critically

1. Services from depository institutions have become similar since deregulation. Why is there any need for different forms of depository institutions?

2. Credit unions are not-for-profit institutions. They return profits to members. Why wouldn't everyone place their money only in credit unions?

3. Do you think payday loans and currency exchanges take advantage of those who do not have access to other forms of financial services? Why or why not?

4. How does the fact that the government backs many forms of depository institutions affect the confidence of consumers about their deposits?

Make Academic Connections

5. **SOCIAL SCIENCE** Until late in the twentieth century, the financial world was dominated by men and not ethnically diverse. Contact a large bank and learn what policies they have in place to guarantee and encourage equal opportunity careers, for both genders and all races, in the banking profession. List some of those policies.

6. **HISTORY** Although services offered seem similar today, there was once a great difference between thrift institutions and banks. Find out more about the way these institutions arose to meet a particular social need. Write a one-page report about the beginnings of savings and loans, credit unions, and mutual savings banks.

chapter 1 assessment

Chapter Summary

1.1 Introduction to Banking

A. Banks are financial intermediaries that safeguard, transfer, exchange, and lend money. Commercial, retail, and central banks are three main types.

B. Mergers, technology, and competition have reshaped banking.

1.2 Role of Banks in the Economy

A. Banks safeguard our money through various business practices that protect, record, and evaluate banking transactions and businesses.

B. Banks expand the economy by transferring and lending funds to creditworthy borrowers, thus supporting markets and providing economic stimulus for jobs.

1.3 How the Banking System Works

A. Banks make money on the spread between interest paid and received. Bank assets include earnings and investments. Deposits are liabilities. ROA and ROE are two ratios used to measure a bank's profitability.

B. Bank deregulation brought expansion of customer services. New services banks offer to stay competitive involve credit cards, new types of loans, smart cards, online banking, and mobile banking.

1.4 Other Financial Institutions

A. Depository intermediaries include banks, savings and loan associations, mutual savings banks, and credit unions. Most of these are backed by the government.

B. Nondepository institutions include insurance companies, trust companies, brokerage houses, loan companies, and currency exchanges. Most of these are private firms not part of the national banking system.

Vocabulary Builder

Choose the term that best fits the definition. Write the letter of the answer in the space provided. Some terms may not be used.

a. asset
b. central banks
c. commercial bank
d. creditworthy
e. depositor
f. depository intermediary
g. deregulation
h. equity
i. financial intermediary
j. identity theft
k. liability
l. liquid asset
m. medium of exchange
n. niche market
o. nondepository intermediary
p. profit
q. retail bank
r. return on assets (ROA)
s. return on equity (ROE)
t. spread
u. wholesale bank

____ 1. The difference between interest paid and interest received
____ 2. A private company that does not receive deposits but sells financial services
____ 3. Government banks that regulate and manage money supply
____ 4. The ratio of net income to total assets
____ 5. Most common form of government-backed corporate bank
____ 6. To banks, deposits represent this type of obligation
____ 7. The loosening of government control
____ 8. Anything of value that can be readily exchanged
____ 9. Revenue minus cost
____ 10. An agreed-upon system for measuring value of goods and services
____ 11. Net income ÷ Total equity
____ 12. Total assets − Total liabilities

Review Concepts

13. Why are banks called financial intermediaries?

14. List

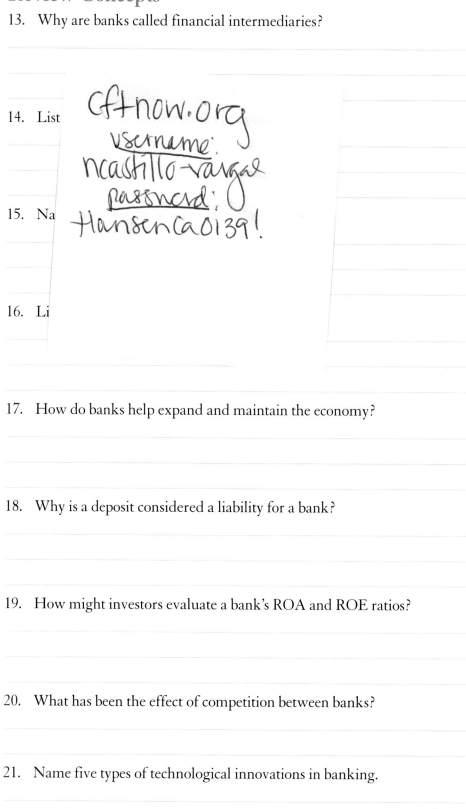

15. Na

16. Li

17. How do banks help expand and maintain the economy?

18. Why is a deposit considered a liability for a bank?

19. How might investors evaluate a bank's ROA and ROE ratios?

20. What has been the effect of competition between banks?

21. Name five types of technological innovations in banking.

22. Name two types of thrift institutions.

23. What is a nondepository financial institution?

Apply What You Learned

24. Why are banks regulated and protected by government?

25. What are advantages and disadvantages of mergers in banking?

26. How did deregulation ultimately result in more banking services for consumers?

27. Would consumers be better off if all public utilities, including electric and gas companies, were deregulated so that the marketplace could set prices?

28. Consumer debt is higher than ever in the United States. What would happen if people suddenly stopped borrowing from banks?

29. How did the U.S. mortgage crisis affected both the U.S. economy and the international economy?

30. If private, nondepository loan companies charge higher interest than depository institutions backed by government, how do they stay in business?

Make Academic Connections

31. **CRITICAL THINKING**   Most insurance is bought to protect against the possibility of loss, except life insurance. Everybody who buys life insurance eventually dies. Explain how life insurance works.

32. **ADVERTISING**   Analyze five bank advertisements from a variety of media, such as newspapers, magazines, radio, television, billboards, and the Internet. What do banks do to get your business? Keep a journal for one week, noting each advertiser, the services being advertised, and a basic description of each ad. Make a chart that shows your analysis.

33. **LAW**   *Usury* is the practice of charging extreme interest rates. From your library or the Internet, find out more about usury limits, what they are, how they work, and what the usury limits are in various states. Write a one-page report summarizing what you learn.

34. **ETHICS**   ATM fees are a source of revenue for banks. If you use an ATM from a bank different from your own, you may be charged a fee for the transaction both by the bank that owns the machine and by your own bank for processing the transaction. Does this seem fair to you? Why or why not?

35. **ETHICS**   Some lenders target the neediest consumers. The recent mortgage crisis was fueled, in part, by qualifying borrowers for loan amounts that exceeded their realistic ability to meet monthly payments. Likewise, payday loans charge exorbitant interest rates with high processing fees. Are the terms and conditions offered by these lenders fair and reasonable? Why or why not?

36. **CAREERS**   Visit the website of a large regional bank. Find out what opportunities the bank offers to prospective employees. Make a list of some of the positions available and the training and experience required.

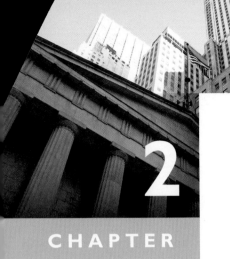

2

Development of the U.S. Banking System

iStockphoto.com/MarioGuti

climbing the ladder

From Web Content Consultant to Documentation Manager

While his children slept on the flight home from a hectic week at a Florida amusement park, Reza reflected on his career. After college, he had accepted a position at a diversified financial institution. Working as a web marketing consultant for the annuity and mutual funds division, his job involved developing and executing online marketing initiatives. Reza supported multiple products that were advertised on a variety of websites. He developed web content and designed site layouts. Ensuring that the written and visual elements complemented each other and functioned smoothly were a critical part of this position.

Reza had realized he could enhance his job security by working in a variety of areas. Having a broader base of experience also would allow him to expand his personal network.

Next Reza had accepted a job as an implementation technical consultant in the company's credit card division. Reza was responsible for assessing data technology needs, file specifications, and delivery methods. He streamlined processes and met with internal customers to determine electronic reporting formats for products.

Realizing he wanted to move higher in the organization, Reza routinely reviewed internal job postings for supervisory positions. He had been delighted to pass the rigorous interview process for a job as a business technology supervisor in his company's trust division. In this role, Reza was responsible for application systems analysis and programming activities. After leading teams to conduct feasibility studies and time and cost estimates, Reza assigned members of his group to complete various components of the projects.

Reza's stellar reputation as an effective supervisor had led to a job offer as a network security manager. His team was responsible for developing systems and procedures that protected host and network systems from unauthorized access. He managed the creation of firewall security standards and intrusion detection procedures. The team perpetually evaluated the information technology (IT) infrastructure to identify new areas of risk.

After the birth of his twins, Reza had decided to scale back on his hours at the office. By working in his current position as an online training documentation manager, Reza was able to work from home three days a week. The flexibility in his schedule helped him and his wife manage childcare needs. In this position, Reza is responsible for overseeing the content development of online training courses, updating existing online courses, and writing and maintaining operational procedures.

Upper Rungs to Consider

Now that his children were older, Reza realized it was time to find a challenging onsite position. Management positions that Reza planned to look for included technology integration, IT project management, and network operations.

Preparing for the Climb

Over the course of a long career, are there ways to occasionally scale back to handle temporarily demanding life needs? What is the best way to stay involved in your field to make it easy to reenter the field?

2.1

Creation of a National Currency

Learning Objectives

2.1.1 Identify different types of currency.

2.1.2 Explain how currency evolved through the early days of the United States to what it is today.

Key Term

- currency

Banking Scene

When Katie Conlon finished high school, an aunt gave her a $100 bill for graduation. While writing a thank you note to her aunt, Katie took a good look at the bill. She had never thought too much about cash. How and why did currency start circulating in the United States? What part of the government prints money? Katie started checking the Internet to learn more. What websites would be good places to start looking?

2.1.1 WHAT IS CURRENCY?

Money is a *medium of exchange* for people to use to trade things of value. Anything from fur to grain to metal can fill that role. In most places of the world, some form of money is the agreed-upon medium of exchange. So what is meant by the term *currency*?

Most people associate the word with paper money, and they're right. Strictly speaking, **currency** is all media of exchange circulating in a country. This definition includes coins as well as paper money. In today's society it also includes credit instruments, such as bonds, checks, cashier's checks, and other types of loan papers.

Classifying Currency

To keep terms straight, most economists make some other distinctions, dividing the term currency between coins, called *metallic currency*, and paper money or credit instruments, called *paper currency*. There are further terms for paper currency, depending upon who issues it. *Government currency* is money printed by a government. In some countries, banks issue notes against their reserves called bank notes, which are referred to as *bank currency*. Checks are also a form of currency, and they are called *deposit currency*, because that is how their value is redeemed.

Shifting Meanings

As with many financial concepts, the idea of currency has changed. Before World War I (1914–1918), many countries had governments that did not issue paper money. Paper currency meant only notes issued by large banks. In the United States, however, paper currency meant the money that the government printed, and nothing else. Following the war, the idea of currency began to take on the broader sense in use today. In part, this wider sense was the result of changes in banking and economics that circulated a lot more forms of valuable paper, including the various credit instruments comprising the idea of currency today.

✔checkpoint

What is currency?

2.1.2 THE GROWTH OF AMERICAN CURRENCY

An account of the earliest days of American currency is generally a history of a mixture of types of money. The colonists, who came from many European countries, used the currency of their homelands. In the early days, some settlers also used shells and nails to trade for what they needed, making them a kind of coinage. Pretty quickly, various types of money, both coins and paper, were circulating among the settlements that would one day rise up and create a nation.

Colonial Cash

Coins were the most common medium of exchange. Some British-type coins were minted on American soil as early as the 1650s, but few colonists

iStockphoto.com/Ken Cave

trusted them. Foreign money was much more common. Though the colonies did use English pounds and shillings, a Spanish dollar called the *real* was the most popular. Higher in silver content than other coins, the real was the most trusted form of currency in America. Early American coins were imitations of reals.

There was always some form of paper money in the colonies, too. Much of it consisted of English or other foreign bank notes. Most of this paper money could be redeemed for coins, which were trusted far more than paper certificates.

During the Revolutionary War, the Continental Congress issued paper money to buy desperately needed supplies. Few people had confidence in this currency. In fact, the scornful phrase "not worth a continental" referred for many years to any worthless item.

Currency in the United States

After the Revolutionary War, the new United States decided to replace the many colonial coins then circulating. The Mint Act of April 1792 authorized $10, $5, and $2.50 gold coins; $1, 50¢, 25¢, 10¢ and 5¢ silver coins; and 1¢ and 1/2¢ copper coins. The U.S. mint began operation in 1794, but many of the foreign coins remained in circulation well into the 1830s.

The U.S. government did not issue paper currency until 1861. Before then, bank notes from two chartered Banks of the United States and from many different state banks were the only paper currency in use.

The multiple types of currency often caused problems. During the crisis of the Civil War, people became so concerned about the value of money that some stores even issued their own currency. The National Currency Act of 1863, later rewritten as the National Banking Act of 1864, established standards for currency. It also taxed state bank notes, making them unprofitable. State banks gradually got out of the business of issuing currency, and a system of national currency came into being. Problems with the money supply persisted, though, and in 1913 the Federal Reserve Act established the basic banking system in use today.

U.S. Government Paper Currency Today

Amount	Portrait on Front
One dollar note	George Washington
Two dollar note	Thomas Jefferson
Five dollar note	Abraham Lincoln
Ten dollar note	Alexander Hamilton
Twenty dollar note	Andrew Jackson
Fifty dollar note	Ulysses S. Grant
One hundred dollar note	Benjamin Franklin

Five hundred, one thousand, five thousand, and ten thousand dollar notes have been unavailable from the Treasury since 1969. Last printed in 1945, these large denominations are still legal tender, although most are in the hands of collectors.

Sometimes there is a need for currency to evolve to reflect the state of the economy it serves. In 2006, there was a debate in the United States whether to discontinue the penny. A number of factors propelled this debate forward. As the price of zinc escalated, it cost one-and-a-half cents to produce a one-cent penny. As the cost of living increases, the relative value of the penny decreases. Despite these quantitative arguments, the penny continues to circulate in the United States economy.

More Than a Medium of Exchange

Currency does more than serve as a medium of exchange. Currency can provide a means for a country to provide recognition for individuals or states, or events of historical significance to a country. For example, from 1999–2008, the U.S. Mint issued quarters commemorating each of the 50 U.S. states.

Each state governor was allowed to decide how the quarter design process would work in his or her state. One state, Massachusetts, held a competition among elementary school students to allow children the opportunity to participate in the design of the state's commemorative quarter. In addition to highlighting the particular characteristics of each state, the quarters also created additional demand for coinage. Collectors often strive to obtain the complete series of the coins, which they save in their personal collection. Coins that remain in private collections are removed from circulation, thus increasing the need for additional coins.

In contrast to the somewhat frequent design changes of U.S. coins, the portraits featured on United States paper currency have remained constant since 1928. Individuals of historical significance, who are no longer alive, are featured in the portraits. To meet evolving security needs, in 1996 some design changes were made to dollar bills to combat counterfeiting.

NET KNOWLEDGE

Sometimes the past is honored in the present. Visit the United States Mint site and learn about the $1 coin series commemorating personal contributions of Native Americans. How do you think Native Americans and the rest of American society feel about these coins? Another collectible series commemorates our national park system. Launched in 2010, the National Park Quarters series will continue through 2021. Five quarters a year are issued in this series, each one commemorating a different national park.

What other groups of people, events, or landmarks can you think of as the subject for a series of commemorative coins?

✔checkpoint

What was the most common medium of exchange in Colonial America? When did the U.S. government begin to issue paper currency?

assessment 2.1

Think Critically

1. Why was early American currency a mixture of forms of money?

2. Outline the early history of money in the U.S. economy.

3. Why might people have distrusted the value of paper currency issued by the Continental Congress during the Revolutionary War?

4. Why might currencies issued by the many state banks have caused confusion before the Civil War?

5. List some reasons that might prompt design changes in currency.

Make Academic Connections

6. **HISTORY** Another form of currency that didn't hold its value was currency issued by the Confederate States of America during its rebellion against the Union in the Civil War. Use the library, the Internet, or other research sources to learn more about Confederate currency. Write a one-page report that explains the problems that the Confederacy had with its currency and why the currency couldn't hold its value. What are specimens of Confederate currency worth today?

7. **SOCIAL STUDIES** The U.S. Bureau of Engraving and Printing is responsible for printing currency for the U.S. government. Incorporated in the design of each note are symbols that represent ideas from American philosophy and identifying features of the particular note. Visit the Bureau's website at www.bep.treas.gov/ to learn more. Choose a note of some denomination, and create a chart or graphical representation that interprets and explains the symbols and features and what they mean.

8. **TECHNOLOGY** Both metallic and paper currency are so common in society that hardly anyone gives them a second glance. Did you ever wonder how they are produced? Research sources of your choosing and create a written, oral, or computer presentation that explains the process used to make either paper or metallic currency.

Banking Before 1913

Banking Scene

When Katie Conlon moved from her home in New Jersey to attend college in Bloomington, Indiana, she wanted to set up a bank account in town. She saw advertisements for many banks, but two banks caught her eye. BankOne, a national bank, and the Peoples State Bank both offered services that looked more or less the same. What is the difference between a state bank and a national bank? How could she find out?

Learning Objectives

2.2.1 Identify the reasons for the establishment and expiration of both the First and Second Banks of the United States.

2.2.2 Describe the continuing problems that led to the Federal Reserve Act.

Key Term

• Federal Reserve Act

2.2.1 BANKS IN THE YOUNG UNITED STATES

In many ways, democracy in the new United States of America was an experiment. Never before had a country attempted such an enterprise. The young nation had to work its way through many problems of government, trying to find the right balance between the role of the government and the freedom of individuals. In a similar way, banking in the early United States also had an experimental quality. Some of the history of U.S. banking was a process of trial and error, and some of the issues were the result of struggles between competing ideas—just as in the nation at large.

The First Bank of the United States

George Washington's Secretary of the Treasury, Alexander Hamilton, believed that without a strong central government and a strong bank, the new nation would eventually fail. Hamilton encouraged the new government to accept and pay with interest not only the debts of the Revolutionary War, but also to assume responsibility for debts individual states incurred in the struggle. In this way, the federal government established itself as the final authority for the economic security of the new nation.

Hamilton also urged the creation of a Bank of the United States. Thomas Jefferson, who believed creating such an institution gave too much power to too few people, fiercely opposed him in this idea. Over Jefferson's objections, the bank was chartered in 1791.

The first Bank of the United States was not an institution of government. The bank was privately held. Although the government owned about 20 percent of the bank, the rest was in the hands of private investors and foreign governments, to the continuing dismay of those who opposed it.

Digital Art/Corbis

As the chief depository of the U.S. government, the bank gained power. By 1805, the bank had eight branches. Its bank notes became the most common form of currency circulating in the United States. It exercised control on state-chartered banks, not by law but by demanding that state banks redeem their bank notes with gold or silver when they were deposited in the First Bank of the United States. Thus, the bank almost accidentally performed the role of a central bank. As the nation grew westward, more people resented the control of powerful Eastern bankers. When the bank's charter expired in 1811, there was not enough political support to renew it.

The Second Bank of the United States

Within five years, conflicting state bank policies and changing economic conditions caused Congress to reconsider. In 1816, Congress granted the second Bank of the United States a 20-year charter. After a slow start, the bank began to do well under its president, Nicholas Biddle.

Biddle deliberately improved upon the central banking functions of regulating credit and the money supply, but had to do so by restraining state banks, who then saw the U.S. bank as an enemy. A new class of entrepreneurs and developers who thought regulation of money and credit supply not in their interest was gaining power. Rising resentment of what people saw as an aristocracy again spelled trouble for the bank.

President Andrew Jackson took office in 1828 and was an unyielding opponent of the bank. Jackson's chief rival, Senator Henry Clay, tried to renew the bank's charter four years early in 1832, hoping to make the renewal an election issue. Jackson vetoed the bill, arguing that the bank represented "the advancement of the few at the expense of the many." The bank did indeed become a campaign issue, but Jackson trounced Clay in the election.

The bank's charter still had four years to run. Determined to kill the bank that he saw as unconstitutional, Jackson forced the withdrawal of government funds from it, moving money instead to a number of state banks, which came to be called his "pet banks." The Second Bank of the United States weakened and died when its charter expired in 1836.

One World

The Bank of England

The Bank of England, one of the oldest central banks, was nationalized in 1946. The bank advises the government on monetary issues, but its freedom to act independently is limited. The bank implements the chosen monetary policy and performs other central banking functions, such as funding public borrowing, issuing bank notes, and managing reserves. It also deals with international banking issues on behalf of the government.

Think Critically What are advantages of a central banking system entirely under the control of the government? What are the disadvantages?

Why did the two first U.S. National banks fail?

2.2.2 STEPS TOWARD CENTRAL BANKING

In the absence of a national banking system, state banks grew in number and influence. Private banks sprang up, each with its own policies and currency. This fragmented system supplied money for the economy, but without some overriding control, chaos with credit and the money supply reigned. The Independent Treasury System, a network of federal offices that handled U.S. government money, could not manage the banking system adequately. State banks being unable to issue the new currency found it necessary to purchase it for gold from the newly formed national banks.

The National Banking Act of 1864

After the Civil War, rampant inflation threatened the entire economic system. The National Banking Act of 1864 was enacted. It established the office of the Comptroller of the Currency to issue charters to national banks. These banks were authorized to issue national bank notes. Each time a bank issued national currency, it was required to purchase an equivalent amount of U.S. government bonds. This caused problems as the country was in a growth period and banks had to decide whether they were going to issue currency or make loans with the money they had on hand. State bank currencies died out because high taxes were assessed on them. To survive, state banks expanded their deposit functions and other services.

Continuing Issues   Although the National Banking Act helped by establishing a national currency, it still did not address regulation of the credit and money supply, nor did it guarantee the safety of banks. Money supply problems occurred repeatedly, including crises and bank failures in 1873, 1883, 1893, and 1907. In 1913, the Federal Reserve Act created a system to stabilize the banking system. As part of the central banking system, the Federal Reserve provided a check collection system and flexible currency.

What was the purpose of the National Banking Act of 1864?

assessment 2.2

Think Critically

1. Do you agree with Hamilton or Jefferson about the creation of a private bank to handle government banking? Explain your reasoning.

2. How did conflicting political views ultimately cause the demise of the first two Banks of the United States?

3. Prior to the Federal Reserve Act of 1913, what factors made the banking system and the economy unstable?

Make Academic Connections

4. **TECHNOLOGY** Counterfeiting is an ongoing problem associated with paper currency since the government first began printing it. Visit the U.S. Bureau of Engraving and Printing's website at www.bep.treas.gov/ to learn about anticounterfeiting measures. What challenges does modern technology present and what steps does the Bureau take to meet them?

5. **HISTORY** The battle between Hamilton and Jefferson over the Bank of the United States led to the formation of political parties. Find out how. In what way did the disagreement between Hamilton and Jefferson over the bank reflect two fundamentally different views of the union of states? How did this tension affect the growing economy of the United States?

6. **COMMUNICATION** In some ways, the argument over power and influence of monetary policy that raged in the early 1800s is still with us. Conduct a poll of classmates, friends, relatives, or your community members to find out whom the public thinks controls the economy. Ask how their opinions have changed as a result of the banking crisis of 2008. Compile your results as a class, interviewing at least 50 total subjects.

Modern Banking

Banking Scene

Before she left for college, Katie Conlon's grandmother gave her a check toward her education and told her to put it in a "good, safe bank." Then her grandmother told Katie stories of her own childhood during the Great Depression, including how her father had lost his savings when a bank went out of business. "Could that happen today?" Katie wondered. What sources could she use to learn about the Great Depression?

Learning Objectives

2.3.1 Explain why Congress established the Federal Reserve System.

2.3.2 Identify recent challenges faced by the banking system.

Key Terms

- reserve liquidity
- Great Depression
- margin
- bank run
- Federal Deposit Insurance Corporation (FDIC)
- inflation
- stagflation
- recession

2.3.1 A TRUE NATIONAL BANKING SYSTEM

In the half century before the Federal Reserve Act of 1913, America became an industrial powerhouse. This massive industrialization sometimes caused problems with the banking system as the demand for credit and money was high. The National Banking Act of 1864 put a reserve system in place, with small banks able to borrow reserves from city banks, which could in turn borrow from central reserve city banks. (*Reserves* are a percentage of deposits that are set aside to help with liquidity drops.) However, this reserve system was not flexible. Sudden economic downturns could cause a chain reaction, with a few banks inflicting stress on the entire system because there was not enough reserve liquidity, or ways to convert the reserves readily to cash. Reserves at this point only applied to national banks and to those state banks who chose to become members of the Fed. They did not change until the 1980s, with the passage of the Monetary Control Act and the Garn-St. Germain Depository Institutions Act.

Fed services, at this point, were made available to member banks as part of their membership. State non-member banks acquired Fed services through correspondent banks.

The Federal Reserve Act of 1913

After a severe economic panic in 1907, Congress formed a bipartisan group (made up of members from both political parties) to study the problem. The Federal Reserve Act in 1913 founded a system of central banking that was both adaptable and flexible. A board of directors controlled district reserve banks from which member banks could borrow money to meet demand. The original Federal Reserve Board consisted of presidential appointees, the Secretary of the Treasury, and the Comptroller of the

At the time of its founding, the Federal Reserve was hotly criticized by many who felt that its makeup was dominated by bankers, who would act only in their own interests and ignore the "common man." The final structure of the Federal Reserve represented a compromise on these issues.

Think Critically

If you were a member of the Federal Reserve Board, how would you separate your own interests from the good of the country's economy?

Currency. Ten-year terms for appointed members removed the responsibilities of the board from partisan politics.

The Federal Reserve handled the government's central banking function, conducted bank examinations, and decided whether banks could borrow money from the Federal Reserve. The board based its decisions on whether the banks were being run responsibly and whether extending the loan would put stress on the banking system at large. In this way, banks came under the control of an organization whose job was to monitor and protect the entire banking system. It was also in the interest of member banks to conduct their own operations in such a way as to satisfy the Reserve Board. Thus, the United States at last had a federal institution to manage monetary policy.

The Federal Reserve has changed since its beginning in 1913, both in structure and in operation, largely as a result of the crisis of the Great Depression. Today, the Federal Reserve plays a key role in the economy.

Banks in Crisis

The **Great Depression**, which began in 1929 and extended worldwide until about 1939, was the worst and longest economic crisis of Western industrialized nations during the twentieth century. The stock market crash in October of 1929 brought about near-collapse of the economic system in the United States and other nations. Many banks and their customers were its victims.

Ironically, the failure was caused in part by success. The economy was roaring in the 1920s, and the stock market was booming. The market was so attractive, in fact, that everyone wanted in, whether they had the money available or not. People and companies borrowed money to buy stocks or bought them on credit. Many stocks were bought on **margin**, or for a fraction of their price. They were then resold at a profit, without the full purchase price of the stock ever having been paid. This practice led to risky investments and speculation. When the market began to fall in September 1929, nervous investors began to sell their stocks. In October, the panic spread, everyone tried to dump stocks, and the market collapsed. There was no money to pay what was owed on margins or on anything else.

In addition, many banks had also invested in the stock market. Banks that did not fail outright were pressed to their limits and had no money for further loans or investments. Businesses failed, and people were forced out of work. They could not pay back loans from banks, further worsening the position of financial institutions. Hence, the entire economy spiraled rapidly downward. American ties to Europe and continuing economic problems after World War I spread the depression worldwide.

People rushed to their banks to withdraw what money they could. Deposits are liabilities, and no bank keeps enough reserves to cover all liabilities. When many people try to withdraw their money at once, a bank run takes place, and many such runs occurred.

Stock Montage/Archive Photos/Getty Images

Bank failures threatened the entire nation, and depositors in most failed banks lost all their money. On March 6, 1933, after a series of major bank failures, newly elected President Franklin D. Roosevelt closed all banks by proclamation. He declared a *bank holiday* in order to save the remaining assets of banks still in business and to let people calm down, as he tried to assure them that the government could help.

The Banking Acts of 1933 and 1935

Within four days after President Roosevelt declared the bank holiday, Congress passed the Emergency Banking Act of 1933. This law, also called the Glass-Steagall Act, massively reformed the nation's banking system. Among other things, it separated commercial banking from investment banking to protect assets, and it required bank holding companies to be examined by the Federal Reserve. Perhaps most importantly, it established the Federal Deposit Insurance Corporation (FDIC), which guarantees deposits against bank failures. The amount guaranteed originally was $2,500 per depositor, per bank. This amount has been raised in increments over the years to $250,000, and sometimes it is even more for special kinds of accounts or ownership categories. These actions restored public confidence in the nation's banking system. Banks reopened, and three quarters of them survived.

The Banking Act of 1935 made further refinements by expanding the monetary controls of the Federal Reserve and changing the structure of the Federal Reserve Board. The Secretary of the Treasury and the Comptroller of the Currency were removed, and board member terms were lengthened. These two acts, with some modifications made later, prevented the massive banking failures of the 1930s from recurring during the twentieth century.

✔ checkpoint

What brought about the creation of the Federal Reserve in 1913? What is a bank run?

2.3.2 RECENT BANKING

The basic banking system remained unchanged until 1980. During the 1980s and 1990s, several acts were passed that affected banking. Changes in the way the Federal Reserve deals with Congress and in the way it prices its services to member banks fine-tuned the system. The Federal Reserve and its chair became more independent of government. Its primary goal is to promote general economic health more than any particular policy. Challenges posed by inflation, recession, and modernization have changed banking dramatically from the business it was in Roosevelt's time. As a result of this legislation, all banks and savings and loans are required to maintain reserves at the Federal Reserve and all Federal Reserve services must be available to all banks and savings and loans at explicit pricing.

Inflation and Banking

Inflation contributed to bank changes that occurred in the 1970s and 1980s. Inflation is a rise in general prices, including a rise in the supply of money and incomes. You might think that an increase in money supply and incomes is a good thing, but what tends to happen is that prices go up as well. A sustained increase in costs and money supply leads to money having less purchasing power. For example, in 1932 a wool sweater cost $1.00 and a gas stove cost $19.95. A factory worker earned about $17.00 per week and an accountant earned $45.00. The problem is that in periods of severe inflation, prices tend to rise faster than earnings. When earnings catch up, the overall cost of living has risen, and so it becomes true that "a dollar isn't what it used to be." How well could that accountant live on $45.00 per week today?

Banking Math *Connection*

Did you get a 13% raise this year? Most people didn't. If inflation is running at 13%, you would need a raise of that rate just to break even. If inflation continues to rise for a few years, it can have a ruinous effect. Calculate the cost of 13% inflation for five years on the cost of a $15,000 car.

Solution

The formula for calculating one year's rise is

(Original cost × Inflation rate) + Original cost = Year 1 cost
   ($15,000 × 0.13)   + $15,000   = $16,950

To calculate for five years, you can't just multiply 13% by five (65%) and use that as the rate, because the original cost changes (compounds) every year. The calculation must be repeated five times, using the year 1 cost in place of the original cost for year 2, and so forth.

($16,950.00 × 0.13) + $16,950.00 = $19,153.50   Year 2 cost
($19,153.50 × 0.13) + $19,153.50 = $21,643.46   Year 3 cost
($21,643.46 × 0.13) + $21,643.46 = $24,457.11   Year 4 cost
($24,457.10 × 0.13) + $24,457.10 = $27,636.52   Year 5 cost

Although there are many theories about what causes inflation, economic problems usually also occur. In periods of runaway inflation, no one can keep up, because the value of money does not match the value of goods. It takes more and more money to buy fewer and fewer things. In addition, money put aside earlier no longer has the buying power it had when it was saved.

Just such a cycle occurred in the 1970s and 1980s. Prices, wages, and interest rose rapidly, partly because of an excess of easy credit and money supply. During this same period, banks struggled because the law limited the amount of interest they could pay. Faced with more attractive options, depositors put their money elsewhere, and banks again began to have trouble. Although inflation was rising, the economy as a whole was not doing especially well, producing an unusual circumstance called stagflation. A combination of a stagnant economy, high inflation, and high unemployment lead to stagflation. During the 1970s, inflation was about 14 percent per year.

To combat inflation, the Federal Reserve tightened the money supply and allowed interest rates to rise. A severe recession followed, but inflation fell and has remained low. A recession occurs when there is a decline in total production lasting a minimum of two consecutive quarters (at least six months). The 1990s saw the longest period of sustained growth in U.S. history.

Root causes of stagflation during the 1970s included the rising cost of energy and food. By the end of 2007, there was concern that the U.S. economy, subjected to sharp increases in prices for energy and food, was heading toward stagflation. Most economists are now calling the crisis the Great Recession. The spillover effect of the subprime mortgage crisis also caused consumers to slow down their spending.

Deregulation

Laws, including the Monetary Control Act of 1980 and the Garn-St. Germain Depository Institutions Act of 1982, were passed in the early 1980s to let banks compete more freely with other financial firms, opening the doors to the services available today. Not all of the effects of deregulation were good, however. Some financial institutions were allowed

Tech Talk

Document Management System (DMS)

Information in banking is a moving target. Laws and regulations change. Interest rates change. Bank account offerings and fees change. How can a bank efficiently inform employees about changes? How can customers access current offerings at a bank? A document management system (DMS) provides a streamlined approach for managing and updating documents. A DMS has a repository, a content server, and content applications. Together they provide information storage, information management, and end user access.

Think Critically   Do an Internet search for document management systems in the banking industry. Review the products vendors offer. Study how a DMS could improve efficiency in one of your particular areas of interest. Share your findings with the class.

to make unwise loans and investments. Many savings and loan institutions (S&Ls) took advantage of new regulations to invest in commercial real estate and speculative loans. When the recession of the mid-1980s struck, these S&Ls failed. Because the Federal Savings and Loan Insurance Corporation (FSLIC), similar to the FDIC for banks, could not cover all the losses, the government intervened. U.S. taxpayers had to pay for the policies of both the government and the officers of the failed S&Ls.

The mortgage crisis that came to the forefront during the summer of 2007 can be attributed, in part, to a loosening of lending oversight standards. This loosening began in the early 1990s but did not produce adverse effects in the economy until 2007. This illustrates the fact that economic decisions made today may not show consequences until much later. By trying to encourage a growth in homeownership through creative lending strategies, many participants in the mortgage industry helped fuel the growth and distribution of risky mortgage products. Because homeowners were given access to mortgages that exceeded their realistic ability to make payments, they began to finance more of their daily expenses through the use of credit cards. As other investment products were developed based on both poorly performing mortgage products and on credit card debt, when the mortgages began to fail and when people stopped making credit card payments, the investment products based upon them failed also. As the number of non-performing investment products grew, it became increasingly difficult for consumers to access credit. This led the U.S. government to institute a $700 billion bailout package to help troubled lenders. An in-depth explanation of the mortgage crisis, the credit crisis, and the subsequent Emergency Economic Stabilization Act of 2008 is provided in Chapters 8 and 9.

The Revolution Continues   During the first decade of the twenty-first century, various economic downturns prompted the Federal Reserve to drop interest rates multiple times in hopes of stimulating the economy. Evolving technology facilitated the passage of Check Clearing for the 21st Century Act (Check 21), which allowed using substitute checks to process checks electronically. Mergers changed the banking industry constantly. The mortgage crisis, the credit crisis, and federal intervention to rescue large financial institutions on the brink of failure all contributed to changes in banking. Although much of the basic structure of the banking system remains essentially as it was in 1913, the business of banking, with its rapid communication, its global information exchange, and its marketing focus is much different from the banking industry of an earlier age.

checkpoint

Why is inflation a potentially serious economic threat? Why were banks deregulated in the early 1980s?

assessment 2.3

Think Critically

1. Why couldn't Congress just allow a free market to determine monetary policy?

2. Why do you think the Federal Reserve Act attempted to remove the members of its board from the pressures of partisan politics?

3. How did consumer fear help cause the bank failures of the Great Depression?

4. Why is inflation particularly hard on those who save money well?

Make Academic Connections

5. **MATH**   Inflation is still with us, although the rates are far lower than they were 30 years ago. Anticipating inflation is part of financial planning. If this year's inflation rate is 2.7%, and you placed $2,000 in a savings account at the beginning of the year earning 2% interest, how much must you deposit in the account at the end of the year to hold the same purchasing value?

6. **POLITICAL SCIENCE**   Find out more about how Roosevelt reshaped society during the Great Depression. Although controversial, Roosevelt's efforts brought about the government you recognize today. Choose research materials to write a paragraph about how Roosevelt transformed the nation, listing some of the reforms.

chapter 2 assessment

Chapter Summary

2.1 Creation of a National Currency

A. Currency includes all circulating media of exchange in a country. It may include metallic currency (coins) and paper currency (government currency, bank currency, deposit currency, and other credit instruments).

B. There were many forms of currency in early American history. After the Revolutionary War, bank notes from many sources circulated. After the Civil War, forms other than U.S.-issued currency were taxed out of existence.

2.2 Banking Before 1913

A. Both the First and the Second Banks of the United States were private institutions that ultimately died. Banks were largely unregulated until the Civil War.

B. The National Banking Act of 1864 eliminated many forms of currency and moved toward a central banking system. Money supply problems persisted.

2.3 Modern Banking

A. Congress established the Federal Reserve in 1913. It was the first official central banking system in U.S. history.

B. The Great Depression brought many bank failures. Banking reform acts saved the industry. Challenges from inflation and changes from technology characterized latter twentieth-century banking.

Vocabulary Builder

Choose the term that best fits the definition. Write the letter of the answer in the space provided.

a. bank run
b. currency
c. Federal Reserve Act
d. Federal Deposit Insurance Corporation (FDIC)
e. Great Depression
f. inflation
g. margin
h. recession
i. reserve liquidity
j. stagflation

____ 1. Ways to quickly convert banks' reserves to cash
____ 2. Combination of a stagnant economy and high inflation
____ 3. Legislation that created a system to stabilize the banking industry
____ 4. A decline in total production lasting a minimum of two consecutive quarters (at least six months)
____ 5. Circumstance when many depositors withdraw money at once
____ 6. All media of exchange circulating in a country
____ 7. Agency that guarantees bank deposits
____ 8. Worst economic crisis in U.S. history during the twentieth century
____ 9. Collective rise in money supply, incomes, and prices
____ 10. Stocks bought for a fraction of their price, and then resold at a profit, without the full price of the stock ever having been paid (encouraging risky investments and speculation)

Review Concepts

11. Why did Alexander Hamilton urge the founding of the first Bank of the United States?

12. Why did Thomas Jefferson oppose founding the First Bank of the United States?

13. How did the First and Second Banks of the United States exert control over other banks?

14. Why did the First and Second Banks of the United States fail?

15. How were banks regulated between 1836 and the Civil War?

16. Why did state banks eventually stop issuing their own currency?

17. Why did Congress establish the Federal Reserve system?

18. What caused massive bank failures during the Great Depression?

Apply What You Learned

19. In what ways does the disagreement between Hamilton and Jefferson about banking policy still exist today?

20. Outline the history of banking in the U.S. economy.

Make Academic Connections

21. **MATH** Calculate the loss of real value in a $10,000 savings account if inflation is 10% a year for 3 years versus the loss of real value if inflation remains around 3%. How much less would that savings account be worth if inflation goes up? (For this exercise, do not consider interest paid.)

22. **MEDIA** Collect stories about interest rates, the Federal Reserve, inflation, banking, the effects of the mortgage crisis, and current economic conditions from various news media. Take notes from stories on electronic media such as radio, television, and the Internet. Use these notes in a class discussion about economic trends.

23. **HISTORY** Thomas Jefferson was an American hero, but his opponent on the bank issue was also a fascinating man. Use research materials of your choice to write a two-page character sketch of Alexander Hamilton, focusing not only on biographical facts but on traits that made him both an effective and resented spokesperson for his opinions.

24. **ART** Use printouts from the Internet or photocopies of library materials to create a collage of images from the Great Depression. In your collage, try to convey a sense of the economic conditions of the time.

25. **RESEARCH**   Research the ramifications of the subprime mortgage crisis of 2007/2008. List the impact on U.S. municipalities, the U.S. economy, and international economies.

26. **GOVERNMENT**   *Seigniorage* is the term used to describe the profit the government makes from manufacturing coins. As part of the effort to support its goal of being self-supporting, the Mint calculates the profit on each coin produced. The Mint also strategizes about how to respond to competitive threats that will decrease the demand for currency. Visit the Mint's website and review its most recent annual report. List defined competitive threats and list which coins are profitable and which are not. Be prepared to discuss with the class the two focuses of the Mint: (1) It serves the needs of the public by managing and issuing coins. (2) It views the public as its customer.

27. **RESEARCH**   The mortgage crisis that began in the summer of 2007 began because it became increasingly easier for buyers to qualify for loans. Research lending standards online and provide a brief description of how lending standards were lowered over time.

28. **CURRENT EVENTS**   One method the U.S. Treasury uses to avoid counterfeiting currency is to educate the public about the features of currency. Visit the Department of the Treasury Bureau of Engraving and printing website to learn about recently released security features. Compare the security features on an updated $5 bill and an older $5 bill. List the ways that you can use the new security features to quickly note a potential counterfeit bill.

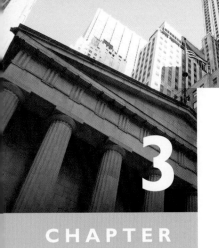

CHAPTER

3

The Federal Reserve System

iStockphoto.com/traveler1116

skills that pay dividends

Understanding Public Policy and Its Impact on Business

Money flows through the economy. It allows people to trade products and services at a fair value. With money as a medium of exchange, products and services can be exchanged directly between individuals, businesses, and governments without the intervention of third parties.

Government exists to protect people from each other, to protect people from private interests, and to further the ideas that society holds valuable. Government also provides the legal framework to ensure that protections are provided in an organized way. Through legal requirements, the government mandates accountability. Individuals and corporations are legally responsible for their actions and they are required to comply with existing laws.

It is important to understand how these concepts intersect to achieve the goal of economic stability in a thriving society. One example of government policy impacting business is energy conservation. Increased public concern over the condition of the environment and the impact of global warming has been steadily gaining momentum.

The Environmental Protection Agency (EPA) began an energy conservation program called Energy Star, which is a voluntary labeling program, in 1992. Products that are energy efficient and reduce the emission of greenhouse gases can earn an Energy Star rating. In 1996, the United States Department of Energy (DOE) entered into a joint partnership with the EPA for the Energy Star program. This joint effort resulted in a substantial increase in the number of products that are eligible for an Energy Star rating. In 2014, it was estimated that households using Energy Star products could save about $34 billion on their utility bills.

Another method of promoting energy conservation is through tax incentives. Hybrid vehicles, which are powered by both batteries and fuel, achieve higher fuel efficiency and lower emissions than standard vehicles. To encourage consumers to begin using hybrid vehicles, the government developed an Alternative Motor Vehicle Credit.

This credit is structured to jump start purchases of hybrid vehicles by providing the largest amount of credit to consumers who purchase the vehicles closest to their release dates. The tax credit allows consumers to reduce the amount of federal tax owed by the amount of the credit.

The money consumers save through utility bill reductions and tax credits is money they have available to spend or invest. Government policies, which reflect the goals of the voting public, are designed to influence consumer behavior through financial incentives.

When government establishes policies that subsidize an industry, as is the case for hybrid vehicles, it affects the growth and development of the industry. If consumers are eager to help the environment and receive a tax credit, they will purchase hybrid vehicles. This increases demand for hybrid vehicles and encourages more companies to manufacture them.

Develop Your Skill

Research the tax incentives homeowners with mortgages receive. Determine whether mortgage tax credits subsidize the real estate market.

3.1

Structure of the Federal Reserve System

Learning Objectives

3.1.1 Identify the organization of the Federal Reserve System.

3.1.2 Explain how the Federal Reserve influences banks and the economy.

3.1.3 Describe proposed reorganization of the Fed.

Key Terms

- member bank
- District Reserve Bank

Banking Scene

After opening an account at People's State Bank, Kareema stopped at a drive-through restaurant for a soft drink. Waiting to pay, she happened to glance at the bill in her hand. At the top of her bill, she saw the words "Federal Reserve Note." Why, she wondered, are these bills called Federal Reserve notes? Kareema resolved to find out more about the Federal Reserve System. Where might she start?

3.1.1 STRUCTURE OF THE FED

The Federal Reserve was created in 1913 to respond to problems with the nation's changing money supply. Now you will look more closely at the modern Federal Reserve System, learn who makes it up, what the system does, and how it operates. The "Fed," as it is often called, functions as the government's banker, providing a range of financial services both to the government and to all financial institutions. It also supervises banks, conducting examinations to identify risk or bookkeeping problems. The Federal Reserve manages monetary policy as well, hoping to benefit not only banks but also the economy at large.

The Federal Reserve is a uniquely American approach to central banking. It is a combination of public and private policymakers working together to control the nation's monetary policy, supervise banks, and provide financial services to the government and banks. The Federal Reserve is set up like a private corporation, with member banks holding stock in their District Reserve Bank. The President of the United States nominates candidates for the Board of Governors. The U.S. Senate confirms nominees. The Federal government appropriates no money for the Federal Reserve. Its income is derived from financial services and

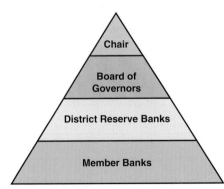

interest on loans to its member banks. Any money made above the cost of providing services is turned over to the U.S. Treasury. Think of the structure of the Federal Reserve as a pyramid, with member banks as the base, District Reserve Banks in the middle, the Board of Governors near the top, and the Chairman at the very peak. Each of these levels depends upon information and action from other parts to hold up the system.

Member Banks

Any bank that is part of the Federal Reserve System is known as a member bank. All national banks must be member banks of the Federal Reserve System. They must purchase stock in the District Reserve Banks in their regions. This stock cannot be bought or sold, and it does not offer control of the District Reserve Bank. It does convey voting rights, however, for directors of the District Bank, and it also pays a 6 percent dividend. State-chartered banks are not required to be members of the Federal Reserve System, although they may choose to become member banks if they meet requirements. Investment banks are currently not required to be member banks.

District Reserve Banks

District Reserve Banks carry out banking functions for government offices in their area, examine member banks in the district, decide whether to loan banks funds, recommend interest rates, and implement policy decisions of the Board of Governors. There are twelve regional District Reserve Banks, located in Atlanta, Boston, Chicago, Cleveland, Dallas, Kansas City, Minneapolis, New York, Philadelphia, Richmond, San Francisco, and St. Louis. As of February 2016, there were 25 branch offices supporting the regional offices. The district and regional branches are listed at the right.

Each district bank is governed by a nine-member board of directors, six of whom are nonbankers elected by member banks. The Board of Governors selects the three other board members. Each board also elects the president of its district bank, subject to approval by the Board of Governors.

District Bank	Branch Bank
1. Boston, MA	
2. New York, NY	Buffalo, NY
3. Philadelphia, PA	
4. Cleveland, OH	Cincinnati, OH
	Pittsburgh, PA
5. Richmond, VA	Baltimore, MD
	Charlotte, NC
6. Atlanta, GA	Birmingham, AL
	Jacksonville, FL
	Miami, FL
	Nashville, TN
	New Orleans, LA
7. Chicago, IL	Detroit, MI
8. St. Louis, MO	Little Rock, AR
	Louisville, KY
	Memphis, TN
9. Minneapolis, MN	Helena, MT
10. Kansas City, MO	Denver, CO
	Oklahoma City, OK
	Omaha, NE
11. Dallas, TX	El Paso, TX
	Houston, TX
	San Antonio, TX
12. San Francisco, CA	Los Angeles, CA
	Portland, OR
	Salt Lake City, UT
	Seattle, WA

The Twelve Federal Reserve Districts

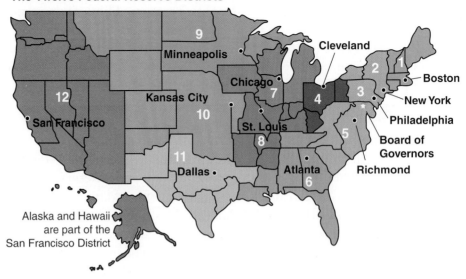

The Federal Reserve officially identifies Districts by number and Reserve Bank city.

In the 12th District, the Seattle Branch serves Alaska, and the San Francisco Bank serves Hawaii. The System serves commonwealths and territories as follows: the New York Bank serves the Commonwealth of Puerto Rico and the U.S. Virgin Islands; the San Francisco Bank serves American Samoa, Guam, and the Commonwealth of the Northern Mariana Islands. The Board of Governors revised the branch boundaries of the System in February 1996.

Source: Federal Reserve System

Board of Governors

The President of the United States selects members of the Board of Governors, subject to consent of the Senate. Each of the seven governors serves a 14-year term, one beginning January 31 of every even-numbered year so that terms are staggered. The Board of Governors is the policy-making arm of the Federal Reserve Board, and its decisions control monetary policy. The Board of Governors oversees the District Reserve Banks and also controls mergers, bank holding companies, U.S. offices of international banks, and the reserves of depository institutions.

The Chair

The President also selects the chair and vice-chair of the Federal Reserve from the membership of the Board of Governors, subject to confirmation of the Senate. The chair and vice-chair each serve a four-year term, but no limit is set on the number of terms. The current chairman, Janet Yellen, began her four-year term on February 3, 2014. She served as the Vice Chairman of the Federal Reserve from 2010 to 2014. Prior to 2010, Janet Yellen was President and Chief Executive Officer of the Federal Reserve Bank of San Francisco, Chair of the White House Council of Economic Advisors under President Bill Clinton, and Professor at the University of California, Berkeley, Haas School of Business.

Xinhua News Agency/Getty Images

The Federal Reserve structure allows for both central control of monetary policy and regional control of district and member banks. Thus, the Federal Reserve, though a central bank, has a decentralized structure that bases policies on both national and regional concerns through close communication.

checkpoint

What are the four structural elements of the Federal Reserve?

3.1.2 FUNCTIONS OF THE FED

The Federal Reserve serves as the central banking authority of the United States, managing the banking system of the country. The five main functions of the Federal Reserve are to serve as the government's bank, to serve as a bank for other banks, to supervise and regulate bank operations, to protect consumers' credit rights, and to ensure that the financial system remains stable through judicious use of monetary policy. The first four functions are described below. Monetary policy is discussed in detail in Lesson 3.2.

The Government's Bank

The U.S. government performs many financial actions through the Federal Reserve. Tax payments to the Internal Revenue Service go to accounts in Federal Reserve banks. From these accounts, the government makes payments to employees, to Social Security recipients, to military personnel, and for other expenses associated with the government.

In addition, Federal Reserve banks perform some services for the government that add directly to its income. The Federal Reserve is responsible for selling and redeeming various government securities, such as savings bonds, treasury bills, treasury notes, and treasury bonds.

The Banks' Bank

One of the main reasons the Federal Reserve was created was to serve as a reserve bank for other banks to ease shortages of cash or to credit banks that have an excess. The Federal Reserve also processes payments between banks. Originally, this function developed to speed the collection of checks, but the task expanded to processing payments for other large accounts, such as payroll accounts and payments for large manufacturing orders. Today, this role also includes not only paper checks, but also electronic funds transfers, the means by which most large transactions move.

Bank Supervision

The Federal Reserve supervises and regulates all member banks. Agencies such as the Office of the Comptroller of the Currency and the FDIC participate in regulatory activities as well. State banking authorities also conduct supervisory activities, so that banks, whether members of the Fed or not, are supervised to ensure responsible banking practice. For international banks operating in the United States, the Federal Reserve ensures fair competition and communicates with central banking authorities in other countries to promote consistent policies.

Protecting Consumers

Consumer protection is another function of the Federal Reserve. Bank examiners monitor whether customers are treated fairly in terms of fees, prices, penalties, and even advertising. Banks must show that they offer and perform their services, including making loans, on an equal opportunity basis.

What are the primary functions of the Federal Reserve?

3.1.3 Proposed Reorganization of the Fed

The financial crisis the United States began to experience in the latter half of 2007 helped spur discussion regarding whether the banking regulation system should be reorganized. A number of federal agencies, including the Fed, regulate portions of the banking industry. There is some overlap between agencies and there are some areas not covered by federal oversight. For example, the Fed, the FDIC, the Office of the Comptroller of the Currency, and the SEC are all involved in banking regulation.

In response to the need for reorganization, the Treasury Department proposed a plan for reorganizing the management of domestic financial markets. This plan acknowledged that, given the evolving nature of financial markets and the way that financial institutions overlap in products offered, a new system was required to respond quickly to market needs. For example, as financial institutions routinely sell diverse products covering securities, banking, and insurance, regulations were needed to manage those areas in a cohesive fashion. Following are some highlights of the report.

President's Working Group on Financial Markets (PWG) Originally established in 1988, this group was responsible for communicating across agencies to help ensure a healthy stock market that inspired investor confidence. Inter-agency communication was achieved by having leadership representatives from the Treasury, the Fed, the SEC, and the Commodities Futures Trading Commission serve on the PWG committee. The expanded goals of the PWG include lessening system-wide risk to financial markets, improving the integrity of financial markets, improving protection for consumers and investors, and enhancing the competitiveness of financial markets.

Payment and Settlement Systems Oversight Used to transfer funds between businesses, financial institutions, and consumers, the payment and settlement systems help keep the economy moving by making sure money is accurately sent and received. The proposed revisions would include a uniform method for regulating these systems.

Insurance Historically operated under state regulation, the proposed plan recommends establishing an organization to federally regulate insurance providers who opt in to the federal program. Federal oversight would help meet the needs of companies that provide insurance on either a national or international basis.

Futures and Securities Separating the regulation of futures and securities made sense in the 1930s when the regulations were established. However it does not make sense in today's market. As products and markets have converged and as international trading has increased, there is a need to regulate futures and securities together. To achieve this objective, the proposal recommends merging the Securities and Exchange Commission (SEC) and the Commodity Futures Trading Commission (CFTC). One regulatory body would provide a more agile response to the changing needs of the marketplace.

As this report was first released in March 2008, and as the report in its entirety recommends a multitude of changes that cut across many federal, state, and private entities, it will be some time before the recommendations can be considered and acted upon. In 2010, the idea of merging the SEC and CFTC was revisited as part of the Dodd-Frank Act but once again wasn't approved in an effort to deal with larger issues that the Dodd-Frank Act was created to resolve.

✔checkpoint

Why is consideration of reorganizing the Fed such a complicated task?

assessment 3.1

Think Critically

1. Why do you think only national banks are required to be members of the Federal Reserve System?

2. Why are Federal Reserve District Banks distributed across the nation?

3. Why did the Treasury Department feel the need to initiate reorganization of the management of domestic financial markets?

4. List four areas of economic management that are facing possible reorganization based on the Treasury Department's recommendations.

Make Academic Connections

5. **EDUCATION** Visit the Federal Reserve Board of Governors' website. From the Site Map link, find the District Reserve Bank that serves your area. Find and visit that bank's site, and discover what materials it makes available for citizen education. List those resources here.

6. **BIOGRAPHY** One of the most influential Federal Reserve chairs in recent history has been Alan Greenspan. Use resource material of your own choosing, and write a one-page report on the life and career of this powerful figure. Include reflections on his comments in the fall of 2008 when he acknowledged that relying on the "self-interest of lending institutions" to behave in a way that made businesses self-sustaining was a gross miscalculation and contributed to the 2008 financial crises.

Monetary and Fiscal Policy

3.2

Learning Objectives

3.2.1 Explain how the Fed conducts monetary policy.

3.2.2 Identify how fiscal policy affects the economy.

3.2.3 Explore criticisms of monetary and fiscal policy.

Banking Scene

Kareema was delighted to get so many outfits for the fall on sale. She'd heard a lot of talk regarding how "money was tight." This was causing many customers to cut back on their spending. Because fewer people were buying clothes, she could get many discounted items. She was happy to get the sale prices, but she wondered what it meant that "money was tight." How can she learn more about the supply of money in the economy? Which government agencies influence the supply of money? Where should she begin her research?

Key Terms

- monetary policy
- Federal Open Market Committee (FOMC)
- Taylor rule
- fiscal policy
- adverse feedback loop

3.2.1 MONETARY POLICY

The most significant function of the Federal Reserve is conducting monetary policy. The goals of the Federal Reserve's monetary policy are to maintain economic growth, to stabilize prices, and to keep international payments flowing smoothly. Federal Reserve actions affect the amount of reserves banks hold, as well as the money supply, which in turn affects the economy.

Open Market Operations   The Fed buys and sells securities issued by the Treasury Department or other government agencies. These are called *open market* sales because the Fed does not control with whom it is doing business in the sales, but trades at a profit or loss in order to accomplish monetary control. These transactions affect the *federal funds rate*, the rate at which banks borrow from each other. When the Fed wants to increase reserves, it buys securities. When it wants to decrease reserves, it sells them. Although this is the most powerful tool of the Fed, these adjustments are short-term and may take place within either days or hours.

Primary Dealers   There is a select group of 20 dealers that the Fed works with to buy and sell securities. These primary dealers must be either broker-dealers that are registered with the SEC or commercial banks that are regulated by supervisors of federal banks. To qualify as a primary dealer, certain capital standards must be met and a certain volume of business must be maintained. Primary dealers engage in a competitive bidding process each time new securities are offered on the open market.

Setting Reserve Requirements   The Fed adjusts the portion of total deposits that banks must keep on hand in their vaults or at the Federal Reserve. Higher reserve requirements result in less money in circulation. Reserve requirement changes are the least frequently used monetary tool of the Fed because changing the reserve requirements fundamentally affects the operations of banks.

Adjusting the Discount Interest Rate   The Fed indirectly affects interest rates at large. The *discount rate* is the rate of interest that the Federal Reserve charges banks for short-term loans. Other interest rates often rise or fall with the discount rate. The Federal Open Market Committee (FOMC) makes discount rate decisions. The committee consists of the seven-member Board of Governors (which includes the Chairman of the Federal Reserve), the Chairman of the New York District Reserve Bank, and presidents of four other District Reserve Banks who serve on a rotating basis. Although legally required to meet four times annually, the FOMC generally meets about eight times per year. Policy changes, when needed, are decided during the meetings.

The Federal Reserve determines necessary interest rate changes in response to economic conditions. A staff compiles and analyzes large amounts of data for support. Economics is an inexact science. The Federal Reserve had avoided the catastrophes of the 1930s until 2008. As a result of the financial crises of 2008, challenges abound for the Fed and other financial regulatory agencies.

Adjusting Monetary Policy

Tinkering with monetary policy does not occur in a vacuum. FOMC members provide input, through discussion and votes on actions. The market then responds to FOMC actions. During early 2008, market observers had hoped the Fed would cut interest rates by one percent. They thought a one percent cut would help keep inflation at bay. However, the Fed decided to cut rates by three quarters of a percent. (Combined with prior interest rate reductions, this cut led to a two percent rate cut in a two-month period.) The Fed has continued to lower interest rates since 2007.

Illustrating that setting monetary policy is not an exact science, two members of the FOMC voted against the three quarter percent interest rate reduction. Even experts do not always agree on the most effective course of action. The three quarter percent rate cut was enough, in the short term, to help improve stock market performance and to improve the international value of the dollar. In essence, the markets gained confidence and responded favorably to the Fed's efforts to help stabilize the economy through interest rate reductions. Adjusting interest rates is one of the many components of monetary policy. Predicting the impact of these adjustments is not straightforward.

Developing Monetary Policy

Did you ever consider all the parties who review, analyze, and try to predict the overall state of the economy? In addition to government staffers and investors, college professors also are interested not only in the economy's performance, but in what drives that performance.

A Stanford University professor, John Taylor, published the Taylor rule in 1993. In simplified terms, the Taylor rule provides ideas for how to use short-term interest rates to achieve the goals of a central bank. These goals include keeping the economy stable and controlling inflation.

The Taylor rule recommends looking at how the economy is performing relative to three targeted indicators. Inflation, full employment, and short-term interest rates are the indicators. When inflation is high or when the economy is above its targeted full employment rate, the Taylor rule suggests that having a high interest rate, which in turn would decrease the money supply, is a good mechanism for restoring the economy to its targeted levels.

The rule provides a simplified method for assessing and forming monetary policy. The rule has some limitations, including not being comprehensive enough to capture the essence of a complex economy and not being able to incorporate decisions that might be made to manage specific risks. Nonetheless, it is often included as part of the analytical and decision-making process of those who set monetary policy.

New Tools to Manage Monetary Policy

In order to help combat the financial crisis that began to appear in the economy during the summer of 2007, the Fed developed three new tools to help manage monetary policy. Term Auction Facility (TAF), Term Securities Lending Facility (TSLF), and Primary Dealer Credit Facility (PDCF) are the new tools.

There are a number of factors that set these tools apart from each other. The fees charged to the borrower for using the tools, how long the loan will last, the type of financial institution that can use the loan, and the type of collateral that can be used to secure the loan all contribute to the differences between the loans.

- **Term Auction Facility (TAF).** Commercial banks can borrow money from the Fed for a maximum of 28 days. Types of collateral for these loans can vary.

- **Term Securities Lending Facility (TSLF).** Treasury securities can be borrowed by primary dealers. The loans, which last up to 28 days, can be secured by a broader range of collateral than TAF loans.

- **Primary Dealer Credit Facility (PDCF).** Primary dealers can take out loans for up to 120 days. A larger group securities than the TSLF securities will be accepted as collateral.

To avoid having these loans increase the total amount of money in the economy, each time the Fed issues one of these loans, the Fed sells an equal amount of Treasury securities. The TSLF and PDCF were initially planned as short-term measures.

✔checkpoint

Why is it hard to predict the impact of monetary policy adjustments?

3.2.2 FISCAL POLICY ●

Just as the Federal Reserve System dominates monetary policy, Congress and the President control fiscal policy and are considered co-equal with the Fed in economic decision making. Congress and the President attempt to smooth economic ups and downs by manipulating the federal budget to create enough demand for goods to keep people working but not so much as to cause inflation. This process controls the total demand for goods and services by managing government spending and the amount of taxes collected. This economic management is called fiscal policy. Administered independently of the Fed's monetary policy, fiscal policy involves adjusting budgetary deficits or surpluses to achieve desired economic goals.

"Priming the Pump" in an Economic Downturn   When the economy experiences high unemployment and little or no business growth, the federal government attempts to add jobs and stimulate business by "priming the pump," or cutting taxes. Theoretically, doing so gives businesses and individuals more money to spend, which results in increased demand for goods and services. Expanded demand causes industries to manufacture more products, hire additional employees, and invest in new buildings and equipment. The expansion thus stimulates the economy. This policy is often referred to as *Keynesian economics* for John Maynard Keynes, who is credited with developing it to address the economic crisis during the Great Depression.

In addition to cutting taxes, which impacts workers' current and future paychecks, sometimes the government issues tax rebates. In effect, rebates provide a retroactive reduction in the level of taxation. They provide a partial refund on previously paid taxes.

During the second quarter of 2008, the U.S. government started issuing tax rebates. By using the rebates to pump $168 billion into the economy, the government hoped to stimulate the slow U.S. economy.

According to economists, tax rebates do not always provide the anticipated stimulus. While studying the affects of a 2001 tax rebate, which ranged in value from $300 to $600, Matthew D. Shapiro and Joel Slemrod, both University of Michigan economists, concluded that only about 20 percent of people spent their rebates on new purchases. A majority of taxpayers either put their rebate money into savings or used it to pay off debt.

Slowing the Boom Economy   In contrast, when the economy is prosperous, demand can exceed supply. This causes prices to increase and, unless stopped, leads to *inflation* when rising prices decrease the value of money.

When this happens, the government uses the opposite policy. It cuts spending, raises taxes, or uses a combination of the two. As a result, consumers and businesses have less money to spend, reducing demand and stabilizing prices.

✔checkpoint

Explain Keynesian economics.

3.2.3 CRITICISM OF MONETARY AND FISCAL POLICIES • • •

Both monetary and fiscal policies have their critics. The two policies often work at cross-purposes. In general, monetary policies seek to control inflation and tolerate relatively high unemployment to achieve their goal. In contrast, fiscal policy appeals to politicians who want to keep the economy vigorous and growing even at the cost of moderately higher prices.

Monetary policy is relatively more agile than fiscal policy. It is easier for the Fed to change bank reserve requirements than to go through the fairly cumbersome process of changing legislation to alter taxes. It is quicker for the Fed to adjust the amount of money flowing into the economy by buying or selling dollars on the open market than altering the level of taxes.

Monetary policy has a downside. If the flow of cash into the economy is too severely restricted, consumers and businesses cannot afford to borrow. This results in a decline in spending and investments, leading to a failure to sell products—especially "big ticket" items such as new homes, automobiles, and appliances. Factories close. As the economy cools off, more and more

branching out

Skip the Bank, Come to the Store

Retailers were licking their chops hoping to feast on the tax rebate checks that the U.S. government began to distribute during April 2008. The checks were part of a $168 billion dollar economic stimulus package. In an effort to capture the entire rebate check from as many customers as possible, retailers developed a variety of incentives. A number of grocery chains offered a 10% bonus for rebate checks used to buy gift cards—therefore a $600 rebate check could be redeemed for $660 of groceries. Some department and clothing stores offered similar bonuses. One electronics retailer, happy to settle for a portion of the rebate check, required that a portion of the check be used for a purchase at its store. It would then load the remaining balance onto a prepaid credit card that could be used at other retailers.

Think Critically Is it ethical for retailers to try to get consumers to tie up their stimulus checks with just one store? How would being obligated to spend a large portion of a rebate check at just one store impact the speed with which the stimulus is felt in the economy?

workers are laid off, and the downward plunge picks up momentum. This cycle is often called an **adverse feedback loop**.

An example of an adverse feedback loop began to occur during the fourth quarter of 2007. By the end of that year, about 8 percent of people who had home loans were either late in making payments or in the midst of foreclosure. Some banks wanted to have a smaller portion of their assets tied up in home mortgages. Because the market was unstable and so many home loans were in default, banks began to ask for larger down payments. They also began to cut way back on home equity loans.

With less money available to spend, consumers began to change their consumption patterns. Buying habits at the grocery store changed. Instead of buying convenient, single-serve packages, they bought in bulk. Entrees shifted from expensive meats to less expensive pastas. Other buying patterns also shifted. Instead of buying designer clothing, store brands were bought. In lieu of going out to the movies, movies were rented.

Although consumers who are caught in an adverse feedback loop may continue to meet their basic needs, they do so in the least expensive way possible. This reduces the total amount of money flowing through the economy.

Fiscal policy has created deep misgivings and endless controversy. Many economists doubt that the federal government can regulate the economy by raising or lowering taxes and expenditures. In addition to being clumsy and time-consuming, these methods involve enormous uncertainties. Fiscal policy is especially difficult to use for stabilization because of the gap between the recognition of its need and its implementation by the President and Congress. For example, the tax cut proposed by President John F. Kennedy in 1962 to stimulate the economy was not legislated until 1964.

Both policies are based on predictions. Even made by experienced economists, predictions are just that—forecasts of what *could* happen.

✔checkpoint

What is an adverse feedback loop?

assessment 3.2

Think Critically

1. How does increasing a bank's required reserve result in less money circulating in the economy?

2. Why doesn't the U.S. government legislate the value of money and set interest rates by law?

3. Explain the Taylor rule.

4. List and define three new tools for managing monetary policy.

Make Academic Connections

5. **ECONOMICS**   The website of the Federal Reserve Bank of New York lists current primary dealers. Review the list and determine whether the status of any primary dealers has been or will be impacted by changes that have occurred in overall market conditions. List your thoughts below.

6. **RESEARCH**   A tax rebate was issued in April 2008. Go online to research the effect of the rebate on the economy. Be prepared to discuss with the class whether you believe rebates are an effective stimulus tool.

3.3

Consumer Protection

Learning Objectives

3.3.1 Explain the various acts that protect consumer rights.

3.3.2 Understand how enforcement responsibilities are shared across agencies.

Key Terms

- Truth in Lending Act (TILA)
- Equal Credit Opportunity Act (ECOA)
- Fair Credit Reporting Act (FCRA)
- Fair Debt Collection Practices Act (FDCPA)
- Dodd-Frank Act
- Consumer Financial Protection Bureau (CFPB)
- Government Accountability Office (GAO)

Banking Scene

Kareema decided to open a new credit card to take advantage of the customer reward program at her favorite clothing store. She was shocked to see all the forms and all the fine print she had to read and sign off on before getting a credit card. There was a lot of discussion regarding interest rates and finance charges. Kareema wondered why there was so much information on the forms. Who decides what information should be included on the forms? Where can she get help to understand what's on the forms?

3.3.1 CREDIT TRANSACTION PROTECTION

An important role of the Fed is to protect consumers. This protection is ensured when the Fed establishes and enforces regulations that promote fairness in the treatment of consumers by private businesses. Financial transactions of consumers are usually protected by consumer protection laws. Protected credit transactions run the gamut from debit cards, car leases, and mortgage loans to ATM transactions.

Credit policies are not always easy to understand. Prior to the 1960s, the interpretation and usage of these policies created opportunity for consumers be treated unfairly or made it difficult for some consumers to understand and obtain credit. In a wave of consumer protection legislation during the 1960s, '70s, and '80s, Congress enacted several important laws to guarantee the rights of consumers. These disclosure laws require that details of lending agreements be specified in writing. Other laws require far more than disclosure, guaranteeing equal access to credit for qualified consumers, accurate credit reporting, and freedom from unfair or deceitful collection practices. Banks are required not only to conform to federal and state laws, but also to document their compliance. In 2010, Congress enacted the Dodd-Frank Act, which afforded additional protections to consumers.

Truth in Lending

Credit cards are the most common form of open-end credit account that are not secured by a home. The **Truth in Lending Act (TILA)**, Title I of the Consumer Credit Protection Act of 1968, was landmark legislation.

Amended many times, it guarantees that all information about costs of a loan is provided in writing to consumers. Items that must be disclosed include the following.

- Total sales price
- Amount financed
- Annual percentage rate (APR)
- Variable rate information
- Total payments
- Schedule of payments
- Prepayment policies
- Late payment policies
- Security interest

In addition, the act provides for a right of rescission for certain types of loans, which allows a consumer to change his or her mind about a loan until midnight of the third business day following the signing of papers.

In 2008, the TILA was amended to include unfair, abusive or deceptive lending and servicing practices. This was a direct result of the mortgage crisis. These pending amendments involve ensuring that interest rate increases, discounted promotional rates, and all payments are applied fairly.

Equal Credit Opportunity Act

The Equal Credit Opportunity Act (ECOA) prohibits the use of race, color, religion, national origin, marital status, age, receipt of public assistance, or exercise of any consumer right against a lender as a factor in determining creditworthiness. If a credit request is denied, the law also requires that the lender provide the reasons for the denial upon request.

Fair Credit Reporting Act

The Fair Credit Reporting Act (FCRA) aims to protect the information that credit bureaus, medical information companies, and tenant screening services may collect. First enacted in 1971, the legislation provided the first legal oversight of the credit information industry. The FCRA mandates the following:

- Consumers must be told what is in their file and who has had access to the information.

- Consumers must be told if information in their file has been used against them.

- Consumers can dispute inaccurate information in their reports. The agency must investigate disputes within 30 days.

- Inaccurate information must be corrected or deleted.

- Credit bureaus cannot report information more than 7 years old in most cases, or more than 10 for bankruptcies.

- Access to consumer files is limited.

- Consumers must authorize the release of reports to employers.

- Lenders cannot obtain medical history or use medical history to determine a credit applicant's worthiness of obtaining a loan.

- Consumers can seek damages for violations of the law.

- By standardizing the information included on credit reports, bias is removed from the reports. These unbiased credit reports enable a broader spectrum of consumers to receive credit.

- A company cannot share customer contact information with its affiliates unless the consumer is offered an easy way to opt out of the solicitation.

- All businesses that hold a consumer account must develop an identity theft prevention program to thwart attempted identity theft.

Fair Debt Collection Practices Act

The **Fair Debt Collection Practices Act (FDCPA)** protects consumers from unfair collection techniques. Third-party collectors may not use deceptive or abusive tactics as they try to collect overdue bills. Such collectors may not contact debtors at odd hours, call repeatedly or in a harassing manner, or threaten them in any way, even with legal action, unless it is actually contemplated. Nor may collectors reveal the debts or collection actions to other people, such as employers, in an attempt to embarrass the debtor. Penalties are prescribed for violations of the act.

The Dodd-Frank Act

President Barack Obama signed the Dodd-Frank Wall Street Reform and Consumer Protection Act (the **Dodd-Frank Act**) into law on July 21, 2010. The legislation was proposed and enacted in response to the financial crisis of 2008. The law created the **Consumer Financial Protection Bureau (CFPB)**, which set clear rules for financial firms to follow and which also has the authority to enforce compliance with them. Other features of the Dodd-Frank Act include ending "too big to fail" bailouts; creating a council to identify specific risks private sector companies might pose, thus warning of potential problems that could threaten economic stability; eliminating loopholes that permit risky and abusive financial practices; providing shareholders with input into executive compensation and corporate affairs; mandating transparency and accountability for credit rating agencies; and allowing regulators to pursue financial fraud, conflicts of interest, and manipulation of the system by special interests. The Act also ends *risk-based pricing,* in which a business offers less-favorable credit terms to a consumer with a relatively weaker credit score. Businesses that use this pricing are required to provide a notice to consumers before they commit to the transaction.

Other Legislation

The laws described in the previous section form the foundation of consumer protection, but there are many other laws that apply as well.

- **Fair Credit Billing Act.** An amendment of TILA, it specifies fair procedures for resolving billing disputes and prevents creditors from taking adverse action until the dispute is resolved.

- **Fair Credit and Charge Card Disclosure Act.** Also an amendment of TILA, it requires credit and charge card issuers to provide information about open-end credit in direct mail or telephone solicitations. Credit card issuers must advise consumers of all fees prior to assessing the fees.

- **Home Equity Loan Consumer Protection Act.** Also amending TILA, it requires lenders to make appropriate disclosures about open-end loans that are secured by homes and places limitations on such plans.

- **Credit Repair Organization Act.** Prohibits credit repair companies from misleading consumers about their services and costs and requires agreements to be in writing.

- **Gramm-Leach-Bliley Act.** Compels banks and other financial institutions to protect the privacy of consumers. Institutions must develop written policies, notify consumers of them, and allow consumers the opportunity to "opt out" before a bank can sell some forms of personal information to others.

In addition to these federal regulations, many states have enacted similar laws intended to protect the rights and privacy of consumers.

Housing and Real Estate

A number of acts have been passed to ensure consumer protection in real estate and housing. These acts include the Flood Disaster Protection Act of 1973, the Real Estate Settlement Procedures Act of 1974, the Home Equity Loan Consumer Protection Act of 1988, and the Home Ownership and Equity Protection Act of 1994. Requiring flood insurance for designated areas, mandating that real estate settlement costs be disclosed to consumers, and protecting against exploitative real estate lending practices are protections provided under these acts. Lenders are also required to clearly list all terms for home equity loans and to limit rates and fees on home equity loans.

Educating the Public on Their Rights

The Fed offers a variety of brochures on its website aimed at educating consumers, in easily understandable language, about their rights. The brochures span topics from shopping for a mortgage, identity theft protection, and understanding credit scoring to information on leasing a car. To serve as broad an audience as possible, and to keep pace with the changing demographics in the United States, many of these brochures are also offered in Spanish.

Ethics in Action

The Fair Credit Reporting Act focuses on privacy rights of individuals. Privacy rights are an inherent part of the American psyche. The 2001 Patriot Act, enacted as a way to help combat the potential financing of terrorism, put into effect a number of policies that enabled government agencies to obtain personal financial information about citizens. By issuing requests either through the Foreign Intelligence Surveillance Act (FISA) or through national security letters (NSLs), government agencies are authorized to obtain this personal financial information without the knowledge of affected citizens. The financial institutions providing the financial information to the government are prohibited from revealing the requests to affected account holders. Although the Patriot Act was reauthorized by Congress in 2006, certain provisions to the Act are being challenged in court. The premise of the challenges is whether the First Amendment rights of citizens are being unlawfully violated. Litigation on this issue is pending.

Think Critically

Is it ethical for the government to obtain confidential information about citizens without the knowledge of citizens? When do national security concerns supersede individual privacy rights? How should oversight of government agencies occur in this situation?

Name three pieces of lending legislation that amend the TILA.

3.3.2 ENFORCEMENT OF POLICIES OUTLINED IN ACTS • • •

Authority for enforcing consumer protection acts varies with the individual law and the government agency associated with it.

Shared Responsibilities

In addition to the Federal Reserve Board, agencies that share enforcement responsibilities include the Federal Deposit Insurance Agency (FDIC), the Securities and Exchange Commission (SEC), the Office of Thrift Supervision (OTS), the Federal Trade Commission (FTC), the National Credit

Union Administration (NCUA), the Office of the Comptroller of Currency (OCC), Consumer Financial Protection Bureau (CFPB) and the Commodity and Futures Trading Commission. These agencies have specific areas of responsibility and work together jointly on various aspects of enforcement.

In addition, audits are conducted to test compliance at banks and other financial institutions. Examiners typically review randomly selected loan files for completeness of documentation. They also watch for patterns of credit granting and denial, look at the way disputes are resolved, and check to see that privacy regulations are being observed.

One such audit was conducted in January 2008 by the **Government Accountability Office (GAO)**. The GAO is the auditing arm of Congress that helps ensure that federal laws and policies are implemented properly. The 2008 audit was a comprehensive study of the banking industry's compliance with the fee disclosure requirements of the Fed.

The report indicated that for more than 20 percent of the branches included in the survey, it was difficult to easily obtain complete information about account terms and conditions. In response to the issuance of the report, numerous government agencies with oversight and implementation responsibilities have pledged their support to make sure customers can easily obtain all banking fees and terms.

Why are so many agencies involved in enforcing consumer protection?

assessment 3.3

Think Critically

1. What factors brought about consumer protection laws?

2. How might incomplete disclosure in an advertisement about a car loan have misled consumers before passage of the Truth in Lending Act? Give an example.

3. Why is it in a bank's best interest to provide complete disclosure in a lending agreement and documentation of compliance with all lending laws?

4. Some bankers feel that the banking industry is overregulated. What probably leads them to feel this way?

Make Academic Connections

5. **COMMUNICATION** Work in teams to conduct a poll of at least 30 people. Find out how many of them have examined their credit reports in the last 12 months. How many of them have been the victim of an erroneous entry in a credit report? How many are aware of key provisions of FCRA?

6. **PROBLEM SOLVING** Conduct research to learn what information you should include in a letter of dispute to a consumer reporting agency. Draft a sample letter to a consumer reporting agency disputing a charge for an unpaid dental bill from a dentist of whom you've never heard.

7. **CONSUMER AFFAIRS** Review the privacy policy of a local bank's website. Report your findings.

Role in Determining Banks' Financial Health

3.4

Banking Scene

Kareema was visiting her Grandma and they decided to order pizza. Grandma said she was short on cash and was going to run to the bank. One minute later, Grandma reappeared with cash. Puzzled, Kareema asked her how she got to and from the bank so quickly. With a wry smile, Grandma indicated that the "bank" was a secret stash under her mattress. Having lived through the Great Depression and the crash of the banks, Grandma was leery of banks. Kareema wondered how banks stayed secure today. What safeguards are in place to keep banks secure?

Learning Objectives

3.4.1 Explain the regulatory process and how it works.

3.4.2 Explain the CAMELS rating system for evaluating bank safety.

Key Terms

- charter
- Call report
- System to Estimate Examinations Ratings (SEER)
- CAMELS rating

3.4.1 OVERSIGHT RESPONSIBILITIES OF THE FED

The banking crisis that began during the second half of 2007 caused many people to be quite concerned with the stability of the nation's financial markets. How does the Fed work to promote the stability of the banking system? Congress gave the Fed the jobs of regulating and supervising the banking system. The Board of Governors writes banking regulations. These regulations provide a blueprint of appropriate business practices for banks.

Enforcing the rules is the responsibility of the 12 Reserve banks. Enforcement of a variety of financial institutions is required. International corporations that do banking in the U.S.,

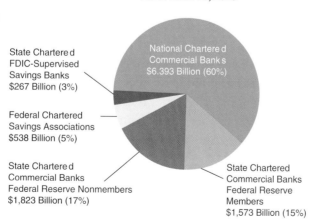

Deposits of FDIC-Insured Commercial Banks and Savings Institutions by Charter Class As of June 30, 2015

State Chartered FDIC-Supervised Savings Banks $267 Billion (3%)

Federal Chartered Savings Associations $538 Billion (5%)

State Chartered Commercial Banks Federal Reserve Nonmembers $1,823 Billion (17%)

National Chartered Commercial Banks $6.393 Billion (60%)

State Chartered Commercial Banks Federal Reserve Members $1,573 Billion (15%)

Excludes U.S. branches of foreign banks

Source: Federal Deposit Insurance Corporation

state-chartered member banks, and bank holding companies are under the supervision of Reserve banks.

The Fed has help supervising banks. The FDIC, the OTS, and the OCC also supervise banking institutions. The pie chart on page 81 helps clarify relative dollar volumes.

The Review Process

The Reserve banks ensure that each bank complies with state and federal legal requirements. They also make sure that each bank adheres to its own internally developed methods for conducting business. Most importantly, the Reserve banks make sure that each bank has sufficient reserves to handle outstanding loans and the risks associated with those loans.

A bank is given permission to operate as a business based on its charter, which is a legal approval to operate a business as a bank. Charters are issued by a government authority. The specific agency that issued the charter is responsible for regulating the bank. The table below clarifies some of these relationships.

Supervising Authority	Type of Institution
Federal Reserve	State banks (that have joined the Fed)
	Bank holding companies
Office of Thrift Supervision	Savings and loan associations
	Thrift holding companies
Comptroller of the Currency	National banks
Federal Deposit Insurance Corporation	State banks (that have not joined the Fed)
Consumer Financial Protection Bureau	Banks, credit unions, securities firms, payday lenders, mortgage-servicing operations, foreclosure relief services, debt collectors and other financial companies operating in the United States

Size and structure of the financial institutions dictate the frequency of on-site reviews. Member banks, which are state banks that have chosen to become members of the Fed, usually receive an on-site review annually. Small banks, with assets of less than $250 million, might only be reviewed every 18 months. For some state member banks, the Fed may alternate on-site reviews with the overseeing state.

Processes and technologies are in place to streamline the off-site monitoring of banks. Actual reports that banks must complete on a regular basis vary by the size and scope of the bank. Larger banks with more diversified activities are required to complete more reports.

To make sure that bank reports and supervision are performed in a uniform manner, the Federal Financial Institutions Examination Council (FFIEC) was established by Congress in 1978. Membership on the council includes representatives from the Federal Reserve Board of Governors, the Comptroller of the Currency, the National Credit Union Administration, the FDIC, and the OTS. By having members from a variety of agencies, the FFIEC fosters information sharing between state and federal agencies with the common goal of providing consistent methods for banking supervision.

Each quarter, banks are required to complete a Consolidated Reports of Condition and Income, or Call report. This report is the basis for the

Uniform Bank Performance Report. By comparing current financial ratios to past financial ratios, the Uniform Bank Performance Report highlights any changes in a bank's performance. Declines or startling changes in performance trigger investigation by the supervising agencies.

The **System to Estimate Examinations Ratings (SEER)** is an automated system that analyzes and compares historical supervisory ratings of banks with their Call report data. SEER provides an additional method of capturing changes in financial performance that may require supervisory intervention. SEER data can also be used to track trends within the banking industry.

✔checkpoint

Why is the authority that issued a bank's charter important in the ongoing operations of the bank?

3.4.2 THE SCORE CARD

After each on-site review is completed, the Fed issues a rating for the bank. Examiners use the **CAMELS rating** system to evaluate six criteria of safety and soundness. Each letter stands for one of the criteria: **C**apital adequacy, **A**sset adequacy, **M**anagement, **E**arnings, **L**iquidity, and **S**ensitivity to risk. Risk evaluation measures whether a bank makes good decisions in lending money. CAMELS ratings are not public information. The agency that issues the rating has proprietary rights to the rating. Banks cannot release their CAMELS rating to third parties without first obtaining approval from the agency that issued the rating. This issue became prominent when insurance companies began to ask banks for their CAMELS rating prior to providing them with insurance.

Maintaining Balance in the Banking System

Banks are required to get permission from the Fed before they can acquire another bank, introduce new products, or diversify. This mandatory approval process enables Reserve banks to make sure that regulatory requirements are met. The permission process also gives the Fed an opportunity to ensure there will be sufficient competition in the regional market.

Trust Generates Trust

It takes a great deal of mutual trust for all parties in an economic system to keep investing in a system. Each investor needs to be assured that every other investor will act within a predefined and universally accepted way. Banking regulations make a code of conduct explicit and mandatory. This gives investors assurance that their money will be carefully and honestly managed. This trust allows money to keep flowing through the system. Regulations can be revised to reflect needs of society and still maintain the safeguards necessary for ethical and safe practices.

Regulations That Encourage Private Investors to Aid Ailing Banks

A variety of privately financed entities, including private equity firms, hedge funds, and mutual funds, were willing to provide capital to distressed banks during the recent mortgage and credit crises. Regulations that were in place during April 2008 allowed these investors access to the banks' books, including some confidential banking records. By being allowed to carefully examine banks' financial status before investing in them, privately financed companies could obtain a solid understanding of actual financial positions of the bank. Knowing what they were getting into allowed private equity firms the ability to negotiate the terms of their investment and to invest with a clear understanding of any risks associated with their investment.

During the savings and loan crisis that occurred during the late 1980s and early 1990s, private investors did not have the same level of open access to the books of banks. This lack of access discouraged private investment firms from providing capital to help save failing savings and loans.

Future Regulations That May Facilitate Private Investment

Some market watchers think the government should make additional regulatory changes to further encourage private equity investors to help save banks.

Current regulations cap the percent that a private equity firm can invest in a bank at less than 10 percent of shares. There is a belief that by increasing that cap, private equity firms would be more willing to invest in banks. An increased percentage of ownership would provide stronger shareholder voting power. With stronger voting power, firms would feel they have more control over future management of the bank.

Another potential change would impact banking acquisitions. Currently, when one bank acquires another, any bad loans held by the acquiree must be written off immediately by the acquiring bank. This requires a lot of up-front capital from the acquiring banks. Similarly, a large amount of capital for bad debt is a disincentive for many potential investors.

The potential change would allow bad debt held by the acquiree to be written off over time. This would lessen the amount of capital an acquiring bank would need to provide. By lessening the immediate financial exposure of the acquiring bank, the proposed change would lower the hurdle for acquiring a bank.

Why is society interested in encouraging banks to help other ailing banks?

assessment 3.4

Think Critically

1. What is a charter?

2. What does the acronym CAMELS represent?

3. How does the Uniform Bank Report help regulators?

4. Why is trust necessary in the banking system?

Make Academic Connections

5. **LOCAL GOVERNMENT** Interview a local bank representative and ask about the review process at his or her bank. Find out which regulatory agencies participate in the review and the frequency of the reviews. Inquire how the bank's asset level affects the frequency of the review schedule. Summarize your findings below.

6. **RESEARCH** Copies of Call reports are available to the public at the FFIEC website. Access the website and look up the most recent Call report for your bank. Scan the report to obtain an idea of the completeness of the data collected. Does the thoroughness of the data collected make you, as a consumer, feel more confident that your bank is closely regulated? Be prepared to discuss your thoughts and feelings with the class.

3.5

International Banking and the Federal Reserve System

Learning Objectives

3.5.1 Explain the role of the Fed in international banking.

3.5.2 Discuss how the Fed works to keep the dollar strong.

3.5.3 Review how countries work together to provide a stable international banking economy.

Key Terms

- Strength of Support Assessment (SOSA)
- ROCA score
- fixed exchange rate
- flexible exchange rate
- balance of payments
- Federal Reserve System Open Market Account (SOMA)
- U.S. Treasury Exchange Stabilization Fund (ESF)

Banking Scene

Kareema had spent a few years saving money for her upcoming vacation to Europe. She had carefully planned her budget to cover transportation, lodging, food, admittance to attractions, and some spare money for spontaneous "fun" activities. She had recently read that the value of the dollar had declined relative to the euro. She began to worry about her expenses. Realizing the dollar would buy less on her trip, she was examining her budget to see where she could cut back. Why did the dollar weaken?

3.5.1 AN INTERDEPENDENT GLOBAL ECONOMY

Globalization has led to increased interdependency between nations. Food, raw materials, medicines, electronics, and vehicles are just a few of the products that flow between borders. Money is required to enable these transactions. A mutually acceptable method needs to be in place so that nations that use different currency can exchange funds across international borders.

Just as products flow across borders, financial instruments flow across borders. U.S. monetary policies affect the global economy just as financial actions of the global economy affect the U.S. economy. Foreign-owned banks operate in the United States and U.S.-owned banks have offices in foreign countries. The Fed works, sometimes in conjunction with other U.S. agencies or with central banks of other countries, to promote stability in international financial markets. Efforts include supervising international banking, minimizing disruptions in currency value, and sponsoring internationally focused learning sessions.

Supervision of International Banks

There are multiple ways that the Fed regulates foreign banking. U.S.-chartered banks that operate in foreign countries are regulated by the Fed. Banks that are chartered in a foreign country and transact business in the U.S. are also regulated by the Fed.

Federal regulation of foreign banks was formalized with the International Banking Act of 1978 (IBA). To ensure a level playing field between international banks and domestic banks, this act gave the same powers to foreign banks that U.S. banks have. On the flip side, foreign banks are subjected to the same restrictions as U.S. banks.

Nearly 20 years later, this act was amended with the passage of the Foreign Bank Supervision Enhancement Act of 1991 (FBSEA). Under FBSEA, foreign banks are required to obtain the approval of the Fed before opening offices in the U.S. In determining whether to approve these applications, the Fed considers how stringently the bank is regulated in its country of origin, the overall financial health of the bank, and whether the bank and its country of origin actively seek to fight money laundering.

Sometimes the Fed partners with other U.S. supervisory agencies to carry out regulations. Two sets of rankings have been established to help with this process. The Strength of Support Assessment (SOSA) reflects how well a foreign bank is able to provide appropriate guidance, oversight, and financial backing to its U.S. offices. A composite score of performance in four distinct areas is a ROCA score. The areas included in this score are **R**isk management, **O**perational controls, **C**ompliance, and **A**sset quality.

Stabilizing Currency Values

Promoting full employment, price stability, and economic growth is the common goal of many monetary authorities in various countries.

Banking Math *Connection*

With a flexible exchange rate, currency values change relative to other currencies. The following chart shows the values of a few currencies relative to the dollar as of February 2016. These rates were listed in the Foreign Exchange Rates section of the Federal Reserve. Find how many euros equal 1 U.S. dollar.

Country	Denomination	$US February 2016
Australia	dollar	0.714
EMU members	euro	1.115
India	rupee	68.129

Solution

$$\frac{1 \text{ euro}}{1.115 \text{ \$US}} = \frac{x \text{ euro}}{1 \text{ \$US}}$$

$$1.115\,x = 1$$
$$x = 1 \div 1.115$$
$$x = 0.90 \text{ euros}$$

Therefore, 1 $US will buy 0.90 euros.

Foreign exchange methodologies have changed through the years. From about the mid 1940s until the early 1970s, the U.S. dollar was at the center of international currency exchange. Under a fixed-rate exchange system, the United States needed to maintain the dollar price of gold at about $35 per ounce. The United States would buy and sell dollars to stay at or near the $35 rate. In turn, other countries were required to maintain the value of their currency relative to the U.S. dollar at a set amount. Only a one percent variation in value was allowed.

A fixed exchange rate is a bit of an artificial system. A monetary valuation of one country's currency is tied to the valuation of another country's currency. Sometimes the decision is made to maintain the international currency value at the expense of some other monetary goal—such as maintaining full employment, price stability, or economic growth.

A flexible exchange rate enables currencies to fluctuate based on market conditions. To fully understand flexible exchange rates, an understanding of balance of payments is necessary.

Balance of Payments

Countries monitor the total amount of goods and services that leave their country. They also monitor the amount of goods and services that enter their country. Each country looks at the overall total of its imports and exports. It also monitors the amount of goods and services it trades with individual countries. The balance of payments is a record of all the exchanges of goods and services that occur between two countries for a specified time period.

A flexible exchange rate allows currency values to move up or down in response to changes in the balance of payments. If Country A sends more goods and services to Country B than it receives from Country B, then Country A has a surplus in the balance of payments with Country B. As a result of this surplus, Country A's exchange rate increases relative to Country B's. Therefore, Country A's currency can buy Country B's goods more cheaply. Likewise, Country B will find it more expensive to buy the goods of Country A.

Tech Talk

Electronic Funds Transfer

Like many businesses and private individuals, the Federal Reserve System uses electronic funds transfer (EFT) to make and receive payments. The Fed has its own system, called Fedwire, with special capabilities. Fedwire connects the Federal Reserve, the Treasury, other government agencies, and more than 9,500 financial institutions. In 2014, an average of 547,939 daily payments totaling approximately $3.5 trillion took place over the Fedwire network. This is compared to an average of 430,000 daily payments totaling about $1.5 trillion back in 2000. The Federal Reserve by law must charge for its Fedwire services and it prices them according to cost.

Think Critically
In what ways does Fedwire strengthen the entire Federal Reserve System? Why might the law mandate a charge for this service?

✔checkpoint

How would a balance of payment deficit affect Countries A and B?

3.5.2 KEEPING THE DOLLAR STRONG

In the mid 1970s, the U.S. transitioned from a fixed exchange rate to flexible exchange rates for managing international currency stability. The Fed helps maintain the international value of the dollar through foreign currency operations. The FOMC provides guidance to the Fed when it buys or sells U.S. dollars. The goal of stabilizing the international value of the dollar is to maintain a stable currency value to encourage international trade. Countries who wish to conduct business with the U.S. want a clear understanding of the profits and/or risks associated with the trades. Knowing that the value of the dollar will remain relatively stable allows foreign investors to predict the amount of profit or risk they will experience.

How do actions of the Fed stabilize the dollar? If the value of the dollar is falling, the Fed may purchase dollars by selling foreign currency. This tightens the supply of dollars on the open market, which causes the value of the dollar to increase. If the value of the dollar is high and the Fed wants to lower it, the Fed may buy foreign currency with U.S. dollars. This increases the supply of U.S. dollars in the marketplace, which lowers the value of the dollar. The Fed seeks to maintain a steady balance of Federal Reserve balances. When the Fed sells foreign currency, it *sterilizes* the impact of the sale by purchasing an equivalent amount of U.S. currency. Sterilization is necessary to maintain the federal funds rate at the target set by the FOMC. The account the Fed maintains international reserves in is the **Federal Reserve System Open Market Account (SOMA)**. The account the Treasury maintains international reserves in is the **U.S. Treasury Exchange Stabilization Fund (ESF)**.

As the U.S. Treasury and the Fed work in close cooperation on decisions and policies affecting foreign currency issues, they also share responsibility for maintaining the levels of foreign exchange reserves in the U.S. This shared responsibility results in a generally equal division of reserve holdings. For example, in February 2016, the Federal Reserve had just over $4.2 billion in its SOMA account and the Treasury had about $92 billion in its ESF account.

✔checkpoint

Why is the Fed interested in stabilizing the value of the dollar?

3.5.3 INTERNATIONAL COOPERATION

Many countries realize their dependence on and vulnerability to international market conditions. In addition to trading products across borders, countries or citizens from one country may directly invest in businesses in another country. One example of this direct investment is when foreign investors purchased mortgage-backed securities during the U.S. mortgage crisis. These investors were hoping to make a profit by purchasing the securities at a discount. By doing this, foreign investors held a significant number of U.S. mortgages.

To foster a spirit of trust, and to develop laws that ensure transactions are carried out in good faith and honestly, a number of organizations have formed over the years that are designed to make banking safe and mutually beneficial across international borders.

International Monetary Fund (IMF) Representatives from 188 member countries work together to promote economic growth among member countries. The IMF takes actions to encourage the stability of the financial exchange markets. Sometimes the IMF will lend money to a country that needs help with its balance of payments. The IMF also seeks to avoid money laundering in an effort to avoid financing terrorism.

Bank for International Settlements (BIS) The BIS is a bank for central banks. Serving the central banks of 60 countries (and not private entities), BIS focuses on fostering international monetary and financial stability. A variety of products aimed at helping central banks invest and manage their foreign assets is offered by BIS.

Asia Pacific Economic Cooperation (APEC) The 21 members of APEC are referred to as "member economies." APEC encourages economic growth in the Asia-Pacific Region. The U.S. is a member of APEC.

International Banking Seminars Since 1997, the Federal Reserve Bank of Chicago has organized international conferences on banking. By bringing together people who develop policy and people who do economic research, the seminars provide a cross section of ideas regarding issues that cut across many aspects of international banking. Recent seminars have focused on "Globalization and Systemic Risk," "International Financial Instability: Cross Border Banking and National Regulation," and "Credit Market Turmoil of 2007–2008: Implications for Public Policy."

 **checkpoint**

How does bringing together policy makers and researchers to examine a common topic facilitate smooth transactions for international banking?

assessment 3.5

Think Critically

1. Explain the key concepts of the International Banking Act of 1978.

2. What does the acronym ROCA mean and how does it relate to SOSA?

3. What is the balance of payments?

4. Name the account for international reserves maintained by the Fed and by the Treasury.

Make Academic Connections

5. **EDUCATION** Visit the website of the Chicago Federal Reserve. Review recent seminars on international banking and see what seminars are planned for the future. Be prepared to discuss how the seminars reflect past, current, and future concerns of the industry.

6. **ECONOMICS** During the third quarter of 2007, the international value of the dollar fell. During that time, one euro could buy $1.4065. Prior to that time, one euro could not buy more than $1.4. One result of the falling dollar value was that products manufactured in America were less expensive to citizens of countries whose currency was strong relative to the dollar. This increased American exports. Research the current international value of the dollar relative to the euro. List it below. Also explain how the dollar's international value affects the overall economy.

chapter 3 assessment

Chapter Summary

3.1 Structure of the Federal Reserve System

A. The Chair oversees the Federal Reserve Board, which oversees the 12 District Reserve Banks, which monitor and serve the member banks.

B. The Fed is the U.S. government's bank, a bank for banks, and a supervisory organization.

3.2 Monetary and Fiscal Policy

A. Monetary policy adjusts bank reserves and influences interest rates for economic stability. The Federal Reserve is the author of monetary policy.

B. Fiscal policy is the Congress and President's way to control the economy.

3.3 Consumer Protection

A. Four main laws (TILA, ECOA, FCRA, and FDCPA) provide the foundation for consumer protection in lending.

B. Banks are required to document their compliance with all applicable state and federal regulations.

3.4 Role in Determining Banks' Financial Health

A. The Fed, the FDIC, OTS, and OCC share oversight duties.

B. Quarterly Call reports summarize banks' performance.

3.5 International Banking and the Federal Reserve System

A. The Fed supervises U.S. banks with offices abroad and foreign banks with offices in the U.S.

B. The Fed and the Treasury work to keep the dollar strong.

C. Multiple organizations foster international economic development.

Vocabulary Builder

a. adverse feedback loop
b. balance of payments
c. Call report
d. CAMELS rating
e. charter
f. District Reserve Bank
g. Equal Credit Opportunity Act (ECOA)
h. Fair Credit Reporting Act
i. Fair Debt Collection Practices Act (FDCPA)
j. Federal Open Market Committee (FOMC)
k. Federal Reserve System Open Market Account (SOMA)
l. fixed exchange rate
m. flexible exchange rate
n. Government Accountability Office (GAO)
o. member bank
p. ROCA score
q. Strength of Support Assessment (SOSA)
r. System to Estimate Examinations Ratings (SEER)
s. Taylor rule
t. Truth in Lending Act (TILA)
u. U.S. Treasury Exchange Stabilization Fund (ESF)

Choose the term that best fits the definition. Write the letter of the answer in the space provided. Some terms may not be used.

____ 1. A report banks are required to complete quarterly that reflects their performance

____ 2. A rating of how well a foreign bank is able to provide appropriate guidance, oversight, and financial backing to its U.S. offices

____ 3. A record of all the exchanges of goods and services that occur between two countries for a specified time period

____ 4. Protects consumers from unfair collection techniques

____ 5. Guarantees that all information about a loan is provided in writing

____ 6. When the monetary valuation of one country's currency is tied to the valuation of another country's currency

____ 7. The government body that makes decisions about discount interest rates

____ 8. A theory about using short-term interest rates to achieve the goals of a central bank

____ 9. Legal approval to operate a business as a bank

Review Concepts

10. Name the four organizational components of the Federal Reserve System.

11. What five functions does the Federal Reserve perform?

12. Describe the structure and purpose of the FOMC.

13. How does Keynesian economics relate to fiscal policy?

14. Explain the role of an adverse feedback loop in the recent credit crisis.

15. How does the balance of payments impact a flexible exchange rate?

16. Why is it significant which government agency issued a bank's charter?

17. How does the SEER report help regulators?

18. Why is the government interested in helping private investors aid banks that are struggling?

_____

_____

_____

_____

19. Describe the membership and objectives of the IMF.

_____

20. Why did the U.S. transition from a fixed exchange rate to a flexible exchange rate?

_____

_____

Apply What You Learned

21. What is the advantage of distancing the Federal Reserve System from politics?

_____

_____

_____

22. Why is inflation a constant concern of the Federal Reserve Board?

_____

_____

23. Describe the differences between monetary and fiscal policy.

_____

_____

24. As of February 2016, the Australian dollar was worth $0.714 U.S. dollars and the Indian rupee was worth $68.129. How many Australian dollars and Indian rupees would a U.S. dollar have bought at that time?

_____

25. Name four consumer protection laws related to lending.

26. How would it help the banking industry if the amount a private equity firm could invest in a bank was increased beyond 10 percent?

Make Academic Connections

27. **POLITICAL SCIENCE**   If inflation is such a concern, why not just stabilize the economy by imposing wage and price controls? Wages and prices have occasionally been frozen before in emergency situations. Should wage and price controls be permanently established? Write a paragraph that summarizes your opinion.

28. **SOCIAL STUDIES**   Choose one of the laws discussed in Lesson 3.3, Consumer Protection. Prepare a detailed report on its history, its provisions, and its effect on the lending industry. Write a three-page report on what you learn.

29. **RESEARCH**   Consumer protection also applies to student loans. In September 2008, the *New York Times* reported that seven student loan companies were required to develop a $1.4 million dollar fund to help educate students and their parents on student loans. The companies were cited for misleading advertising practices, including sending students marketing materials that looked like they came from the federal government. Research any new cases where the government intervened to protect consumers' rights. Prepare a one-page report to summarize your findings.

4 Money and Interest

zefart/Shutterstock.com

skills that pay dividends

The choice of computing methods—from calculators, to cell phones, to spreadsheets, to online services—has made it extraordinarily easy for you to enter data into a computing device and get an answer. Whether doing multiplication to calculate the cost of buying enough pizzas for a Little League team or performing complex analytical functions to determine the economic performance of a business, you can get a machine to provide an answer.

Do people using electronic calculators understand the concepts behind the computations? If electricity failed and batteries were not available, could most people manually calculate the answers? Maybe not, given the scores from U.S. students during a recent International Student Assessment that indicated 15-year-old U.S. students performed less well on math than peers from 23 other countries.

The ability to mentally perform a "ballpark" calculation for financial transactions enables you to think on your feet. You will be able to quickly assess the reasonableness of the results you see on your screen. By having a rough idea of what an answer should be, you can catch errors early on.

In the banking industry, percentages are used in a variety of ways. Calculations that use percentages include simple interest and mutual fund performance.

Simple interest is calculated by multiplying the beginning amount, or principal, by the interest rate and by the duration of the investment. The interest rate is expressed as a percentage. The duration of the investment is expressed, in decimal form, in relation to a year. A three-month investment is 25 percent of a year, or 0.25 years. A 21-month investment is 1.75 years.

Mutual funds are comprised of a variety of distinct investments that have various degrees of risk and varying maturity dates. Typically the investments are diversified across a number of different industries to minimize the exposure caused by a downturn in any specific industry. The performance of each investment in each industry contributes to the performance of the fund as a whole.

Mutual fund returns are expressed based on the performance of each industry in the fund. For example, the fund may state that 50 percent of its results are based on performance of the airline industry, 30 percent on the performance of the pharmaceutical industry, and 20 percent on the performance of the software industry. Stated another way, half of the fund is invested in the airline industry, a bit less than a third is invested in the pharmaceutical industry, and one fifth of it is invested in the software industry.

Develop Your Skill

Create a quiz on percentages that has 10 values and 10 percentages to calculate. Exchange papers with classmates and complete the quizzes. Grade the quizzes and see who had the greatest percentage of correct answers.

4.1

The Money Supply

Learning Objectives

4.1.1 Explain how the money supply is measured.

4.1.2 Describe the two types of money.

Key Terms

- money supply
- liquidity
- aggregate measures
- commodity money
- fiat money
- fractional reserve system

Banking Scene

When Elizabeth Axtell paid for her gasoline fill-up, she received a 10 dollar bill as change. She happened to notice that on the bill someone had written, "Happy Birthday, Betty!" This greeting on the bill caused her to think of all the places the bill had traveled and all the people who had handled the bill. As she put the bill away, she wondered how much money there is circulating out there at any given moment, and she resolved to learn more about it. How might Elizabeth begin to define "out there"?

4.1.1 WHAT IS THE MONEY SUPPLY? • • • • • • • • • • • • • •

As you learned about the creation of a national currency and problems throughout the nineteenth and early twentieth centuries with the money supply, did you wonder where money comes from? Why can't the government just print more money? What would happen if it did?

The Federal Reserve was established to solve currency problems and manage the money supply. Its adjustments are indirect, and because banks are private institutions, the Fed doesn't simply command the money supply. The Federal Reserve influences the conditions under which banks do business and sees that those banks abide by banking regulations. You may be surprised about what money really is in the United States. You will get a sense of how much money is out there, what it is doing, and how its movements are measured. You will also learn more about how banks and the Federal Reserve work together to create and manage money.

The Concept of Money Supply

Even after state currencies disappeared and a national monetary system was in place, serious problems with the banking system occurred in 1873, 1883, 1893, and 1907, resulting in bank failures and large-scale economic problems. The crisis in 1907 caused Congress to commission a study group, which ultimately led to the establishment of the Federal Reserve.

The source of these problems was the money supply. The money supply is defined as the liquid assets held by banks and individuals. These assets include all the money in circulation as well as money held in banks or in

Photodisc/getty images

other financial institutions. This money is moving in the economy from place to place and person to person. The flow of money—and the amount of it flowing—has a direct effect on how the economy performs.

The basic idea is simple: if there is too much money around, prices rise to the point of inducing problematic inflation. If there is too little money around, there is not enough to meet needs and a "credit crunch" slows the economy. If the economy slows too much, commerce spirals down, jobs are lost, less and less money moves, and so forth. The trick is to keep the money supply and economy growing at a stable rate so that wealth spreads, yet without inducing inflation. Unfortunately, there are so many factors in a complex economy that providing steady growth is not easy.

Expanding the Money Supply

Why might extra money in the economy cause inflation? Assume you have an income of $4,000 per month that meets your basic needs. Suddenly, your income jumps 15 percent to $4,600. What would you do with the extra money? Most people would probably buy things. That seems like a good thing, doesn't it?

Now assume you own an electronics store. If a large rush of customers came in demanding laptops, how would you respond? Consider the following questions: What would happen to prices of laptops? Why? What would happen to the supply of laptops? What effect might that have on prices? If prices for all goods and services also went up, what would be the net effect on your 15 percent increase in income compared to what it actually buys?

The supply of laptops will decrease, thus causing prices to rise. If prices for all goods and services go up, the 15 percent increase in income will actually buy less. If this trend continues for a period of time, it can result in inflation.

Measuring the Money Supply

Defining the money supply as all the money in circulation, all the money held by banks, and all the money held by individuals may not be detailed enough to track the ebb and flow of money. Liquidity is a measure of how quickly things may be converted to something of value like cash. Liquidity is variable, depending on the nature of the asset or liability. Your savings account is not as liquid as coins in your pocket, but it is more liquid than a certificate of deposit that doesn't mature until next June.

All the money in all types of accounts is part of the money supply. However, some types of money are more liquid than others. To estimate money's movement, economists and the Federal Reserve use various measures. These measures, called M1, M2, and MZM, take into account various types of money and various circumstances of liquidity.

Measure	Explanation
M1	Money that can be spent immediately. M1 includes currency (paper and metallic) and various types of checking accounts, including nonbank travelers' checks, standard checking accounts, and NOW (interest-bearing) accounts.
M2	All the money in M1 plus short-term investments, such as small savings accounts (less than $100,000), money market accounts, and money market mutual funds.
MZM	Money at zero maturity. Represents all available liquid money. It is M2, minus time deposits, and includes all money market funds.

As a result of the Humphrey-Hawkins Act, also known as the Full Employment and Balanced Growth Act of 1978, the Fed set semi-annual target rates for the money supply. Investors interpreted these target rates as an indicator of what the Fed planned to do with the money supply. For example, if the Fed released a low M1, investors might think short-term interest rates would be decreased to increase the money supply. (When consumers earn less return on the money in savings accounts, they may decide to take money from savings and make a purchase. This releases more money into the economy.) As of July 2000, the Fed stopped setting target ranges for the money supply.

Taken together, these aggregate measures, which add up the components of the money supply, are used to estimate the size of the money supply.

Tech Talk

Measuring Nontraditional Forms of Money

How do "electronic money" and automated payment systems affect the money supply and monetary policies? These nontraditional forms can alter the measurement of the money supply, which in turn could shift the way monetary policy is implemented. Most consumer electronic money falls easily into the M1 demand-deposit category, and it has already begun to be measured as such. But as these services grow, they may alter the definition of certain monetary instruments. Economists rely less on the M1 and M2 measures than they once did, and some think they are relatively unimportant.

Think Critically
Why are the M1 and M2 measures becoming less important? How does changing technology also alter the Federal Reserve's supervisory task?

M1 is sometimes referred to as the "base" money supply. M2 and MZM give some indication of potential demand on the money supply. Historically, it was believed that increasing growth of the money supply accompanied a strengthening economy, while decreasing growth of money implied a slowing economy.

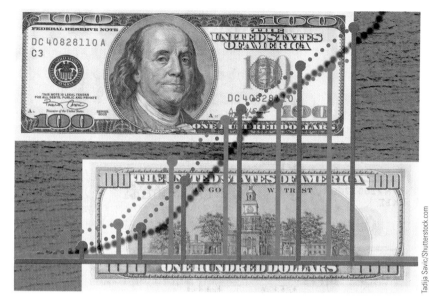

Over time, M1 and M2 became less reliable indicators of financial performance. As financial offerings expanded, with the introduction of products like NOW accounts, the relationship between economic performance and the values of M1 and M2 weakened. NOW accounts allowed consumers to earn interest on service-free checking accounts so long as they maintained a minimum balance. Shifts in the economy, including changes in interest rates, prompted customers to shift their investment strategies. As investments moved from traditional savings accounts to the stock market, the value of M2 decreased. Stocks and bonds are excluded from M2 measurements. Therefore, although consumers still had their money working for them, the value of the money was not reflected in M1 or M2.

A fourth measure of the money supply, M3, was in use from 1971 until March 2006. M3 was the most comprehensive measure of available money and included all the money in M1 and M2 plus large deposits, such as agreements among banks and institutional money market funds. A surge in M3 indicated an excessive amount of money was available. As access to money became easier, costs rose and inflation occurred. Some who study economic trends believe that an unusually rapid growth of M3 was a predicator of a possible depression.

None of these measures alone is a safe predictor of inflation. Other factors such as supply, demand, labor, resources, and political events also play a role in determining the rate of inflation.

✔checkpoint

What makes up the money supply? Why do economists use different measurements to track the money supply?

41.2 THE NATURE OF MONEY

To understand where the money supply comes from, how it moves, and how banks and the Federal Reserve influence it, you need to understand what money in the United States really is. Although the monetary system has remnants from long ago, it is also a modern "agreement" dating from the 1930s. Two essential ideas dominate the monetary system. One is the idea of *fiat money*, and the other is the idea of a *fractional-reserve system*.

Two Types of Money

Why does money have value? Money is a medium of exchange—something with an agreed-upon value used for trade. Today that agreed-upon value is strictly a convention of the government and has no necessary relationship to the value of gold, silver, bushels of grain, feathers, or any other commodity. A dollar is worth a dollar because everyone agrees that it is, not because it is backed by an amount of precious metal somewhere. Historically, there are two types of monetary systems.

Commodity money is based on some item of value—for example, gold or precious stones. Coins, the oldest form of currency, had some value because of the metal in them. Bank notes were originally issued to represent holdings of precious metal and became the first paper currency. The notes had value because they could be exchanged for an actual amount of a valuable commodity. Although many of the symbolic ideas and concepts associated with commodity money remain in play, commodity money is not generally in use today.

Fiat money is money that is deemed legal tender by the government, and it is not based on or convertible into a commodity. The word *fiat* refers to any order issued by legal authority, and in the case of U.S. money, the

iStockphoto.com/zoom-zoom

authority is the Federal Reserve as created by Congress. Take a look at a dollar bill. It announces that it is a Federal Reserve note. According to recent estimates, it costs about 6.2 cents to produce a dollar bill, and you cannot take Federal Reserve notes to the bank and exchange them for gold or silver. What makes Federal Reserve notes valuable is that they are the only kind of money the government will accept for payment of taxes and for payments of debts related to court actions. They are, in short, the official currency of the United States.

Fiat money makes sense as a medium of exchange. If you and some friends agreed to use certificates you made for value between you, and you all abided by that convention, your currency system would work. Saran might be willing to trade you a DVD for two of the certificates, which you might then give Luisa for an hour of raking leaves. Luisa might use them to buy a basket of flowers from Dawn for Saran, and Dawn might offer you two certificates to care for her dog while she's away. As long as you all agree on the relative values, the system works. In the case of the national system, the government enforces what is acceptable currency, and the Federal Reserve, banks, and market influence its value. In any case, there is no longer silver in a quarter, though everyone agrees that it is worth 25 percent of a dollar.

The Fractional-Reserve System

One of the key concepts in understanding how money is created and manipulated arose almost a thousand years ago. Some people say "modern" banking began in England around 1200. At that time, people began to pay goldsmiths to store precious metals safely. The goldsmiths charged a fee for this service. When people left gold or silver, the goldsmiths gave them receipts, indicating that the holder of the receipt had deposited a certain quantity. Soon, people began to use these receipts as a medium of exchange, because trading them was a lot simpler than going to the goldsmith, getting the gold, and giving it to the person owed. It was easier just to give the receipt. These receipts were the first bank notes in England, and became a form of paper currency.

The goldsmiths quickly got into the business of lending the gold and silver they had on deposit, charging interest for the loans. That business was good, so goldsmiths began to pay interest to attract deposits. This business practice initiated the *spread* in banking.

The goldsmiths also noticed something else. Not everyone wanted their gold back at the same time. Therefore, the goldsmiths adopted a fractional-reserve system whereby they needed to keep back, or reserve, only a fraction of the total gold that had been deposited—just enough to cover those who might want to withdraw their gold. They could also lend notes, thus making more money without actually having gold to back it up. The paper notes in circulation eventually exceeded the reserves of gold that the goldsmiths actually held. In effect, money was "created" without changing the amount of gold.

Although what the goldsmiths noticed was based on a system of commodity money, some of the same principles apply today. First, even though Federal Reserve notes are fiat money, money is created in more or less the same way. Second, a fractional-reserve system is still in use today, and adjusting its requirements is one way that the Federal Reserve controls the money supply.

✔checkpoint

What is fiat money? What is meant by fractional reserve?

"communicate"

Interview several people from various walks of life. Ask them what they think makes our money valuable. Write a short report listing the various opinions (right or wrong), and share the ideas with your class.

assessment 4.1

Think Critically

1. Why are there more elements to the money supply than just the money that is actively circulating?

2. Why do different parts of the money supply need to be measured differently?

3. Why must the government enforce the value of fiat money by requiring its use for settling private debts in court or for transactions with the government?

4. What would have happened to the English goldsmiths if for some reason everyone had wanted their gold back at the same time? What could the goldsmiths have done?

Make Academic Connections

5. **HISTORY**   Besides fiat money, the U.S. government has issued other types of money, such as silver certificates. Find out what a silver certificate is, when the last one was issued, and what one is worth today. Record your findings here.

6. **MATH**   The Federal Reserve requires banks to hold a reserve on customer deposits subject to checking. For example, assuming the Federal Reserve required a reserve of 3% on the first liabilities between $9.3 million and $43.9 million and 10 percent on all amounts above that. If a bank had $91 million in such deposits, what was the amount of required reserves?

Money Creation and Circulation

4.2

Learning Objectives

4.2.1 Describe how money is created by bank activities.

4.2.2 Explain how money circulates in the U.S.

Key Terms

- primary reserves
- secondary reserves
- excess reserves
- multiplier effect

Banking Scene

As Elizabeth Axtell pulls away from the gas station, she thinks about how currency circulates. She also begins to wonder more about the origin of money. She knows the government prints it, of course, but under what circumstances? How does the money supply grow? What would you tell her?

4.2.1 HOW MONEY IS CREATED

How money is created and how currency is printed are two different things. The Bureau of Engraving and Printing performs the task of printing currency. No matter how much the Bureau prints, it isn't actually considered part of the money supply until a commercial bank or other financial institution calls for it in exchange for amounts on deposit in the reserve account of the Federal Reserve. Money is actually created by the interaction of the demand for it, banks' use of it, and the Federal Reserve's supply and control of it.

Banks and other financial institutions play a key role in the creation of money by transacting their business. Banks earn much of their profit by lending. The lending function, however, does much more than earn money for the bank and its stockholders. Because of the function of the Federal Reserve and the banking system as a whole, banks actually "create" and circulate money as they do business.

Deposits and Reserves

Your deposits are liabilities for the bank that holds them, because the bank will have to give your money back to you. In order to guarantee that the bank will have money on hand to cover its liabilities, the Federal Reserve requires banks to hold money in reserve. Only a portion of the total amount of deposits is required to be reserved. **Primary reserves** consist of *vault cash* (cash on hand) and the required percentage amounts on deposit in the Federal Reserve District Bank. A bank may have other reserves as well, called **secondary reserves**, including securities the bank purchases from the federal government and deposits that are due from other banks. Secondary reserves are used to meet liquidity needs, which include customer requests for withdrawal amounts and money needed for new loans.

Excess reserves are reserves held by a bank beyond its reserve requirement. Excess reserves, which are amounts that exceed primary and secondary reserves, are the resources a bank uses to create money through its business transactions. These excess reserves are amounts for which there is no immediate demand. The bank may go into the Fed Funds market and put them to work overnight by lending them to another institution that has a need for them. Or the bank may purchase a repurchase agreement from the Federal Reserve if the FRB is making such an offer through its open market operations.

The Multiplier Effect

To understand the role banks play in creating money, consider again the fractional-reserve system. Remember that a bank needs to keep on hand only part of its total liabilities, and that liabilities always exceed reserves. This fractional-reserve system works just as it did for the goldsmiths long ago. Money on deposit, minus the reserve requirement, can be loaned to customers. When it is, new deposits are created. These new deposits go out to customers as loans and create more deposits, thus expanding the amount of money in the system. This phenomenon is called the multiplier effect.

Suppose you deposit $1,000, and the bank has a 10 percent reserve requirement. That leaves $900 that may be loaned out to someone. That $900 may be used to buy something, and the seller will probably end up depositing that $900 in another bank. (It could be the same one, but use a different one for the sake of the example.) Of the $900 deposited in the second bank, 10 percent is reserved, leaving $810, which the second bank will lend and will thus end up deposited in a third bank. Your original $1,000 deposit has

Banking Math *Connection*

Calculate the total amount of money "created" from a deposit of $15,000 as it moves through four cycles of deposit. Assume a reserve rate of 10 percent.

Solution

The formula for calculating the money available from a deposit is

Deposit − Reserve = New Deposit

Repeat the operation for each deposit, then total the new deposits.

Deposit 1: $15,000 − $1,500.00 = $13,500.00   0.10 × $15,000 = $1,500.00
Deposit 2: $13,500 − $1,350.00 = $12,150.00   0.10 × $13,500 = $1,350.00
Deposit 3: $12,150 − $1,215.00 = $10,935.00   0.10 × $12,150 = $1,215.00
Deposit 4: $10,935 − $1,093.50 = $ 9,841.50   0.10 × $10,935 = $1,093.50

Total Deposits = $46,426.50

These four deposits result in the "creation" of more than $46,000 available for use in the money supply.

resulted in deposits in three separate banks totaling $2,710. Of this total, $1,710 was "created" by the transactions.

Now, of course, your bank must have enough total reserves to cover the $900 check it wrote for the loan when the second bank presents that check for payment. Your bank must also be prepared to give your original $1,000 back to you if you decide to withdraw it. It may use excess reserves for this money, or money from its cash flow of other business, or it may borrow from the Federal Reserve or other sources. Estimating the amount of reserves needed at a particular point in time is critical to banking, although it is impossible to do so with complete accuracy. The bank can't absolutely know when you will want your money, and it can't absolutely know when someone wants a loan. Banks follow the money supply and the economy as closely as they can in order to anticipate their liabilities and reserve needs. In order for all these transactions to pay off, the bank must be making a solid profit on the money it lends. That $900 loan and others like it must earn enough income to defray the costs of creating money. Banks that make poor judgments about the type and amount of loans they extend may find themselves in trouble. If enough banks get into trouble, the whole system could be in jeopardy. Overseeing sound banking practices is one of the important functions of the Federal Reserve, as shown by this example.

 checkpoint

Why must banks keep money on reserve? What is the multiplier effect?

4.2.2 HOW MONEY CIRCULATES

Banks move money. Not only do they move money, they create it by making deposits in other financial institutions so the monetary system as a whole expands.

Transfers and Circulation

As you considered the multiplier effect in the last section, did you get the sense that there's a lot going on as money moves? If you did, you're right. That simplified example showed only one small deposit at work. It did not consider the millions of customer and commercial transactions taking place every day, nor did it consider transactions flowing from banks and the Federal Reserve that make up the reserves any of the banks were holding. It also did not show the effect of the loans themselves on the economy, what products might have been purchased

with the borrowed money, or what jobs depended upon them, so that the people holding those jobs could also make deposits—and thus fuel more expansion. All these transfers and transactions, as well as simpler movements of currency, such as bills passing as change, constitute the circulation of money.

If you look again at the elements of the money supply, you notice that M1, M2, and MZM represent so many potential transactions that the circulation of money is a complex phenomenon. Of course, most large transactions do not actually involve the movement of physical currency. Most, including creation of deposits at banks and at the Fed, involve *ledger entries*. A record of the transaction appears, just as you record your deposits and spending in your checking account. Many of these records are now entirely paperless.

The Fed and Fiat Money

It is important to remember what money is and isn't. When banks "create" money with deposits, it comes from somewhere. Where it comes from is the theoretical idea of the money supply, which is possible because of the fiat system. The Federal Reserve manages this fiat system, and it adjusts required deposits in bank accounts at the Federal Reserve to affect the money supply and banking system accordingly. The Fed has the option of contracting the money supply by raising reserve requirements if the economy seems to be overheating. If banks must hold more in reserve, there is less available to lend. Similarly, by lowering reserve requirements, the Fed expands the money supply by making more money available to create deposits. Although these options are available, the Fed very seldom uses changes in reserve requirement rates to implement monetary policy. Open market operations is the tool it uses most frequently to implement monetary policy. The Fed also influences bank activity by controlling interest rates.

One World

U.S. Currency Abroad

Of the $1.39 trillion worth of Federal Reserve notes estimated to be in circulation during 2015, at least two-thirds were held by people from abroad. Though their governments have their own money and may not be part of our fiat system, many people around the world use U.S. Federal Reserve notes and coins as a medium of exchange for both local and international business.

Think Critically Why might U.S. currency be seen as valuable in other countries? Why might people who have no direct business with anyone in the United States value U.S. currency?

When investor confidence is shaken because of the perception of a high degree of turmoil in the economy, the Fed can take steps beyond adjusting both the reserve requirements and interest rates.

Money as an IOU

Did you know that you hold an IOU from the government? A dollar bill in your hands represents an obligation of the government to provide something of value to you. Because it is fiat money, the government promises not a quantity of gold, but a pledge that the note will be good in the United States. The item of value being provided to you is the guarantee that it will be accepted for payment of taxes and settlement of debts.

Because money is an IOU in this way, it is also a liability on the Federal Reserve's books. When the Federal Reserve makes a loan and thus creates a deposit in a bank's account at the Reserve, it has "created" more currency (and may call for actual paper money to support it). Required by law to balance the books, the Fed buys and holds *treasury securities* from the government itself as pledge against the IOUs it has issued. These securities are what back your currency, although they would be paid in Federal Reserve notes. Because the fiat money system is a closed system, the full faith and credit of the U.S. government is what actually backs your bill. As long as the government is operating and able to maintain the system, its IOU to you (its money) will be a valuable medium of exchange.

✔checkpoint

What circulates money in the United States? What backs the currency in circulation in the United States?

assessment 4.2

Think Critically

1. Why can't banks and the Federal Reserve just create money at will so that all people will have what they need?

_____

_____

2. Why do some people say that money is "borrowed into existence?"

_____

_____

3. Why is the stability of the U.S. government such a large factor in the monetary system?

_____

_____

Make Academic Connections

4. **MATH**   Revisit the Banking Math Connection on page 106. Recalculate the amount of new deposits created as a result of an original deposit of $15,000 and a required reserve rate of 12 percent instead of 10 percent. How much less money does this reserve rate create in deposits? Why would making such a change slow the economy?

_____

_____

_____

_____

_____

_____

5. **BIOGRAPHY**   Other factors influence the money supply as well, including government actions and policies. Two giants in economics, John M. Keynes and Milton Friedman, had differing opinions. Choose one of these men and write a one-page biographical sketch, outlining his principal ideas.

6. **COMMUNICATION**   With a classmate, discuss ways that the information in this chapter has changed your understanding of currency. Summarize your discussion.

Interest and Interest Rates

Banking Scene

When Elizabeth Axtell bought her car, she shopped for a loan as well as a vehicle. Most car dealers finance through a bank or through the carmaker's financial company, and rates should be compared. A week after selecting her rate, she saw that it had increased. Though she felt satisfied with the deal she got, she wondered why interest rates change.

Learning Objectives

4.3.1 List factors that affect interest rates.

4.3.2 Explain which factors the Federal Reserve affects.

Key Terms

- federal funds rate
- discount rate
- prime rate

4.3.1 INTEREST RATES AND BUSINESS • • • • • • • • • • • • • •

In the discussion of how money is created to expand the economy, little mention of interest rates has appeared. Yet interest rates are the primary way banks make money and the focal point of almost everything they do. Bankers are not creating money purely from the goodness of their hearts. Banks are businesses, and businesses depend on profit to survive. The money supply and the economy are linked closely to interest rates. Generally, when rates are high, money is said to be "tight" and business tends to slow, because it costs more to acquire capital. When rates drop, more credit is accessible, and the economy tends to gather speed. Interest rates play a critical role in determining what the economy is doing.

iStockphoto.com/morganl

Factors Affecting Interest Rates

Contrary to what many people believe, the Federal Reserve does not decide interest rates. Its actions influence them, and the Fed does indeed attempt to nudge rates up or down in the interest of its monetary policy. But forces that determine interest rates are not completely under the Fed's control.

Market forces determine most interest rates. Banks are free to charge whatever rates they want for most of their transactions with customers (within legal limits), but it is a balancing act. Setting a higher rate for a loan does bring in more income, but it also tends to drive away business. Banking is more fiercely competitive than ever, and the lower the rate banks can charge on the money they lend, the more customers they are likely to have.

The economic conditions at large help determine interest rates too. If the demand for capital is high, interest rates tend to rise like any other prices. If they rise too far, demand falls off. The inflation outlook influences rates as well, as both savers and investors look for higher rates when they fear that inflation will erode the value of what they earn. Bankers are no different from any other investors in this regard.

The cost of money itself is a factor, and here the Federal Reserve's monetary policy matters. The Federal Reserve impacts two rates.

© ArchMan/Shutterstock

The federal funds rate is the amount of interest charged for short-term, interbank loans. The Fed influences the federal funds rate by setting a target rate. If the banks are selling federal funds for a rate that is in excess of the target, the FRB open market operations will enter the market and sell repurchase agreements for U.S. government securities that it owns at a higher rate. This action reduces the ability of banks to create money.

Banks are constantly monitoring and adjusting their reserves to make sure they can cover their liabilities, both those required by the Federal Reserve and those that occur in day-to-day banking. They often borrow or lend funds to each other to make those adjustments.

The discount rate is the interest rate that the Federal Reserve sets and charges for loans to member banks. The Fed controls the discount rate. This rate is not to be confused with the prime rate, which is the rate that banks charge their best and most reliable customers. Most major banks use the movement of the discount rate to determine their individually established prime rate, but is important to note that these are not the same rates.

Changes in these rates affect the amount of money banks are willing to borrow to maintain reserves. If rates rise, it discourages borrowing, so lending activity slows. When rates fall, banks may feel safe to lend more to earn more. The goal of these rates is to implement monetary policy by affecting reserves, which in turn affect the money supply, which affects the economy.

What interest rates does the Federal Reserve control or affect?

4.3.2 MONETARY POLICY AND INTEREST RATES

The goals of the Federal Reserve's monetary policy are to maintain economic growth, to stabilize prices, and to help international payments flow. Adjusting reserves, setting the discount rate, and influencing the federal funds rate are the tools it uses to achieve its goals.

The Federal Reserve sets the discount rate, but it only influences the federal funds rate. Using open market operations, the Fed buys and sells government securities, paying for them by making a deposit in the selling bank's Federal Reserve account. When it sells the securities to commercial banks, it withdraws their cost from the commercial bank's account at the Federal Reserve. In this way, reserves are increased or decreased, affecting the rate that banks charge each other for interbank loans. The Federal Reserve may buy or sell securities to yield a higher rate than the federal funds rate in order to achieve its goals, without taking gain or loss into consideration.

 checkpoint

How does the Federal Reserve influence the federal funds rate?

assessment 4.3

Think Critically

1. Why do you think so many people believe that the Federal Reserve controls interest rates?

2. Why does the prime rate so often move up or down with the discount rate?

3. Why would it not be a good idea if the government completely controlled the money supply?

4. How does the Fed's use of open market operations reflect a free-enterprise economy?

Make Academic Connections

5. **COMMUNICATION** Poll people outside your class to see what they think is the dominant factor affecting interest rates. Make a table that shows your survey results. What percentage of the total number of people you poll thinks the government sets interest rates?

6. **CRITICAL THINKING** Visit the St. Louis Federal Reserve Bank's website listing of prime interest rates from 1929 to the present. Make a graph showing average interest rates for five-year periods. What might you infer about the economy at various times from the data on your graph?

chapter 4 assessment

Chapter Summary

4.1 The Money Supply

A. The money supply consists of liquid assets held by banks and individuals. The supply includes money in circulation and money held by banks and other financial institutions. Various measures track the money supply.

B. The United States uses a fiat system of money in which the value of money is declared and guaranteed by the government. The system still operates on a fractional-reserve system, left over from commodity money systems.

4.2 Money Creation and Circulation

A. Banks use their excess reserves to create money. By loaning the money not required to be reserved, new deposits are created. The multiplier effect expands the amount of money in the money supply.

B. Money circulates by means of the millions of transfers associated with the various elements of the money supply that occur daily, including consumer transfers, interbank transfers, and Federal Reserve-to-bank transfers.

4.3 Interest and Interest Rates

A. Market factors control interest rates, although the Federal Reserve influences them.

B. Federal Reserve activities affect the cost of money to banks, thus affecting the size of reserves and the money supply.

Vocabulary Builder

Choose the term that best fits the definition. Write the letter of the answer in the space provided. Some terms may not be used.

a. aggregate measures
b. commodity money
c. discount rate
d. excess reserves
e. federal funds rate
f. fiat money
g. fractional-reserve system
h. liquidity
i. money supply
j. multiplier effect
k. primary reserves
l. prime rate
m. secondary reserves

____ 1. The liquid assets held by banks and individuals
____ 2. Interest rate that the Fed charges for loans to member banks
____ 3. Currency based on some item of value, such as gold or precious stones
____ 4. Tools used to estimate the size of the money supply
____ 5. Interest rate banks charge their best and most reliable customers
____ 6. Cash on hand and the required percentage amounts on deposit in the Federal Reserve District Bank
____ 7. Phenomenon that creates new deposits from lending
____ 8. Interest charged for short-term, interbank loans
____ 9. Practice of reserving only part of a deposited quantity
____ 10. Money deemed legal tender by the government, but not based on or convertible into a commodity
____ 11. Measure of how quickly things may be converted to something of value like cash

Review Concepts

12. What are the components of the money supply?

13. Identify and define two types of money.

14. List three measures of the money supply and describe them.

15. List and define three types of bank reserves.

16. How does the multiplier effect create new deposits?

17. Why might Federal Reserve notes be thought of as IOUs?

18. What actually backs the currency of the United States?

19. What is the difference between the discount rate and the prime rate?

20. What factors determine interest rates?

21. How do interest rates influence the quantity of money available in the economy?

Apply What You Learned

22. Why is an expanding money supply generally a good thing?

23. What are the dangers of a money supply that expands too rapidly?

24. Under what circumstances is it a good idea to contract the money supply?

25. What are the dangers of contracting the money supply too much?

26. How does adjusting the reserve requirements cause the money supply to expand or contract?

27. Why would a booming economy affect the demand for money?

28. Why do banks want interest rates to remain low?

Make Academic Connections

29. **MATH**   Calculate the total amount of money "created" from a deposit of $10,000 as it moves through three further cycles of deposit. Assume a reserve rate of 8 percent.

30. **HISTORY**   Many people objected strongly when the United States adopted a fiat money system (and some still object today). Learn more about the gold standard and how it established currency values. Write a one-page summary of what you learn.

31. **COMMUNICATION**   If economics is a science, and economic data are measurable, why is there so much disagreement about the best way to handle the economy? Collect statements from 10 people about the best thing that could be done to help the economy and why their ideas would help. Which of them seem to make the most sense to you and why?

32. **ECONOMICS**   Find current information about the money supply at the Federal Reserve website. Examine this data and draw conclusions about the growth of the money supply. Do your conclusions seem to match the current state of the economy?

CHAPTER 5

Deposits in Banks

Deposit here

iStockphoto.com/RapidEye

climbing the ladder

From Trust Associate to Trust Department Director

Kisho, the trust department director for a large bank, is reviewing the presentation he plans to give to a group of employees who are either new hires or recent transfers into the trust department. Preparing an overview of trust department job functions has caused Kisho to reflect upon his own career.

When he began his career as a trust associate, he was responsible for maintaining designated trust liquidity levels for trust clients. Using clients' standard letters of direction, Kisho determined the appropriate trade actions that were needed to maintain daily authorized liquidity levels. He was also responsible for identifying any type of recurring activities in daily processing that could lead to corporate liability. Sometimes he recommended processing changes to reduce liability.

Kisho's curiosity regarding the most effective way to invest to maximize trust performance led him to his next position as an investment analyst in the institutional trust department. By working on investment modeling, performance analysis, and risk analysis across all asset classes, Kisho gained a deeper understanding of trust performance.

Software selection and management was a critical part of Kisho's job. He kept current on new software developments in risk management, returns-based analysis for marketable securities, and holdings-based analysis.

After learning all about how trust asset decisions are made and managed, Kisho decided to learn more about compliance. In his next position as a trust auditor, Kisho participated in the bank's trust audit programs to identify regulatory requirements, assist in the establishment of internal controls, and help other departments with periodic compliance reviews. The position helped Kisho increase his personal network by maintaining relationships with external auditors and bank examiners.

Kisho spent three years earning a chartered financial analyst (CFA) designation through evening coursework. This helped Kisho land his next position as a portfolio manager. In this role, he was responsible for managing trust account assets to maximize investment return relative to an acceptable amount of risk. He also assisted with developing short- and long-term investment strategies that satisfied management needs and met customer investment objectives.

Currently, as trust department director, Kisho manages a high volume of complex trust accounts and achieves aggressive sales goals. He is responsible for the execution of the terms of any complex plan servicing the trusts of high-net-worth individuals. As some of these trusts are multigenerational trusts, managing the relationships among all parties involved requires tact and discretion.

Upper Rungs to Consider

One facet of his current position that Kisho particularly enjoys is being involved with the community and with professional organizations to keep current on relevant events. He enjoys interacting with a wide variety of people and plans to monitor job postings to look for a position as a marketing director or as a relationship development director.

Preparing for the Climb

Maintaining a strong and diverse personal network is important for career advancement. What steps can you take to expand your personal network?

5.1

Deposit Accounts

Learning Objectives

5.1.1 Define transaction accounts and identify major types of checking accounts.

5.1.2 Define time deposits and identify major types of savings accounts.

Key Terms

- transaction account
- demand deposit
- Check 21
- time deposit
- statement savings account
- money market deposit account (MMDA)
- certificate of deposit (CD)

Banking Scene

Rosa Lopez is preparing to open a checking account at a local bank. She knows that there is a wide variety of checking accounts, and that similar accounts may have different names at different banks. She has decided to collect information from various banks in an effort to find an account that will best suit her needs. To do so, she plans to make a list of questions about how she expects to use the account. Using answers to her questions, Rosa hopes to be able to match her requirements to account features offered by banks. What kind of questions about her own needs should Rosa include in her list?

5.1.1 MAKING YOUR DEPOSIT

You have studied the big picture of how the national banking system works to keep money circulating. Now you will walk through the local bank doors and look more closely at various types of accounts available to individual consumers. Although each bank may use different names for the various accounts offered, most banks offer similar accounts. A bank may assign "marketing names" to accounts as a way of distinguishing itself from its competitors. Features and fees may vary, but the essential services are the same with a few exceptions. Federal and state regulations require banks to provide explanations of their fees and policies.

Transaction Accounts

Deposit accounts fall generally into one of two categories: *transaction accounts* and *time deposits*. A transaction account is an account that allows transactions to occur without restrictions on the frequency or the volume of transactions. Many transaction accounts are demand deposit accounts, those that are payable on demand whenever the depositor chooses. The total funds in transaction accounts affect the money supply because of their high liquidity. Transaction accounts are a large component of M1. These demand deposits require banks to hold reserve funds, because the money could be transferred immediately at the direction of the account holder.

The most common form of a transaction account is a *checking account*. The account holder withdraws money from the account by means of a check, which is a written notice to the bank to pay a named person a specified amount from the account. Checking accounts offer customers quick access to their money, provide a convenient way to pay bills, and facilitate transferring funds to other institutions. Prior to writing a check, customers need to have sufficient funds in the bank to cover checks written and any fees to be deducted. Because there are many kinds of checking accounts from which to choose, consumers can find accounts that best meet their needs.

Historically, checks were paper documents. During the 1970s, direct deposit and auto debit, two forms of electronic funds transfer (EFT), began replacing checks. More recently, advances in Internet sophistication, as well as increased Internet experience among consumers and businesses, have prompted a shift to electronic checking. Online banking, which incorporates electronic checking, provides an assortment of streamlined account management services. These services range from accounts summary information through electronic bill pay.

Checking Accounts

Checking accounts have various characteristics. All are generally classified according to their ownership—single or joint. An *individual account*, sometimes called a *single account*, is owned by one person. A *joint account* has two or more owners, each of whom has equal and independent access to it. There are two different types of joint accounts. One, held by *tenants in common*, is frequently used by business partners. The approval of all owners is required to make withdrawals. The *joint tenancy* account, used by two or more persons wishing to have co-owner accounts with others, allows each co-owner to make deposits and withdrawals independently. Joint tenancy accounts may be used by siblings, roommates, spouses, domestic partners, or any individuals who have a consumer partnership. A joint tenancy account provides the *right of survivorship*, which gives a surviving owner the right to the account's assets upon the other owner's death.

Check 21 is federal legislation that allows banks to electronically process check information. This new category of negotiable instrument, a *substitute check*, has been in effect since October 2004. Consequently, photographic replications of the front and back sides of checks are commonly returned to customers who have check return included in their checking account services.

The names of checking accounts can differ from one bank to another. Regardless of the name, checking accounts can be categorized by their characteristics.

Basic Basic checking accounts offer a few simple services for minimal cost. These accounts may vary considerably in set fees and services, and most do not pay interest. Some may have no charges as long as a minimum balance is maintained, but most have a basic fee and price extra services per item. For example, you may have a set number of checks or deposits allowed per month, and all transactions beyond these incur an extra charge. Extra charges may also be incurred for automated teller machine (ATM) and debit card transactions. The return of canceled checks may have an associated fee, or may not be an option at all.

There are numerous forms of basic checking accounts with different names, but the same fee-for-service principle applies. Generally, a basic checking account is ideal for those who don't plan to keep a high balance.

Free This checking account usually requires a minimum balance but waives certain fees, such as ATM and per-check fees. Fees are charged to consumers who fail to maintain the minimum balance.

No Service Charge This account, which may charge for ATM withdrawals, has no other service fees and no minimum balance requirement. Minimum balance requirements for free checking accounts should be compared for brick-and-mortar banks and online banks. Some online banks have lower minimum account requirements than brick-and-mortar banks.

Interest-Bearing These checking accounts vary widely. They do pay interest on the balance deposited in the account, but usually only if the balance is maintained at or above a required level. Generally, the higher the interest offered, the higher the minimum balance required. Minimum balance may be calculated based upon the average balance in the account each day of the month, or it may be a preset level. If the balance falls below the level on any day of the month, higher service charges apply.

Georgejmclittle/Shutterstock.com

Express Designed for people who prefer to bank by ATM, telephone, or online, this account usually offers unlimited check writing, low minimum balance requirements, and low or no monthly fees. However, teller fees as high as $6 a visit, or a flat monthly fee of $8 or more for teller visits, are charged. These accounts are popular with students and younger customers who don't want to spend a lot of time on banking.

Lifeline This account offers low minimum deposit and balance requirements as well as low monthly fees and a limited number of written checks per month. This type of account may be attractive to low-income customers. Some states require banks to offer such accounts.

No-Frills Many banks offer special checking deals if you are age 55 or older or are a student. The benefits may include the following.

- Free personal checks
- Free cashier's or traveler's checks
- Increased use of ATMs

- Better rates on loans and credit cards
- Discounts on a variety of items such as travel

Asset Management   Many banks have this advanced type of checking account that offers the convenience of one account to take care of typical banking and investment needs. The account usually provides unlimited check-writing privileges and a comprehensive end-of-year statement that documents the year's transactions. Requirements include a higher minimum balance to open and an annual fee.

Online Banking   Online banking services are available as either independent accounts or as an additional service to standard brick-and-mortar accounts. Due to their lower cost structure, online banking accounts may offer lower minimum balances and fewer fees than traditional banks. Online banking services, either through an online bank or as part of a brick-and-mortar bank's package of services, offer a variety of services ranging from consolidated management of multiple accounts through automated bill payments.

Mobile Banking   Transactions from mobile devices may include balance inquiries, payment requests, and check deposits. Information that banks can automatically send to customers includes paycheck deposit alerts, bounced check notifications, and large transaction notifications. These mobile services can be linked to a variety of checking accounts.

ATM Fees   Fees for using an ATM should be carefully assessed. Depending on the type of checking account, consumers have the potential to incur two fees when using an ATM that is not affiliated with their own bank. A single transaction may prompt the non-member bank to charge one fee and the member bank to charge another fee.

Consumers should look closely at the services included with their checking account as well as the fee structure for the account. A basic account may actually cost more money to operate than another type of account if there are transaction-based fees. In the same way, the interest earned on an interest-bearing account may not be enough to offset the higher cost of fees if the balance maintained is fairly low, especially if it falls below the minimum balance requirement. Account regulations for each account as well as account usage patterns should be carefully considered. Finding a good match between the two can result in cost savings.

Other Demand Deposit Transactions

Other transactions are also categorized as demand deposit transactions, such as traveler's checks, money orders, automatic transfer service (ATF) transactions, and electronic funds transfer (EFT) that make automatic withdrawals or transfers to pay bills without writing checks. Most checking accounts also allow access to deposits via ATMs, electronic banking, and debit cards.

Some banks allow account access through mobile phones. Debit card transactions function like check transactions, except that no check is written. All deposits to cover these transactions are called *checkable deposits*, as are the funds deposited in checking accounts.

 **checkpoint**

What is a transaction account and why is it a demand deposit?

5.1.2 TIME DEPOSITS

Time deposits are deposits that are held for, or mature at, a specified time. Generally, time deposits include savings accounts, money market deposit accounts, certificates of deposit (CDs), and various bonds. Time deposits are less liquid than checkable deposits. There are no reserve requirements imposed by the Federal Reserve on time deposits.

Savings Accounts

The most common time deposit account is the savings account. For time deposits, banks may require up to a seven-day notice from a depositor who wants to withdraw money. In contrast, demand deposits require no notice. As a practical matter, most banks don't impose the prior notice requirement for savings accounts, but they reserve the right to do so. Savings accounts valued at less than $100,000 are part of the M2 money supply.

Passbook savings accounts, which helped build the banking industry, provided a ledger of activity that the teller updated when the customer made deposits or withdrawals. This traditional type of savings account has all but disappeared, replaced by statement savings accounts. Both types of accounts allow you to make deposits in person, by mail, electronically, or by direct deposit.

Statement savings accounts provide a monthly or quarterly computerized statement detailing all account activity, including interest credited and fees charged. This type of account is the industry standard. Often, statements are combined with those of other accounts held at the bank, providing a complete and clear picture of all banking activity.

Savings accounts are among the safest places to put money. Accounts are insured by the Federal Deposit Insurance Corporation (FDIC) up to $250,000 per depositor, per bank. For high net worth individuals with more than $250,000 to keep in a bank account, any deposit amounts exceeding a combined total of $250,000 at a single banking company should be transferred to a bank owned by a different company. As interest income on savings accounts is relatively low, high net worth individuals would probably invest their money in products providing a higher yield than savings accounts. If liquidity is needed, then savings accounts are a good option.

Money Market Deposit Accounts

Money market deposit accounts (MMDAs) offer a higher rate of interest than savings accounts, but they usually require a higher initial deposit to open an account. In addition, minimum balance requirements to avoid the imposition of fees are also higher. The FDIC insures MMDAs for amounts up to $250,000 per depositor. The bank invests money market deposits in a variety of savings instruments. Similar accounts, called *money market mutual fund accounts*, invest the money in mutual funds. Although they are not insured, banks make most of these investments in safe, short-term savings instruments with high credit ratings.

Liquidity of these accounts is not as high as savings accounts. You may be restricted to six transactions per month. Only three of them may be checks, and you may have to wait up to three days to get your money.

Certificates of Deposit

Certificates of deposit (CDs) are certificates issued by banks that guarantee the payment of a fixed interest rate until the *maturity date*, which is a specified date in the future. Banks offer CDs with maturity dates from seven days to ten years. Generally, the larger the amount of the CD and the longer the term, the greater the interest rate.

Some CDs offer fluctuating rates. Variable rate CDs are often linked to the prime rate and may offer an interest rate at a predefined percentage rate less than the prime rate. For example, a variable rate CD might offer interest at 2.25 percent less than the prime rate. Some CDs offer *bump-ups* that provide the opportunity to increase the interest rate on the CD when interest rates rise. A *callable* CD is one that can be called in at the discretion of the issuing institution. Be sure not to confuse the callable date with the maturity date.

Usually, the rate for CDs is higher than the rates offered by money market or savings accounts. For the vast majority of CDs the maturity date is fewer than 18 months. You can get your money before the maturity date if you need to, but you will pay an interest penalty, anywhere from three to six months' worth of interest, if you withdraw the money early.

Certificates of deposit are quite safe, as the FDIC insures them for amounts up to $250,000 per depositor, but they are not very liquid. Consumers should consider the maturity date when investing in CDs, because the interest rate remains the same on fixed rate CDs. If interest rates rise, the CD rate will not earn as much

Peshkova/Shutterstock.com

branching out

Walmart

Realizing that a substantial number of its customers do not have traditional bank accounts, Walmart developed creative ways of providing financial services. Walmart partnered with a variety of third parties to provide bank-like services to its customers. By developing these partnerships, Walmart was not required to go through the regulatory processes and approvals required of banks. The Walmart MoneyCard is one example of a product developed as a result of a partnership. The MoneyCard allows customers to set up direct deposit of their payroll checks onto their Walmart MoneyCard. When the MoneyCard is used for a transaction, the stored value of the money on the card is used. The MoneyCard is not a credit card. No credit check or bank account is required. There can be fees for reloading the card, for monthly card maintenance, and for assorted administrative costs that a customer may elect to use. Under certain circumstances, specific fees may be waived.

Think Critically
How does the entry of a retail outlet with the consumer reach of Walmart affect competition within the banking industry?

as other forms of time deposits. But if interest rates fall, locked-in CD rates can be an advantage. Depositors must also decide how long they are willing and able to tie up their money.

Sometimes *brokers* sell callable CDs. You should understand which bank issued the callable CD. The FDIC insurance rates of $250,000 apply to each depositor at each lending institution. Knowing which institution issued a CD will help you or your bank's customers avoid exceeding the $250,000 limit at an institution.

Credit Union Products   Credit unions offer both transaction accounts and time deposits. These holdings usually represent shares in the credit union rather than deposits. A *share-draft account* is much like a checking account, a *share account* is essentially like a savings account, and a *share certificate* is equivalent to a certificate of deposit.

✔checkpoint

List three types of time deposits. Which of these are exempt from reserve requirements?

assessment 5.1

Think Critically

1. Why does the Federal Reserve require reserves for demand deposits but not for time deposits?

2. How might competitive pressures have led to different types of checking accounts?

3. Why have passbook savings accounts disappeared?

4. What factors should be considered when contemplating a certificate of deposit?

Make Academic Connections

5. **COMMUNICATION**   With a partner, make a list of questions you need to ask to help determine your checking account needs. Compare various types of checking accounts and focus your questions on what you now know about differences in checking accounts. Come up with at least four questions, and then compare lists with those of other pairs.

6. **MATH**   According to a Federal Reserve study, Americans wrote an estimated 18.3 billion checks and made nearly 123 billion electronic (noncash) payments in a recent year. This reflects a steady trend to shift away from checks in favor of electronic payments. At that time, the population of the United States was about 314 million. Using those figures, how many checks and how many electronic payments were written per capita in a year in the United States?

5.2

Interest-Bearing Accounts

Learning Objectives

5.2.1 Explain how interest is calculated.

5.2.2 Discuss why compound interest is the most powerful savings tool.

5.2.3 Describe how interest rate variations can impact consumer behavior.

Key Terms

- interest
- compound interest
- annual percentage rate (APR)
- annual percentage yield (APY)

Banking Scene

As she considered what type of checking account to open, Rosa Lopez felt it would be a good idea to open a savings account as well. She looked for advertised interest rates for accounts and certificates of deposit, and began to consider how those rates would affect her savings over time. She wanted to design a chart or table to compare rates and intervals at which interest would be paid. Then she would fill it in with sample numbers. How would Rosa design such a chart or table?

5.2.1 IN YOUR INTEREST ● ● ● ● ● ● ● ● ● ● ● ● ● ● ● ● ● ● ●

It might not always be good to be called a "calculating person," but when it comes to your finances, you had better be. Banks offer interest on many deposit accounts, and they charge interest on loans they make. Understanding these calculations is absolutely necessary to analyzing your own finances. Whether it's money coming to you or money you're paying to borrow, interest will likely be a major factor.

Interest is the price paid for the use of money. The bank is using your money when you deposit funds. In some cases, the bank pays you for the use of your money. If you borrow from a bank or other financial institution, you pay to use that money, and interest is the amount you pay. Interest is almost always expressed as a rate or percentage of the total amount of money in use, and it is calculated over time.

Calculating Interest

To calculate simple interest, you must know the amount of money that is being used. This beginning amount is called the *principal*. The basic formula for calculating interest is $P \times R \times T = I$, where P is principal, R is rate, T is time, and I is interest. Rate is expressed as a percentage. Time is expressed in years or parts of years. Portions of a year are expressed as a decimal value. For example:

$$P \times R \times T = I$$

six months is 0.5 years
nine months is 0.75 years
a year and a half is 1.5 years

Banking Math *Connection*

Calculate the simple interest earned on a savings account in nine months that begins with a deposit of $5,000 and pays 0.06 percent interest.

Solution

The formula for calculating interest is

Principal × Rate × Time = Interest
$5,000 × 0.006 × 0.75 = $22.50

If you had such an account, you would have earned $22.50 in interest, giving you a balance of $5,022.50. This example assumes no compounding and that the interest is paid at the end of the nine months, which might not reflect conditions of an actual account.

Interest in the Real World

Calculating simple interest provides an idea of the process, but in the real world there are some complexities. Banks calculate the interest they pay on a fixed interval. Interest may be paid once a year (annually), every six months (semiannually), every three months (quarterly), or any other interval as defined in the account regulations. If the bank paid 0.06 percent interest on a $5,000 account semiannually, at the end of six months $15.00 would be added to the account. For the next six-month interval, the beginning principal would not be $5,000 but would be $5,015.00. Interest would now be earned on the higher amount. Adding interest to the principal and paying interest on the new total is called paying compound interest. It is the most powerful savings tool.

Tatiana Popova/Shutterstock.com

✔checkpoint

What do the terms in the formula $P \times R \times T = I$ stand for?

5.2.2 THE POWER OF COMPOUNDING

Compound interest "starts over" with a new principal every time interest is paid, adding the paid interest to create a higher principal on which interest is paid in the next interval. For example, assume you loaned $10,000 to your cousin for three years at a simple interest rate of 5 percent per year. You'd make $500 in interest the first year, $500 in interest the second, and $500 in the third, for a total of $11,500.

Assume you put the same $10,000 in a bank account paying 5 percent interest compounded semiannually. You'd get back $11,597.10. In effect, that's a rate of 5.3 percent per year.

	Simple Interest 5%		Compound Interest 5%	
Time	*Interest*	*Principal*	*Interest*	*Principal*
6 months	$250	$10,000	$250.00	$10,250.00
1 year	250	10,000	256.30	10,506.30
1½ years	250	10,000	262.70	10,769.00
2 years	250	10,000	269.20	11,038.20
2½ years	250	10,000	276.00	11,314.20
3 years	250	10,000	282.90	11,597.10
Total	**$1,500**		**$1,597.10**	

The algebraic formula for calculating compound interest is $F = P(1 + R)^n$, where F stands for future value, P is principal, R is rate, and n is the number of intervals. There are many online calculators that will compute compound interest for you, but understanding the idea behind compound interest is very important.

Larger principals and longer terms have a more dramatic effect, especially if regular additions are made to the principal, as on a regular savings plan. For example, if you put $20 a week in a savings account earning 5 percent interest compounded annually, at the end of five years you would have deposited $5,200, but your balance would be $6,033.99.

APR and APY

Two terms you may encounter when evaluating interest are APR and APY. Both allow you to compare interest. **Annual percentage rate (APR)** is the nominal rate on which interest is calculated per year. In the example above, both investments have an APR of 5 percent. Another measure gives a better comparison. The **annual percentage yield (APY)** represents the effect of compounding. In the example above, the APY of the simple interest is 5 percent and of the compounded interest is 5.3 percent. APY varies according to the APR and the frequency of compounding. APY is mandated as the required quotation by the Truth in Savings Act. Although banks may elect to present an APR, they must present the APY.

✔checkpoint

Why is compound interest such a powerful savings tool?

5.2.3 INTEREST RATES IMPACT CONSUMER BEHAVIOR ● ● ●

Savvy consumers who want to make money in a fairly low-risk environment have profited from understanding the spread of interest points in the marketplace. The spread is the variation in value of two competing interest rates.

Jelica Videnovic/Shutterstock.com

By using sophisticated online software that analyzes and summarizes the highest interest levels offered by assorted savings institutions, these consumers are constantly moving their money among various accounts to obtain the highest interest available at any point in time. In some cases, these consumers will borrow money on a credit card, at either low or no interest introductory rates, and use those borrowed funds to gain interest in a high-yield online account. Consumers who use these tactics are often referred to as *rate chasers*.

Financial institutions that offer high interest rates are hoping to attract long-term customers. Many of these banks are now trying to obstruct rate chasers by increasing the minimum deposit required to open a high-yield account.

✔checkpoint

Why do financial institutions try to obstruct the efforts of rate chasers?

assessment 5.2

Think Critically

1. Why is it important for consumers to compare interest rates on bank accounts and other interest-bearing instruments?

2. How does the frequency that interest is compounded change the effect of compounded interest rates?

3. Why is APY a more useful measure for comparing interest rates than APR?

Make Academic Connections

4. **MATH** Marie Broussard puts $10 a week in a savings account. At the end of two years, how much more would Marie have in savings if she found an account that paid interest of 5½ percent instead of 4½ percent per year, assuming both accounts compound annually?

5. **HISTORY** Conduct research on the history of paying and receiving interest. Write a one-page report on the earliest beginnings of the practice.

6. **TECHNOLOGY** Online financial calculators are useful tools, performing complex calculations quickly. Find three such calculators on the Internet and describe the particular features, advantages, and disadvantages of each.

Flow of Deposits

5.3

Banking Scene

Rosa Lopez has decided which services she needs for her checking and savings accounts. Now her task is to choose accounts that match her needs. With so many banks, so many accounts, and so many similar but not identical names, collecting information on specific offerings is complicated and time consuming. How would you recommend Rosa pursue this task most efficiently?

Learning Objectives

5.3.1 Explain the complexity of forces that influence the flow of deposits.

5.3.2 Identify limitations of the Federal Reserve's influence of the flow of deposits.

Key Term

- interbank transactions

5.3.1 A COMPLEX PATTERN

You go to work, get your check, and deposit it in the bank. Your employer wrote that check against funds deposited in the company's bank, and the money for those deposits came from somewhere too. The next time you are in a bank or waiting in a drive-through, look around and multiply the process by everyone you see. Then multiply the process by the millions of people at work in the United States, using thousands of banks. If you are starting to get a picture of a complex flow of deposits rocketing around the nation, you are getting the idea.

The Federal Reserve, or Fed, came into being to serve as the nation's central bank. The money supply is sometimes adjusted by the actions of the Fed. Because banking is so important, it may be easy to assume that the government is running everything, but that is not really how it works. In addition to new money and the easing or tightening of credit, the flow of deposits also includes all the money circulating in the day-to-day cycle of economic life. Money doesn't just mean currency. It includes checks, ledger transfers, and credit.

The Economic Engine

The economy is the engine that drives the flow of deposits. Basic economic principals of supply and demand for goods and services move money through banks. In a way, the movement of money is like the movement of communication through phone lines and satellite services. Individual transmissions may not be very complicated, but many are happening at once, and they may be going in many different directions. At the same moment you deposit your check at the bank, someone else cashes his or hers across town. In addition to these small transactions, banks

Tech Talk

Cup of Java?

Many banks offer interactive tools on their websites, such as interest calculators of various types. Have you ever wondered how they work? Many of them run by means of Java, a programming language specially designed to run small applications, called "applets," over the Internet. Advantages of Java are that it works with any operating system, such as Windows or Macintosh, and that it allows for distributed processing, so the software need not reside on your computer.

Think Critically   Why do you think interactive tools on bank websites have become so popular? Search online for bank sites that offer interactive tools. List at least five useful tools you find.

themselves, just like you, may have changes in cash-flow needs. Maybe revenues are down, or expenses are up, or maybe business is so good they need more money to support it. The transactions that occur when banks make or receive deposits from each other or from the Fed are called **interbank transactions**. It is not always easy to predict the results of these transactions, but the best predictor is the past. That is why economists, banks, and the Federal Reserve pay close attention to recording and analyzing economic statistics.

In fact, the economy as a whole plays a far greater role in determining how money is moving than does the government. Market forces are a primary determinant of interest rates. Fluctuations in interest rates are caused by variations of capital needs, individual tendencies toward saving or spending, and on inflation-related effects.

Disintermediation of funds also affects the economy. *Disintermediation of funds* occurs when depositors take their money out of bank accounts and

invest those funds directly into capital markets. The term also captures the activity that occurs when companies, seeking financing, go directly to capital markets to secure the financing. In both instances the traditional role of a bank—accepting deposits from one group and providing loans to another group—is diminished. This financing method increased during the 1980s and 1990s. However, during the credit squeeze that began in 2007, the trend began to reverse. At that time, mutual funds began to seek financing directly from banks in an effort to maintain the required liquidity of their funds.

✔checkpoint

What is the greatest factor in the flow of deposits? Why do economists track and analyze so much data?

5.3.2 DEPOSITS AND THE FED ● ● ● ● ● ● ● ● ● ● ● ● ● ● ● ● ● ● ●

Whether the money supply is expanding through the creation of new money or contracting as credit tightens, supply and demand for money affects deposits. The Federal Reserve also has an effect on deposits. For example, the Federal Reserve sets reserve requirements. If reserve requirements are high, banks must hold back more money and consequently have less to lend. If reserve requirements are low, more money may be available for loans. Still, there are reasons not to overestimate the power of this capability.

- Federal Reserve requirements do not change very often and are not as much a factor in bank lending as general economic conditions.

- Federal Reserve requirements only apply to the M1 money supply (checkable deposits that are already moving freely). Other parts of the money supply are operating entirely by means of market forces, and though less volatile, are not under the Fed's control.

- The Fed does not control other forms of commerce. Much wealth today is generated by nonbank financial institutions, such as stockbrokers and the securities and other instruments they trade, which are a form of money themselves. These instruments, the institutions that sell them, and the policies they have in place are not controlled by the Federal Reserve, though they affect the economy at large.

In general, the money supply is determined by the supply and demand for credit. Although the Federal Reserve responds to these conditions, it does not necessarily create them.

Adjusting the Money Supply

It is true that the Fed does have an influence on the money supply and the flow of deposits, most frequently through its *open market operations*.

- **The Federal Reserve can put more money in the economy.** To do so, it buys U.S. government securities on the open market. The Fed buys these securities by using money that is part of the Fed's balance sheet. The sellers of the securities deposit money from the Fed in financial institutions. Thus, deposits flow from money on the Fed's balance sheet into bank accounts. By generating funds from the sale of government securities, banks then have more money to lend, and the money supply expands as a consequence of the multiplier effect.

"**communicate**"

Conduct a survey among 20 friends, family members, and classmates to examine consumer attitudes. Ask these questions:

1. How much do you consider the economy at large when making purchase and loan decisions?

2. What do you think the present state of the economy is, and what are its prospects for the next year?

Based on responses to your survey, write a two-page report describing the economic mood of the country.

- **The Federal Reserve can effectively take money out of the economy.** If the Fed feels it needs to slow the economy, it sells the Treasury securities it holds. There is a market for them because of their security. When it sells the securities, the money comes from bank deposits, thus leaving less in the system at large. The money the Fed receives for the securities is removed from the economy, as it does not go into a bank account of any kind. It effectively disappears.

In addition, the Fed can adjust the discount rate, which is the rate it charges banks for loans. If the discount rate is low, banks are more likely to borrow money to use to make money. If the discount rate is high, just like consumers, banks are less likely to borrow.

The Banking Business

Governmental measures influence but do not entirely control the flow of deposits. Banks are businesses and do what they can to make a profit. Deposit flow is determined by the needs of all businesses, bank and non-bank, moving money around in the banking system. Banks move money from themselves to consumers, back and forth among themselves as a function of normal business or borrowing funds from each other, and back and forth from the Federal Reserve, in a constant flow of deposits. They function just as you do but on a larger scale, moving and using or even borrowing money to acquire things they need.

✔checkpoint

How does the Federal Reserve influence the flow of deposits?

assessment 5.3

Think Critically

1. Why is it sometimes hard to predict the flow of deposits in the banking system?

2. How might political or national events affect the flow of deposits in the banking system?

3. Do you think the government should have more direct control of the economy and thus the flow of deposits? Why or why not?

4. Give examples of daily economic activities that are more likely to have predictable effects on the flow of deposits.

Make Academic Connections

5. **GRAPHICS** Create a graphic representation or flow chart of how money is added to or removed from the economy by the Federal Reserve. What activities should be included in the representation?

6. **SOCIAL STUDIES** How do current economic conditions affect social conditions in our country? Explore the effect of the economy on daily life in the United States. Write a one-page personal essay about the ways you believe the state of the economy affects how we live, the values we hold, the way we spend our time, our political opinions, our career choices, and other aspects of our lives. Incorporate information about how the credit collapse of 2008 affected your family's life. These ideas may be personal opinions, but try to express them clearly and be sure to give reasons for your thinking.

5.4

Deposit Regulations

Learning Objectives

5.4.1 Describe deposit account documents.

5.4.2 Identify and explain basic deposit account rules.

Key Terms

- governing documents
- overdrawn
- stale check
- post-dated check

Banking Scene

When Rosa Lopez opened her checking and savings accounts, she was given a variety of brochures explaining the features and benefits of each account. She was also given a list of rules and regulations pertaining to her accounts—detailed documents that included legal language and were printed in small type without graphics. Why was it important for Rosa to read these documents carefully, even though she had a clear picture of account features, charges, and interest rates?

5.4.1 DEPOSIT ACCOUNT DOCUMENTS

The relationship between a financial institution and its customers is more than a business relationship. It is also a legal relationship that offers rights and imposes responsibilities on each party. Banks document these rights and responsibilities. When an account is opened, customers receive documentation outlining the rights and responsibilities associated with the account.

State and federal governments require banks to provide this documentation to customers so that questions about account policies and procedures have clear answers. These documents protect both the consumer and the bank from misunderstanding and loss.

The Federal Reserve, in its regulatory capacity, along with state and sometimes local governments, perform reviews to ensure that deposit account documents are specific, complete, clear, and used appropriately. All banks must comply with various state and federal consumer laws, including laws about fairness and full disclosure. Several documents are typically included in this document package.

- **Account rules** explain characteristics of each type of account. They include definitions, requirements, restrictions, and other information associated with each account.

- **Deposit rate schedules** list interest rates for various types of accounts that are in effect at the time.

- **Fee schedules** show all charges that apply to each specific type of deposit account.

- **Check hold policies** explain when deposited funds will be available for use by the consumer. Usually, deposited funds are credited provisionally, until full and final payment is received. In most cases, funds are available for use immediately, but the bank may charge back to the account any amount that is uncollectible.

- **Disclosure statements** provide full information about bank policies, such as electronic funds transfer policies, lending policies, interest crediting, and compliance with banking regulations. These statements are required by law.

- **Opting out options** allow you to notify your bank that you do not authorize the bank to share your personal financial information, such as average account balance, with any other businesses. Using this option can also keep the bank from sharing information with other divisions within the bank. For example, you may prohibit the bank from sharing your personal information with the financial planning division of the bank.

Deposit account documents are sometimes collectively called governing documents. Banks are free to change them, but they must give customers written notice of changes.

Why are governing documents necessary?

5.4.2 Account Rules

The statement of account rules supplied for each account provides a detailed explanation of the policies, procedures, requirements, and agreements applying to that account. It is usually very specific, spelling out what is expected of both the customer and the bank.

Reference to Governing Documents   The bank notes that account holders agree to abide by the rules as set forth in the rest of the governing documents. The bank also states that it may change the rules at any time and acknowledges its responsibility to provide updated documents to account holders.

Signature Policies   Banks keep the signatures of all parties to an account, whether it is held solely or jointly. Signature policies spell out who may do what, both in terms of the account as it exists when it is opened and in the event of inconsistencies, disputes, or the death of parties. Usually, in the event of disputes among parties, the bank refuses to pay items on the account until the parties resolve the dispute. The bank notes that it has no responsibility for a dispute, its resolution, or its choice to freeze the account. Orders to freeze accounts may originate due to the death of an account holder, lawsuits filed against account holders, or bankruptcy proceedings.

Some consumer advocates believe that many governing documents are made deliberately hard to read so that consumers won't read them. Banks argue that precise legal language is necessary to protect both themselves and consumers.

Think Critically

Would you support legislation that required account rules to be written in "plain English"? Why or why not?

Opening and Closing Accounts   Policies governing opening accounts may include a specified minimum opening deposit, the presence of the person opening the account with proper identification, and the right not to open an account for a person if the bank so chooses. The bank also reserves the right to close an account at its discretion.

Resolution Form   When opening an account for a business that is set up as a limited liability company (LLC), a corporation, or a partnership, the business may need to provide the bank with a *resolution* form. This form grants authority for specified individuals to manage account transactions on behalf of the business.

Deposit Collection   This provision is similar to federal regulations concerning funds availability except that it goes further in explaining the effect of uncollected deposits on the account. The bank notes that it is not responsible for collecting deposits beyond using reasonable care in their processing. This statement often notes exactly when deposits are credited. For example, deposits made after 3:00 p.m. may be credited during the next business day.

iStockphoto.com/YinYang

Overdraft Policies   When an account has insufficient funds to meet its obligations, it is **overdrawn**. Depending on the account type, the bank may pay the obligation or return the check to whoever presented it. If an account holder has multiple accounts within a bank, the bank might transfer funds between accounts to cover overdrafts. An *overdraft* occurs when withdrawals are greater than deposits. Fees are charged for overdrafts. A reference to the fee schedule usually appears in the statement of account rules.

Minimum Balance/Service Charges   The bank specifies the exact fee schedule for service charges when an account fails to maintain a minimum balance.

Withdrawal Policies   Requirements for withdrawing funds from the bank vary by account type. They include maturity dates and penalties for early withdrawal of time deposits, making withdrawals in person, identification needed at withdrawal, and various other requirements for withdrawing funds.

Check Policies   These policies relate to the accurate dating of checks and their timely deposit or presentation. A stale check is dated six months or more before it is presented for payment or deposit. A post-dated check is dated later than when it was written. A bank may refuse to honor either.

Account Statement Policies   These policies deal with the bank statement. They state what is and is not included with each statement, the account holder's obligation to review the statement in a timely manner, and the discrepancy handling process.

Other Policies   Account rules usually include assorted bank policies. Stopping payment of a check, handling inactive or dormant accounts, and reimbursement of expenses incurred by the bank on the account holder's behalf are a few examples of policies covered in this section.

Waivers   Account rules may also contain notices about various waivers, such as the customer's agreement to waive protest of dishonored items and the bank's willingness to waive certain fees. The bank's waiver does not prevent it from enforcing the same provision(s) that it had waived previously.

Governing documents and account rules serve as the legal basis for the relationship between you and your bank. If you do not like a provision or some of the account rules, you are free to choose another bank. Most account and deposit regulations are fairly similar from bank to bank. In their precision and specificity, they protect the bank and the consumer.

Federal Reserve Regulations

Just as banks enforce account rules on consumers, the Federal Reserve imposes a number of requirements on banks or depository institutions. These may apply to transaction accounts as well as time deposits.

Regulation DD   This policy implements the Truth in Savings Act of 1991. It requires banks to disclose the interest rate paid and the fees charged on deposit accounts to enable consumers to make informed decisions. The purpose of providing this information is to allow consumers to make comparisons among depository institutions.

In May 2005, Regulation DD was amended to require that banks provide explicit disclosure regarding the details of overdraft protection. Under this amendment, banks must clearly list all fees associated with overdraft protection services on banking statements. Final amendments to this rule, which became effective in July 2006, discuss which disclosures must be included in marketing materials related to overdraft protection.

Regulation D   This regulation requires banks to maintain adequate reserves for the funds they have on deposit. Regulation D defines the types and number of transactions that the bank may allow on time deposits, such as savings accounts and money market accounts. Check or debit overdraft, preauthorized automated transfers, preauthorized electronic debit, and automatic or assisted phone transfers are limited to six per month. Balance inquiries, loan payments, and all transactions from a checking account do not count as part of these transactions.

"communicate"

Multiple federal agencies use a similar naming structure for regulations. For example, "Regulation D" is used by both the SEC and the Federal Reserve. For the SEC, Regulation D covers exemptions from registration requirements. For the Fed, Regulation D defines bank account reserve requirements. Use the Internet to find another overlap. Prepare a PowerPoint chart that clearly explains the difference in regulations with the same name. Be sure to include an easy-to-understand reference to the agency listing the regulation.

Regulation CC This is known as the Availability of Funds and Collection of Checks regulation. Regulation CC sets the schedules under which banks must make funds deposited into transaction accounts available for customer withdrawal. Usually, the maximum time to clear a check deposited into a checking account is two to five business days. Business days are defined as Monday through Friday, except most federal holidays. Some types of deposits require a next-day availability. To meet the requirements of Regulation CC, a bank must:

- Provide consumers who have transaction accounts, such as a checking account, with disclosures stating when their funds will be available for withdrawal.

- Post a notice of the bank's availability policy pertaining to consumer accounts. The posting is required in the bank as well as at all ATMs.

- Include a notice of funds availability on the front of all *preprinted* deposit slips. It does not have to appear on blank counter deposit slips.

Many financial institutions have been cited for violating various parts of Regulation CC. Thus, it is important for a bank to ensure it is in compliance with the requirements of Regulation CC.

In October 2004, Regulation CC was amended to include the Check 21 Act. As noted in Lesson 5.1, Check 21 authorized the use of electronic checks as a viable negotiable instrument.

Regulation E Electronic funds transfers, or EFTs, are regulated under Regulation E. EFTs are commonly used for direct deposit of paychecks or preauthorizing repetitive monthly payments of a consistent amount (like authorizing automatic payment of monthly health club fees from your checking account). Regulation E is designed to protect the rights of consumers who use EFT and to outline the responsibilities of financial institutions providing EFT. Consumers must receive EFT disclosures prior to making their first EFT transaction. Information to include in the disclosures includes:

- Limits of a consumer's liability and of an institution's liability if unauthorized EFT transactions occur

- Descriptions of the type and number of transactions that can be made

- ATM fees that can be incurred when using the bank's ATMs as well as the ATMs of other banks

- Contact information for reporting unauthorized EFTs

How do governing documents and account rules differ?

assessment 5.4

Think Critically

1. Why do banks supply a separate set of account rules as part of the governing documents for each account?

2. Do you think most people carefully read the documents associated with their bank accounts? Why or why not?

3. Why does the government feel it is necessary to require that written copies of documents related to bank accounts be provided to customers?

4. In what circumstances might a bank waive a fee it had charged?

Make Academic Connections

5. **SOCIAL SCIENCE**   Learn more about consumer protection and the banking industry. Using research materials of your choice, make a timeline showing key events in the growth of fair and reasonable banking practices.

6. **PROBLEM SOLVING**   If you had a dispute with a bank, how would you resolve it? What approaches would you take, and what further actions would you pursue if you could not come to an agreement? List steps that you would take to resolve a disagreement over an uncredited deposit, for example.

chapter 5 **assessment**

Chapter Summary

5.1 Deposit Accounts

    A. Transaction accounts, like checking accounts, are demand deposit accounts that allow unlimited transactions.

    B. Time deposits include savings accounts, money market deposit accounts, and certificates of deposit.

5.2 Interest-Bearing Accounts

    A. Interest is the price paid for the use of money. Simple interest is calculated with the formula $P \times R \times T = I$.

    B. Compounding greatly expands the power of interest. The formula for calculating compound interest is $F = P(1 + R)^n$. APR represents the annual percentage rate, and APY represents the annual percentage yield.

5.3 Flow of Deposits

    A. The flow of deposits includes all economic transactions, not just those between banks and the Federal Reserve.

    B. The Federal Reserve influences the flow of deposits, but supply and demand have a greater influence on deposit flows.

5.4 Deposit Regulations

    A. For each account, banks provide a package of governing documents that include account rules, deposit rate schedules, fee schedules, check hold policies, and disclosure statements.

    B. Account rules list detailed policies. The Federal Reserve imposes requirements on banks through various regulations.

Vocabulary Builder

a. annual percentage rate (APR)
b. annual percentage yield (APY)
c. certificate of deposit (CD)
d. Check 21
e. compound interest
f. demand deposit
g. governing documents
h. interbank transaction
i. interest
j. money market deposit account (MMDA)
k. post-dated check
l. stale check
m. statement savings account
n. time deposit
o. transaction account

Choose the term that best fits the definition. Write the letter of the answer in the space provided. Some terms may not be used.

____ 1. Price paid for the use of money

____ 2. Effective rate of interest when compounding is factored in

____ 3. Savings account earning a competitive interest rate from invested deposits

____ 4. Deposit held for or maturing at a specified time

____ 5. Account that allows transactions to occur at any time and in any number

____ 6. Deposit payable on demand whenever the depositor chooses

____ 7. Savings instrument with fixed interest rate and fixed maturity date

____ 8. Return calculated by adding interest to principal for next interval

____ 9. Nominal rate on which interest is calculated per year

____ 10. A transaction made between banks

____ 11. Account-specific documents outlining the legal rights and responsibilities of both the bank and the account holder

____ 12. A check that is dated six months or more before it is presented for payment or deposit

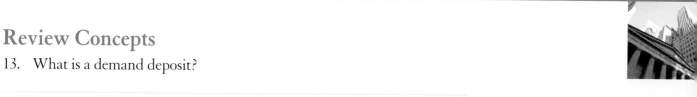

Review Concepts

13. What is a demand deposit?

14. Name three forms of demand deposits.

15. What is a minimum balance?

16. Name three types of time deposits.

17. Why are savings accounts not subject to the Fed's reserve requirements?

18. Describe a certificate of deposit and its maturity date.

19. What do the letters in the formula $P \times R \times T = I$ represent?

20. Explain the basic idea of compound interest.

21. What is the difference between APR and APY?

22. What is the most significant factor influencing the flow of deposits in the United States?

23. Name five main types of documents typically supplied with new accounts.

Apply What You Learned

24. Why are transaction accounts the most liquid of all funds?

25. What factors should a person consider when choosing an account?

26. Why is the annual percentage rate an ineffective measure for comparing accounts?

27. Why won't the Federal Reserve's monetary policies completely control the flow of deposits in the U.S. banking system?

28. Why must banks provide customers with documents such as account rules, and how do account rules protect both banks and consumers?

29. How do Federal Reserve regulations protect consumers?

Make Academic Connections

30. **ADVERTISING** Collect advertisements for checking and savings accounts that appear in print media. Evaluate the ads in terms of attractiveness, clarity, quality of product, and overall effectiveness. What makes a fair and good advertisement?

31. **MATH** Calculate the interest earned on a three-year certificate of deposit (CD) with an initial value of $12,500 earning 5½ percent, compounded annually. What will be the final account balance? Then calculate the interest earned on a one-year CD with an initial value of $5,000 earning 7 percent compounded semiannually. What will be the final balance?

32. **DESIGN** Create a marketing brochure for a checking account. Select what features your account will offer, choose what type of customer you would like to attract, decide on a name, and design a brochure that will effectively and fairly present the features. You may wish to gather real brochures to use as models.

6 Negotiable Instruments

skills that pay dividends

When speaking to a group of people, it is important to have a clear idea of your topic and the purpose of your presentation. Know your audience and what actions you want them to take.

When giving a presentation to a specific group of people, research the composition of the audience prior to developing the presentation. Anticipate the concerns of audience members and proactively plan to address those concerns. For example, are you speaking to a company's employees at their place of work to introduce your bank to the employees? If so, where are the employees in their careers? Are they new college graduates just getting accustomed to managing a large salary who need advice on checking, savings, and investment accounts? Are they employees who are mid-career who are interested in starting a savings plan for their children's college educations? Knowing who the audience members are will allow you to customize your presentation to address their specific needs. It will enable you to bring the appropriate product literature for distribution.

Show the audience that you are a credible source of information and have a thorough understanding of the material you present. Your knowledge of the topic should extend beyond what you present. Then, when questions or discussions occur, you will have additional knowledge that you can share. When the audience knows that you are fully aware of the implications of what you are recommending, they can be sure you have the skills to protect their interests.

Make sure any presentation tools you use are easy to understand. All visual tools should be concise with clearly identified titles.

Engage your audience by using humor or personal experiences that evoke a positive emotional response.

Be direct in your closing. Ask if anyone has questions, concerns, or issues that need clarification. Ask the audience to take the action you intended. In the workplace example, you could ask audience members to open new accounts at the close of the presentation.

These same techniques can be adapted for addressing an individual. If you need to give an impromptu presentation to an individual client who enters the bank, have a brief list of screening questions available. These questions can help you direct the customer to clearly define his or her thoughts, needs, and preferences. You can then tailor the discussion to meet those needs and suggest the appropriate products.

Develop Your Skill

Select a product you will need to explain to customers. Prepare a persuasive presentation to describe the product to a customer. Give your presentation to classmates and solicit feedback on the strengths and weaknesses of the presentation.

6.1

Types of Negotiable Instruments

Learning Objectives

6.1.1 Define the term negotiable instrument.

6.1.2 Identify different types of negotiable instruments.

Key Terms

- negotiable instrument
- bearer instrument
- draft
- bill of exchange
- promissory note

Banking Scene

Midori Akita is finishing her career as a postal worker and moving from her home in New York to a small town in Florida. She will receive a monthly pension check from the government. The government wants her to use direct deposit to receive these payments. As she prepares for her new life in Florida, Midori must consider many options about the best ways to receive, transfer, and handle her money. When moving, how does someone learn about the financial choices they need to make in their new location? How can they research them before they move?

6.1.1 NEGOTIABLE INSTRUMENTS ● ● ● ● ● ● ● ● ● ● ● ● ● ● ● ●

Money circulates around the banking system every day, 24 hours a day, seven days a week. The flow of deposits that carries both national and international economies moves constantly. In what forms does that money move?

When most people think of money, they think of cash, but only a small part of the money that moves in this country is cash. Increasingly, ledger entries add to one account and subtract from another without actual currency changing hands. Today, electronic transfers of one kind or another create these entries. Most large transfers within the banking industry have taken place this way for years. The electronic world is increasingly apparent to consumers, as electronic payment systems are becoming a routine part of retail businesses as well. Money can also move to and from people in the form of *negotiable instruments*, such as checks, drafts, and other written documents of value

A negotiable instrument is a written order or promise to pay a sum of money, either to a specified party or to the person who holds it. Negotiable instruments include drafts, bills of exchange, and some promissory notes, but the most common form of negotiable instrument is a check.

What Is Negotiable?

Don't let the word *negotiable* in *negotiable instrument* confuse you. The word means transferable. Consider that a check, like money, is a medium of exchange. The "negotiation" that goes on refers to the transfer of the instrument from one party to another. That transfer may mean passing the instrument between two people, or from one bank to another, or even from one country to another. The recipient or holder of the instrument negotiates the instrument in order to obtain its value. For example, your company gives you your paycheck. By signing your name on the back of the check, or *endorsing* the check, you are transferring the title of the check. Endorsing the check has made it negotiable and it can be deposited in your bank. Then you have use of its value.

Unless you and the bank agree that the instrument is negotiable, you won't be able to use it. The negotiation, however, may be restricted by one party or another in the transfer. As you might imagine, banks have a great interest in seeing that the negotiable instruments they receive for deposit are genuine and worth their assigned value. Most of the terms of negotiation relate to making certain an instrument does indeed possess real value, so that the bank in which you deposit it can negotiate the instrument to get the value from it just as you did.

interesting *facts*

The first documents that might be called checks appeared in Europe in the late 1650s.

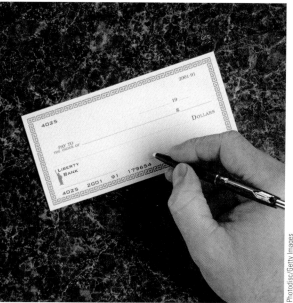

What Is an Instrument?

In the broadest sense, almost any agreed-upon medium of exchange could be considered a negotiable instrument. A Federal Reserve note is a written promise to pay on demand a certain value to the person who owns it. Certificates of deposit, bonds, treasury bills and other securities, and even a winning lottery ticket may also meet that definition. In day-to-day banking, a negotiable instrument usually refers more narrowly to checks, drafts, bills of exchange, and some types of promissory notes.

✔checkpoint

What is a negotiable instrument? What is the most common form of negotiable instrument?

6.1.2 FORMS OF NEGOTIABLE INSTRUMENTS • • • • • • • • • • •

A negotiable instrument is a written order promising to pay a sum of money. It may be a **bearer instrument**, which is payable to the *bearer* (whoever holds it), or it may be an instrument with highly specified terms, including the date of maturity and the intended recipient. What makes it negotiable is that it can be used for value and is a medium of exchange.

Checks

Checks are the most common form of negotiable instrument and are the preferred method of payment for many debts. They offer convenience for both writer and recipient, a relatively high degree of safety, and a record of transactions. They are accepted for most transactions when supported by appropriate identification, and their common and recognizable form makes them a part of normal life for most people. There is a huge industry devoted to the printing, transporting, safeguarding, and processing of checks around the country. The Federal Reserve provides some of these services, but there are many private companies involved as well.

The standard features of personal checks are the following:

- **Check number** is the number of the check being written.

- **Date** is the date the check is written. Checks are payable on demand and cannot legally be predated or postdated.

- **Payee** is the receiver of the funds. This line directs the bank to "pay to the order of" a specified party.

- **Amount** spaces allow for the amount of the check to be entered in both numbers and words, to minimize errors. In the event the words and numbers don't match, the amount written in words takes precedence.

- **Signature** is a valid signature of the maker of the check. Banks will not negotiate checks without a signature.

- **Memo** is an optional entry to note the check's purpose or other information.

- **Identification numbers** give the check number, the bank number, and the account number. They are printed with magnetic ink in machine-

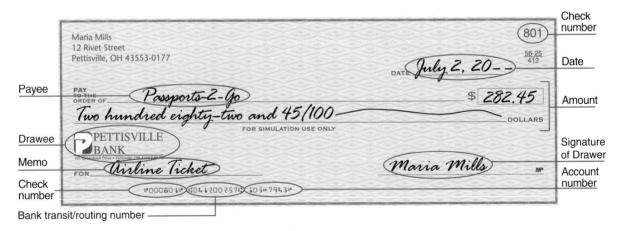

readable characters, called magnetic ink character recognition (MICR) numbers.

- **Drawee** identifies the bank that maintains the account and holds the funds of the person or business that is writing the check.

- **Drawer** is the person who is writing the check.

When you write a check, you may issue it to the person whose name is on the payee line, but you are really writing it to your bank. You are giving the bank instructions to pay the sum "to the order of" the recipient.

As a percentage, check use per person declined in the United States by about 45 percent between 2003 and 2012. In 2012 the Fed processed about 18.3 billion checks. In 2003, the Fed processed about 37 billion checks. Increased use of electronic payments has reduced the number of checks written.

Drafts

A draft is similar to a check. In fact, a check is one form of a draft, but there are other forms. A draft is an order signed by one party (the *drawer*, or drafter) that is addressed to another party (the *drawee*) directing the drawee to pay to someone (the *payee*) the amount indicated on the draft. The payment may be at sight or at some defined time. If you (the drawer) were writing a draft, you would be directing your bank or other institution (the drawee) to pay the payee of the order the sum shown on the draft. The process is similar when you write a check. The terms for writers and receivers of drafts are the same as those used for checks. In fact, some credit unions provide "share drafts" instead of checks for their members. Most drafts are used for the purchase of goods and services when the transaction goes beyond the bounds of U.S. banking law.

Jason Stitt/Shutterstock.com

Bills of Exchange

A bill of exchange is a negotiable and unconditional written order, such as a check, draft, or trade agreement, addressed by one party to another. The receiver of the bill must pay the specified sum or deliver specified goods on demand or at a specified time. Bills of exchange are a common form of internationally negotiable instruments.

Promissory Notes

A promissory note is a written promise to pay at a fixed or determinable future time a sum of money to a specified individual. You might not regard promissory notes as negotiable instruments, but it is easy to see why they are. Suppose you wrote an IOU to LaTasha for 10 dollars. LaTasha, as it happens, owes Jamal 10 dollars. Why couldn't LaTasha just give Jamal your IOU? You pay Jamal the 10 dollars, and everyone comes out even. That is exactly what happens when certain promissory notes are used as negotiable instruments. These two-party documents are legally binding documents with many specified terms that may vary widely. For example, you might obtain a mortgage loan from ABC Mortgage Company, which might then sell the mortgage note to DEF Finance, which now owns your obligation.

Such trading practices on short-term notes make up a large part of a rapidly moving investment economy. *Commercial paper*, a short-term (270 days or fewer) note or draft issued by a corporation or government, is a common investment instrument. Remember that fast-moving overnight loans between banks make up a segment of the money supply.

 **checkpoint**

List the standard features of a personal check.

Banking Math *Connection*

Do you balance your checkbook? Undetected errors can cause problems. Your bank statement of October 15 says you have $1,114.72 in your account. Your checkbook register shows $1,146.57. You have made one deposit, written two checks, and visited the ATM once since the statement was printed.

Solution

Begin with ending balance from the Oct. 15 statement. $1,114.72

Add deposit made since the date of the bank statement.

Oct. 22	$954.00	954.00
		$2,068.72

Subtract checks and debits in your check register not shown on the bank statement.

Oct. 15	Check 1114	$125.00	
Oct. 21	ATM	90.00	
Oct. 26	Check 1115	707.15	
		$922.15	922.15
			$1,146.57

Your calculation agrees with your checkbook register. If the account doesn't balance, recheck your math, compare deposit slips and checks for entry errors, check for outstanding checks that haven't cleared, and check automatic withdrawals or fees that you may not have recorded.

assessment 6.1

Think Critically

1. How is a negotiable instrument different from cash?

2. Before electronic payments became widely used and accepted, why did people like to use checks?

3. Why can a promissory note be considered a negotiable instrument?

4. What risks might be associated with negotiable instruments?

Make Academic Connections

5. **MATH**   According to a study released by the Federal Reserve, there were 122.8 billion electronic (noncash) payments in a recent year. The total value of noncash payments was $79 trillion. Debit cards accounted for 38% of the payments and 2% of the value. Credit cards accounted for 21% of the payments and 3% of the value. ACH transactions were 18% of the payments and 61% of the value. Checks (paid) were 15% of the payments and 33% of the value. Prepaid cards, including electronic benefits transfers, were 7% of the payments and 1% of the value. Calculate the number and amount of each type of noncash payment.

6. **TECHNOLOGY**   Working in teams, list every company or group you can think of that might be involved in the business of preparing or processing checks. Which of these groups might successfully adapt if electronic payment systems displaced checks? Which might go out of business? What effects might these changes have on the economy and the banking system?

Presenting Checks for Payment

Key Terms

- elements of negotiability
- holder in due course
- blank endorsement
- restrictive endorsement
- full endorsement
- qualified endorsement

Banking Scene

After moving to her new neighborhood in South Florida, Midori Akita opened a checking account at a nearby bank. She used her final paycheck from the Postal Service to open the account. Her account representative politely requested two separate forms of identification, including one with a photograph. Midori knew that the bank needed to be certain of both the check and its depositor. What was the bank trying to determine?

6.2.1 ELEMENTS OF NEGOTIABILITY

A check is a negotiable instrument. When you present a check to a bank for payment, the bank must assure that the check meets certain legal requirements. These conditions are commonly called elements of negotiability. The Uniform Commercial Code, Articles 3 and 4, covers notes, drafts, and checks. Every state has adopted these legal guidelines. They require a written, signed, unconditional promise or order to pay a fixed amount on demand or at a defined time to the holder in due course. This is the person or financial institution that acquires a check or promissory note received in good faith as payment and is entitled to payment by the drawer of the check or note.

When you bring a check to a bank to cash or deposit, the elements of negotiability directly affect how the bank looks at the check, the maker of the check, and you. After all, if the check you deposit turns out to not be a legal negotiable instrument, the bank is not going to get paid and neither are you.

Written

The first requirement for a negotiable instrument is that it must be written. Remember that the law surrounding negotiable instruments grew up long before electronic payment systems. In addition, written documents are easily transferable and universally recognized as legally binding. If a document conforms to the law, it is a negotiable instrument.

You might be surprised to note that there is no legally prescribed form for a check. A check is a written order to pay someone. There is not even a necessity that the "document" be written on paper. If all proper information were present, the check would be honored. There are old stories of checks written on various materials, tax payments made with "the shirt off one's back," or even written on a person's actual back. Whether these tales are true is hard to prove, but they illustrate that the information on the document is what matters, not the medium on which it is written.

Of course, checks written on shirts would wreak havoc in the automated check-processing system. Standards created by the American Bankers Association and the American National Standards Institute (ANSI) govern the size and placement of information on checks, as well as paper thickness, colors, and security features. Checks typically come in one of three sizes— the standard, personal-check size and two larger sizes common for payroll. These standards are for the industry's benefit, but they do not determine negotiability.

Signature

A document must be signed by a person capable of making the order or promise for it to be a negotiable instrument. Legally, a check is not payable if it does not bear the drawer's genuine signature. The bank that paid such a check would be liable, not the drawer. Like any legal document the signature must be valid, but it does not necessarily need to be human. Machine signatures are perfectly acceptable if the bank obtains a resolution or agreement that liability for forgery resides with the customer using the machine.

Unconditional Promise or Order

To be negotiable, an instrument must make an unconditional promise or order to pay. First, the promise or order must be explicit. Authorizing a payment or acknowledging a debt is not enough. Second, the promise or order must be unconditional. Reasoning for this rule has to do with transfer. If the order to pay is conditional, a third party, who has no control or relation to any conditions set, may not be able to obtain the instrument's value. If its value cannot be transferred or obtained, an instrument is not negotiable.

Sum Certain

A negotiable instrument must state clearly on its face the principal amount to be paid, and it must be a monetary value. Although interest may be referenced, as may other documents regarding fees and charges, the principal sum in a note or order must be defined.

Payable on Demand or at a Defined Time

If a negotiable instrument bears no instruction as to when it is due, it is payable on demand, that is, immediately. It may show a time when it is payable, such as a promissory note does, but that must be a defined time. Checks are commonly payable on demand.

Words of Negotiation

Remember that *negotiation* applies to the ability of the holder to obtain its value, not to conditions or terms. Words of negotiation are instructions about how the instrument's value may be obtained. *Pay to the order of Keshia Smith* lets the instrument be negotiated by Keshia Smith with her endorsement, or to whomever she may later assign it. *Pay to the order of Cash* makes the instrument a bearer instrument, valuable to anyone who has it regardless of endorsement.

When you hand a check across the counter, the bank's representative will quickly check for all six elements of negotiability. Banks spend considerable time and effort training employees to understand and identify these elements. Recognizing them not only protects against fraud, but also allows the bank or other institution to know exactly how to handle a negotiable instrument.

 **✔checkpoint**

What is meant by "elements of negotiability"?

6.2.2 ENDORSEMENT AND IDENTIFICATION

When you present a check to the bank for payment or deposit, the banker will assure that the check has been endorsed. Although the maker of a check may have created a perfectly negotiable instrument, the actual negotiation of it involves the transfer of both the instrument and its value. *Endorsement* of the instrument allows it to be negotiated, not only by you but by other parties later. After all, if the instrument cannot be used by others, it is not really negotiable. After you have endorsed the check, the teller may ask to see identification, especially if you seek cash or are depositing only a small part in your account (known as a *cash back transaction*).

Types of Endorsement

There are four primary types of endorsement, and each affects the degree of negotiability of the instrument. Some of these endorsement types have varying names, but they mean essentially the same thing.

Blank Endorsement   A blank endorsement, sometimes called an *open endorsement*, is the least secure of the four main types of endorsement, but it is also the most negotiable. It is simply the signature of the holder.

For example, assume a check has been written to Maria Mills. Maria simply writes her name in the endorsement area on the back of the check and does what she wants with the check thereafter. Maria must take care of this check, however. Once she signs it, the check could be cashed by anyone. A check with a signed blank endorsement is a bearer instrument and is as good as cash to anyone who can find someone to accept it. It is a good idea not to endorse a check with a blank endorsement until the very moment you intend to cash or deposit it. Your signature implies that you have negotiated the check, and if you sign it and lose it, anyone who finds it may cash it.

Perhaps Maria intends to pass the check to someone else. Assume the check is for $100.00, and Maria happens to owe her cousin Martina exactly $100.00. Maria could use a blank endorsement and simply give the check to her cousin. Martina could then endorse it again and deposit or negotiate the check as she pleases. Martina's endorsement is called a *secondary endorsement*. In fact, checks may receive multiple secondary endorsements as they work their way back to their originating banks.

The blank endorsement is the most common type of endorsement, and millions of people negotiate checks on a daily basis with it. However, you must handle checks that have blank endorsements with the same care you use with cash.

Restrictive Endorsement   The holder of a check may wish to prescribe a little more carefully how the check is negotiated. A restrictive endorsement limits the use of the instrument to a means specified by the endorser. In theory, a restrictive endorsement ends further negotiation of the check. The most common restriction is "For Deposit Only," which limits the negotiation of the endorsed check to deposit in an account. By ending the instrument's transferability, a restrictive endorsement renders the instrument no longer negotiable.

Restrictive endorsements do not necessarily guarantee the end of negotiation, though. Perhaps an inattentive teller may not respond to the restriction properly, or perhaps the check might be deposited into another account other than that of the intended payee. Such cases are more common when business accounts are involved, or when the payee has many accounts. More restrictive endorsements such as "For Deposit Only, Hobbit Corporation" provide greater protection. Specifying the name of a particular account if a company has multiple accounts restricts negotiation more effectively.

A *split deposit* occurs when a depositor designates that a single check should be divided to have portions of it deposited in different accounts.

Full Endorsement   A full endorsement transfers the check to another specified party. From there, its negotiability depends on what that party does with it. Sometimes called a *special endorsement*, a full endorsement limits neither the transferability nor the further negotiability of the check. Suppose again that Maria Mills owes her cousin Martina $100.00. She could just endorse the check with a blank endorsement. She could just cash the check and hand

canbedone/Shutterstock.com

Martina the cash. She could also use a full endorsement to transfer the check completely to Martina. In effect, it is just the same as if Martina had been the original recipient of the check. Martina must endorse the check whenever she wishes to negotiate it further, and she has the same range of options that Maria did. What the full endorsement provides is protection for the endorsed check. No one but Martina can use the check next.

Of course, negotiability is also determined by the next holder. Martina has to find a bank that will accept Maria's check, and she must identify herself and endorse the check to the satisfaction of the bank. If it is a different bank from Maria's, Martina's endorsement also acts as an *accommodation endorsement*, guaranteeing that the bank will eventually collect the money from Maria's account, wherever it may be.

Qualified Endorsement   A qualified endorsement is an attempt to limit the liability of the endorser without limiting an instrument's further negotiability. The words "without recourse" appear in the endorsement, intending to move the instrument along without incurring liability if the check is no good. A qualified endorsement often guarantees payment if the person of primary liability does not pay.

Although qualified endorsements are not common, persons acting as a representative for others may use them. If, for example, a lawyer representing Martina Mills received a check for funds owed to her, the lawyer might simply transfer the check to her by endorsing it as with a full endorsement but adding the words "without recourse." If the check were no good, assuming the lawyer had met other legal requirements for endorsement, neither Martina Mills nor any later holder of the check could require the lawyer to make good on the check.

The deposit agreements in the governing documents cover in detail when deposits are accepted, when funds are available from them, and what happens in cases in which the funds cannot be collected. Every account holder, especially those who receive checks from many sources, should be thoroughly familiar with the rules of his or her own bank.

Types of Endorsements

Blank Endorsement	Restrictive Endorsement	Full Endorsement	Qualified Endorsement
ENDORSE HERE *Maria Mills* DO NOT WRITE, STAMP, OR SIGN BELOW THIS LINE	ENDORSE HERE *For Deposit Only* *Maria Mills* DO NOT WRITE, STAMP, OR SIGN BELOW THIS LINE	ENDORSE HERE *Pay to the order of Martina Mills* *Maria Mills* DO NOT WRITE, STAMP, OR SIGN BELOW THIS LINE	ENDORSE HERE *Pay to the order of Martina Mills, without recourse* *Maria Mills* DO NOT WRITE, STAMP, OR SIGN BELOW THIS LINE

Identification and Check Acceptance

Does the bank really care who you are if you present a check made out to Maria Mills and want to cash it? It sure does. Check fraud is a serious issue for banks, and there are ways that banks and companies work to prevent it. One of the ways banks protect themselves is to require adequate identification.

Banks may require as much or as little identification to cash or deposit a check as they wish. Some banks even require fingerprinting. The greatest risk to banks comes from personal checks cashed by new customers or noncustomers. A bank may charge fees for noncustomers, even for checks drawn on that same bank. It may make different rules for customers and noncustomers, and it may refuse to cash a check about which it is doubtful. Sometimes these policies make people feel they are being treated poorly, but a bank must balance customer service and risk management. When a bank cashes your check, it is essentially giving you money it has yet to recover, so it has a great interest in making sure you are who you say you are and that the check is genuine.

✔checkpoint

Name the four main types of check endorsement.

Ethics in Action

You are walking down the street and notice a $20 bill. No one is around, and there is no way you can determine who might have dropped it. You congratulate yourself on your good fortune, feel sorry for the person who lost it, pick up the money, and go on your way. The next day, as you walk to your bank to deposit your paycheck, you notice a blue piece of paper on the curb. It's a check for $20, in good shape, made out to John Dolan, whom you don't know. The check is drawn on your bank, and Dolan has placed a blank endorsement on it.

Think Critically

How is the check different from the $20 bill? How is it the same? Knowing this check is a bearer instrument, what will you do with it? Discuss the issue with classmates.

assessment 6.2

Think Critically

1. How do elements of negotiability provide for the transfer and use of a negotiable instrument?

2. Why do the words "pay to the order of" play such an important part in negotiability?

3. What role does endorsement play in the negotiability of checks?

4. If you were cashing a check at a bank and were asked to supply a fingerprint, would you be offended? Why or why not?

Make Academic Connections

5. **COMMUNICATION** Create a PowerPoint presentation on types of endorsements for checks. In your presentation, indicate the advantages and risks of each type as they apply to both safety and negotiability.

6. **SOCIAL STUDIES** Being able to open and maintain a checking account is a basic skill critical to participation in American economic life. Should such business skills be a required part of public education? What basic business skills should be taught? Write a one-page paper in which you clearly identify your opinion on these issues and provide logical reasons to support it.

Processing Checks

6.3

Banking Scene

As Midori Akita adjusted to her new life in Florida, she received a check in the mail from a brother-in-law in upstate New York as a retirement gift. She considered cashing it, but then remembered the account rules for her new account and thought it might be easier to deposit the check. Still, her account rules noted that there might be a "hold" on the funds until the check cleared. Why might banks have such policies? What do you think is a reasonable time for a hold to occur?

Learning Objectives

6.3.1 Identify key laws that make today's check-clearing process possible.

6.3.2 Explain the sequence of events as a check is processed for payment.

Key Terms

- float
- transit number
- returned check

6.3.1 A NATIONAL SYSTEM OF PAYMENT

Electronic payments and checks are not only common forms of negotiable instruments, they are a way of life in the United States. Electronic payments and checks are far safer and more convenient than cash for bill payment. The legal status of electronic payments and checks makes them a dominant force in the economic life of the nation. Both can provide proof of payment. Enhanced technology and communications have made the processing of checks more efficient and accurate. Although electronic payments have surpassed check payments, check payments remain a fact of economic life and the banking system.

The Legal Structure of the Check Payment System

For a massive system of check processing to work, there must be clear and coordinated cooperation among banks. In the United States, with its unique blend of private and public institutions in the banking system, check payment depends upon the legal foundations that set up and maintain the banking system itself. Although many state and federal regulations govern the banking industry, five key legislative acts most critically affect the check-processing system.

Federal Reserve Act of 1913 In establishing the structure of our banking system, the Federal Reserve Act of 1913 also established the fundamental relationship between the Federal Reserve and banks, as well as among banks. The Act created a national check-collection system and other rules for payments. Today, the Fed is deeply involved in check collection and plays a leading role in the industry. It has fostered technological advance,

"communicate"

Take a poll of your friends and relatives to see how many have charge cards, debit cards, contactless payment cards, or banking services through their cell phone. Ask them which method they use most often and why. Compile the results and write a short analysis of why these forms of payment are so popular.

beginning with automatic sorters more than 40 years ago and continuing through the latest state-of-the-art technology. The Fed has also used its regulatory authority to influence applicable legislative acts by Congress. In addition, the Federal Reserve has helped set and apply standards for checks and the technology that processes them. Not only the backbone of the banking system, the Federal Reserve is an up-to-the-minute participant in the check processing and collection system.

Uniform Commercial Code of 1958   The Uniform Commercial Code (UCC) of 1958 established a consistent code for commercial law transactions. Adopted eventually by all 50 states, the UCC largely eliminated the wide variation of legal regulation that could hamper the national payments system. Articles 3, 4, 5, and 9 of the UCC pertain to banking and negotiable instruments and contain terms, definitions, and regulations, many of which form the foundation of account agreements.

Expedited Funds Availability Act of 1987   The Expedited Funds Availability Act (EFAA) of 1987 was passed to combat an abuse of the check-payment system practiced by a few banks. When checks were deposited, these banks did not credit the accounts until long after the checks had been paid by the banks on which they were drawn. Although the banks had credit for the checks in their funds, they would not make payments on them, creating in effect a "float" fund for their use at the expense of their customers. The EFAA directed the Federal Reserve to set rules that balanced the needs of consumers with the need for banks to protect themselves from uncollectible checks. Federal Reserve Regulation CC established these rules and procedures.

Check 21   In October 2004, a federal law was passed to enact Check 21. To streamline check processing, banks can take a picture of the front and back of a check and transmit images of the check to other banks. This image allows pertinent financial data to be exchanged so the value of the check can be obtained. The image also enables a bank receiving a check image to produce a substitute check, or paper copy, of the check. Copies of the image can also be included on monthly account statements which are sent to account holders. Check 21 eliminates the need for the processing of paper checks. Like a paper check, a substitute check or a digital image of a check can be used for proof of payment.

Electronic Check Conversion   Electronic check conversion is distinct from Check 21. Electronic check conversion allows a billing party, whether a utility, a retail outlet, or any other business, to use the information on a check to initiate an electronic funds transfer (EFT) from your account. Your check, which may be returned to you (if you are at a retail business) or destroyed, is not the payment form. The EFT is the method of payment. Businesses are required to inform consumers when an electronic check conversion will occur.

Consumer rights vary according to the method of payment. Checks, substitute checks, and electronic check conversion have distinct rights associated with them.

✔checkpoint

Why does the check processing and collection system depend on the Federal Reserve?

6.3.2 CHECK PAYMENT AND PROCESSING

What happens to your check after you write it and give it to the payee? The process of adjusting various accounts and returning checks involves several steps.

1. Suppose you write a check for $95.50 for this month's electric bill. You are the drawer or maker of the check. The electric company is the payee. Your bank, A National Bank, is the drawee.

2. The electric company deposits your check in B National Bank. If the drawer and the payee of a check have the same bank, that bank handles the processing in-house. About 30 percent of all check clearing ends here. If the banks are different, the processing continues.

3. B National Bank puts a magnetic code on your check showing the dollar total and sends it on to the Federal Reserve or other intermediary. Note that B National Bank has *not* credited the electric company's account for $95.50 yet, because the check has not cleared.

4. The Federal Reserve clears about one-third of the nation's checks. There are several large private banks, called *correspondent banks*, that also clear checks, and some have created check-clearing corporations. The check is sorted, and the bank ID and the dollar amount are read from the magnetic codes.

5. The Federal Reserve or intermediary credits B National Bank $95.50 in its account at the Federal Reserve. All financial institutions using the Fed to clear checks have an account at the Federal Reserve. Correspondent banks also have accounts at the Fed. Your check is then sent on your bank, A National Bank. At this point B National Bank has been credited with the $95.50, but A National Bank has not paid out anything. Thus, for this brief period, both banks count the same funds. These funds are called **float**, and they distort the money supply and reserve figures.

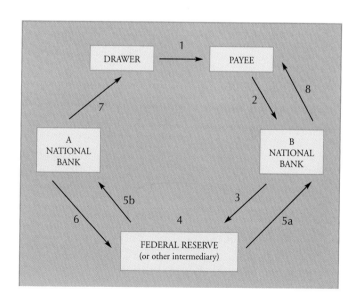

6. A National Bank pays the Federal Reserve $95.50 and debits your account $95.50. If

your account doesn't have $95.50 in it, the check is returned unpaid to B National Bank, and ultimately, to the electric company. Penalties may be applied by the bank as well as the electric company.

7. In the past, the canceled check, which is your original check that was processed by both the check-cashing location and your own bank, was returned to you. Today you are likely to receive an image of the check or a transaction summary with your bank statement. Actual return of physical paper checks is nearly obsolete because it is more costly than the digital-imaging systems banks use.

8. Finally, B National Bank credits the electric company's account for $95.50. This may have happened earlier in the process, depending on B National Bank's policies for deposits. The entire process usually takes two to five days, and banks are required to make a depositor's funds available within five days.

These steps may vary somewhat if a correspondent bank or other intermediary is used, or if along the line the check is converted into an electronic transaction rather than moving physically through the system.

The millions of checks written daily create a lot of float. Float has several causes, and each has a separate name. *Malfunction float* is caused by machine breakdown. *Transportation float* refers to delays in moving checks from one place to another. It occurs most often in winter. *Holdover float* occurs when banks are slow in processing transactions. Some banks have been accused of deliberately holding checks to create float to earn short-term interest. Electronic check processing has greatly reduced float.

iStockphoto.com/bluecinema

Transit Number

To aid in the check-processing procedure, a transit number is printed at the bottom left-hand corner of a check (see page 154). The **transit number** is a nine-digit number that identifies the bank that holds the checking account and is responsible for payment. It was created in 1910 by the American Bankers Association (ABA) and is also known as the *routing number*, *transit/routing number*, and *ABA number*. Transit numbers are issued to only federal or state chartered financial institutions that are eligible to hold an account at a Federal Reserve Bank. The transit number system also now identifies participants in automated clearing houses, EFT, and online banking.

EDI Implementation

Computers "talk" to each other by means of conventions, called protocols, for information exchange. EDI is an acronym for electronic data interchange, a set of standards for business-to-business exchange of information. As technology improves and extends further into the banking business, implementation of EDI becomes more critical to run such applications as online banking, smart card applications, and other forms of electronic commerce.

Think Critically Research EDI systems. What challenges do you think might be involved with implementing EDI?

Other Types of Check Processing

Banks may encounter checks that require special handling and processing. One example is the *postdated check*, which is a check that is dated later than the date on which it is actually written. The rules on processing postdated checks vary by state, depending on whether the state follows the Uniform Commercial Code (UCC). According to the UCC, a postdated check is allowable as long as the bank customer gives the bank advance "notice" of the check, including the check number, account number, amount, date, and to whom the check is payable. If proper notice is given, the bank, not the customer, would be liable for damages if the check is cashed before the date on the check. States not following the UCC may consider these checks illegal.

Another kind of check that requires special handling is a returned check. A check written on an account that does not have adequate funds to cover it and which is returned unpaid to the person who deposited it is a **returned check**. It is also known as a *bounced check* or an *NSF* (nonsufficient funds) *check*. Policies for processing returned checks vary, but overdraft fees usually apply. If a check does not clear the bank the first time it is processed, some banks will automatically process it a second time. Many banks offer an overdraft protection program. For a fee, which can range from $17 to $36, the bank will cover the amount of the returned check. In some cases, there will be an extended overdraft fee of up to $36 if the account remains in the negative for a certain number of days. The bank stipulates that the overdrawn account must return to a positive balance within 30 days.

✔checkpoint

What is float? What causes it?

assessment 6.3

Think Critically

1. Could banks in the same city create an independent check-clearing network that didn't use any intermediaries? Why or why not?

2. How does the foundation of the Federal Reserve make a national check-clearing system work more smoothly?

3. Why does the Federal Reserve work to limit float?

4. Why does advanced technology minimize float?

Make Academic Connections

5. **MATH** According to the Federal Reserve, during one five-year period, average float decreased from $774 million to about $133 million. What percentage decrease does this drop represent?

6. **CRITICAL THINKING** You have a roommate who routinely writes checks before receiving a paycheck. Your roommate claims the money will be deposited by the time the checks clear. Make a list of practical reasons why this idea is not a good one and the consequences it could bring.

Changing Forms of Payment

6.4

Learning Objectives

6.4.1 List modern forms of payment systems.

6.4.2 Explain how banks and other financial institutions use automated forms of payment.

Banking Scene

Although Midori Akita had long had the option of having her paycheck deposited electronically, she had never used it, preferring to have the check in her hands. Now living in Florida, she is considering having her retirement checks go to her new bank through direct deposit. What questions might she ask about EFT?

Key Terms

- charge cards
- credit cards
- cash cards
- debit cards
- smart cards
- person-to-person payments (P2P)
- radio frequency identification (RFID)

6.4.1 CONSUMER PAYMENTS

Checks used to make up the largest volume of payments in the United States, but that has changed rapidly since 2003. Other forms of payment now exceed the use of cash in dollar volume for transactions. With more rapid and more secure electronic capabilities, growth in electronic forms of payment is likely to alter forever the way payments are made and processed. The banking system already is adapting to these changes, but some of the newest possibilities also pose challenges for the existing system.

The growth of varied forms of payment is a product of two phenomena. One is the entrepreneurial spirit. Merchants and banks have always looked for ways to increase revenue. Providing alternative payment methods increases business by making purchasing easier. Revenue is further increased when fees, including credit card fees, are charged for the use of the new methods. Along with this opportunistic spirit, advancing technology is supporting creative, convenient, rapid, and efficient forms of payment. Banks and the banking system are adapting to meet this evolution.

Charge Cards

Today's credit card industry grew from the use of charge cards. Because of the similarities, it may be easy to confuse the two. With charge cards, a consumer must pay the account in full at the end of the month. Most of the monthly bills are paid by check, with the card issuer doing the recordkeeping. Charge cards, in effect, lend the amount of purchases for a month. Originally charge cards were store cards, but eventually third-party companies formed networks of participating businesses to expand the market.

Credit Cards

Credit cards allow consumers to pay all or part of their bills each month and finance the unpaid balance. Because of limits on interstate banking, credit cards did not become big business until banks devised a system using two banks (the card issuer's and the retailer's) that met regulations. Then the business exploded to become the competitive and powerful economic force it is today. To make the system work, the credit slips (or records of them) function more or less like checks. The retailer sends the slips to its own bank, which pays the retailer, records the transactions, and sends the slips to a clearing system. The clearing system routes them to the issuing bank, which pays the retailer's bank and collects from the consumer. In 2014, Visa held the largest market share of credit and debit cards.

Cash Cards

Cash cards are commonly used at an automated teller machine (ATM). Consumers can get cash, make transfers and deposits, or perform almost any other banking function at the machine by inserting the card and entering a *personal identification number* (PIN). Banks encourage the use of cash cards, as they are less expensive than human tellers and are usually available 24 hours a day. Some banks even charge for the use of a human teller in an effort to encourage ATM or online banking to hold down costs. Internetworking of different bank computers has made cash cards a way of life in the last 20 years, but the simple cash card is beginning to disappear. The same functions are often combined on a card that is also acceptable to retailers for payment. These cards are, in effect, debit cards.

Debit Cards

Taking advantage of current computer networking technology, debit cards transfer money from a person's designated account to the account of the retailer.

nexus 7/Shutterstock.com

A debit card allows an immediate *point-of-sale* (POS) transaction. The consumer swipes the card through a magnetic reader, enters a PIN, and authorizes the transfer. A record of the transaction appears on the consumer's bank statement, and the bank usually charges a monthly fee for use. Debit cards are rapidly growing in popularity as consumers become more comfortable with them. Checks still travel nicely by mail, but debit cards may replace them for point-of-sale transactions.

Smart Cards

Smart cards are credit, debit, or other types of cards with embedded microchips. The microchips store values and, unlike magnetic strips, use the embedded logic to change values and record transactions. Smart cards enable a wide variety of "electronic purse" programs. The use of smart cards has grown rapidly in Europe but is just beginning to take off in the United States. Retail, security, and customer loyalty programs frequently use smart cards. Eventually, smart cards could combine all plastic-card functions on a single card.

Bill Payment Services

There are multiple ways for consumers to streamline the way they pay businesses. Bill payment services vary in the methods used and fees assessed. Many consumers who have bank accounts use the bill pay option offered as a free service by their bank. After a consumer authorizes a payment, the bank transfers the funds electronically, if the business is set up to receive electronic payments. For businesses not equipped to receive electronic payments, banks will print out and mail a check to the business.

Some third-party services allow consumers the opportunity to direct all bills to the service—whether a paper bill or an electronic bill. The service then pays all bills after receiving authorization from the consumer. This eliminates the need for the consumer to receive, sort, and manually pay bills. Charges for this type of service vary. Sometimes a monthly fee is charged in addition to a fee for each transaction.

Some credit card services allow consumers to preauthorize repetitive monthly payments to third parties, like cell phone or Internet providers. This service is often provided free of charge. It is best to use this service for bills that have the same value each month.

Person-to-Person Payments

Online systems have been developed to allow consumers to pay each other directly for a product. The businesses that facilitate these person-to-person (P2P) payments provide an Internet platform for payment transfers. The businesses generate revenue by charging a fee for serving as the payment intermediary. The service fee may be either a flat rate, be based on a percentage of the value of the sale, or be a combination of both. Prominent P2P systems facilitate international payments that include currency conversions.

Highly developed P2P systems may compete with services historically provided by banks. Offering branded credit cards, money market investment accounts for balances held in their system, and tracking deposits and payments are services that may be offered by P2P providers. There are significant differences involved when dealing with a P2P provider versus a bank. For example, the money market account offered by a P2P provider is not protected

NET KNOWLEDGE

Using P2P payments may be a convenient way to pay for the goods and services you buy. To use this payment method safely, the Federal Deposit Insurance Corporation (FDIC) suggests that before signing up with a P2P service, you gather information about fees involved, privacy practices, when the money will be charged to your credit card or deducted from your account, its policy on resolving errors and disputes, and whether it is a bank or a non bank company. Go online and identify a P2P service. Then analyze the company's offerings using the five criteria above. Make a chart showing your findings.

by FDIC insurance, whereas a money market deposit account at a bank with FDIC insurance is protected.

Contactless Payments

There are multiple technologies available that enable consumers to make a payment without having their credit or debit cards make physical contact with the credit card reader. The technology used most frequently in the U.S. for contactless payments is **radio frequency identification (RFID)**. RFID, which is also known as *automatic identification and data capture (AIDC)*, uses a transponder to convey identifying information including the account holder's account or balance information and the fees being assessed to the account by the business for products or services.

RFID is appealing to consumers and businesses alike. The chips that carry account information can be embedded in a variety of products including key chains, credit cards, and cell phones. Without having to fiddle with the proper orientation of a credit or debit card to insert it in the reading device, transactions can occur more quickly. As RFID technology is commonly used instead of cash for low-value transactions, the need to make change is eliminated. Commuters who encounter tollbooths or mass transit payment turnstiles also appreciate the convenience provided by RFID.

Deferred Payments Processed by an Intermediary

A number of companies are available to serve online consumers who either don't want to use their credit cards online or who do not have either a traditional credit card or bank account. Sometimes the services provided by these intermediaries are called *electronic wallets, digital wallets, virtual wallets,* or *online wallets*. Methods used by intermediaries include allowing a consumer to preload a card that is later activated online to pay for merchandise, letting a consumer make a purchase that the intermediary bills for later, or helping a consumer make a direct payment for an online purchase by using the funds in their online banking account. Similar to P2P remuneration, the intermediary may charge either a flat rate, a rate based on the percentage of the sale, or a combination of both.

Biometrics

Biometrics refers to using a distinct individual characteristic to uniquely identify a specific person. Fingerprints, retina scans, and voice recognition are some of the more common sources of biometric data. Fingerprint data was in use for a number of years at various grocery food chains. It was also being tested at gas stations. After initially linking credit account data to a

One World

Internationally, biometrics have become widely accepted as a method for safeguarding financial security, substituting for the traditional passwords used to secure accounts. In Japan, cell phones equipped with fingerprint sensors are widely used for mundane through sophisticated financial transactions—from ordering fast-food to accessing bank accounts. In Australia and Indonesia, banks use employees' fingerprints to provide access to secure areas. A large bank in Mexico processes up to a million transactions a day for nearly 20 million customers using fingerprint technology that secures accounts.

A new generation of mobile biometric technologies combines voice and facial recognition to provide a "mobile identity" for users. The voice-plus-facial-recognition technology is more user-friendly for users than the fingerprint sensors because it involves the familiar camera and voice-recording functions on a cell phone. According to biometrics industry experts, this familiarity will be the key to user acceptance of the technology.

Think Critically

What experience, if any, do you have with biometric technology? Would you favor using a form of biometrics to secure your accounts over traditional passwords? Why or why not?

fingerprint, consumers were able to pay their grocery checkout bill or their fuel bill by placing their fingerprint on a fingerprint reading scanner.

Banks are in the process of adopting biometrics. In the U.S., current applications focus on employee verification. For example, a retina scan may be performed to confirm the identity of an employee who is servicing an ATM. Other countries have adopted biometrics for customer service measures. For example, in Japan, a retina scan may be performed on ATM users to confirm their identity.

Tyler Olson/Shutterstock.com

The Need for Caution

Experts recommend using a credit card as the source for online payments. Credit cards usually offer limited liability for false or disputed charges. Resolving disputed charges that are paid for from a bank account or a prepaid card can be more difficult than resolving erroneous bills paid for from cash or bank accounts. Consumers should also be careful that any networks used to authorize online bill payment are secure.

Name ten payment systems other than cash or check.

6.4.2 BANK PAYMENTS

Innovations that are changing payment methods for consumers are also changing bank processes. Not only have banks implemented systems for recording and processing new forms of consumer payments, they have also developed innovative systems for conducting their bank-to-bank transactions and internal operations.

EFT

EFT is an acronym for *electronic funds transfer*. Funds transfers occur between banks, between banks and the Federal Reserve, between banks and the government, and between banks and consumers.

Direct Deposit   One common form of EFT is direct deposit. A law was passed by Congress in 1996 that required most federal payments to be made by EFT. To encourage compliance with this law, the government established Electronic Transfer Accounts (ETAs). For recipients of federal accounts who do not have or cannot qualify for a typical bank account, these low-cost accounts allow recipients to receive their payments electronically. These accounts also help ensure recipients can receive their payments in the event of a natural disaster that requires them to evacuate their homes. For EFT recipients, a statement arrives instead of a check, and the overhead cost of processing checks is eliminated. Safety, accuracy, and immediate use of the funds are reasons that many people prefer direct deposits.

The Financial Management Service (FMS), which is a bureau of the United States Department of the Treasury, annually distributes more than one billion payments valued at more than $2.4 trillion. In 2013, FMS made more than 96 percent of its disbursements by EFT. FMS data indicates that each paper Social Security check payment costs $0.92 more than each EFT payment.

GoDirect In April 2005, FMS began a marketing campaign called GoDirect to encourage recipients of federal funds to receive payments by EFT. Now, it is the law that all federal funds payments be processed via direct deposit to either a bank or credit union or to a Direct Express Master Card. The card has no fees associated with it and the funds on the card have FDIC insurance.

As the government is such a large distributor of funds, these programs help drive EFT further into the psyche of American consumers. This makes consumers more receptive to efforts by private employers to encourage direct deposit as well.

Automated Clearing Houses

Many transactions are handled by *automated clearing houses* (ACHs). The Federal Reserve led the development of ACHs in the 1970s and still operates most of them. Magnetic tapes exchanged among banks read streams of data into computers, ideal for large volumes of smaller payments such as payrolls or recurring payments. Although ACH technology is older and slower than online transfer, the cost per transaction is considerably less.

Online Transfers

For instant movement of high-volume amounts, banks and the Fed use interbank online transfers. These online EFTs take place via dedicated networks not for public use. The transfers are usually time sensitive, so the instant and final transfer of these funds is critical. *Fedwire*, the funds transfer system run by the Federal Reserve, handles transfers for federal funds, interbank dealings, and securities transactions. In September 2014, Fedwire handled more than 555,000 transactions per day at an average daily value of $3.7 trillion. Fedwire transactions are increasing, up from 537,000 transactions per day at an average daily value of $2.7 trillion in 2007. Another online system for private-sector transactions is the *Clearing House Interbank Payment System* (CHIPS), which specializes in large-dollar transactions for international business. CHIPS is the largest private-sector U.S.-dollar funds-transfer system in the world, clearing and settling an average of $1.5 trillion in cross-border and domestic payments daily. At the end of each day, banks settle their accounts by transferring money to accounts at the Federal Reserve.

Check 21

Digital-imaging technology is the technology that enabled Check 21 legislation. Significant cost savings have been achieved by eliminating storage, recordkeeping, postage, and labor costs associated with paper checks. Instead of saving the actual processed check, a digital photo of the check becomes the document of record. A bank may send a customer

interesting *facts*

According to the National Automated Clearing House Association (NACHA), in 2014, the largest ACH payment originator was Wells Fargo & Company, with transactions totaling about $4.1 billion. The largest recipient of ACH payments was Bank of America with transactions totaling about $1.8 billion.

reduced images of checks or merely a record of checks processed. If a customer needs a canceled check, the image can be retrieved from digital storage.

Check 21 was introduced in 2004. As of third quarter 2006, the Fed processed about 17 percent of its checks with Check 21 technology. As of 2010, all checks are processed using Check 21. Check 21 has enabled the Fed to consolidate regional check-processing centers. In 2003, there were 45 check-processing offices. In 2008, there were 18 check-processing offices. As of 2010, there is only one check-processing office located in Cleveland, Ohio.

Front view of a substitute check

Back view of a substitute check

Source: The Federal Reserve

 **checkpoint**

Name three systems banks use for funds transfers.

assessment 6.4

Think Critically

1. Why do you think banks are interested in new payment systems?

2. Why might banks choose not to use up-to-the-minute technology for funds transfers or internal operations?

3. What are the advantages of Electronic Transfer Accounts (ETAs) to payment recipients?

4. How do digital-imaging techniques eliminate float?

5. How do P2P systems help stimulate the economy?

Make Academic Connections

6. **ECONOMICS** The technological innovations that have enabled new payment methods, ranging from bill payment services through biometrics, have created many new business opportunities for the intermediaries who develop the platforms that provide the services. There are, however, some industries that will experience a decline in the demand for their services as a result of the new technologies. Select two new technologies and one old technology and research how businesses providing the technologies are performing. Provide a brief description.

7. **COMMUNICATION** Interview someone who works in the banking industry. Learn that person's thoughts about the future of payment systems. Summarize your findings in a brief report to the class.

chapter 6 assessment

Chapter Summary

6.1 Types of Negotiable Instruments
A. A negotiable instrument is a written order or promise to pay a sum of money to a specified party or to the person who holds it.
B. Checks are the most common form of negotiable instrument. Other forms include drafts, bills of exchange, and promissory notes.

6.2 Presenting Checks for Payment
A. Elements of negotiability call for a signed, unconditional promise or order to pay a defined sum on demand or at a defined time.
B. Types of endorsement include blank, restrictive, full, and qualified.

6.3 Processing Checks
A. The Federal Reserve Act of 1913, the Uniform Commercial Code of 1958, the Expedited Funds Availability Act of 1987, and Check 21 provide the legal framework for today's check-payment system.
B. Checks travel a circuit among drawer, payee, banks, and the Federal Reserve or other clearing house. Postdated and returned checks require special processing.

6.4 Changing Forms of Payment
A. Technological developments have fueled innovations in payment options.
B. ACHs, Fedwire, and CHIPS are computer systems that transfer high volumes of transactions between banking entities.

Vocabulary Builder

a. bearer instrument
b. bill of exchange
c. blank endorsement
d. cash card
e. charge card
f. credit card
g. debit card
h. draft
i. elements of negotiability
j. float
k. full endorsement
l. holder in due course
m. negotiable instrument
n. person-to-person payment (P2P)
o. promissory note
p. qualified endorsement
q. radio frequency identification (RFID)
r. restrictive endorsement
s. returned check
t. smart card
u. transit number

Choose the term that best fits the definition. Write the letter of the answer in the space provided. Some terms may not be used.

____ 1. A negotiable and unconditional written order
____ 2. Certain legal requirements that a check must meet
____ 3. Negotiable instrument payable to whoever holds it
____ 4. Endorsement that limits further negotiability
____ 5. Commonly used at an ATM to perform banking functions
____ 6. Endorsement that transfers the check to another specified party
____ 7. Least secure type of endorsement
____ 8. Transfers money directly from buyer's bank account to merchant's account
____ 9. A written order or promise to pay a sum of money to a specified party or the person who holds it
____ 10. Card with embedded microchips
____ 11. A card that requires consumers to pay off purchases each month
____ 12. The technology that enables contactless payment
____ 13. When consumers pay each other directly for a product
____ 14. A check that is returned due to insufficient funds

Review Concepts

15. What is a negotiable instrument?

16. What does *negotiable* mean as it applies to negotiable instruments?

17. List the six elements of negotiability for a legal negotiable instrument.

18. Identify four types of endorsement and explain the effects of each on a negotiable instrument.

19. Briefly explain the check-clearing process.

20. Why might you want to use a postdated check?

21. What is a transit number? What is its purpose on a check?

22. List ten types of consumer payments other than cash.

23. Give several examples of electronic funds transfer (EFT).

24. What are automated clearing houses?

25. What is the benefit to banks of using digital imaging technology in the check-clearing process?

Apply What You Learned

26. How are negotiable instruments similar to money?

27. Why are there specific legal requirements for an instrument to be negotiable?

28. When you cash a check, why does the bank care whether or not you are the actual payee?

29. What personal factors might cause someone to use a bill payment service?

30. Why is float harmful?

31. How has technology affected the forms of payment used by consumers?

Make Academic Connections

32. **MATH**   Alan's bank statement shows a balance of $674.32. Since the statement date, Alan had deposits of $800.00 and $50.00. He has visited the ATM for withdrawals of $20.00, $50.00, and $20.00, and he has written checks for $42.11, $79.80, $600.00, $81.50, and $174.00. His checkbook register shows a balance of $556.91. Is his account properly balanced?

33. **COMMUNICATION**   Why do government programs, like GoDirect, that utilize advanced technology, have a significant impact on the behavior of businesses and consumers? Explain your thoughts in a two-page persuasive paper that gives clear reasons for your findings. Distinguish between direct business impact and the more subtle impact of increased familiarity leading to increased adaptation.

34. **ART/DESIGN**   Develop a brief PowerPoint presentation to explain to someone unfamiliar with the Internet their online payment choices.

35. **TECHNOLOGY**   Learn more about encryption, one of the ways in which computer networks protect their data. What are the main methods, advantages, and issues surrounding secure data transmission today?

36. **SOCIAL STUDIES**   The growing availability of personal and financial information troubles many people. In groups, research privacy issues as they apply to banking and the Internet. Present a report on current problems, possible solutions, and potential legislation about protecting consumers' privacy.

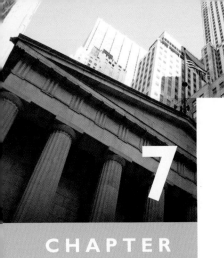

Bank Loans

iStockphoto.com/Javi_indy

climbing the ladder

From Loan Service Clerk to Credit Card Risk Specialist

As he packed up the mementos in his office to move to the bank's new downtown headquarters, Vladimir was flooded with memories of prior positions he held at the bank.

By working his way through his first years of college as a loan services clerk, Vladimir obtained an initial understanding of how a bank processes loans. For new loans, he was responsible for processing research requests and for preparing mortgage participation certificates. He also managed the general ledgers for customer loans and corresponded with customers whenever necessary.

During his first few college cooperative education assignments, Vladimir worked as a commercial loan documentation specialist. He prepared all loan documentation and booked loans into the loan system. Coordinating loan details with title companies, tax service companies, and government filing agencies was another duty. He also carefully reviewed all loan-related documents for errors or fraud.

For his final two cooperative education assignments, Vladimir had worked as a collections associate. This position gave him early exposure to the importance of learning to live within a budget. Dealing with clients who were financially overextended because they bought more than they could afford showed Vladimir how tough it could be to get out of debt.

As a collections associate, Vladimir had been responsible for making outbound phone calls to delinquent card holders. He had also handled incoming phone calls from the same account holders. Vladimir used various software tools, including skip trace software, to locate delinquent cardholders. As the bank had provided training on the legalities associated with tracking down debtors, Vladimir conducted his searches within the appropriate legal constraints.

When talking with delinquent card holders on the phone, Vladimir often encouraged them to make an immediate payment over the phone. He communicated with bank personnel and debt counselors regarding delinquent accounts.

After graduation, Vladimir began working as a credit card risk specialist. He helped analyze loan product mix, losses, and whole loan sale performance. He performed statistical analyses to help guide underwriting practices. He also made recommendations regarding how to optimize profit and minimize credit loss exposure. Updating the credit risk software, including the credit scorecard module, was another duty. An important part of his job was to develop strong relationships with sales and product managers so they would appreciate the value of his risk-based analyses.

Upper Rungs to Consider

Vladimir wanted to apply his skills and knowledge on a broader level. He was researching a position as a collections and loan servicing manager. If he took that role, he would be responsible for managing the entire loan-servicing department. Primary responsibilities would include ensuring loan losses were minimized and meeting regulatory requirements.

Preparing for the Climb

Managing personal credit prudently is critical to financial stability. Many employers check credit scores during the hiring process. What steps can you take to proactively manage your credit and your credit score?

7.1

Consumer Loan Theory

Learning Objectives

7.1.1 Explain asset transformation and modern portfolio theory.

7.1.2 Describe components of consumer lending.

7.1.3 Explain nonloan sources of bank revenue.

Key Terms

- asset transformation
- modern portfolio theory (MPT)
- adverse selection
- captive borrower
- moral hazard
- credit rationing

Banking Scene

Jamar Brown wants to buy some equipment for a house-painting business he is starting this summer. He has put together a basic business plan regarding how much he will spend on equipment and how much he will charge for each job. He has lined up his first three customers. He applied for a $5,000 loan at the bank, but they have only approved a $2,500 loan. Jamar wondered why the bank would not approve his entire loan amount. What do you think?

7.1.1 MANAGING A BANK'S PORTFOLIO

Loans make up a large percentage of bank revenues. Three general categories of loans are consumer loans, mortgage loans, and commercial loans. The pie chart below provides a further breakdown of the types of

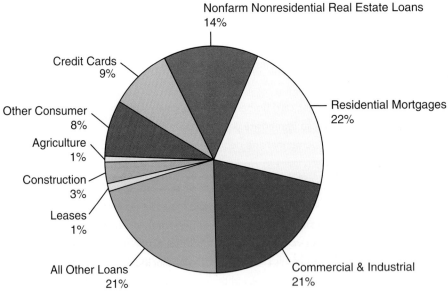

Loan Portfolio Composition
December 31, 2015

- Nonfarm Nonresidential Real Estate Loans 14%
- Credit Cards 9%
- Other Consumer 8%
- Agriculture 1%
- Construction 3%
- Leases 1%
- All Other Loans 21%
- Commercial & Industrial 21%
- Residential Mortgages 22%

Source: FDIC

loans that banks provide. As you can see from the chart, at the end of 2015, 36% of the loans were real estate-related mortgages and loans.

Loan Balances in the United States

At the end of the fourth quarter of 2015, total loans and leases from FDIC-insured institutions amounted to nearly $16 trillion. This was an increase of about 2.7% over the previous year. Of this amount, roughly $4.4 trillion was secured by real estate, a 4.9% increase. Home equity loans dropped 5.5% to $465.1 billion. The largest percentage increase in real estate loans came in the construction and development category, which increased 15.3% to $274.9 billion. Farm loans increased 4.5% to reach $81.5 billion. Commercial and industrial loans increased by 7.4% to $1.85 trillion. During the same period, (non-real estate) loans to individuals totaled to about $1.5 trillion. More than half of this amount, $756.5 billion, was credit card loans. About 1% of all loans were less than 90 days overdue while 2% of all loans were more than 90 days overdue.

Asset Management

Banks are financial intermediaries. They attract money in the form of deposits. Money leaves banks through loans. Bank income is generated through interest and fees.

Asset transformation refers to using deposits to generate revenue by putting deposits to work via loans. The largest component of bank revenue comes from loans. Some revenue is generated by securities investments.

Deposits are bank liabilities because they could be withdrawn by a customer at any point in time. Loans are bank assets because they represent money that the bank will receive back in the form of principal and interest payments. When banks transform liabilities (deposits) into assets (loans), asset transformation has occurred.

For a bank to be profitable, it must astutely engage in asset transformation. Returns need to be generated with minimal risk. There should be a staggered process of making loans, the expiration of loan payments, and investment maturity dates.

Modern Portfolio Theory

In 1952, Harry Markowitz developed the concept of modern portfolio theory (MPT). This theory states that within any portfolio of investments, diversification should be used to spread out risk. Diversification should include variation by industry and variation in maturity dates. Maintaining a diversified portfolio shields investors from downturns in a particular industry. Ideally, a downturn in one industry, which leads to reduced profits in that industry, would be offset by increased profits in a different industry. In this way, a relatively stable level of return can be achieved within a diversified portfolio.

Another type of diversification that occurs within a portfolio is the staggering of maturity dates of securities within a portfolio. This allows portfolio managers to assess, on a rotating basis, whether to reinvest in a particular security. This ongoing reassessment of the value of particular securities encourages adaptability. As market conditions change, portfolio managers can adjust the particular mix of assets included in a given portfolio. Variations in maturity dates trigger a perpetual review, on a rotating basis, of the securities within a portfolio.

The loans held by a bank are essentially a portfolio of assets. How those assets are selected, managed, and maintained affects the stability and profitability of the bank. Loan diversification, both by type and by maturity date, helps stabilize the performance of the bank's loan portfolio.

checkpoint

What is asset transformation?

7.1.2 CONSUMER LENDING THEORY

Consumer loans comprise a specific portion of a bank's loan portfolio. Consumers represent a specific market segment for bank loans. Consumer loan theory has evolved as part of the methodology for developing profitable consumer loan portfolios.

Loan Selection

Revenue from loans is the primary income source for banks. Therefore, banks are very selective in deciding the type of customer with whom they will do business. Years of experience have taught bankers some key lessons regarding which type of lending situations are desirable and which are not.

If a bank has the opportunity to lend $25,000 to two customers and can charge one customer an 8 percent interest rate and can charge another customer a 12 percent interest rate, which customer would it want to secure? Remember that loan interest rates are determined by overall economic conditions, the prime rate, and the amount of risk associated with the loan. **Adverse selection** is the concept that the borrowers who are most willing to accept a high interest rate are the same borrowers who are most likely to default on their loans. So if the first customer is offered a $25,000 loan at an 8 percent rate because he or she has a strong credit history with good collateral, it is because the person is very likely to repay the loan on time.

If an 8 percent interest rate is available on a $25,000 loan, why would a borrower consider paying 12 percent interest for the same amount of principal? Suppose this borrower wants to start a side catering business and needs $25,000 to buy equipment. This borrower has a weak credit history. Because he is just starting the business, it is unknown how much revenue will be generated by the business. But because he is very passionate about the business idea, he really wants to start the business. He thinks the business will grow and lead to financial independence. Without an initial loan, he cannot start the business. He believes so strongly in the idea that he is willing to risk other assets to get the start-up capital. He will gladly pay 12 percent interest, even though he knows similar loans are available for 8 percent interest. The bank is unsure about the profitability of the business because the business is new. As many new businesses fail, there is a relatively high risk of loan default. To help offset the financial exposure of default, the bank charges a higher interest rate on the loan. Adverse selection led the high-risk borrower to accept a loan with less-favorable terms.

Some segments of borrowers are more likely to prefer one type of lender to another. For example, if a car company has a lower loan qualification standard than a bank, then a consumer with a relatively weak credit history might opt for auto financing from a car company. Because it is easier for a consumer with a weak credit history to obtain a loan from the car company, then that consumer is a **captive borrower** relative to the car financing company. On the flip side, when higher-risk customers migrate to the auto company for a loan, then the auto loan company will have a higher default rate. This is another example of adverse selection.

Moral hazard occurs when borrowers take greater risks if they think the harm they will incur from those risks will somehow be minimalized. In the case of high-risk individual borrowers willing to accept a high loan rate, if they have assets they are willing to surrender to the lender because of loan default, then they may accept the high-rate loan. Moral hazard, as applied to industries, has a similar connotation. In early 2008, when the government intervened to rescue Bear Stearns, there was a great deal of concern whether other financial companies would continue to engage in high-risk behavior because they knew the government would provide a safety net if they got into trouble. Many would argue, to decrease moral hazard, the government should not intervene to rescue firms that engage in high-risk behavior.

Banks can decide on an appropriate customer base. Not everyone who applies for a loan receives a loan. Sometimes banks will loan someone a portion of the requested amount. When banks refuse to provide a loan, or when they lend less than the customer requested, they are engaging in **credit rationing**. By carefully allocating how their deposit funds will be used, banks are maintaining the stability of their portfolios.

Downstream Loan Profit

Banks do not always keep loans. They often sell loans on the secondary market. *Securitization* of loans occurs when individual loans are pooled together. These combined loans can then be sold as securities.

The individual return rate for each loan and the individual risk associated with each loan is combined into a collective return rate and a collective risk rate for the pool of loans. Sometimes banks issue these securities directly. Sometimes banks sell individual loans to an intermediary who pools the loans and issues securities based on the pooled loans. When sold to an intermediary, banks achieve profits from the loans in two ways. The first method is by charging loan origination fees to the borrower. The second method is by selling the loan for a slightly higher principal than the original loan. The buyer of the loan gets, in effect, a slightly lower interest rate than the original loan. The securitized loans are then sold to investors. Securitization can occur for any type of consumer loan including vehicle loans, education loans, and miscellaneous loans.

checkpoint

What is adverse selection?

7.1.3 ADDITIONAL SOURCES OF BANK REVENUE • • • • • • •

In addition to generating revenue from astutely managing loan portfolios, banks also generate revenue from charging a variety of fees. For instance, according to *The Wall Street Journal*, banks earned $31.9 billion in overdraft revenue in 2013.

Off-Balance Sheet Activities

Banks offer a number of services that generate revenue but that are not included on their *balance sheets*. A balance sheet lists a company's net profit, owner's equity, assets, and liabilities. Balance sheets are prepared at least annually and, for public companies, are public documents. As public documents, they are seen not only by company management, but also by investors. In contrast, off-balance sheet activities are not seen by investors.

Off-balance sheet activities include overdraft protection and assorted letters of credit. Consumer lending can generate fees from overdraft protection. Fee-based letters of credit are used both domestically and internationally to facilitate obtaining a loan or transacting business. There are a variety of forms of overdraft protection. A checking account can be linked to either a savings account or a credit card. If an overdraft occurs from the checking account, funds are transferred from the linked account. Although charges for this fund transfer vary, some banks charge $9 each day that a fund transfer is required. Consumers may be enrolled in an occasional overdraft protection line, which offers a short-term loan so that payments are paid when customers don't have the money in their

Credit cards are a form of consumer loans. Private-label credit cards are for a particular retailer and can only be used in the stores of the retailer issuing the card. Although a retailer may promote its own credit card, the company that issues the credit card bears responsibility of owning the loans associated with the cards. Following market trends of providing consumers with easy access to credit, numerous retailers installed kiosks in their stores so that customers could sign themselves up for a new instant credit card. The kiosks provide either a temporary credit card or a permanent plastic card to use right away. When customers have a higher amount of credit available to them, they often spend more money while shopping.

Think Critically
Why do stores want to increase the number of private-label credit card holders? Why do the private-label issuers want to enroll more credit card holders?

accounts. The charge can be as much as $36 and the account must be brought back to a positive balance within 30 days.

Overdraft protection can also be linked to a home equity line of credit, also called a *flex line*. Charges for flex lines vary but may include no application fee or charges in the first year. Additional years may require a fee to maintain the flex line. Although fees vary, a $65 annual fee to maintain a flex line is typical. Some institutions may charge a fee if the flex line is closed down too quickly. The interest rate on flex lines vary.

Other Revenue Sources

There are other fees a bank may charge. Account service charges, safe deposit box rental, ATM charges, insurance sales fees, and trading fees are examples of additional fees. Account service fees vary by account, but may include charges for a certified check, researching past transactions, verbal funds transfer, counter checks, and returned checks.

✔checkpoint

What are three methods of providing overdraft protection?

assessment 7.1

Think Critically

1. What are the two key ideas of modern portfolio theory?

2. Explain why people raised concerns about moral hazard when the government intervened to help out Bear Stearns. What are the long-term concerns with moral hazard?

3. How do banks earn revenue by selling loans?

4. What is the advantage to banks of off-balance sheet activities?

Make Academic Connections

5. **RESEARCH** Conduct Internet research and look up various account fees at three local banks. Compare the charges assessed to accounts. Summarize your findings and be prepared to share them with the class. Also be prepared to discuss which accounts provide the best value for your particular needs and why.

Consumer Loans

Banking Scene

Jamar Brown needs a better truck for his house-painting business. He has saved $2,000 for a down payment and has researched the kind of truck he wants. In addition to his business loan, he now needs to consider a truck loan. He wants to find the best loan with terms that are right for his situation, but he is not sure where to start. What questions should Jamar ask himself as he prepares to seek a loan?

7.2.1 INSTALLMENT LOANS

Loans have always been at the center of the banking business. Lending is the foundation of the banking industry, the lifeblood of all business, and critical to the working of our economic system. Loans, when responsibly used and administered, are a powerful financial tool. Like any powerful tool, they can also be dangerous when used without proper knowledge.

With increasing competition among banks and financial institutions, a wide array of loan products is available. Most consumer lending falls under two categories: installment loans and open-end loans.

Installment loans are perhaps the most familiar type of consumer lending product that banks offer. An installment loan is a loan for which the amount of the payments, the rate of interest, and the number of payments (or length of term) are fixed. Installment loans are repaid on a periodic basis. Monthly payments are typical. An installment loan contract is a legal document obligating both parties to the written terms, so it is important for consumers to read and understand every word carefully.

Personal Loans Personal loans do not require that a specific purpose be stated. You might take out a personal loan for a vacation, optional medical procedures such as cosmetic surgery or dental work, or almost anything you choose. There is an almost unending variety of terms and schedules for personal loans, based on the consumer's credit rating and the specific type of loan he or she seeks. There are many types of installment loans available, usually marketed according to purpose.

Vehicle Loans Automobile loans may be the most common type of installment loan. After the automobile price is settled, the trade-in value and down payment negotiated, and the deal established, consumers can finance the remaining balance with an installment loan. Although manufacturers have financing available through their own corporations, banks often offer competitive rates and establish relationships with dealers to provide the service. With installment loans, the term and payments are fixed and scheduled based on the principal and the interest rate calculated on the balance. A better credit rating typically results in a lower interest rate. The *Truth in Lending Statement*, required to be given at the time of signing, should be carefully read by buyers to help protect their rights.

Home Equity Loans Home equity loans are an increasingly popular form of lending. These loans, based upon the difference between what a home is worth and how much the homeowner owes on a first mortgage, are in effect second mortgages. This type of loan generally carries a low interest rate, and interest charges may be tax deductible.

When home values drop, as they did in the aftermath of the mortgage crisis, many homeowners have mortgages that exceed the market value of their homes. In these cases, home equity loans are not an option.

Education Loans Education loans help many students achieve an education they might not otherwise be able to afford. In many cases, loans are backed or subsidized by the government. Stafford loans for students and PLUS loans for parents are examples of government-backed programs. If the borrower for some reason defaults, the government may pay these loans.

Because of government backing, there is less risk to the lending bank, so interest rates are often lower than those available for other loans. Students are not required to make payments while they are in school. Payments begin once a student is out of school. If the student meets certain need-based requirements, the government will pay the interest that accumulates on the loan until student payments begin. Employers may also help arrange loans through credit unions or the employer's bank for continuing education programs for employees.

Photodisc/Getty Images

Secured and Unsecured Loans

Although there are many types of consumer loans, they all fall into one of two categories. A secured loan is one in which some item of value backs the loan in case the borrower defaults on the loan. The item that secures the loan is called collateral. The bank could use the collateral, if necessary, to recover the financial loss of an uncollected loan. For example, if you take out an auto loan, the lender typically has a lien on the car, a legal claim to the property to secure the debt. The car will go to the lender if you fail to make the payments, and the lien is noted on the car's title.

Collateral offers the bank a degree of safety for its loan. In theory almost anything agreed to between borrower and bank could be collateral, but for most loans used to make a large purchase, the purchased item is the collateral. A banker might accept other things of value to secure a personal loan, such as a savings account, CDs, stocks or other securities, a personal possession of value, or any other financial asset. Banks typically don't want an inventory of used cars and diamond rings, though. They examine creditworthiness carefully before granting any loan, secured or otherwise.

An unsecured loan is a loan backed only by the reputation and creditworthiness of the borrower. Sometimes called a *signature loan*, these loans typically are made for smaller amounts than secured loans. There may be exceptions for customers who do large volumes of business with the bank or have a great track record and credit rating. Commercial lending often blends secured and unsecured loans.

Lending Terminology

Loans are legal contracts between lender and borrower, and so they include precise language. With the many types of loans and many varieties of plans within those types, there may be a great deal of variation in details and numerous terms. Although banks are required to disclose the truth about their loans, it is still in the consumer's best interest to read carefully and understand everything in the loan agreement. Reputable bankers explain and answer questions about loan terms. Doing so both helps to promote good customer relations and to ensure a smooth and steady income for the bank.

Some fundamental terminology applies to nearly every loan.

- **Principal is the amount borrowed.** If you need to borrow $12,000 after your trade-in and down payment on a car, the $12,000 is the principal.

- **Interest is the amount you pay to use the principal.** The interest rate is the amount of interest, usually expressed per year as a percentage of the principal, such as 2.9 percent. The annual percentage rate (APR) is one of the most important figures to compare when considering loans. Rates for most installment loans are *fixed rates* for the life of the loan, but in some loans they may be *variable rates*, changing over time. *Indexed rates* are linked to some other rate, such as the Federal Reserve's prime rate (usually plus some other figure) to allow for changes in the economy.

It is important to know how interest is calculated. In some loans, interest is calculated on the declining principal balance as payments are made. In other loans, payments go toward the interest first, and then toward the balance, so there is no advantage in paying off the loan early. In such a case, you may owe more on the principal at the time of payoff than you would have if you had financed with a loan that charged interest on a declining balance.

- **Fees are other charges for the loan.** Examples are application fees, document preparation fees, late charges, and so forth. The loan agreement must specify all fees.

- **The finance charge is the total dollar amount to be paid for the loan.** The finance charge includes all interest calculations, fees, and other costs. It must be disclosed to the consumer. Sometimes the finance charge alone can be misleading. For example, if you borrowed $1,000 for a year with a loan fee of $10 and interest totaling $100, your finance charge would be $110. The APR would be 10 percent if you kept the whole $1,000 the full year, but you probably wouldn't. Assuming that you began to pay the loan back immediately in 12 equal payments of $92.50, you don't have the use of the full $1,000 for the year. The math gets a little tricky, but the actual APR would be 18 percent.

- **Total payments are the total amount a consumer must repay.** They include the principal and the total finance charge. This figure must be disclosed at the time a loan is signed. The total payments figure reveals the effect of an interest rate over time. The APR, the finance charge, and the total payments are the three key figures to evaluate.

- **Payment is the amount the borrower repays each specified period.** The schedule of payments specifies exactly when payments are due and what penalties are assessed if payments are not made on time. Sometimes an *acceleration clause* brings the entire loan due if payments are missed. A missed payment may also be cause for a variable interest rate to increase. Payments are usually monthly and fixed for the life of the loan. Some loans may include a balloon payment (a single large payment) at the end of the loan. Although the balloon payment reduces the payments before it, paying the final large amount may be difficult.

✔checkpoint

What is the difference between a secured loan and an unsecured loan?

_____

_____

_____

Ethics in Action

Some credit card issuers offer teaser rates, extremely low rates for balance transfers or for a brief period of time. Later, the rates may change to normal or even high levels. Credit analysts note that moving your credit accounts too often can hurt your credit rating.

Think Critically

Do you think that offering teaser rates is a misleading policy? Why or why not? Should credit lenders hold it against consumers who take advantage of such offers? Why or why not?

7.2.2 OPEN-END LOANS

Open-end loans are another type of loan with an almost endless variety of applications. The amount owed on an open-end loan is flexible, as is the term. The longer you use the money, the more you pay.

Credit Cards

You may not think of credit cards as forms of consumer loans, but that is exactly what they are. The issuer is lending you the money for a period of time and charging interest for its use. The principal changes as your balance goes up and down, but you are still borrowing and paying interest. Because the balance changes, finance charges vary as well. One variable is the method used to calculate the balance. Some cards offer a grace period, which is an amount of time you have to pay the bill in full and avoid any finance charges. Most cards have an annual fee that is added to the balance. Transaction fees for cash advances or charges for exceeding your credit limit may apply. Some issuers charge a monthly maintenance fee even if you do use the card. Late penalties for bills paid after the due date raise the cost of credit cards, and delinquency rates may raise the APR significantly.

Lines of Credit

Other forms of open-end loans are the various line-of-credit plans that banks may offer. These may include a home equity reserve or an overdraft protection plan. Essentially, these plans allow consumers to establish a line of credit that they may draw on as needs arise. Borrowings may be for any amount up to an agreed-upon limit. As the balance is paid down, more money may be borrowed. Terms of agreement are similar to those of credit cards.

checkpoint

What is an open-end loan?

assessment 7.2

Think Critically

1. Why do you think consumer loans have so many names and forms?

2. What is the difference between the interest and the finance charge of a loan?

3. Why might it be important for consumers to understand their credit card agreements?

4. In your opinion, how many credit cards are too many? Explain your reasoning.

Make Academic Connections

5. **COMMUNICATION**   With a partner, make a list of questions you should ask yourself before deciding whether to take on debt. Include questions about needs, budgets, and possible changes in lifestyle. Convert the questions into a checklist for consumers that offers guidance for responsible borrowing.

6. **RESEARCH**   Have students conduct research among lending institutions to find the current costs involved with a specific type of installment loan. They should choose one of the following to investigate—personal loan, vehicle loan, home equity loan, or education loan—and set a specific amount of money to borrow. Students should report their findings in a short report that includes the typical interest rates offered, the fees that would be involved, the duration of the loan, and the total amount they would pay for the loan.

Granting and Analyzing Credit

7.3

Banking Scene

Jamar's business is booming. He wants his friend Larry to buy a truck, and to work with him painting houses. Larry, who has a poor record of paying off his credit cards, is having trouble getting financing for a new truck. What might Jamar and Larry need to know about the credit-granting process?

Learning Objectives

7.3.1 List steps in the credit-approval process.

7.3.2 Identify major criteria in a person's credit rating.

Key Terms

- underwriting
- subprime rates
- consumer reporting agency (CRA)
- FICO score

7.3.1 GRANTING CREDIT

Every borrower represents a potential risk to the lender. If you can't or don't pay off any loan you have, you not only ruin your credit rating, but you hurt the bank as well. In fact, bad loans of various types are the number one reason banks get into financial trouble. Banks have to make sound decisions when it comes to granting loans, and they need defined methods of doing so. According to the FDIC, a *net charge-off* is the total of loans and leases removed from a balance sheet because they are uncollectible minus any funds from prior charge-offs that were collected. At the end of the third quarter of 2014, net charge-offs were about $9.2 billion, down from about $25 billion at the end of the third quarter of 2011. Banks need to lend wisely to avoid risk exposure that can lead to large losses.

Before a bank is willing to advance its money (or more accurately, its customers' money) to you, it takes a number of steps to minimize the likelihood of a bad decision. Most of these steps are part of a well-defined policy of risk management.

Risk Management

Risk management for bankers is the practice of minimizing financial loss through effective policies. Banks face risks in operations, credit, liquidity, legal and regulatory compliance, and even marketing matters. Regarding credit granting, risk-management policies include consideration of the bank's overall financial position, reserve requirements, cash flow, and ratio analyses of liabilities and assets. These factors all influence the credit-granting process, determining how flexible a bank can afford to be in granting credit. In addition, a bank's risk-management policies are carefully scrutinized by bank examiners during an audit. Sometimes legal requirements complicate these issues. Banks must document that they comply with the law in such areas as extending credit fairly and equally throughout the community.

Credit-Approval Process

To ensure credit-granting decisions are made in an accurate, efficient, and fair manner (and to be able to document them as such), well-run banks have written credit-approval procedures. Procedures and the specific standards for them may vary depending upon the type of loan. Variations from bank to bank also occur. Some of these steps may be combined, or for large loans may have several cycles of processing and underwriting for approval. Some of the procedures may be automated, such as with an online application, but the essential credit-approval process follows some basic steps.

- **Application.** The first step in the credit-approval process is obtaining a complete and accurate application. This may seem self-evident, but it is critical, for much of the later processing of the loan depends upon the information provided here. It is not unusual for a credit application to fail because it lacked an important detail or gave inconsistent information. Even something as basic as a name can cause confusion. Is it George Walker Bush, George H. Bush, George Bush, Sr., or George Bush, Jr.? A Social Security number may clear up such problems, but an incorrect digit could ruin everything. A loan officer or other representative often works with the customer, guiding him or her through the application and clarifying exactly what information and what degree of detail is necessary. Often bank representatives help consumers with this step as part of a loan analysis or a needs analysis. This process helps consumers decide what kind of loan may best meet their needs.

- **Documentation.** The next step for the bank is gathering the necessary documentation for the loan. Some of this information may come from the application itself, depending upon how detailed it is. Other information includes such items as a credit report, employment verification, bank account information, appraisal of properties for secured loans, and so forth. Sometimes preliminary approval is granted based on these documents.

- **Processing.** The bank builds a loan file, as the loan officer verifies statements on the application and checks information on all documentation the bank receives. The processing time depends upon the type and amount of the loan and the credit history of the applicant. The loan officer may ask for explanations or seek further information during this step.

- **Underwriting.** When all required information has been gathered and verified, the loan officer forwards the loan file for underwriting, or reviewing the loan for soundness. The underwriter's job is to make sure the loan is a prudent use of bank funds. The underwriter reviews the application package to make sure it is complete and makes an evaluation of the loan based on the assembled documentation. Underwriters evaluate the three Cs: *collateral, capacity,* and *credit reputation*. Collateral refers to the security (if any) required for the loan. Capacity refers to the ability to repay, based on income, job history, and amount currently owed. Credit reputation, or credit history, is a record of how well the applicant has repaid debt in the past. Based on these factors, the underwriter approves or disapproves the loan.

Today, underwriting is increasingly automated. Sophisticated software programs provide statistical analyses and models based on vast quantities of data. Banks may sometimes grant a loan to applicants who don't meet standards, grant a loan with certain conditions, or offer a loan at subprime rates. **Subprime rates** are those higher than normal to offset the increased risk represented by a less-than-perfect borrower. The days when a banker might offer a loan based on acquaintance are disappearing. Many banks have less flexibility in underwriting than they once did, although they may offer more programs to meet varying needs.

- **Closing.** At the closing, a bank representative discusses and explains the terms of the loan, and the borrower signs the documentation that has been prepared. Included with the documentation are disclosure statements required by law.

- **Funding.** When the documents are signed, the bank either adds the funds to the borrower's account or issues a check.

Not all of these steps are followed for every type of loan nor in this exact order. However, some form of credit-approval process takes place for every loan, whether it is a credit card application through the mail or a loan officer working face to face with the consumer.

What is underwriting?

7.3.2 ANALYZING CREDIT

When an underwriter (whether human or electronic) looks at your loan application, one of the key factors considered is your credit history. It is fairly easy to verify your income, how long you have had your job, and how much the car you want to buy is worth. It is not so easy, however, to predict how people will pay bills. The best way to predict the future is to see how a person has done in the past.

Consumer Reporting Agencies

A **consumer reporting agency (CRA)** is a company that compiles and keeps records on consumer payment habits and sells these reports to banks and other companies to use for evaluating creditworthiness. Sometimes called credit bureaus, CRAs include information about whether individuals have been sued, arrested, or have had financial judgments issued against them by a court. The three largest consumer reporting agencies are Equifax, Experian, and TransUnion, but there are many such agencies. Among the three largest, records on almost every conceivable use of credit by every American exist. These comprehensive records form the foundation of credit analysis. Most credit reports contain the following types of information.

- **Personal data** includes names (including former ones), Social Security number, addresses, and employment history. Similar information for a spouse may also appear.

- **Accounts history** includes detailed history of active credit accounts, such as names and addresses of creditors, when an account was opened, co-signers, accounts status, whether the manner of payments (MOP) is timely, and whether the account is in default or a judgment has been issued. These records for active accounts typically show 24–36 months of history, and creditors keep reporting as long as the account remains open. Banks and credit unions, credit card companies, mortgage companies, finance companies, and department stores report this information regularly.

- **Delinquent accounts** are sometimes the only accounts reported to a consumer reporting agency. In these cases, the same sort of information as described above appears, as well as the current status of the delinquent account. Utilities, insurance companies, doctors, and landlords are typical reporters of this data.

- **Public records** include bankruptcies, judgments, liens, divorces, child-support arrearages, and criminal records. Private companies track and sell this data to credit bureaus.

- **Inquiries** are records of all who have requested a copy of the credit report within the last year. Although consumers have little control over these records, too many inquiries in a year can appear as if a consumer is having trouble obtaining credit.

With the enormous volume of credit records, errors inevitably enter into some records, and sometimes they are the first evidence of identity theft. Credit investigations have been criticized as not always being reliable.

Although credit bureaus are private organizations, consumers are entitled to a free credit report each year from each of the three major credit agencies. As TransUnion, Equifax, and Experian each issue their own report, it is a good idea to review a report from each agency annually. By checking reports annually, consumers can learn whether anyone has tried to open an account in their name. This is one way to detect identity theft. There are other ways to obtain free credit reports as well. Discover now includes your credit score each month with your statement. If there are any significant changes in your credit score, a credit report should be obtained immediately.

The Fair Credit Reporting Act guarantees consumers the right to review and dispute information in the reports. Consumers should be persistent in resolving errors and they should keep good records of all communication regarding error resolution efforts. In some instances, it can take more than five years to resolve errors.

Tech Talk

Online Identity Verification

With identity fraud on the increase, lenders and businesses are looking for ways to be certain customers are who they say they are, especially in online applications. Some applications use networking technology to link credit applications directly to consumer reporting agencies to aid in verification.

Equifax's eIDverifier™, for example, was among the earliest software programs that asks for verification information beyond Social Security number, driver's license number, and address. The program asks consumers to answer a multiple-choice questionnaire that is created from their own credit histories, answers to which only genuine consumers would know. These answers are compared to the Equifax data, and only if they match can the consumer move forward with the transaction.

In 2006, Recombo, a company that provides electronic signatures for electronic contracts, formed a partnership with Equifax. By using the eIDverifier, Recombo can improve the safety of its web-signing documents.

Think Critically
Search the Internet for more information about online identity-verification systems, and write a short report on your findings. Does the use of such systems increase your confidence regarding online security? Why or why not?

"communicate"

Go online and search for a free credit report. Get your credit report from several agencies. When reports are received, compare the results. Share with the class the nature of any discrepancies you find in the reports and actions you plan to take to resolve the discrepancies.

Credit-Scoring Systems

A credit-scoring system can provide an efficient and unbiased method of evaluating credit. For many years, banks have used credit-scoring systems to evaluate the potential creditworthiness of loan applicants. These scores place a numerical value on the performance or status of an applicant in various categories. Income, debt, age (as long as it is not used to discriminate), years on the job, and even whether one has a telephone are the kinds of factors a credit-scoring system evaluates. The points in each category are added for a total score. There are many such systems in use, typically requiring a minimum score to qualify an applicant for a loan.

FICO

The FICO credit-scoring system developed by Fair, Isaac and Company, Inc. has come to dominate the dozens of credit-scoring systems in use. The FICO score is a three-digit number that credit granters can use in making a loan approval decision. Using a sophisticated model, the FICO system weighs all categories of information, with the importance of factors depending on the amount and type of information available on the person being evaluated. The FICO system excludes income and the type of credit for which the applicant has applied. Also excluded are race, ethnic background, religion, gender, and marital status, all of which are prohibited by law from being factors used to make a credit decision. FICO uses the following criteria in its ratings. Percentages are approximate.

- **Payment history (35 percent)** includes a consumer's track record on many types of accounts, including credit cards, installment loans, mortgages, and other types of borrowing, as well as public records on collections, bankruptcies, judgments, and wage attachments. Details on late payments and how many accounts have no late payments appear.

- **Amounts owed (30 percent)** include the total amounts owed on all accounts, the types of accounts that are open, how many of those accounts have balances, whether certain types of accounts have balances, how much of a credit line is in use, and how much is still owed on installment loans compared to the original loan value.

- **Length of credit history (15 percent)** considers how long accounts have been established and how long it has been since each was in use. In general, a long, solid credit history increases the FICO score.

- **New credit (10 percent)** is often sought by people in financial trouble. Although shopping for the best rate is a good idea, too much new credit is a sign of overextension. FICO considers how many new accounts exist, how long since a new account was opened, how many recent requests for credit have been made, and what recent credit history shows.

- **Types of credit (10 percent)** are evaluated, including what types of accounts exist and how many there are of each. A "healthy mix" of credit yields a higher score than a dependence on a single type of credit account.

Photodisc/Getty Images

FICO scores range between 300 and 900, with about 620 being the point below which consumers may be regarded as high-risk. The sophisticated (and secret) FICO scoring system is not without critics. Some analysts say that potential creditors depend too much on it, rather than carefully weighing all factors. FICO is not responsible for errors in content.

Consumers can obtain their FICO scores online, but they may need to pay for them. Just as each credit agency generates its own credit report on each consumer, each credit agency generates a separate FICO score on each consumer. FICO scores can vary by as much as 50 points among the three credit agencies. As FICO scores are generated based on information in credit reports, consumers need to be sure that their credit reports are accurate at each of the three agencies. Because FICO scores affect consumers' interest rates, ideally they should know their FICO score well in advance of applying for loans. With advance knowledge of a negative FICO rating based on erroneous information in a credit report, consumers can try to correct the information in the credit report prior to applying for a loan.

 checkpoint

What is a consumer reporting agency?

assessment 7.3

Think Critically

1. Why might underwriting standards vary among banks?

2. How do subprime rates offset the risk associated with borrowers who have less-than-perfect credit?

3. How might a stranger having your Social Security number ruin your credit rating?

4. Do any of the categories of personal information on a credit report strike you as being a violation of privacy? Discuss.

Make Academic Connections

5. **CRITICAL THINKING**   Critique the methods and concepts of credit investigation described in this lesson. Then, working in groups, design a credit-scoring system that produces a maximum score of 100. Assign point values to at least six types of information. State the weight of each type of information and how relevant you believe each is in predicting likelihood of payment.

6. **CONSUMER AFFAIRS**   Visit at least three noncommercial websites that provide information about how you can correct errors on your credit report. Summarize your findings.

Cost of Credit

Banking Scene

Jamar has established a strong credit record through timely payments on his business and truck loans. While at the bank, his loan officer asks whether he would also like to apply for a business credit card. He doesn't know if this is a good idea. She offers him several possibilities and options. Jamar has also seen many such offers in the mail. What should Jamar consider before he applies for a business credit card?

Learning Objectives

7.4.1 Identify key factors in the cost of credit.

7.4.2 Explain the impact of negative credit ratings on consumers.

Key Terms

- revolving credit
- sum-of-digits method
- previous-balance method
- adjusted-balance method
- average-daily-balance method
- predatory lending

7.4.1 WHAT CREDIT COSTS

More than ever, the nation's economy runs on credit. Not only is it the foundation of banking income, it is also the engine that makes possible growth and development throughout the economy, bringing into being the standard of living you know today. Credit is a convenient tool for consumers to use to enhance their lives. At the end of 2014, consumer credit was growing about 6 percent annually.

Like any tool, credit can be dangerous if misused. In December 2015, total U.S. consumer credit was $3.5 trillion. The portion of the total that could be attributed to revolving credit was $936 billion. **Revolving credit** is a line of credit that has a maximum limit. It can be used on an ongoing basis until the limit is reached. When the balance (or a portion of the balance) is paid off, the credit can be used again until the next time the maximum is met. Credit cards are an example of revolving credit.

The easy availability of credit that results from fierce competition among lenders has allowed some consumers to accumulate more debt than they can manage. Instead of cutting back in a financial pinch, they simply add more debt to cover the shortfall. Eventually this can lead to disaster. Understanding the cost of credit and knowing how it is calculated helps consumers use it wisely. Banks want and need to make money on loans, but they have no interest in struggling to collect debt or losing what they lend in default. For this reason, banks have an interest in promoting consumer education. Many banks offer information on the best use of credit, and they are required by law to make full disclosure of the costs.

Reviewing APR and Finance Charge

The annual percentage rate (APR) is the amount of interest charged on the loan principal expressed as a yearly figure. APR does not include annual fees, transaction fees, penalties, loan origination fees, or other such costs.

The APR is a key aspect of comparing credit costs. Understanding the total finance charge depends on how interest charges are applied. How does the principal change? Lenders can calculate interest in many different ways, as long as they explain clearly what they are. Some methods are more advantageous to consumers than others. Finance charges may be very different, depending on which method is used.

Sum-of-Digits Method Sometimes the interest gets paid first, so paying ahead saves the consumer no money. This payment structure has essentially built-in prepayment penalties, which may be fixed charges or may be based on the sum-of-digits method. This method takes the total finance charge, divides it by the number of months in the loan term, and assigns a higher ratio of interest to the early payments. For example, consider a 12-month loan. By adding 12 + 11 + 10...+1, calculate that the sum of the digits 1 through 12 is 78. In the first month, 12/78ths of the total payment goes to interest. In the second month, 11/78ths, the third month, 10/78ths, and so on. Although the total cost to the consumer is the same, there is no advantage to paying early, because the interest is front-loaded.

Below is a chart showing the sum-of-digits method for a $1,000 loan that has a 6 percent interest rate and a $30 loan-processing fee. For this loan, the total financing charges are $90 ($60 for interest and $30 for loan processing). The total loan cost—comprised of principal, interest, and the loan processing fee—is $1,090. Monthly loan payments are $1,090 ÷ 12 = $90.83.

If the loan repayment were calculated as a simple combination of principal and interest, then each loan payment of $90.83 would be comprised of

Month of Loan Payment	Numerator for Month	Denominator for Month	Ratio of Payment Applied toward Interest	Monthly Loan Payment	Amount of Payment Applied to Interest	Amount of Payment Applied to Principal
1	12	78	0.15	$90.83	$13.97	$76.86
2	11	78	0.14	$90.83	$12.81	$78.02
3	10	78	0.13	$90.83	$11.64	$79.19
4	9	78	0.12	$90.83	$10.48	$80.35
5	8	78	0.10	$90.83	$9.32	$81.51
6	7	78	0.09	$90.83	$8.15	$82.68
7	6	78	0.08	$90.83	$6.99	$83.84
8	5	78	0.06	$90.83	$5.82	$85.01
9	4	78	0.05	$90.83	$4.66	$86.17
10	3	78	0.04	$90.83	$3.49	$87.34
11	2	78	0.03	$90.83	$2.33	$88.50
12	1	78	0.02	$90.83	$1.16	$89.67

$7.50 interest and $83.33 of principal. Therefore, if a consumer paid off a loan in eight months, he or she would expect to achieve a savings of $30 in interest and finance charges ($7.50 multiplied by four months). However, with the sum-of-digits method, the interest payment is front-loaded. Therefore, a consumer who pays the debt off after eight months only achieves a savings of $11.64. Summing the amount of payment applied to interest for months 9 through 12 provides a total of $11.64.

This method of calculating payment is sometimes referred to as the *Rule of 78*. The name derives from how the denominator sums for a one-year period. The same method of interest calculation can be used on loans of any duration. The denominator used in the calculations would be the sum of the total months. For example, a 15-month loan would have a denominator of 120.

Previous- and Adjusted-Balance Methods For open-ended credit, the finance charge is based on the rate multiplied by the balance. How the lender computes the balance matters in terms of the total finance charge. Some creditors take the amount owed at the beginning of the billing cycle and calculate interest on that figure, regardless of payments or charges. This method is called the previous-balance method. Others subtract payments made during the billing cycle but usually don't count purchases. This method is called the adjusted-balance method.

Average-Daily-Balance Method Probably the most common method is the average-daily-balance method. The balances for each day of the billing

---

Banking Math *Connection*

What portion of a credit card payment goes toward the principal? Suppose you have a balance of $1,500 on a credit card. Your minimum payment is 4 percent, or $60, on a card with an APR of 18 percent. How much of that payment will go toward paying the interest?

Solution

The formula for finding the interest is

$$\text{Rate} \div 360 \times 30 \times \text{Balance} = \text{Interest}$$

Rate is the APR, in this case 0.18. Dividing it by 360 gives the rate per day, or 0.0005. Multiplying this figure by 30 provides the rate per month, and multiplying that product by the balance gives the interest.

$$\text{Rate} \div 360 \times 30 \times \text{Balance} = \text{Interest}$$
$$0.18 \div 360 \times 30 \times \$1,500 = \$22.50$$

In this example, $22.50 goes toward interest, and only $60.00 − 22.50 = $37.50 goes toward reducing your balance. It is going to take a long time to pay off the balance. Consumers should always pay as much beyond the minimum payment required as they can afford.

Cheryl Savan/Shutterstock.com

cycle are added and then divided by the number of days in the billing cycle to yield an average figure on which the finance charge is calculated.

Minimum Payments

Most credit cards require a minimum payment of about 4 percent of the unpaid balance every month. The minimum payment was increased from 2 percent because of guidelines issued by federal legislators at the end of 2005. To help consumers avoid a perpetual cycle of debt and to save on interest payments over the long term, consumers are now required to pay at least 1 percent of the principal amount. The other 3 percent of the minimum payment is applied to interest and fees. Prior to this legislation, consumers could make a minimum payment of just 2 percent. A 2 percent payment only covered interest and fees and did not contribute to the reduction of principal. Lower minimum payments increase bank profits, but contribute to greater consumer debt. Although paying the minimum payment keeps the account in good standing, it doesn't reduce the principal much.

Term

For installment loans, length of term also affects the total finance charge. Lenders must disclose the total payments. This figure along with the APR and the finance charge helps consumers evaluate the cost of a loan accurately. The following chart shows loan costs for three possible $6,000 loans.

Repaying the loan over a longer period reduces the monthly payment considerably. It also increases the total payments for this installment loan.

	APR	Length of Loan	Monthly Payment	Total Finance Charge	Total Payments
Creditor A	14%	3 years	$205.07	$1,382.52	$7,382.52
Creditor B	14%	4 years	$163.96	$1,870.08	$7,870.08
Creditor C	15%	4 years	$166.98	$2,015.04	$8,015.04

So which loan is the best deal? The answer depends upon the individual consumer's needs and abilities. The least expensive loan is the shortest one with the highest payments. Perhaps a larger payment won't fit your budget, so paying a little more to use the money longer is a wiser decision than saddling yourself with a payment that is difficult to make. The consumer's credit rating may dictate which interest rate is available. Knowing and understanding the details of the cost of credit is critical for consumers.

Why is it a good idea for consumers to pay more than their minimum balances on open-ended credit accounts?

7.4.2 THE IMPACT OF CREDIT

Could you imagine our society without the availability of credit? Our economic system would collapse almost overnight. Yet too much debt is not good for the economy, either. The more debt consumers take on, the less they can buy. The less they buy, the slower the economy. If the economy slows, jobs may be lost, and the spiral of recession deepens. Healthy economic growth depends upon healthy use of credit.

Overextension

Consumers become overextended when they take on more debt than they can really afford. Some consumers mistakenly believe that if a bank approves them for credit, that must mean they can afford it. They take on two, three, four, five, or more new credit cards, thinking that they will have only a small balance on each without really totaling up the costs. They may be able to make minimum payments, but their overall debt load increases.

The effect of overextension on personal finances can be disastrous. If an emergency arises or a situation changes, such as a job loss, some consumers are suddenly in real trouble. A snowball effect may occur as late charges, penalty interest rates, and other fees apply.

One consequence of overextension is a ruined credit rating. Documentation of most credit problems stays in a consumer's file for at least seven years. During that time, new opportunities such as a great deal on the perfect house, an auto loan at an advantageous rate, or needed orthodontia may be inaccessible. In addition, with disposable income going to service debt, day-to-day life becomes more difficult. If you are barely making minimum payments and energy prices rise dramatically, your entire budget may collapse. Consumers have a responsibility to inform themselves about credit costs and use credit wisely.

Responsible Lending

Predatory lending occurs when lenders create problems for consumers by making credit too easily available without regard to the borrower's ability

iStockphoto.com/sturti

to pay. Fierce competition and the growth of subprime lending rates have led some banks to relax their underwriting standards. Regulations aimed at reducing predatory lending have been revised. These regulations will be discussed in Chapter 8.

In the long run, excessive consumer debt is not in banks' interest. Banks need creditworthy customers, and practices that ruin the credit ratings of people serve no one. Collecting debt is expensive, if not impossible, on loans that are in default. Responsible lenders not only evaluate credit carefully and disclose costs as required by law, but they help consumers make the best choices for their own particular situations. Customer service representatives will take the time to explain terms and answer questions fully. Still, the lending business is increasingly market driven, and consumers must understand and choose carefully the best use of financial resources.

Credit Counseling

Numerous agencies for credit counseling, both profit and nonprofit, exist to help overextended consumers. Most of their plans involve reorganizing debts and sometimes renegotiating terms. Banks and other creditors will often accept such arrangements rather than lose their money altogether. Consumers should look carefully, though, because some credit-counseling companies are simply looking for ways to offer more subprime loans or to make a profit from doing what the informed consumer could do alone. In extreme cases, a consumer may seek protection from creditors by declaring bankruptcy. Because doing so may have long-term consequences, professional legal advice is a worthwhile investment.

checkpoint

Why do some consumers become overextended?

_____

_____

_____

_____

_____

assessment 7.4

Think Critically

1. How can a consumer find the best deals on credit?

2. What factors should consumers consider when choosing a loan?

3. In your opinion, why has there been rapid growth in subprime lending?

4. What danger signals might indicate to a consumer that he or she is becoming overextended?

Make Academic Connections

5. **ART/GRAPHICS**   Design a chart that a person could use to compare loan products. Include spaces for all relevant information and factors.

6. **MATH**   Assume a $3,000 balance, a 16 percent APR, and a 2 percent minimum payment requirement. How much is the minimum payment? How much of the minimum payment will go toward reducing the balance?

7. **RESEARCH**   Investigate credit-counseling agencies on the Internet. Summarize your findings of at least three types.

7.5

Bank Loans and Policy

Learning Objectives

7.5.1 Explain how loans affect a bank's income.

7.5.2 Describe the purpose of a bank's loan policy committee.

Key Terms

- liquidity risk
- credit risk
- market risk

Banking Scene

As a new borrower, Jamar Brown has become interested in bank loans. Jamar has gotten partial approval for his house-painting business loan and complete approval for his truck loan. Larry's parents had agreed to co-sign a loan so Larry could buy a truck to help out with Jamar's business. Jamar now wonders about the risks that banks take in making loans and the guidelines banks follow in determining whether to approve an application. What risks do banks face? Who sets the policy affecting loan decisions?

7.5.1 LOANS, THE "BOTTOM LINE," AND LIQUIDITY • • • •

A bank's main business is lending money, which is the source of its profits. Loans represent the largest portion of a bank's interest-earning assets. A bank earns profits by obtaining funds from savers at a cost to the bank (interest paid) and by lending those funds at a cost to consumers (interest received). To be profitable, a bank must carefully manage the loans it makes to ensure that more interest comes in than goes out and that its loans are repaid in a timely manner. Loan customers range from individuals to families, individually owned and other small businesses to giant international corporations, and small to large governments—even foreign ones. A bank frequently has more requests for loans than it can finance using depositor funds. To be able to make these loans, the bank itself raises additional funds by borrowing. If the bank can charge higher interest rates on the loans it makes than the rates it pays on the loans it obtains, it can still profit from lending in this way.

Loans and Income

Loans have a direct impact on a bank's income, because the interest charged on them is its major income source. Therefore, managing its loan programs is crucial to a bank's "bottom line." Interest rates on loans must be set carefully. The loan policies a bank sets must protect its income. Approving questionable loans could lead to *default*, or failure to repay a loan as called for in the loan contract. Default, in turn, leads to lower income. Policy that is too strict can also result in lower income if it prevents the bank from using its funds to make loans and subsequent interest income. Therefore, a bank's income depends on how well it manages its loans. While attempting to increase income, however, banks can never ignore liquidity.

Loans and Liquidity

For a bank, *liquidity* means having the funds to meet its obligations when required. Its liquidity requirement is tied to both the deposit function and the credit function. Customers expect their bank to meet their legitimate needs for credit and to make funds available to them. Several loan factors affect the lending bank's liquidity.

- **Loan term.** *Term* refers to the length of time until the borrower pays off the loan. Short-term loans produce profit more quickly than long-term loans.

- **Interest rate.** Higher interest rates result in more profit than lower ones.

- **Loan type.** Interest on consumer installment loans is generally paid monthly, but some business loans are paid only once a year.

- **Collateral.** Specific property that secures the loan is called *collateral.* If the borrower defaults, the bank has the right to sell the collateral to liquidate the loan.

Overemphasizing liquidity by keeping large amounts of currency on hand as protection against possible increases in customers' demand for withdrawals reduces a bank's ability to make profits from loans. This would impair its credit function and decrease its profit. In making decisions on loan applications, banks consider the impact that their loan mix—individual versus business, short-term versus long-term, and so on—will have on their liquidity.

Wollertz/Shutterstock.com

Liquidity Risk Liquidity risk refers to the risk that a bank will have to sell its assets at a loss to meet its cash demands. A sluggish market can prevent the sale or limit the funds bank assets can generate. Some assets are highly liquid and have low liquidity risk (stock of a publicly traded company), but others are highly illiquid and have high liquidity risk (a house).

Credit and Market Risk

By its very nature, lending money is risky. A bank is never certain that it will get back the money it has loaned out. A bank faces two types of risk when it puts its funds to profitable use through lending: credit risk and market risk.

Credit Risk A primary risk in bank lending is credit risk, the bank's estimate of the probability that the borrower can and will repay a loan with interest as scheduled. To limit credit risk, banks must carefully screen loan applicants, set and apply loan policies, and monitor outstanding loans.

Market Risk The risk that an investment will decrease in price as market conditions change is called market risk. General changes in economic conditions can increase or decrease an asset's value. An example of market risk is the fluctuation in interest rates and in the stock markets. To avoid market risk, a bank must invest its assets wisely. Liquidity risk and market risk are highly correlated.

Digital Vision/Getty Images

Loan Decisions and Trade-Offs

Making loan decisions is a difficult process that generally requires weighing one factor against another. For example, a short-term loan generally has low risk and represents relatively quick liquidity, but it is likely to have a low interest rate and thus produce a relatively low profit. A long-term loan has a higher interest rate and thus increases profit but involves more risk and liquidity concerns. High interest rates could increase income but could also decrease it if the rate causes borrowers to take their loan needs elsewhere. Knowing how to analyze these and other factors helps determine the profit a bank can make from its loans.

✔checkpoint

How do credit risk and market risk differ?

7.5.2 LOAN POLICY COMMITTEE

All banks must have a *lending policy*, which is a written statement of the guidelines and standards to follow in making credit decisions. A bank's board of directors through membership on its *loan policy committee* sets its lending policy. The loan policy committee is actively involved in the credit function in the following ways:

- Ensures that the bank's outstanding loan portfolio meets the needs of its customers and its community and that it complies with the Community Reinvestment Act

- Sets the maximum amount that an individual loan officer can approve and the combinations of higher authority needed for larger amounts

- Determines the types of loans that the bank will or will not consider

- Periodically reviews or audits the bank's loan portfolio to ensure that proper procedures are being followed and no undue risks are being taken

Rawpixel/Shutterstock.com

- Tightens credit standards when conditions dictate

- Implements policies that set loan collateral, loan maturities, maximum lending to various business types, and standards for down payments according to type of loan

- Authorizes all loans for which the amount exceeds the authority of any combination of loan officers to make

The lending policy is generally reviewed annually or as the need arises. It establishes rules such as minimum credit standards for new loans, the process used to check applicants' credit history, the documents required as part of the application, the interest rate for various loan types and risk types, the bank's loan mix, and the treatment of past-due and delinquent loans. Note that the *loan policy committee* sets the guidelines that the *loan committee* follows in evaluating, approving, or rejecting loan applications. They are usually two separate committees.

The lending policies must be fairly administered and standardized for all applicants in a category. For example, when administering commercial loans, lending policies often dictate that banks first evaluate five factors to help measure the risk of such loans. First, *cash flow* is considered to determine whether the business will generate sufficient cash flow to service the loan. *Liquidity* is as important for a borrower as it is for the bank. *Leverage* denotes the amount of debt the business already has. Policy also considers the *collateral* that secures the loan. Finally, the applicant's *management* of its business is also a factor. Based on the analysis of these five factors, the loan committee would decide to approve or reject the loan application. This procedure would be the standard for processing all commercial loans.

Bank policy must meet the provisions of the Community Reinvestment Act (CRA), the federal law requiring banks to meet the credit needs of the entire communities they serve, including those with low and moderate incomes. A bank's performance in meeting these needs is regularly evaluated by federal agencies, and results are made public. Liquidity enables a bank to meet its CRA obligations.

What is the function of a loan policy committee?

assessment 7.5

Think Critically

1. How do loans affect a bank's income?

2. Why is liquidity risk of considerable importance to a bank's loan policy?

3. How does market risk affect a bank?

4. What role do liquidity, credit, and market risk play when a loan policy committee sets the bank's lending guidelines?

Make Academic Connections

5. **RESEARCH**   Liquidity is a crucial factor for banks. Use the Internet to research liquidity management for a bank, and write a one-page report explaining this process.

6. **COMMUNICATION**   Interview someone in a local bank's loan department. Find out what types of educational loans are available and the bank's policy requirements for them and the typical interest rates involved. Present your findings here.

chapter 7 assessment

Chapter Summary

7.1 Consumer Loan Theory
A. MPT is used to help banks diversify their loan portfolios. Asset transformation enables a bank to generate revenue from deposits.
B. Borrowers who are most willing to accept nonfavorable loan terms are the borrowers that are least attractive as customers. Banks can earn revenues by charging fees that are not reflected on their balance sheets.

7.2 Consumer Loans
A. Installment loans are the most common form of consumer lending. Banks are legally required to explain loan terms.
B. The amount owed on an open-end loan is flexible, as is the term. Open-end loans include credit cards and lines of credit.

7.3 Granting and Analyzing Credit
A. Creditworthiness must be assessed before loans are granted. Application, documentation, and underwriting are steps in this process.
B. CRAs and lenders often use credit-scoring systems such as FICO.

7.4 Cost of Credit
A. The cost of credit varies with annual percentage rate and term, and depends on the method of calculation.
B. Consumers should pay close attention to their credit rating, because poor credit can result in long-term financial problems.

7.5 Bank Loans and Policy
A. Lending allows a bank to make a profit, but it must carefully monitor its policies to avoid liquidity risk, credit risk, and market risk.
B. A bank's loan policy committee sets guidelines used to make loans.

Vocabulary Builder

a. adjusted-balance method
b. adverse selection
c. asset transformation
d. average-daily-balance method
e. captive borrower
f. collateral
g. consumer reporting agency (CRA)
h. credit rationing
i. credit risk
j. FICO score
k. grace period
l. installment loan
m. lien
n. liquidity risk
o. market risk
p. modern portfolio theory (MPT)
q. moral hazard
r. open-end loan
s. predatory lending
t. previous-balance method
u. revolving credit
v. secured loan
w. subprime rate
x. sum-of-digits method
y. underwriting
z. unsecured loan

Choose the term that best fits the definition. Write the letter of the answer in the space provided. Some terms will not be used.

____ 1. Period for which no finance charges accrue if balance is paid in full by due date

____ 2. Occurs when borrowers take greater risks if they think the harm they will incur from those risks will be minimalized

____ 3. Loan with fixed amount of payments, rate of interest, and length of term

____ 4. Loan backed by some item of value in case the borrower defaults

____ 5. Dominant credit-scoring system

____ 6. Loan backed by reputation and creditworthiness of the borrower

____ 7. Company that compiles and sells credit records

____ 8. Item used to secure a loan

____ 9. Reviewing a loan for soundness

____ 10. Loan with flexible principal and term

Review Concepts

11. Give three examples of installment loans.

12. What is a secured loan?

13. When is a consumer considered a captive borrower?

14. What is the difference between the interest rate and the finance charge?

15. Why are credit cards a form of consumer lending?

16. What is a line of credit?

17. List six steps in the credit-granting process.

18. What are the three Cs underwriters evaluate?

19. What is a credit-scoring system?

20. Why are credit investigations sometimes criticized?

21. What five items appear in most credit reports?

22. How does liquidity affect a bank's income?

23. Compare and contrast liquidity, credit, and market risk.

24. Explain the functions of a loan policy committee.

Apply What You Learned

25. Should FICO scores be released to consumers? Why or why not?

26. Why do banks engage in credit rationing?

27. What factors should a person consider before obtaining a loan?

28. Why is it important to pay every bill on time?

29. Why is having many credit card accounts a risky practice?

30. Why do banks offer overdraft protection?

31. Why are banks required to have loan policies?

Make Academic Connections

32. **MATH**   Calculate how much of the minimum payment goes toward reducing the principal on a credit card with a 2 percent minimum payment policy, a $4,000 balance, and an 18 percent APR.

33. **ART/DESIGN**   Prepare a brochure for consumer education that highlights effective ways to choose and use credit. Outline the true costs of credit. Reference government agencies that consumers can contact for more information.

34. **COMMUNICATION**   Interview an executive of a local bank about consumer lending. Ask how portfolio diversification is managed and how regulatory changes and the credit crisis have affected business. Present your findings to the class in an oral report.

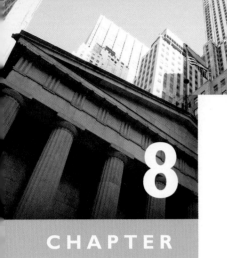

8

Mortgages

Andy Dean Photography/Shutterstock.com

skills that pay dividends

Specific definitions of ethics vary. Most definitions include a sense of what is right or wrong. Cultural and social context affect the definition of what is right or wrong. What one society may deem acceptable may be taboo in another society.

Each individual has a distinct sense of right or wrong. Treating others the way you would like to be treated captures part of the spirit of ethical behavior. This includes kindness that comes even when your knowledge of a topic is superior to someone else's knowledge. By treating people fairly, including helping to educate them about the impact of decisions they are making, you will behave ethically with them. Treating people ethically has the added benefit of fostering long-term relationships. Repeat business is the result of trust and long-term relationships.

Corporations are managed and staffed by individual people working toward the common goal of profitability. Corporations are not societies, but they do have corporate cultures. A corporation can formulate a code of conduct to set the direction and tone for how employees are expected to behave. A code of conduct can delineate how individuals should act relative to each other and how they should perform their duties. It can also address the framework for making decisions and developing solutions in a manner that is consistent with a company's code of conduct.

American society has formalized the collective belief of what is right or wrong by passing laws supporting these beliefs. For example, it is illegal to steal someone else's property.

By providing thorough employee training regarding a company's code of conduct, a company can ensure that all employees understand the code and can apply the concepts implicit in the code into their decision-making. When a code of conduct incorporates the requirements of legal behavior, then employees can behave in a manner that is consistent with legal requirements.

Financial incentives and performance standards need to be constructed in a way that reinforces the code of conduct.

During the mortgage crisis of 2008, each player in the chain knew that the subprime loans were too steep for many homeowners to manage. The loan originators, the underwriters, and the dealers who bought and sold loans in the subprime loan market were motivated by profit. Each participant wanted to obtain a share of this profit even if providing the loan meant that some homeowners would be left with an overwhelming financial burden.

Develop Your Skill

Make a list of five thoughts that would have been on your mind if you were qualifying a customer for a subprime loan. In small groups, share the list with group members. Assign half the group to provide reasons that would relieve your concerns. Have the other half provide reasons that would support your concerns. Reflect together on how easy it can be to justify either side of a situation.

8.1

Mortgage Lending

Learning Objectives

8.1.1 Define a mortgage.

8.1.2 Identify several types of mortgages.

Key Terms

- mortgage origination
- mortgage
- foreclosure
- fixed rate mortgage
- balloon mortgage
- adjustable rate mortgage
- buy-down mortgage
- point
- shared appreciation mortgage (SAM)
- equity

Banking Scene

When Katrina Harris finished college, she found a good job in her career field of web design. After a few years, she paid off her student loans and began to feel more financially secure. She was tired of living in an apartment and began to consider buying her own home. She didn't know anything about mortgages. What kinds of information might she want to research?

8.1.1 WHAT IS A MORTGAGE?

Banks have grown in the nineteenth and twentieth centuries from banks that did business only with other businesses to banks that sought to serve the needs of individuals. Nowhere in the twentieth century has this growth been more evident than in the growth of mortgage lending. Tax breaks, growing equity, rising property value, and a sense of security provide an incentive to undertake long-term debt in the form of a mortgage. The idea of getting a mortgage to buy one's own home is the essence of the American dream, and in good times or bad, owning real estate is one goal that remains constant.

Mortgage lending is a good business for banks, too, although by percentage, it's not as great as it once was. The crush of competition, not only between banks but also from companies who specialize in mortgage lending, has reduced banks' dominance in this field. Mortgage lending is a major source of revenue in banking. Total mortgage lending continues to rise. In 2015, new mortgages secured by real property, called **mortgage origination**, were expected to reach $1.19 trillion, with a forecasted increase of 10% in 2016. While new mortgage originations are expected to rise, the number of refinance originations are expected to decrease. The mortgage business is linked to numerous other segments of the economy, such as construction and durable goods, and often provides a good idea of how the economy is doing as a whole.

The term *mortgage* comes from Old French language and Anglo-Saxon law. It literally means "dead pledge," and it was the most serious obligation one could undertake. At that time, property was conveyed to the creditor, who held it until a debt was repaid and then conveyed it back. If the debt wasn't paid on time, the creditor kept the property. Over time, the idea of the property as security remained, but restrictions eased, and now in almost all cases the borrower has full use and title to the property. Today, a mortgage is a note, usually long-term, secured by real property. Essentially, the mortgage places a lien on the property that is not released until the debt is paid. If the mortgage is not paid, the creditor seeks a court-ordered sale of the property called a foreclosure, and the debt is paid from those funds.

The obligation of a mortgage today is no less serious than it was hundreds of years ago. For most people, the largest and longest debt they will ever incur is a mortgage. It's a serious investment, usually 10 or more times the cost of a new car. Because it usually involves land, a mortgage is tied to the government by deeds and title records. It's also a serious obligation for the lender. Responsible mortgage lending involves a careful review of a borrower's capability and record.

checkpoint

What is a mortgage?

8.1.2 TYPES OF MORTGAGES

There are many names and variations in loan products, and such is the case in the mortgage business as well. Whatever a mortgage is called, though, it essentially falls into one of three general categories: fixed rate mortgages, adjustable rate mortgages, and other forms of financing.

Fixed Rate Mortgages

Fixed rate mortgages, also called *conventional mortgages*, are loans with a fixed interest rate for the life of the loan. Payments on the loan itself (not including insurance and taxes, which may be included in payments) are set for the life of the loan. Terms are set, too. The most common terms are 30- and 15-year terms, but other terms are available.

Consumers are comfortable with fixed rate mortgages because there are few surprises. Once the interest rate is set, it remains the same, and the consumer has a pretty good idea of ongoing housing costs. If interest rates rise, the consumer still pays the original rate, which will look better and better as years pass. If interest rates fall, the consumer might lose money, but he or she has the option to refinance which involves getting a new mortgage at a lower rate. Interest rates are usually highest for fixed rate mortgages.

For banks, a fixed rate mortgage offers a reliable source of income, or more often, a negotiable instrument to resell. There is some risk for the bank, however. If interest rates do rise, the holder of the note is making money on less than a market rate. This risk is the reason why interest rates

"communicate"

Home ownership is often referred to as the American dream. Take an informal poll of as many homeowners as you can to learn about their experiences with home ownership and mortgages.

are usually higher for fixed rate mortgages and why those mortgages are sold and resold, as holders try to maximize revenue.

One type of fixed rate mortgage is called a **balloon mortgage**. In a balloon mortgage, the interest rate and payment stay fixed, but at some specified point, perhaps five years, the entire remaining balance of the loan is due in one single "balloon" payment. Although balloon mortgages allow some people to get mortgages who would not otherwise qualify, they are risky. Few people can pay off a house in five years, so as that balloon payment approaches, they must refinance. If they can't, they are likely to lose their houses and ruin their credit rating.

Adjustable Rate Mortgages

Adjustable rate mortgages (ARMs) are those with rates that change over the course of the loan. Usually the interest rate and payments are fixed for some period of time at the outset but then change according to some index value. Initial rates and payments may be extremely low but are adjusted later to a rate closer to the normal rate, including some addition to make up for an artificially low start. Such *teaser rates* bring in business, but the borrower must make up for it and takes a risk that rates won't rise beyond what is affordable. There are lots of variables with ARMs, so it's extremely important for borrowers to understand their loans thoroughly. The chart on the following page summarizes some of the varying components.

The many possibilities of ARMs offer both opportunity and potential confusion for borrowers. When overall interest rates are low, ARM rates usually don't vary much from conventional rates. In times of rising interest, ARMs may offer a good starting point for those hoping rates will later

ARM Variables

Variable	Definition	Explanation
Interest Rate	The rate the lender charges for the loan, expressed as an annual percentage rate.	Initial rates for ARMs may be close to other rates, or they may be much lower, depending on the lender's product. Eventually, after adjustments over time, they are usually slightly lower than conventional mortgages, dependent on the index. Some ARMs offer a fixed rate for several years at the outset of the loan.
Payment	The amount, usually per month, that a borrower repays the lender. Mortgage payments often include principal, interest, taxes, and insurance.	Payment calculation typically varies with the interest rate, although some lenders may also use a formula that begins with a low payment not related directly to the interest rate. Taxes and insurance, if included, may vary over time in any mortgage.
Index	The measure to which the lender's interest rate is tied. Usually this is a U.S. Treasury security rate plus some figure or percentage.	Each lender may choose any index it wants, and some are better than others for the buyer. Fully understanding the index and its past performance and comparison shopping for ARMs are keys to consumer success.
Formula	The means by which the payment's relationship to index and to principal is calculated.	Each lender may use its own formula, so long as it is clearly specified in documentation. Comparing products side by side and seeing actual payment numbers helps the evaluation process.
Adjustment Interval	The length of time that a given rate and payment are in effect.	Adjustment intervals also vary with each lender's loan product. Some may be as short as three to six months. One year is typical. Whether a long adjustment interval is advantageous to lender or borrower depends upon the formula used and how stable the index has been over time.
Periodic Cap	The maximum amount, usually a percentage, by which an ARM can increase or decrease on an adjustment date.	This feature can protect both lender and borrower from rapid changes in interest rates. For example, a flex limit of one-half percent on any adjustment date keeps change from being too dramatic.
Lifetime Cap	The specified overall maximum or minimum rate of an ARM, regardless of index.	The cap sets a top and bottom interest rate, also called a floor, between which the rate and payment vary. If the floor is 5 percent, and the cap is 12 percent, for example, the rate may not vary outside that range regardless of the index.

fall. If a homeowner plans to be in a house only a few years, an ARM might be an excellent way to get the most house for the least money. A majority of consumers are most comfortable with conventional mortgages. This explains why, historically, they have been the most common type of mortgage.

Other Forms of Financing

Other forms of financing involve various ways that lenders calculate or adjust interest or other values. Most often these vary to suit particular circumstances and offer more flexibility than conventional financing.

Buy-Down   In a buy-down mortgage, the borrower buys down, or prepays, part of the interest in order to get a lower rate. The borrower pays *points* to the lender at the outset, and the lender agrees to lower the rate a specific amount per point. How much the interest drops is agreed to by the lender and the borrower as part of the deal. It's important to understand that a point is *not* an APR percentage point. A point is a value equal to 1 percent of the loan principal. For example, 2 points on a $200,000 home would be 2 percent of $200,000, or $4,000. The principal on the loan remains $200,000, but the interest for the life of the loan would be lowered by some rate agreed to by the lender and the borrower. For its part, the lender usually foregoes some long-term income for the sake of more cash up front. If the lender is planning to sell the note, this may earn the lender more money. The borrower, by paying more up front, may save far more in the long run.

Shared Appreciation Mortgage   Although this form of mortgage is not new, it is having something of a comeback in the competitive lending business. A shared appreciation mortgage (SAM) can lower interest rates for borrowers who agree to share profits with the lender when the house is sold. *Appreciation* is the amount that a house increases in value. With a SAM, the lender receives a part of the appreciation, often 50 percent. Say a borrower buys a house worth $150,000, and when the borrower sells it five years later, it's worth $200,000. The lender would receive a lump-sum payment of $25,000 at payoff in addition to the remaining principal. In housing markets with little appreciation, a SAM can let a borrower get a low-rate loan without costing a lot at payoff. But SAMs also limit profit on the house for the borrower, who must share the appreciation. Sharing housing profits may make it hard for the seller to have a new down payment on another house after paying the lender. In markets that appreciate rapidly, SAMs can be very profitable for banks. SAMs allow borrowers to have a house they might not otherwise be able to afford, as long as they are willing to sacrifice a portion of future profits.

Refinancing   Essentially, refinancing is starting over with an entirely new loan, using part or all of the loan funds to pay off the old mortgage. If interest rates are low, consumers save money by getting new mortgages at lower rates. Banks and other lenders earn money on fees, points, and closing costs of the new loan and add business (usually at the expense of other lenders) at the new rates. Prepayment penalties for the old mortgage may also raise the cost of refinancing, although some states do not allow prepayment penalties on mortgages. Generally, the lower the refinancing rates, the higher the fees and points. Borrowers need to understand and consider all costs carefully.

The process for refinancing is the same as obtaining the original mortgage in most cases, and all steps and underwriting conditions apply. It used to be said that the new interest rate had to be at least two percentage points lower than the old one to make the cost of refinancing pay off, but competition in the business has led to low-cost, zero-point, low-fee offerings from some lenders. Refinancing is also a good time for consumers to consider another type of mortgage if they are unsatisfied or struggling with the one they have.

Home Equity Loans   Home equity loans can be another active area in the lending industry. Equity is the difference between the market value of an item and what is owed on it. Depending on the geographical area and the economy, homes historically appreciated in value 3 to 6 percent or more per year. A home worth $160,000 at purchase might have been worth $185,000 in five years' time.

When home values are appreciating, homeowners can use the difference between what they owe and what their homes are worth to secure a loan. Let's say a borrower purchases a $160,000 house with $20,000 down and after five years has a remaining principal of $135,000. The house appreciates during that time and is now worth $185,000. The homeowner has equity of $50,000. That home equity may be used to secure a loan up to or even beyond the value of the equity.

Home equity loans take one of two forms. One type is a simple loan, a single disbursement of money for the borrowed amount. Another type is a line of credit, sometimes with paper checks or accompanying credit cards. Borrowers have a credit line up to the equity limit. As they pay down the balance, they can add new expenses to the line if they choose.

The mortgage crisis of 2007 and subsequent tightening of credit changed the outlook on home equity loans. As home prices declined, obtaining a home equity loan was more difficult and did not make sense financially for homeowners.

In many respects, a home equity loan is just another consumer loan, but there is a big exception. It's a second mortgage. It is secured by the home. If borrowers are unable to repay the loan, they may lose their homes. In recent years, the easy availability of home equity loans has led some borrowers into trouble. Some irresponsible lenders have also extended credit to people who are not really in a position to repay, a predatory lending practice that can lead to disaster. Responsible lenders underwrite home equity loans carefully, but consumers should be very cautious about borrowing against their largest and most important asset.

Reverse Mortgages   A reverse mortgage is not a mortgage used to purchase a home. It is really another form of consumer loan tied to the appreciated value of a property. In most cases, reverse mortgages are limited to homeowners 62 years or older. With a *reverse mortgage*, a homeowner receives a sum from the lender secured by the value of a home and does not pay the loan back as long as he or she lives there. Typically, a senior homeowner owes less on a mortgage because he or she has been paying on it for many years. Also, the house may well have appreciated considerably since purchase. The lender is repaid, including fees and interest, when the borrower sells or dies. Borrowers may receive their funds in lump sums, a credit line, or a monthly payment direct from the lender, or some combination of the three.

The advantage of a reverse mortgage is that it allows homeowners the opportunity to get cash from the value of their homes without selling and moving. Although loan advances are not typically considered income by the Internal Revenue Service, obtaining a reverse mortgage may affect eligibility in some other government-benefits programs and can affect taxes and estate planning considerably. Equity in the home declines throughout the life of a reverse mortgage, and the homeowner is still responsible for taxes, insurance, and maintenance. As with any loan, there are many variations in features, terms, and lenders, and it's wise to shop for the best terms. This type of loan is usually very expensive in terms of the interest rate. Those considering a reverse mortgage should thoroughly understand all terms of the mortgage, as well as all other aspects of their retirement, financial, and estate planning.

That advice holds true for any type of mortgage from any type of lender. For most people, mortgages represent the largest debt for the largest financial transaction they will ever undertake.

Photodisc/Getty Images

✔ checkpoint

What is the basic difference between conventional and adjustable rate mortgages?

assessment 8.1

Think Critically

1. What incentives make home ownership and the undertaking of long-term debt attractive to consumers?

2. Explain the advantages and disadvantages to the consumer of balloon mortgages.

3. Why might a consumer choose an adjustable rate mortgage over a fixed rate mortgage?

4. What is a *point* and why do some consumers choose to pay points on their mortgages?

Make Academic Connections

5. **HISTORY** Though it may change, land lasts forever. Pick an area, a neighborhood, a small town, a subdivision, or even an individual property and trace the history of its owners. You may need to do some initial research to learn how to conduct a search of county records.

6. **RESEARCH** Refinancing is a big portion of the lending business. Learn more about refinancing using resources such as the Internet, newspapers, and magazines. Write a brief report on your findings.

8.2

Mortgage Loan Processing

Learning Objectives

8.2.1 Describe what is involved in obtaining a mortgage.

8.2.2 Explain the mortgage approval process.

Key Terms

- PITI
- escrow
- loan-to-value (LTV)

Banking Scene

Katrina Harris has done some research on mortgages and now has a better understanding of the loan process. She has been looking at some real estate properties and is now ready to obtain a loan. Where should she begin?

8.2.1 OBTAINING A MORTGAGE

Because of the typical size of the loan, lenders scrutinize mortgage applications closely. The potential risk involved is greater for the bank both in terms of the amount of the loan and the liquidity of the collateral. Banks don't want to own houses.

Lenders typically require a down payment of 5, 10, or 20 percent for a mortgage. (FHA and other government-sponsored loans and programs, which you'll learn about in a later section, may require less.) A larger down payment not only lowers the cost of the monthly payment, it affects how the lender views the borrower. Lenders may make the loan if a down payment is high, even if the borrower's credit rating is not ideal.

In addition, a higher down payment allows a borrower to have more house for the same money. In a healthy lending environment, most lenders don't want a person's housing costs to exceed 25 to 28 percent of gross monthly income. Total debt should not exceed 36 percent, including housing costs. For the same monthly payment, a borrower could get a house worth about $170,000 with a 20 percent down payment, as opposed to one worth $135,000 with 5 percent down. A higher down payment may also avoid a requirement of private mortgage insurance.

PITI

Monthly payments to the lender usually consist of **PITI** or *Principal, Interest, Taxes,* and *Insurance.* These are the housing costs that the lender considers in the loan analysis and are itemized on the monthly mortgage statement.

Principal is the remaining unpaid balance of the mortgage. The figure shown on the statement may not be the payoff amount but merely the remaining principal calculated currently. The payoff figure may differ based on the type and terms of the loan.

Interest is the amount of the monthly payment that goes toward interest. In the early years of a mortgage, this is by far the largest figure. Because interest is usually deductible, the tax advantages of a mortgage make homeownership doubly attractive.

Taxes include local real estate taxes. Most lenders require an amount to be paid to them in advance, called escrow, from which they pay the real estate taxes. Many loans also require an additional amount for an escrow buffer so that the escrow fund never falls below a set level.

Insurance refers to property insurance and sometimes private mortgage insurance. To protect the lender against potential loss, almost all mortgages require the homeowner to maintain adequate property insurance against fire, storms, and other calamities. The lender collects the insurance premium as part of the payment to make sure its security is covered. *Private mortgage insurance* (PMI) protects the lender against loan default. PMI is not typically required for those whose down payment is 20 percent or greater. It can be eliminated once the principal balance reaches 20 percent of the original loan value.

As with all loans, specific terms, methods of calculation, and costs may vary, and it is a good idea for borrowers to have legal counsel about the details of mortgages.

 **checkpoint**

What is private mortgage insurance?

Banking Math *Connection*

Private mortgage insurance (PMI) rates may vary, but a typical PMI rate is ½ of 1 percent of the borrowed principal. The formula for calculating the monthly PMI cost is

$$\text{Rate} \times \text{Principal} \div 12 = \text{PMI}$$

Calculate the monthly PMI cost for a principal balance of $140,000.

Solution

If PMI were required for a principal of $140,000, the calculation would be

$$\text{Rate} \times \text{Principal} \div 12 = \text{PMI}$$
$$0.005 \times \$140,000 \div 12 = \$58.34$$

8.2.2 THE APPROVAL PROCESS

Few things in financial life are as nerve-wracking for many consumers as the mortgage approval process. The many details, close examination of finances, and legal language intimidate many borrowers, producing considerable anxiety. Although the process is detailed, it is getting simpler and certainly faster.

Application, documentation, underwriting based on credit reputation and capacity, and closing are all part of the credit analysis and credit-granting process and are common across loan categories. The process is more detailed for mortgages, largely because the transfer of real property brings into play more legal issues than a simple contract. Here are the basic steps.

- **Application** for a mortgage may be more involved than for other forms of loans, and accuracy and completeness are essential. Unlike many small consumer loans, for which a quick credit check is sufficient, every detail of a mortgage application will be evaluated carefully. Missing, incomplete, or wrong information will delay the process at the very least and may result in denial of the loan.

- **Documentation** for a mortgage loan must also be complete and accurate. Often, it takes some time to assemble full documentation, which usually includes a professional appraisal of the property. Lenders pay attention to the **loan-to-value (LTV)** relationship, which is the value of the loan compared to the value of the asset. Most reputable lenders prefer to lend no more than 95 percent of the appraised value of a house so that their risk is supported. It's not merely a question of what you're willing to pay the seller, but also what the house is really worth that may determine whether you get a mortgage. Other documents include complete credit reports, employment and/or income verification, and verification of existence and source of the down payment. If you borrow the down payment, that debt must be considered as well, and most lenders like to have the down payment deposited for some period of time before the application (60 days is best).

- **Underwriting** is the critical step, as documents arrive and are verified and reviewed. Some lenders have loan processors who verify completeness and accuracy separate from the underwriters, and some combine both

Racorn/Shutterstock.com

functions. As with any loan, *collateral, capacity*, and *credit reputation* determine whether a mortgage is a good investment for the bank. Mortgage underwriters look hard at a borrower's ability to repay as measured by a debt-to-income ratio and the track record of a borrower over a long period of time. Often, underwriters may want more information or a letter of explanation about some circumstance or item in the credit record. Applicants can't hide much from a thorough underwriter, and completeness and fullness on applications is the best approach. Sometimes underwriters may modify the terms of a mortgage one way or another to fit the circumstances. Although mortgage underwriting is becoming automated by software, the underwriting process for mortgages is still the most careful and painstaking part of obtaining a mortgage.

- **Drawing documents** is another carefully considered step in the process. The sale of a home involves many documents between lender and borrower. As you'll recall, many promissory notes are negotiable, and mortgages are often sold for servicing many times. It is essential that all documents be accurate and all terms and requirements met so that the note remains negotiable no matter where it eventually goes. Once the note is signed, the bank prepares the funding.

- **Closing** requires the signing of all documents involving the transfer of the property from one party to another. These documents go beyond the scope of just the mortgage. Closing costs, including fees for application, origination, title search, surveys, appraisal costs, inspections, taxes, attorneys, escrow, and recording are paid, as well as any points and applicable realtor fees. Frequently, a title company, which specializes in researching and transferring property between owners, will handle the closing.

- **Recording** the Mortgage/Deed of Trust at the county recorder's office makes the mortgage public record. Records may be available online, either from a recorder or from another company that compiles such records.

Although the process of obtaining a mortgage is often longer and more involved than obtaining other types of loans, the lending business, like all of the financial industries, is changing. Lenders need to lend money. Prior to the recent mortgage and credit crises, competition among lenders made it easier than ever before for borrowers to apply and be approved. The risk to both lender and borrower is greater for a mortgage than it is for other types of loans. It's best for consumers to understand as much as they can about the process and their own payment capabilities before undertaking a transaction that will have lifelong implications.

What are the basic steps of the mortgage approval process?

assessment 8.2

Think Critically

1. Why is the mortgage loan application process longer and more involved than that for other consumer loans?

2. Why do you think a lender might overlook less-than-perfect credit for a borrower with a large down payment?

3. Why do lenders (or the holders of a mortgage) usually want taxes and insurance included as part of the payment?

4. What types of information do you think are requested on a mortgage loan application?

Make Academic Connections

5. **RESEARCH**   Online mortgage sales are now a big business. Find a mortgage financing website and write a short description of the mortgage loan process used by the financier.

6. **MATH**   Most lenders prefer that a mortgage not exceed 28 percent of your gross monthly income. Assuming that you make $40,000 per year, what is the maximum PITI that the bank would deem acceptable?

Mortgages and the Law

Banking Scene

When Katrina Harris conducted her research on mortgages, she learned about many laws related to mortgage lending. Katrina wondered if any of these laws really applied to her. In what ways do these laws affect Katrina?

Learning Objectives

8.3.1 Describe consumer protection laws that apply to mortgage lending.

8.3.2 Describe laws directly related to mortgage lending.

Key Term

• redlining

8.3.1 CONSUMER PROTECTION LEGISLATION

Numerous laws affect mortgage lending. Parts of consumer protection legislation apply to mortgage lending as well. Most of these laws are designed to protect consumers from unfair practices relating to lending, collecting, or maintaining privacy as described below.

- The Truth in Lending Act (TILA) promotes informed use of consumer credit by requiring disclosures about its terms and costs.

- The Equal Credit Opportunity Act (ECOA) prohibits creditors from discriminating against applicants on the basis of race, color, religion, national origin, sex, marital status, and age.

- The Fair Credit Reporting Act (FCRA) is designed to promote accuracy, fairness, and privacy of information in the files of consumer reporting agencies (credit bureaus).

- The Fair Debt Collection Practices Act (FDCPA) prohibits abusive practices by debt collectors.

- The Gramm-Leach-Bliley Act requires that financial institutions protect the privacy of consumers.

Many of the provisions of these laws apply specifically to the mortgage lending industry. Targeted sections and enforcement specifications for various laws rests within various agencies such as the Federal Trade Commission (FTC), the Federal Deposit Insurance Corporation (FDIC), and the Federal Reserve.

 checkpoint

How do consumer protection laws apply to mortgage lending?

8.3.2 MORTAGE LEGISLATION •

Other laws exist that relate directly to mortgage lending. Complying with this legislation and documenting compliance requires considerable effort and expense on the part of financial institutions. A few of these laws are described below. Most of these laws have been amended numerous times since their passage, and amendments on some of them are pending. Most states also have similar measures, although they may not always be consistent with federal legislation.

Community Reinvestment Act

Congress passed the Community Reinvestment Act (CRA) of 1977 in response to widespread complaints that some banks refused to lend to residents of certain neighborhoods, a practice called redlining. The law requires that banks document their lending decisions and demonstrate an effort to serve their local communities. CRA investments increase home ownership and help stabilize neighborhoods, which is good for the local economy. Periodic government examinations monitor compliance with the law.

Ethics in Action

According to reports throughout the media, Senator Chris Dodd, Chairman of the Senate Banking Committee in 2008, received interest rate reductions on two of his mortgages held by Countrywide. One rate reduction resulted in an annual interest savings of $2,000. The other rate reduction resulted in a $17,000 reduction over the life of the loan. In June 2008, Senator Dodd indicated he had solicited multiple rate quotes from lenders and was unaware of any special treatment.

Think Critically

What extra precautions are required of a politician during financial transactions? What probing questions would be wise to ask to avoid the appearance of favoritism?

Some critics of the law note that the statute is enforced only when banks merge or expand. They point out that the Gramm-Leach-Bliley Act, though imposing new requirements on privacy, weakened the CRA by slowing the cycle of examination for many banks.

Many lenders, however, struggle with the CRA, both in terms of the burden of compliance and their need to follow sound banking practices. It's not always easy to balance the desire to lend liberally in local communities with the need to meet strict (and increasingly inflexible) conditions for making good loans, which are subject to government examination.

Home Mortgage Disclosure Act

The Home Mortgage Disclosure Act (HMDA) of 1974 was a forerunner of the CRA. It requires banks and other financial institutions to record and report data on home lending in order to identify possible discriminatory patterns. As a practical matter, it set into motion the huge recordkeeping responsibilities of compliance regarding home mortgages. In 2013, 7,190 institutions reported data on nearly 14 million home mortgage applications. These data become the basis for statistical analysis and compliance monitoring by various agencies.

Home Ownership and Equity Protection Act

Congress passed the Home Ownership and Equity Protection Act (HOEPA) in 1994 to protect consumers against predatory lending. Provisions of this act also apply to second mortgages and refinancing. If a loan's annual percentage rate (APR) is 10 points higher than a rate on a Treasury Bill for the same length of time (for example, 15 years on a 15-year note), the loan is a high-interest-rate loan, also called a HOEPA loan. Loans with noninterest fees of more than $465 or 8 percent of the loan value are also HOEPA loans. For HOEPA loans, lenders must make disclosures three days before closing, may not pay a contractor directly, may not require balloon payments due in less than five years on most loans, and are limited in the type of prepayment penalties allowed. In some cases, a few lenders deliberately engage in deceptive practices to obtain properties they then resell. HOEPA is intended to discourage such equity stripping and educate those consumers who may not be fully informed.

During July 2008, to address some of the root causes of the mortgage crisis, the Federal Reserve Board announced some new rules under HOEPA. These new rules amend Regulation Z, which is the Truth in Lending Regulation.

These updates govern all mortgage lenders, including lenders not directly supervised by the Federal Reserve. Highlights of these proposed rules include:

- Lenders are prohibited from routinely making loans that exceed a borrower's reasonable ability to pay off the loan. The lender must make sure the borrower can make loan payments based on the highest payment expected in the first seven years of the loan.

- "Stated-income" and/or "stated-asset" loans are prohibited. Lenders are required to verify income and assets prior to making loans.

- Escrow accounts need to be established for real estate taxes and homeowner's insurance for all first-lien mortgage loans. It is the lender's responsibility to establish the account.

- If a payment can change within the first four years, prepayment penalties are prohibited. A prepayment penalty period cannot exceed more than two years for higher-priced loans.

Other revisions include the requirement that good faith estimates of all payments be provided within three days of applying for a loan, that lenders are prohibited from pressuring a real estate appraiser to provide a false estimate of the value of a home, and that *pyramiding* late fees are not allowed. (Late-fee pyramiding occurs when a loan-servicing company continues to charge late fees until all late fees have been paid, even if payments made after the late payments were made in full and on time.)

Advertising requirements have also been revised. Loan features, including rates and monthly payments, must be clearly stated. Seven particularly deceptive practices are prohibited. Lenders are not allowed to state that a payment is "fixed" when the payment can change.

Real Estate Settlement Procedures Act

The Real Estate Settlement Procedures Act (RESPA) was passed by Congress in 1974 in order to combat the engagement of undisclosed kickbacks, inflating the costs of real estate transactions, and the facilitation of bait and switch tactics. The act prohibits kickbacks or reciprocal referrals between lenders and third-party settlement services in the real estate settlement process. It requires lenders to provide a Good Faith Estimate (GFE) to loan applicants within three days of an application in order to disclose all of the fees associated with a real estate loan. The HUD-1 (for purchase transactions) and the HUD-1A (for refinance transactions) is required to be given to the borrower at closing and must disclose all costs associated with the mortgage loan and to whom they are being allotted.

Beginning in January 2010, amendments to the RESPA regulation restricted the amount that fees can increase between the initial Good Faith Estimate given to the borrower at application and the HUD-1 and HUD-1A given to the borrower at closing. Origination charges by the lender cannot increase at all while certain third-party service provider charges (attorney, appraisal, credit reports, etc.) can increase by no more than 10%. If mistakes are made by either the bank or the closing agent, the lender must refund the difference to the borrower after closing.

Should something occur between the distribution of the GFE and the HUD form that changes the cost of the transaction, a changed circumstance may be applied. For instance, a real estate appraiser may charge a higher fee because the property is a two-family dwelling instead of a single-family dwelling. If the lender was not aware of this prior to ordering the appraisal and quoted the single-family appraisal price on the GFE, they can send an updated GFE with the new larger fee. If the lender made a mistake and was aware that it was a two-family property, the lender would have to pay for the difference in the cost of the appraisal report.

In July 2011, the administration and enforcement of Real Estate Settlement Procedures Act (RESPA) was transferred from the Department of Housing and Urban Development (HUD) to the Consumer Financial Protection Bureau (CFPB). A new regulation that combines mortgage disclosures under the Truth and Lending Act and the Real Estate Settlement Procedures Act went into effect in October 2015. This new regulation combines several forms and disclosures into two forms, uses clear language and highlights information to help consumers understand the transactions, and requires the lending institution to provide the closing information at least three days before closing on the loan.

✔checkpoint

What is redlining and what legislation was enacted to address it?

assessment 8.3

Think Critically

1. Why is there a need for consumer protection legislation related specifically to mortgages?

_____

_____

2. What is the purpose of escrow in a mortgage?

_____

_____

3. Why might financial institutions look at mortgage legislation as being burdensome?

_____

_____

_____

4. Which of the laws related to mortgage lending discussed in this section do you believe is most important? What are your reasons?

_____

_____

Make Academic Connections

5. **HISTORY**   Select one of the laws that apply to mortgages and use the Internet to research the history of the law. Present your report to the class.

_____

6. **RESEARCH**   Using the library or Internet, find out what path someone should take if he or she encounters discrimination while trying to obtain a home mortgage loan.

_____

7. **COMMUNICATION**   Talk with a loan officer at your local bank about how mortgage laws affect the officer's job responsibilities. Summarize your discussion below.

_____

_____

Government-Backed Loans

Banking Scene

Katrina Harris learned quickly that she didn't have the resources or the credit history to obtain conventional funding for a home loan. She turned to the government. She had gone to college on government-backed loans, and it occurred to her that there might be similar programs to help new homeowners. What might be a good way for Katrina to start searching for information related to funding sources available from the U.S. government?

Learning Objectives

8.4.1 Explain the concept of government-backed loans.

8.4.2 Identify government-backed programs to encourage home lending.

Key Terms

- Fannie Mae
- Freddie Mac
- Ginnie Mae

8.4.1 WHAT IS A GOVERNMENT-BACKED LOAN?

The government sometimes acts as a partner to the banking industry, as well as to people and businesses. Numerous government programs help banks help people get loans they need.

With these programs, the federal government offers a number of ways to help people obtain financing for worthwhile purposes. In most of these

programs, the banks provide funding and the government absorbs some of the risk. The government backs the loans by promising to repay them should the borrower default. In order to minimize its own risk, the government also examines the borrower's finances and has eligibility requirements for participation. Some states also operate such programs, and consumers can get more information on these and federal programs from prospective lenders. Lenders want to make loans, and they are happy to work with the consumer and government agencies to find financing solutions.

 checkpoint

How do banks and the government work together to provide loans?

8.4.2 Federal Mortgage Programs

The federal government has been administering housing programs since the Great Depression of the 1930s. At that time, many new programs came into being to help people who had lost everything in the crisis. Social Security is probably the most prominent program introduced by President Roosevelt and Congress during that time. Many other programs to help the unemployed, farmers, and others, including those who were struggling with housing, arose as well. The Federal Housing Administration, established in 1934, supported both homebuyers and banks by replenishing funds available for home lending. Today, there are many such programs with varying missions, services, and operations, but the twin benefits of supporting homeowners and backing the banking industry continue.

Federal Housing Administration

The Federal Housing Administration (FHA) is the oldest of the many government agencies working to help homeowners. The banking industry was in trouble during the Great Depression, but it was not the only industry affected. Two million construction workers were out of work, as well as millions of others, and all the businesses they supported with their incomes were faltering. The FHA was an attempt to get the housing industry back on its feet. By guaranteeing loans and providing mortgage insurance, the FHA helped to reverse the tough climate for borrowers. Before the FHA was established, mortgages were typically limited to half of a property's value and had to be repaid in three to five years, typically with a balloon payment. Few people could afford such terms, even fewer in an economic disaster. The FHA made it possible for banks to offer better terms without shouldering all the risk. Helping to pioneer the long-term loans that make homeownership possible, the FHA changed the face of lending.

Today, what was once the FHA is now the Office of Housing, and it is part of the Department of Housing and Urban Development (HUD). It still performs the same services, guaranteeing loans with low down payments—often as little as 3 percent—to help people obtain housing who perhaps could not otherwise afford it. These loans, still called FHA loans, are not direct loans from the program, but they guarantee the lender that the mortgage will be paid. If it isn't, the agency repays the lender. The loans are arranged through lenders and may be fixed or adjustable rate mortgages. The FHA 203(b) loan program for conventional loans is most common, but there are many variations and resources for getting help with the down payment. The mortgage insurance premium is charged up front (usually 2 to 2.25 percent of the loan, with another 0.5 percent per year) and goes to defray the costs of administering the program. Almost anyone can qualify for an FHA loan, subject to some credit and residency restrictions, and there are limits to the size of the loan. The FHA program pioneered the government's entry into the mortgage business and has backed more than 30 million mortgages.

FHASecure

In an effort to help homeowners impacted by the subprime mortgage crisis and resulting ARMs, FHASecure was developed in 2007. Homeowners who are struggling to meet their ARM payments can participate in FHASecure to refinance their homes with a government-insured mortgage. To participate, homeowners must have enough income to make regular mortgage payments on the refinanced loan.

Fannie Mae

The Federal National Mortgage Association (FNMA) was so often referred to by its acronym that the corporation came to be referred to as Fannie Mae, which is now its registered trademark. Fannie Mae also began as a result of the Depression. It was created in 1938 to help lenders find funds to make available for mortgages. If the FHA was a source of help for consumers, Fannie Mae was a source of help for lenders. Fannie Mae is a government-chartered corporation that buys mortgages from the originating institutions and either keeps them or exchanges them for securities that it guarantees.

The effect is that there is a pool of money available to lenders for mortgage loans. In the Depression, this made money available quickly to lenders to expand the available funds, as it still works today.

To participate, lenders must be licensed to originate mortgages, have a net worth of at least $250,000, be bonded and insured, and have written policies for underwriting and loan servicing, among other requirements. Although once a part of the FHA, Fannie Mae is now an independent corporation.

Freddie Mac

The Federal Home Loan Mortgage Corporation, nicknamed Freddie Mac, operates a similar program. Freddie Mac also buys home mortgages from banks and other lending institutions and combines them into large groups, selling interest in the groups to investors. Expanding the market for mortgages as negotiable instruments in this way expands the amount of funds invested in the lending and housing businesses. Created in 1970 as a fully independent corporation, Freddie Mac has financed a significant number of mortgages in the United States since its beginning. Like Fannie Mae, Freddie Mac also lends for multifamily dwellings and rehabilitation projects. Freddie Mac also invites lenders to participate, with eligibility requirements similar to those of Fannie Mae.

Tech Talk

Fannie Mae DU and Freddie Mac LP

As underwriting of mortgage loans becomes increasingly automated, government-chartered agencies that work with private lenders have developed tools for their lending clients. Fannie Mae's Desktop Underwriter (DU) and Freddie Mac's Loan Prospector (LP) are two automated systems that are helping streamline the underwriting communications between agencies and the client lenders.

The desktop programs are based on statistical models of FHA underwriting data to create an automated scoring system specifically designed with FHA criteria in mind. As a result, these customized automated underwriting systems streamline the often cumbersome process of working through the agencies and the FHA. The systems are FHA approved and can return a routine underwriting decision and conditions within an hour. Lenders enter data from their own sites, using a standard Residential Loan Application. Although they are not the only ways to get FHA approval for Fannie Mae and Freddie Mac funds, these two software programs are the wave of an interconnected future in underwriting.

Think Critically
What type of information had to be factored into the DU and LP programs in order for them to be reliable? What are some elements of the underwriting process that make it difficult to automate?

The Combined Impact of Fannie Mae and Freddie Mac

A *government-sponsored enterprise* (GSE) is a business that receives some legal exemptions and privileges from the federal government, which, in effect, lowers its operating costs. Due to a lower cost structure, a GSE can charge lower interest rates. GSEs also have an implicit guarantee of the government as a backer. This implicit guarantee fosters greater confidence within the business community. Both Fannie Mae and Freddie Mac are GSEs.

Fannie Mae and Freddie Mac either own or guarantee about $5 trillion of mortgages in the U.S., about 60% of the total. According to *The Wall Street Journal*, in a nine-month period that concluded at the end of March 2008, Fannie Mae and Freddie Mac lost a combined total of $11 billion.

Although not stated outright, investors have historically relied on an implicit guarantee from the government of loans from these companies. Because together they represent such a large portion of the U.S. mortgage market, steps were taken to stabilize these companies.

Ginnie Mae

A third government initiative, unlike the other two, remains part of the federal government. The Government National Mortgage Association, called Ginnie Mae, is part of the Department of Housing and Urban Development (HUD). Originally an arm of the FHA, it split. It neither buys nor sells mortgages, but it backs securities issued by holders of pools of mortgages. By guaranteeing the worth of the securities, Ginnie Mae attracts investors, and the pool of funds for mortgages remains high. Ginnie Mae encourages funding for FHA, Veterans Administration (VA), and other low-income housing, assuring that there will be funds available for these programs.

Veterans Administration

Loans from the Department of Veterans Affairs (DVA) have helped millions of people serving in the armed forces obtain government-backed loans with low down payments. Veterans may get loans with no down payment, no prepayment penalties, and negotiable interest rates. Similar to the FHA loan program, VA loans allow qualified veterans to buy, build, remodel, or refinance a home. In general, to qualify for a VA loan, a person must meet one of the following criteria.

- Have served 181 days of active duty between 1940 and 1981 or 24 months for those who served after 1981, or discharged with a service-related disability in less time (certain exceptions apply for Gulf War veterans)

- Have served six years in the National Guard or Selected Reserves, completing all weekend and active duty time

- Be an unremarried spouse of a service person killed in action or who died of a service-connected disability

- Be a spouse of a prisoner of war or a service person missing in action

In some cases, the VA may declare other persons eligible, such as Public Health Service officers, merchant seamen with WWII service, members of service academies, and others.

NCSHA

At the state level, many programs also exist that help families buy homes. The National Council of State Housing Agencies (NCSHA) is a national organization of Housing Finance Agencies (HFAs) throughout the states that provide and administer programs for lower-income and other people who seek help at the state level to buy or renovate a home. There is an HFA in every state. There are also 350 affiliated profit and nonprofit agencies that work in this field. These agencies and firms have a variety of programs for affordable housing.

Other Government-Backed Loans

There are many other government-backed loan programs as well. For example, the U.S. Department of Agriculture's (USDA) Rural Housing Service offers both direct loans and grants from the government as well as guaranteed loans. Designed for low- and moderate-income rural residents, the program also offers opportunities for lenders and developers by making doing business in rural areas a safer investment. The Farm Service Agency,

Photodisc/Getty Images

formerly the Farmers Home Administration (FmHA), is an agency of the U.S. Department of Agriculture that provides credit assistance to farmers, both by guaranteeing and sometimes making loans. Borrowers are offered 30- to 40-year loans at fixed interest rates as low as 1 percent.

It's not easy to find every government loan program available. The *Catalog of Federal Domestic Assistance* is available in government depository libraries or online from the General Services Administration. It provides information on agencies and programs with which individuals may be able to work.

✔**checkpoint**

How do the FHA and VA make more loans available?

assessment 8.4

Think Critically

1. How do government-backed loan programs help the economy?

2. What benefits do government-backed loans provide to lenders?

3. Why do you think there are limits to the size of FHA loans?

4. How do Fannie Mae, Freddie Mac, and Ginnie Mae make more mortgage funds available?

Make Academic Connections

5. **HISTORY**   Visit the Fannie Mae foundation website and list some of the information it provides.

6. **COMMUNICATION**   Using the Internet or the library, gather information about FHA, Fannie Mae, and VA loans. List some of the requirements and restrictions that must be adhered to when applying for these loans.

8.5

The Mortgage Crisis

Learning Objectives

8.5.1 Describe why mortgages are a sound investment.

8.5.2 Explain the causes and consequences of the mortgage crisis.

Key Terms

- mortgage-backed securities
- negative equity

Banking Scene

Katrina Harris has enjoyed being a homeowner for a few years. Unfortunately, due to a recent illness, which kept her out of work frequently, she was earning less income. As her bills started to pile up, she thought about refinancing her mortgage to lower her monthly payments. There were many loan products available that could help her out—but they seemed almost too good to be true. What should Katrina consider as she investigates these new loan products?

8.5.1 MORTGAGES AS AN ATTRACTIVE INVESTMENT • • • •

Historically, mortgages represented a secure, steady investment for lenders. Interest rates, or in the case of a variable rate loan, the range of interest rates, are predetermined. The payment schedule, typically spread out in monthly installments over a 15- or 30-year period, is predetermined. Lenders could count on a steady flow of revenue from mortgages.

By carefully prequalifying buyers and making sure they purchased a home within their budget, lenders could be fairly certain that loans would be repaid in a timely fashion. As housing prices typically appreciated, if there was a loan default, the house the lender would take possession of would have a higher value than the defaulted mortgage. Therefore, if the lender needed to sell the house because of a default, they could recoup some, if not all, of their loss due to the appreciated house value.

Many lenders who stayed with the traditional methods of maintaining stringent loan-qualifying standards and matching income to house payments managed to remain in strong financial condition during the mortgage crisis. By taking a long-term view of the mortgages they qualified and by focusing

Photodisc/Getty Images

on the overall health of the loan, they made sound, safe lending decisions. Foregoing higher profits associated with higher-risk loans kept these lenders in good condition.

✔checkpoint

Historically, why have lenders considered mortgages a good investment?

8.5.2 THE MORTGAGE CRISIS

Multiple factors contributed to the mortgage crisis. A number of countries, including China and India, which had traditionally been less developed with fewer financial resources than highly industrialized countries, were becoming more advanced. Other countries, including Saudi Arabia, increased their revenues by selling oil. As the productivity of these countries increased, more national income was generated. The individuals and businesses within these countries wanted to invest their newly found wealth and receive a high return on their investments. In the U.S. there was a shift in how banks financed home mortgages. Traditionally, mortgages had been made with money from local deposits. Over time, mortgage financing transitioned from local deposits to money from the bond markets.

At about the same time, the Federal Reserve announced that to stimulate the economy, the federal funds rate would be maintained at about 1%. U.S. Treasury bonds had traditionally been a safe, steady investment with a satisfactory rate of return. However, they became a less attractive investment with the lower interest rate. Other investments, with return rates that moved relative to this rate, also became less attractive.

The lower interest rates made it easy for consumers to obtain many forms of credit, including mortgage loans. Easy access to mortgage loans drove up the demand for houses. Increased housing demand caused housing prices to escalate.

Mortgage-Backed Securities

Lenders do not always hold on to loans. Sometimes loans are sold to other investors. The originating lender sells the loan with a higher principal than the original loan. The buyer receives the interest income on the loan. As the principal amount is slightly higher than it was on the original loan, the effective interest rate is slightly lower. However, even with a slightly lower interest rate, it is still an attractive investment.

There are businesses that pool these individual loans and sell them as a group to other investors. Any risk associated with a specific loan becomes

interesting *facts*

Ignoring FICO can hurt Fido. During the mortgage crisis, the Humane Society experienced an increase in abandoned pets, which they attribute to people leaving them behind when forced to leave their homes. ▧

Photodisc/Getty Images

part of the collective risk of the pool of loans. These pooled loans are called **mortgage-backed securities**. These securities became an attractive investment for investors from countries that had newly found wealth. Dealers who packaged mortgage-backed securities were trying to generate enough securities to meet the increasing demand.

Prior to the mortgage crisis, investors were eager to buy mortgage-backed securities. These investors believed a predictable, safe income stream would be realized from these securities. The monthly mortgage payments made from the groups of homeowners whose mortgage loans were in the pool generated this steady income. What some investors did not realize, however, was that in an effort to meet the increased demand for mortgage-backed securities, many firms had begun to lower loan qualification standards.

As the firms originating these loans planned on selling them very quickly into the mortgage-backed securities market, they became less concerned with the long-term risks associated with loans made to unqualified buyers. The firms that pooled the mortgages believed that in a pool of mortgages, if some were very stable mortgages and some were sub-prime mortgages, the risk would even out.

Lowering Lending Criteria

Traditionally, collateral, capacity, and credit reputation were all considered before a loan was approved. All information on a loan application was verified. LTV ratios were maintained at a maximum value of 95%.

These qualifying criteria changed as loan qualification standards were loosened. A variety of new loans became available that shared the same goal—allowing more people to qualify for mortgages. Some of these loans allowed 100% financing and did not require PMI. The long-term welfare of the borrower and the long-term risk of default were disregarded.

Interest-only loans allow a homeowner to pay only the interest on their loans for the first 3–10 years. After the initial interest-only period, the loan payments will be recalculated to include principal and interest. This recalculation substantially increases monthly mortgage payments. No home equity is built during the interest-only phase of the mortgage.

Stated Income Verified Assets (SIVA) loans enable a borrower to obtain a loan based on stated income, credit history, and verified assets. Claimed income levels do not need to be verified with a W2, tax return, or pay stub.

Stated Income State Assets (SISA) loans allow a customer to merely claim their income level and asset level. No verification is necessary.

No Income No Asset (NINA) loans do not require a borrower to provide either income or asset information. Loan approval is based on property value, credit history, and down payment. Verification of employment history of the prior two years is required. One hundred percent of a mortgage can be financed with a NINA loan.

NET KNOWLEDGE

The HOPE NOW Alliance is an alliance of mortgage-related industries and service providers that is focused on keeping homeowners in their homes. Access the website and identify the mission of this alliance. Choose one of the current programs the alliance offers and explain how it helps homeowners.

No Income, No Asset, No Employment loans require no verification of employment, assets, or income. These loans are also referred to as No Documentation Mortgage Loans (No Doc).

Rating Mortgage-Backed Securities

The Securities and Exchange Commission (SEC) began regulating underwriting firms in September 2007. In July 2008, the SEC released a report citing a failure to adhere to ethical underwriting standards by a number of prominent ratings firms.

The rise in demand for mortgage-backed securities generated an increase in the number of annual ratings. Firms were often either understaffed or had insufficient time to perform a full risk analysis of the securities. Sometimes analysts needed to issue ratings even though they did not have time to complete their analysis. Analysts were expected to assess the risk of a security without knowing who was issuing or selling the security. In some instances, this process of shielding an analyst from the corporate ownership of securities they were analyzing was violated. When analysts knew that the firm's profits could be impacted by a nonfavorable rating, that impacted the rating assigned to the security.

A number of investments received an AAA bond rating even though they were backed by subprime mortgages. An AAA bond rating is the highest rating a security can receive and means that the repayment of interest and principal is expected to be stable and reliable. Many of the mortgage-backed securities that received AAA bond ratings lost a substantial amount of their value.

Who Owns My Loan?

Distressed homeowners who seek out credit counseling may be able to develop a plan that could enable them to make monthly mortgage payments. Sometimes this plan hinges on renegotiating the interest rate that is in effect on their mortgage. Homeowners who have loans that have been sold multiple times and whose loans are now part of some large pool of mortgage-backed securities often have a difficult time determining who owns their mortgage. If they cannot determine who is holding their mortgage, they cannot negotiate new interest rates.

One World

The International Impact of the Mortgage Crisis

Just as a stone thrown in a pond makes a ripple effect throughout the water, the U.S. mortgage crisis sent shockwaves through financial systems across the globe. In April 2008, the International Monetary Fund (IMF) estimated that the U.S. subprime mortgage crisis could cause global losses of about $1 trillion. The euro zone is the second largest economy in the world. In June 2008, the euro zone experienced an inflation rate of 4 percent. The central bank of the euro zone had targeted inflation to be about 2 percent. By July 2008, European banks with investments in securities backed by U.S. mortgages suffered losses. There was a tightening of European lending and a rise in European interest rates as a result of these losses. Countries that exported products to the U.S. received fewer orders because U.S. consumers had less money available to spend on nonessential items.

Think Critically In this age of global financial interdependence, what steps can individual economies take to shield themselves from financial exposure due to investments in other countries?

Negative Equity

Many homeowners have **negative equity** in their home. This means they owe more on their home than its current value. According to the latest Zillow Negative Equity Report, the national negative equity rate fell to 13.4% in the third quarter of 2015 from 16.9% in the third quarter of 2014. This represents approximately 6.5 million homeowners nationwide. More than 30% of American homeowners with a mortgage remain underwater, a stubbornly high rate that is contributing to inventory shortages and holding back a full market recovery. The "effective" negative equity rate, which includes those homeowners with a mortgage with 20% or less equity in their homes, was 30.2% in the third quarter of 2015. Negative equity is steadily decreasing, but analysts believe it is likely to persist at least through the end of the decade.

 checkpoint

List five loan products that were developed to support loosened loan qualification standards.

assessment 8.5

Think Critically

1. What motivated lenders to shift from funding mortgage loans from locally held deposits to funding mortgages with Wall Street financing?

2. Strong relationships within a community help bankers increase their customer base. How would ongoing, personal relationships with customers impact a bank's decision regarding qualifying customers for appropriate loans?

3. Review the description of a AAA bond rating online. What do you think is an appropriate rating for a subprime mortgage-backed security?

4. Look for SIVA, SISA, NINA, or No Income, No Asset, No Employment loans online. Are they still available? List reasons explaining their current level of availability.

Make Academic Connections

5. **COMMUNICATION** The Humane Society, recognizing that the mortgage crisis is preventing people from keeping their pets, has instituted a grant program to help agencies reach out to pet owners with ideas for keeping their pets. These pets are suffering downstream effects of the mortgage crisis. Working in teams, brainstorm ideas for programs that would allow pet owners who are having financial difficulties to keep their pets. Write a description of the program and share it with the class.

chapter 8 assessment

Chapter Summary

8.1 Mortgage Lending

A. A mortgage is a note secured by real property.

B. Mortgage lenders provide many types of loan products for buying a home.

8.2 Mortgage Loan Processing

A. Monthly mortgage payments to lenders usually consist of principal, interest, taxes, and insurance (PITI).

B. Six steps in the mortgage approval process are application, documentation, underwriting, drawing documents, closing, and recording.

8.3 Mortgages and the Law

A. Consumer protection legislation applies to mortgage lending as well as other loans.

B. Lenders must comply with numerous housing-specific laws.

8.4 Government-Backed Loans

A. The government backs some loans by guaranteeing to repay the lender if the borrower defaults.

B. Mortgage programs like FHA loans, VA loans, and others make loans possible to people who might not otherwise qualify.

8.5 The Mortgage Crisis

A. Historically, mortgages were a sound, safe investment because they provided a reliable, steady income stream.

B. The mortgage crisis was caused by a combination of factors including an increased demand for mortgage-backed securities, lowered lending criteria, and bond ratings issued without performing a risk analysis.

Vocabulary Builder

Choose the term that best fits the definition. Write the letter of the answer in the space provided. Some terms may not be used.

a. adjustable rate mortgage
b. balloon mortgage
c. buy-down mortgage
d. escrow
e. Fannie Mae
f. fixed rate mortgage
g. foreclosure
h. Freddie Mac
i. Ginnie Mae
j. loan-to-value (LTV)
k. mortgage
l. mortgage-backed securities
m. mortgage origination
n. negative equity
o. PITI
p. point
q. redlining
r. shared appreciation mortgage (SAM)

_____ 1. Value of loan compared to value of asset

_____ 2. Prepaying part of the interest to get a lower mortgage rate

_____ 3. When banks refuse to lend in certain neighborhoods

_____ 4. Mortgage with changing interest rate

_____ 5. A note secured by real property

_____ 6. A value equal to 1 percent of loan principal

_____ 7. A mortgage in which the entire remaining balance of the loan is due in one single payment

_____ 8. Principal, interest, taxes, and insurance

_____ 9. Conventional mortgage

_____ 10. When the amount owed on a home is more than the current value of the home

Review Concepts

11. What is a mortgage?

12. What is a foreclosure?

13. List four types of traditional mortgages and five types of mortgages associated with the mortgage crisis.

14. What distinguishes the mortgage loans associated with the mortgage crisis from traditional mortgages?

15. Define equity and negative equity.

16. Why is it significant that Fannie Mae and Freddie Mac are GSEs?

17. What is the LTV ratio and why is it important to lenders?

18. What role did bond ratings play in the mortgage crisis?

19. List three consumer protection laws that apply to mortgage lending.

20. What are the consumer and business implications of the Community Reinvestment Act (CRA)?

21. To comply with RESPA, what must lenders disclose to borrowers?

22. How do government-backed loans differ from conventional loans?

23. According to *Inside Mortgage Finance*, subprime mortgages were 20% of all mortgages in 2005 and 2006. In the last quarter of 2007, subprime mortgages were 14% of all mortgages; by the second quarter of 2007, they were only about 8% of the total. What did the drop in the percent of subprime mortgages mean? If this occurred today, how would the drop impact the economy?

24. Explain how a buy-down mortgage works.

Apply What You Learned

25. Under traditional circumstances, why does obtaining a mortgage initiate the most thorough credit review most consumers will ever undergo?

26. What factors does a lender judge in order to assess consumer capability?

27. How did the HOEPA revisions announced during July 2008 help restore stability to the mortgage loan market?

28. Why does the government have an interest in guaranteeing loans for private purposes?

Make Academic Connections

29. **MATH** Calculate the PMI rate for a principal balance of $125,500. Assume the PMI rate is ½ of 1 percent of the borrowed principal.

30. **TECHNOLOGY** Use the Internet to learn more about the impact of technology on the real estate and mortgage industries. Prepare an oral report on what you learn.

31. **HISTORY** Learn more about past discriminatory practices, such as redlining, that led to various consumer protection laws in the mortgage lending industry. Write a one-page report on the topic.

32. **COMMUNICATION** Interview a mortgage lender in your community. Find out what lenders like to see from an applicant, and make a top-ten list of things homebuyers can do to increase their chances of getting mortgages for their dream homes.

Commercial Lending

climbing the ladder

From Commercial Banking Associate to Portfolio Manager

After Hillary sent her youngest child to college, she began to consider how much longer she needed to work and what positions she would like to have before she retired.

Hillary reflected on her past experience. To establish a college fund, Hillary had spent a few years after high school working as a commercial business banking associate. Providing administrative support to commercial lenders, Hillary helped prepare credit memos so loan authorities could make decisions on requests for new credit and renewals. She worked with the bank's small business administration department to prepare loans for closing. She made sure that post-closing requirements were met. If a loan request was denied or modified, Hillary helped prepare a denial letter that complied with government regulations.

The experience Hillary gained in commercial lending helped her obtain summer internships during college as an assistant commercial loan underwriter for the financial services subsidiary of an auto manufacturer. With supervisory oversight, Hillary performed credit analyses for dealer financing products. She evaluated loan requests that included floorplan lines of credit, revolving credit lines, and wholesale lease lines of credit. She helped review existing wholesale relationships to determine if any risk factors had changed.

Hillary's first full-time job after college utilized her prior commercial lending experience. Working as a commercial lending officer, Hillary developed and maintained profitable account relationships. She also managed a small commercial loan portfolio.

Hillary's skill at managing the small commercial loan portfolio led to her current position as a commercial portfolio manager. Working with large loan customers, Hillary formulates credit strategies to enhance business service. Focusing on industry constraints, credit exposure, and the specific needs of each borrower enables Hillary to develop customized loan products. Hillary works with customers to develop performance metrics for their businesses. She helps customers measure actual performance to planned performance. Hillary makes on-site visits to customer locations to assess the ongoing health of the business. Her close working relationship with individual customers helps her proactively identify and manage any potential changes to credit risk. She has developed a strong reputation within the community, which helps her bring new clients to the bank.

Upper Rungs to Consider

Hillary has decided she likes her current job. She excels at it. She is comfortable staying in the job until she retires. However, to help the bank remain competitive in future years, Hillary is going to seek out mentoring and training opportunities to help develop the skills of the next generation of employees.

Preparing for the Climb

To successfully manage commercial loans, it is critically important to have a thorough understanding of the industries in the geographical areas in which you approve loans. What is the best way to develop specialized knowledge for a particular industry or business?

9.1

Commercial Loans

Learning Objectives

9.1.1 List purposes for commercial loans.

9.1.2 Identify types of commercial loans.

9.1.3 Identify types of businesses.

Key Terms

- commercial lending
- term loan
- short-term loan
- factoring
- merchandiser
- manufacturer

Banking Scene

Gloria Velez successfully obtained a house mortgage and was happy with the way that transaction went. Her job sometimes frustrated her, and she began to toy with the idea of starting her own business. To do this, she realized she would need to obtain a loan. Before going very far with the idea, she knew she would have to write some sort of a business plan. What are the components of a good business plan?

9.1.1 THE NATURE OF COMMERCIAL LENDING • • • • • • • •

Just as consumer loans allow you to have things you could not otherwise readily afford, commercial lending makes it possible for businesses to accomplish what they might otherwise never achieve. **Commercial lending**, as its name makes clear, is lending to business enterprises. Commercial lending is for businesses. However, commercial lending practices may apply to individuals as well, such as a person who is buying rental property. Although perhaps less visible to the everyday citizen, commercial lending is actually a larger dollar market than consumer and mortgage lending.

Banks and other financial institutions are keenly interested in the commercial lending market and usually maintain specialists dedicated to working on the commercial lending transactions. Large banks dominate this field, although some small banks establish niches in their own communities. Although the underlying principles of sound lending apply to commercial as well as consumer lending, some of the products and analyses differ in their complexity. The best commercial loan officers understand thoroughly the business their customers are in and look for effective and efficient ways to structure financing. Business needs may be variable as well as complex, and creative financial solutions can make the difference between success and failure.

A private citizen can probably live without debt, however, very few businesses can. One key to success in commercial enterprises is growth, and the careful acquisition and use of debt makes growth possible. Commercial loans are advantageous for lenders, businesses, and the people they serve.

Commercial Loan Purposes

Commercial lending markets and customers may vary widely in size and scope. Whether it's a small one-person printing franchise in your neighborhood or a multinational hotel empire, businesses face many of the same challenges in terms of remaining adequately capitalized. Some of the purposes for commercial lending include the following.

- **Real Estate.** Commercial real estate requirements differ from private residential mortgages, although many of the analyses are similar. Because facilities often need to be developed or redeveloped, and there may be local government issues involved, acquiring commercial real estate is a large and complex process. Even for investing in residential real estate, the lending analysis is not quite so simple as for buying a home and requires a close look at the property as a business asset.

- **Construction.** Closely linked, and often part of the same financing package as real estate loans, construction loans are a significant part of the commercial lending business. The size of construction loans often makes them subject to careful analysis of the value, purpose, and even design of the construction, as well as the overall financial position of the borrowing business. In order to assess whether the construction supports the loan value, underwriters must judge the worth of the building within its business function and its potential market value beyond the business.

- **Equipment.** Most businesses need equipment to operate, and equipment is often the greatest start-up cost of new businesses. Because the value of equipment over time changes, equipment loans are often tied to the overall cash flow, business plan, and financial position of the borrower as well as to the equipment itself. This change in value, called *depreciation*, requires that the loan officer understand fully the function, use, and effective lifetime of the equipment for the business.

- **Operations.** Cash flow is an unending concern of business. Whether funding is needed to purchase inventory or supplies, meet unexpected expenses, or even hold the company over through a difficult time, operations expenses are often part of a commercial lending package. Here, perhaps, is where a loan officer may need the most in-depth understanding of a business to assess the risk adequately. Operations expenses are sometimes seasonal or cyclical, as in agriculture and textile industries, and ongoing patterns of lending and repayment are part of the day-to-day life of these businesses. Many financial institutions involve themselves deeply with client businesses on a daily basis, managing cash flow, lines of credit, debt servicing, and operations costs as part of a total business relationship with the customer.

✔checkpoint

Name four purposes for commercial loans.

9.1.2 TYPES OF COMMERCIAL LOANS

There is a wide range of commercial loan products available, and they offer considerable flexibility. Like consumer loans, commercial loans are secured or unsecured, depending on the type of loan, and vary widely in terms and rates. Businesses, like individuals, have credit ratings, too, and the type and availability of funds depends on their track record and income prospects.

Term Loans

Most **term loans** finance permanent working capital, equipment, real estate, business expansion, or acquisition of another business. Terms and rates vary with the asset securing the loan or the expected life of the asset. Many varieties of commercial loans are available, such as fixed rate, adjustable rate, and balloon loans. Adjustable rate loans operate just as they do in the consumer sector, with rates tied to indexes as outlined in the loan contract, usually including caps and floors. Balloon loans, although somewhat risky for the individual, are more common in commercial lending because they often offer more advantageous rates. As the loan matures, the borrower may sell the property to meet the balloon or may refinance the note. Still, careful analysis is necessary, because business conditions at maturity may be hard to estimate and refinancing can become difficult or expensive.

Short-Term Loans

Most **short-term loans** are for a year or less, and a business may have many of them in sequence or even concurrently to finance expenses. Most short-term loans are used for seasonal or cyclical business costs, such as increasing inventory or maintaining the business until predictable receivables arrive. Short-term financing is a regular part of business, and both small and large short-term loans are common. Depending on the credit rating of the business, short-term loans are frequently unsecured. This may lead to trouble for lenders and borrowers if business goes poorly. Monitoring business conditions and performance is an important part of the loan analyst's job. Most short-term loans require a lump-sum payment at maturity. However, businesses often refinance short-term debt as well, rolling debt servicing into part of their ongoing operations costs.

Tech Talk

Online Help for Entrepreneurs

Owning a business appeals to many people. If you dream of one day owning your own business, you can turn to the Internet for help. The Internet offers vast amounts of information on business opportunities. There are websites that provide guidance for starting a business. Some help you write a business plan and marketing plan and help you track your goals. Many sites can provide information on getting a business loan and help you evaluate your net worth before applying for a loan. Other websites offer businesses for sale across the country. Several websites offer tips, strategies, and techniques to help an entrepreneur find and buy the right business at the right price.

Business owners also may obtain loans online. You can review current interest rates and use the calculator provided on the website to estimate your payments. You can obtain quotes from hundreds of commercial lenders that are more than willing to compete for your business. You can get prequalified, apply for a loan, and get an answer within days. With the help of the Internet, you may be closer than you think to being your own boss!

Think Critically   Would you consider applying for a business loan online? Explain your answer. What are the advantages and disadvantages of using the Internet to obtain a loan?

Lines of Credit

Lines of credit for businesses work just as they do for individuals. The lender provides cash in the form of regular amounts, single disbursements, or a credit account to a business to cover routinely occurring expenses. Credit lines often finance contract work (which may not be paid until complete), inventory, or receivable intervals. They may also be used for day-to-day expenses, depending upon the lender's relationship with the borrower. Essentially, a line of credit is an open-ended loan, and though it has no specific term, its rates and conditions vary with the particular lending agreement.

Real Estate and Equipment Loans

Particular commercial mortgage loans for real estate and equipment are tied to and secured by the asset being purchased. These loans may also vary in terms and rates, but, depending on the equipment or real estate, they are typically long-term notes with 10- to 20-year repayment periods. Usually, the loan-to-value relationship (LTV) is limited to around 75% for real estate and anywhere from 60–80% percent for equipment. Second and third mortgages are also available for commercial real estate in amounts dependent on the first mortgage principal and the property value. However, second and third mortgages affect the overall debt structure of the business.

Contract Financing

Contract financing is secured by the value of a specific contract and allows for an orderly flow of funds to a company or organization performing services under contract. Funds are advanced as the work is performed, and contract payments often go directly to the lender until the obligation is satisfied.

Bridge Loans

Bridge loans are a particular form of short-term loan used to cover expenses until long-term financing is in place. Bridge loans are especially important in start-up enterprises or in complex transactions where many separate purchases, developments, or sales depend upon each other. Timing may be difficult to coordinate in such deals, and bridge loans offer a way to keep the business rolling.

Leasing

Many lenders finance leases for businesses, usually with lease terms of three to five years. The advantage of leasing is that it can allow businesses to possess needed equipment for less total cost than they would be obligated for if they bought the equipment. Lenders review the business and the equipment just as they would any other type of loan. At the end of the lease period, the business might return the equipment, buy the equipment, or renew the lease.

Asset-Based Loans

Another type of financing is called *asset-based lending*. Banks analyze profit and loss (P&L) statements, tax returns, and business plans to make lending decisions based on business income. Lenders of asset-based loans secure the loans with the overall assets of the business, including equipment, inventory, and accounts receivable, rather than just business income or a specific piece of equipment. A form of asset-based lending called factoring advances cash to a business in exchange for its receivables. The amount advanced is usually some percentage of the accounts. The factor then collects the invoices, forwarding the money to the borrower less fees and interest kept by the factor. Most businesses seeking asset-based lending are those that do not easily qualify for other types of loans, such as new businesses without a track record or businesses with high potential that has not yet been realized.

✔ checkpoint

Name five types of financing available to businesses.

9.1.3 TYPES OF BUSINESSES

Businesses can be categorized in a number of ways. Business ownership can be classified as sole proprietorship (one person as the owner), partnerships (two or more persons), or corporations (entities that have the legal authority to their own rights, privileges, and liabilities distinct from those of their members). Another way is to categorize businesses as to whether they are merchandisers (they sell goods or services) or manufacturers (they build items to sell to merchandisers). Merchandisers and manufacturers have similar yet somewhat specialized needs for commercial loans.

Merchandisers

You do business with merchandisers on a daily basis. Think of the local independent shops that sell you groceries, repair your appliances, prepare your income taxes, and sell you ice cream, as well as the services you receive from the plumber, the dentist, the veterinarian, and the hairdresser or barber. These businesses must generate income to support themselves. Income can vary from month to month for some businesses. Consider a small local nursery. Its business is typically seasonal: in the spring and summer, its busiest seasons, it sells trees, shrubs, flowers, lawn equipment, fertilizer, and so on. In the early fall, sales include end-of-season flow-

ers and trees, and perhaps pumpkins, Indian corn, and cornstalks. In the winter, its sales are limited primarily to Christmas trees, greenery, and other seasonal items. Can its income from the spring and summer support the business from fall to spring? Even if the nursery were to close during the winter, it will still have most, if not all, of the following obligations:

- Mortgage or rent payments

- Utilities

- Insurance—property (and health for owners and/or employees if offered)

- Auto loan payments

- Payments for inventory purchased earlier

- Salaries or incentives to keep employees during the downtime

- Income and sales taxes and any employee-related taxes

In addition to these expenses, the company must order inventory for the new spring season.

Managing cash flow is one of the most difficult aspects of running a business, and loans may need to be acquired to help with cash flow.

LuckyBusiness/iStockphoto.com

The time to obtain the best terms for any loan or credit arrangement is to anticipate needs rather than waiting until a crisis arises before seeking out money. In addition to offering loans, bankers have expertise to help business owners plan to meet all of their financial needs and have cash when they need it.

A specific problem for some businesses is extremely costly inventory. The auto industry, for example, maintains expensive inventory. Even a small auto dealer may need 10 versions of a new model (with different features and colors), each of which has a dealer cost of $18,000, or $180,000. Add to this the various other models it must keep on hand to be competitive, with all their versions, and the costs can quickly skyrocket. Banks offer *floorplan loans* to meet the inventory financing needs of such small and mid-sized businesses. These plans include competitive features such as flexible credit limits to accommodate seasonal needs and market fluctuations as well as model-year buildups, plus Internet access to their inventory.

Manufacturers

Although their focus is making or building items for others to sell, manufacturers, whether large or small, have the same basic needs that merchandisers have. They cannot meet orders to make their products unless they have the cash or other arrangements to purchase raw materials that compose their products, support research and development, maintain buildings and equipment, and pay employees.

Manufacturers are affected by industry conditions. For example, in the volatile market for crude oil, the cost of one barrel of oil reached $140 in 2008. Today, the cost of one barrel is about $30. As oil is used both as a raw material in manufactured products and as an energy source to manufacture products, the volatility in its cost affects manufacturing costs across industries. Increased manufacturing costs can drive up demand for working capital loans. Decreased manufacturing costs can lessen demand for loans.

Many banks have loan officers who are extremely knowledgeable about various industries and can help these companies plan their financial needs. These bankers can, for example, suggest ways to make arrangements with suppliers for ordering and managing inventory items.

✔checkpoint

What is the difference between merchandisers and manufacturers?

assessment 9.1

Think Critically

1. Identify three major differences between consumer lending and commercial lending.

_____

_____

_____

2. Why is it essential that loan analysts understand the nature of a business, not just the balance sheets, to determine the soundness of a loan?

_____

_____

_____

3. How is it possible that a bank might make poor loans to a long-time commercial customer?

_____

_____

_____

Make Academic Connections

4. **COMMUNICATION** Interview a realtor to determine the differences between selling commercial real estate and residential real estate. Uncover differences in the lending analysis process for both types of real estate.

5. **SOCIAL STUDIES** Small and new businesses are a vital part of our economy. These businesses could not survive, however, without financial backing. How do you think commercial loans help the economy?

_____

_____

_____

6. **COMMUNICATION** Interview a commercial loan officer. Ask the loan officer to explain the job to you, including required education, experience, and training. Present a brief oral report to the class.

7. **RESEARCH** Identify a merchandising company or a manufacturing company with which you are familiar. Research and describe the type of inventory this company is likely to stock.

9.2 Commercial Credit Analysis

Learning Objectives

9.2.1 Identify basic ratios used in commercial underwriting.

9.2.2 List other items used to evaluate commercial loans.

9.2.3 Explain the importance of disclosure in commercial loans.

9.2.4 Explain the mortgage crisis ripple effect.

Key Terms

- debt ratio
- loan-to-value (LTV) ratio
- debt service coverage ratio (DSCR)

Banking Scene

To prepare for starting her own business, Gloria Velez has developed a business plan. She intends to share this plan with the lender when applying for a loan to finance her new business. Besides the business plan, what other things do you think Gloria will need to provide the lender to help her obtain a loan?

9.2.1 COMMERCIAL CREDIT ANALYSIS TOOLS

Commercial credit analysis is not in principle a great deal different from the process used for consumer loans. The same general steps and ideas apply, but with some modifications. Assessing an individual's employment, income, and current amount of debt is necessary to determine an individual's ability to repay a loan. Analyzing a business can be far more complicated. Past financial statements are studied. Underwriters estimate the likelihood of the business' future success. The relationship between the bank and the company is also significant.

In the case of large corporations, evaluating those prospects can be an extremely complex process. Lenders hire or employ professional financial analysts to carefully study as much as can be determined about a company's financial position. Whether a company is large or small, the financial analysis for a particular loan often comes down to the results of three measurements. Though making the measurements may be complicated, the results determine whether the loan makes sense.

Debt Ratio

Debt ratio for businesses is not much different from the debt ratio of consumers. Debt ratio is the total obligations compared to the total income.

The formula for calculating debt ratio is simple. Debt ratio equals the debt obligation divided by income for some period of time.

Debt ratio = Debt ÷ Income

For example, in a given month, if your income is $3,000 and your monthly debt is $1,500, you have a debt ratio of $1,500 ÷ $3,000 = 0.5, or 50%. If you have a debt ratio of 200%, in which your debt is twice your income, you have a problem. Lenders usually will not consider a candidate with a debt ratio above 40%.

Assessing the debt ratio may be a major task in the case of a corporation, for merely compiling all the numbers can be a large job. Most of the processing of a commercial loan application is an attempt to verify the numbers that the prospective borrower provides.

Loan-to-Value Ratio

Another critical ratio is loan-to-value. The loan-to-value (LTV) ratio is the principal amount of the loan divided by the value of the securing property, just as it is in residential mortgages.

Loan-to-value ratio = Principal ÷ Market value

Lenders for commercial mortgages tend to be more conservative than for residential ones. Lenders look for a loan-to-value ratio of 80% maximum and often will not lend more than 60% of the appraised value.

The principle of loan-to-value gets complicated when you consider other types of business property such as equipment. Unlike real estate, which usually appreciates, or becomes more valuable, most business property depreciates, or loses value. Although depreciation offers tax breaks, it complicates securing a loan. Information technology equipment, for example, which becomes obsolete quickly, depreciates so rapidly that it's virtually worthless in a few years. How much can you get for a used computer? Lenders analyze those types of loans by carefully considering the overall health of company finances.

Debt Service Coverage Ratio

A more sophisticated tool for assessing a company's overall debt structure is the debt service coverage ratio. Used extensively for commercial real estate, it also provides a look at a company's overall position. The debt service coverage ratio (DSCR) compares net operating income to the total cost of debt. Net operating income is gross income minus expenses, taxes, insurance, utilities, and so on. Note that net operating income does not include the cost of debt for mortgages or other debts for equipment, services, and other such things. Compiling these numbers may not be a simple task because there may be many items from many sources to be considered and verified. When net operating income is divided by the total cost of debt, it yields the debt service coverage ratio.

Debt service coverage ratio = Net operating income ÷ Total cost of debt

Consider a small business with a $650,000 net operating income on a gross income of $1 million. Assume that the total cost of servicing the debt of the business, including all principal and interest but not counting taxes or insurance, which were taken out already to derive net operating income, is $520,000. Dividing $650,000 by $520,000 yields a DSCR of 1.25.

A lender wants to see the highest DSCR possible, for the higher the DSCR, the more net operating income is available for debt service. The higher the total debt service cost rises, the lower the DSCR falls. A ratio of less than 1.0 indicates a negative cash flow. Different lenders may require different levels of DSCR. Conservative lenders might seek 1.25 or higher, while other lenders would accept 1.20 or 1.10. Only rarely will a lender accept a DSCR near or below 1.0, and then only when there are strong mitigating reasons, such as other sources of potential income or a clear indication of a future upsurge of net operating income.

 checkpoint

List three analytical tools used to evaluate commercial lending.

9.2.2 OTHER EVALUATION

In order to perform ratio and other analyses of a company's finances, lenders want full access to company financial records. Remember that verification of capability is far more complex and difficult in the case of a business than in the case of an individual. In addition, changing business conditions may alter a company's profitability rapidly. Only by understanding the true nature of a company's financial position can a lender hope to make a sound decision. Typically, lenders want to examine the following:

- Federal and state income tax returns for three years
- Company financial statements for three years (all assets and liabilities and pro-forma profit and loss statements)
- Year-to-date profit and loss and balance statements
- Projected cash flow estimates for at least the coming year
- Valuations and appraisals for collateral used to secure the loan
- Written business plan (for small businesses)
- Personal financial statements of owners (for new or small businesses)

Only by knowing the complete picture can a lender make an informed decision about a loan. As in all of the lending industry, competition has sometimes led lenders to less strict underwriting, which can lead to defaulted loans. Bank examiners review commercial lending policies just as they do consumer loans, and in times when larger numbers of bad loans are being made, examiners conduct more stringent examinations.

checkpoint

Why does a lender need access to a company's financial records?

9.2.3 DISCLOSURES

Unlike consumer lending, most commercial lending is regulated only by the terms of the loan agreement and some state laws. The assumption is that both parties to the loan are business professionals and can comprehend and negotiate the loan agreement with terms to which all parties agree. Still, it is in the interest of the business relationship to make sure that all terms are explained and understood, as both parties seek to benefit from the loan.

Although it is fraud to falsify records for the purposes of acquiring a loan, desperate businesses hoping to refinance large amounts or forestall collapse sometimes provide inaccurate or incomplete information. Sometimes close relationships between lenders and businesses themselves lead to poorly underwritten loans. A financial collapse can doom not only the company that

Banking Math *Connection*

Banks typically use the debt ratio, the loan-to-value ratio, and the debt service coverage ratio to determine if a commercial loan is viable.
Use the following data to calculate each ratio, rounded to the nearest hundredth.

Monthly income	$4,500
Monthly debt	$1,250
Loan principal	$30,000
Market value	$45,000
Gross income	$160,000
Net operating income	$100,000
Total cost of debt	$85,000

Solution

Debt	÷ Income	= Debt ratio
$1,250	÷ $4,500	= 0.28 or 28%

Principal	÷ Market value	= Loan-to-value ratio
$30,000	÷ $45,000	= 0.67 or 67%

Net operating income	÷ Total cost of debt	= Debt service coverage ratio
$100,000	÷ $85,000	= 1.18

undertook the loan, and sometimes the lender, but also the personal finances and even the pensions of employees who had no part in the fraud. It is the ethical and professional responsibility of all parties involved with commercial lending to see that loans are honestly and soundly underwritten.

✔checkpoint

Why isn't commercial lending as heavily regulated as consumer lending?

9.2.4 THE MORTGAGE CRISIS RIPPLE EFFECT

The Office of the Comptroller of the Currency (OCC) conducts an annual survey of national banks to determine trends in lending standards and credit risks as reflected in underwriting practices. The survey that was released in June 2008 reflected trends for about 83% of total loans in national banks. These loans had a combined value of $3.7 trillion.

Tightened Underwriting Standards

In response to the economic uncertainty caused by either nonperforming or under-performing mortgage loans, banks tightened their underwriting standards for both commercial and retail loans. The poorly performing

Ethics in Action

You work as the accountant for a large manufacturing company. The company has fallen on hard times recently due to increased competition throughout the industry. The company is seeking a loan to buy new, state-of-the-art equipment to improve its operations, in turn making it more competitive in the market. After reviewing the company's finances, the president of the company is concerned that it cannot obtain a loan in its current financial state. She asks you to "rework" the financial statements and inflate earnings by reducing some of the recent debt taken on by the company. She thinks this will help secure the loan. The president feels that no harm is done because the company will increase profits in the long run with the new business it will acquire after the acquisition of the new equipment.

Think Critically

Do you agree or disagree with the president? Explain why. If the loan is obtained and financial disaster ensues, whom will this ultimately affect?

mortgage loans affected not just the mortgage loan portfolios directly, but also the investment products that were backed by the mortgage loans.

Reasons banks cited in the OCC study for tightening underwriting standards included a shift in appetite for risk, less market liquidity, the slowing in the residential real estate market, and the overall state of the economy. Specific ways that underwriting standards were tightened include increasing the credit spread for heightened credit risk, increasing the number of conditions written into the loans, lowering LTV ratios, and increasing collateral requirements.

NET KNOWLEDGE

The OCC's annual report on bank lending trends provides a wealth of current information. Go to the OCC website. Briefly review the 2008 report and then search for the most current one that is available. How have lending trends changed? What do you think the reasons are for the changes?

The Federal Reserve conducts a quarterly survey of bank lending practices by soliciting input from senior loan officers. The results of this survey are consistent with the OCC findings. The chart below shows the trend in lending standards from 1996 to 2016.

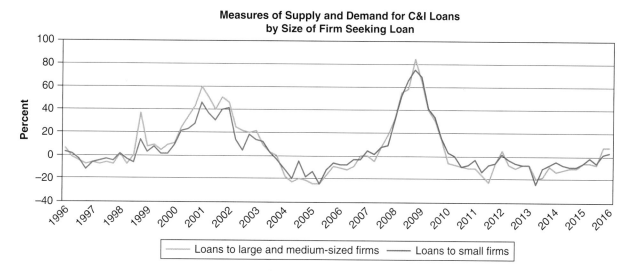

Measures of Supply and Demand for C&I Loans by Size of Firm Seeking Loan

Loans to large and medium-sized firms — Loans to small firms

Net Percentage of Domestic Respondents Tightening Standards for C&I Loans

SOURCE: JANUARY 2016 SENIOR LOAN OFFICER OPINION SURVEY ON BANK LENDING PRACTICES BY THE FEDERAL RESERVE BOARD.

✔ checkpoint

What causes banks to increase underwriting standards for commercial loans?

assessment 9.2

Think Critically

1. Why is the credit analysis process so much more detailed for commercial loans versus consumer loans?

_____

_____

2. What does a company's debt ratio reveal to the lender?

_____

_____

_____

3. What things can a lender learn from reviewing a company's financial statements?

_____

_____

_____

Make Academic Connections

4. **MATH**   Assume that a small business owner has come to you with a loan request. Your careful analysis of the records shows a net operating income of $875,000 and total debt of $798,000, including the new loan. According to the debt service coverage ratio, is this a good candidate for a loan? Why or why not?

_____

_____

_____

5. **RESEARCH**   Locate the website of a commercial lender. Gather some background information on the lender and list some of its services and the various types of loans it offers.

6. **CRITICAL THINKING**   Assume you just obtained a loan to finance new equipment for your business. You later discover that the lender did not disclose all terms of the loan and that your interest rate will not remain fixed throughout the life of the loan as you had discussed. What recourse can you take?

_____

_____

Small Business Loan Programs

9.3

Banking Scene

Gloria Velez learned quickly that she didn't have the resources or the track record to obtain conventional funding for a business loan. She kept her job, but began to work hard on her own time to learn more about running her own business. She turned to the government. She had gone to college on government-backed loans, and it occurred to her that there might be similar programs to help new businesses. What might be a good way for Gloria to start searching the vast amount of information about starting a business available from the U.S. government?

Learning Objectives

9.3.1 Describe the purpose of the SBA.

9.3.2 Explain SBA loan eligibility requirements.

9.3.3 Identify SBA loan options.

Key Term

- Small Business Administration (SBA)

9.3.1 THE SMALL BUSINESS ADMINISTRATION

The Small Business Administration (SBA) offers a number of financial, technical, and management programs to help businesses. The SBA grew out of a Depression-era agency, the Reconstruction Finance Corporation (RFC), a lending program for businesses of any size hurt by the Depression. The Department of Commerce's Office of Small Business, primarily an advisory agency, and RFC functions were combined in 1952 into the Small Business Administration.

The definition of a small business varies. The SBA correlates business size to industry codes that are defined in the North American Industry Classification System (NAICS). A comprehensive table of these codes is available on the SBA website. Classification as a small business is based either on the number of employees or the average annual revenue of a firm. As an example, in wholesale or trade businesses, a small business is one that has 100 or fewer employees. In manufacturing businesses, a small business has 500 or fewer employees.

Of course, small businesses can and do seek financing through many avenues. Commercial lending is available from many sources. Many small or new firms, however, don't easily qualify for standard commercial loans. As in consumer lending, credit scoring is critical in commercial lending. Things may not be easy for those small firms that don't have cash flow or collateral to qualify.

The SBA has an ongoing mission of education and assistance for small businesses. There's nothing small about the project, though. According to the SBA, for the fiscal year 2015, the SBA supported approximately $1.835 billion in lending to America's small businesses.

The financial assistance the SBA provides to small businesses comes in the form of loan guaranties. The loan guaranty program assures a lender that if the borrower defaults, the SBA will repay most of the loan. The SBA guarantees between 50–100% percent of the loan funds depending on the size of the loan and terms.

Borrowers apply to and receive funds from lenders, who must approve the loans. The SBA reviews the loans as well and provides the lender a written authorization of the guaranty. The basic interest rate of the loan is the prime rate as published in *The Wall Street Journal* (WSJ Prime). Lenders establish their own interest rates based on WSJ Prime plus a few percentage points. The SBA does set interest rate maximums for lenders. Payments go to the lender. Although there is more paperwork involved for both borrower and lender, the added trouble allows the lender to make loans it probably couldn't make without the assurance of SBA backing, and borrowers get funding they probably couldn't get otherwise.

Mark Van Seyoc/Shutterstock.com

Lenders are familiar with SBA loans, and many have SBA application forms either on site or posted on their websites. SBA certified lenders are those that work frequently and well with the SBA, and they have some authority to make their own decisions within the program. They also get faster SBA service. The SBA also maintains a preferred lender program for its best and most reliable lenders. In exchange for a lower rate of guaranty, preferred lenders have full authority to approve SBA loans on their own.

Although SBA standards may be more relaxed than those for other commercial loans, applications are still examined for soundness. Neither the SBA nor the lender wants to get stuck with a bad loan.

✔checkpoint

How do SBA loans differ from standard commercial loans?

9.3.2 SBA ELIGIBILITY

Most businesses are eligible for SBA loan guaranties, but the SBA makes a decision on a case-by-case basis, based on the type of program. In general, eligibility is determined by the following.

- **Type of Business.** Businesses must be operating for profit in the United States or its possessions, have reasonable owner equity, and use other financial alternatives, including personal assets of owners. Some types of businesses are ineligible. Charitable or religious groups, real estate investment, lending, pyramid sales plans, gambling businesses, and businesses engaged in illegal activities may not participate.

- **Size of Business.** The SBA has precise definitions of a small business. It must be independently owned and not dominant in its field. When businesses are affiliated, all affiliated parties must meet the size standard for its field of operation, which varies from industry to industry. For example, the miscellaneous store retail size standard is $7.5 million in revenue, while for agricultural farming businesses, $750,000 is the upper limit.

- **Use of Loan Funds.** Although SBA-backed loans may be used for most business purposes, funds cannot be used to finance floor plan needs, to purchase real estate when a commitment has already been made to a developer or for investment, to pay delinquent taxes or to make payments to owners, or to pay existing debt unless it can be shown that refinancing will benefit the business and is not the result of poor management.

Certain other conditions apply in special circumstances, based on the particular field in which the business is engaged.

✔checkpoint

What three factors determine SBA loan eligibility?

9.3.3 SBA LOAN TERMS AND CONDITIONS · · · · · · · · · ·

A borrower seeking an SBA loan must expect to meet all the criteria for a commercial loan. In general, the borrower needs a down payment, which can range from a minimum of 10% to as much as 35%. Most importantly, the borrower needs to demonstrate that he or she has the experience and knowledge required to run the business successfully. The SBA expects that the loan will be repaid from the normal business cash flow and, therefore, joins the lender in seeking full documentation of the operation of the business. As you saw earlier in this chapter, lenders require federal and state income tax returns, company financial statements, up-to-date P&L statements, projected cash flow estimates, personal financial statements of the owners, and a well-written business plan. Like the lender, the SBA wants to see as much collateral for a loan as possible, but it treats collateral as one part of the overall credit picture.

Maximum loan amounts and the size of the guaranty vary with the particular loan program, as do terms and other conditions. Loan terms may vary from 1 to 20 years, depending on the purpose of the loan. Interest rates are set by the lender but are subject to SBA maximums. Whether the interest rate is fixed or variable is also between the lender and borrower. The following sections describe the loan terms and conditions for various SBA lending programs.

7(a) Loan Guaranty

The 7(a) Loan Guaranty program is the SBA's most popular loan program and the foundation of the agency. The name of this program comes from Section 7(a) of the Small Business Act of 1953, which authorized the Small Business Administration to provide business loans and loan guaranties to small businesses in the United States. Businesses can use the funds to expand or repair facilities, purchase equipment or make improvements, finance receivables, or in some cases, refinance existing debt or purchase land or buildings. Although 7(a) loans are not fully guaranteed by the SBA, lenders can apply to the SBA to have a portion of a loan guaranteed against default. Even with a guarantee, borrowers are still responsible for loan repayment. In FY 2015, the SBA approved 63,461 7(a) loans amounting to nearly $23.6 billion. Proceeds from 7(a) loans may be used to establish a new business or to assist in the operation, acquisition, or expansion of an existing business.

7(a) loans have a maximum loan amount of $5 million. SBA does not set a minimum loan amount. The average 7(a) loan amount in fiscal year 2015 was $371,628. With the 7(a) program, the federal government provides an 85% guaranty for loans of $150,000 or less and a 75% guaranty for loans greater than $150,000 (up to a $3.75 million maximum).

According to the January 2016 Congressional Research Service Report, congressional interest in this loan program has increased. Some leaders are in favor of expanding the program. They want to give small businesses access to enough capital so they, in turn, can assist in the economic recovery.

Others, however, are opposed to expansion of the program. They are concerned that the long-term effects of spending programs such as this will increase the federal deficit and thus have an adverse effect on the economy.

SBA Express Loans

SBA Express loan programs offer quick turnaround time on loans, often within 36 hours. They have a maximum of $350,000 and offer a 50% guaranty. These loans typically are used to pay revolving lines of credit (up to a 7-year maturity) or a term loan. Express programs generally follow the 7(a) guidelines. In fiscal year 2015, the SBA approved 32,252 SBA Express loans totaling $2.20 billion. This was 50.8% of the total 7(a) program loan approvals.

504/CDC Loan Guaranty Program

The 504/Certified Development Companies (504/CDC) program is designed for the purchase of fixed assets such as land and improvements. Example projects might include constructing new facilities; modernizing, renovating, or converting existing facilities; and installing street improvements, parking lots, and landscaping.

The loans also might pay for long-term machinery and equipment with a useful life of at least 10 years. With most 504 loans, a private sector lender provides 50% of the project costs. Another 40% of the costs are provided through an SBA CDC. The purchaser provides the final 10% of the project costs as a down payment on the loan. Maximum loan amounts range from $5 to $5.5 million, depending on the project. The minimum loan amount is $50,000.

International Trade and Export Promotion Loans

These programs support firms that engage in business internationally. The International Trade program is a long-term loan (up to 25 years) that aids in the financing of permanent working capital, equipment, facilities, land and buildings, and debt refinance related to international trade. The Export Working Capital program helps provide short-term financing for exporters up to three years but generally one year or less. The financing may be transaction- or asset-based and can also support standby letters of credit for exporters. Both programs have a maximum loan amount of $5 million. They both provide a 90% guaranty, up to $4.5 million maximum. The International Trade program provides up to $4 million maximum guaranty for working capital.

Microloan

The SBA Microloan program makes funds available to nonprofit intermediary lenders to help small, newly established businesses. A microloan has a maximum value of $50,000. The lending intermediary agrees to provide technical assistance and advice, and the borrower

"communicate"

Talk to several small business owners about their experiences as entrepreneurs. Compile a list of pros and cons of owning your own business.

may be required to undergo training or meet planning requirements. Microloans may be used to pay for machinery and equipment, fixtures, and leasehold improvements and to provide working capital. They may not be used to repay existing debt.

CAPLines

The CAPLines loan program supports short-term lending for seasonal, contract, or other cyclical capital needs with either short-term loans or revolving lines of credit. Generally, 7(a) guidelines apply.

Community Advantage 7(a) Loans

The SBA's Community Advantage 7(a) loan initiative was designed to increase lending to low- and moderate-income communities. It offers guaranty of loans up to $250,000 and a streamlined application process. The financial institutions that participate in this program are expected to maintain at least 60% of their SBA loan portfolio in underserved markets. As of September 30, 2015, 74 active Community Advantage lenders had issued 1,757 loans of $225.6 million. According to the SBA, the goal of the program is to "leverage the experience these institutions already have in lending to minority, women-owned and start-up companies in economically challenged markets, along with their management and technical assistance expertise, to help make their borrowers successful."

branching out

Financial Matchmaking with CDARS

The Certificate of Deposit Account Registry Service (CDARS) offers individuals and businesses an easy way to insure their bank deposits. To provide FDIC insurance coverage for deposits greater than $250,000, CDARS redistributes the money in an individual's or business's account to other banks. The redistributed money is invested into CDs valued under $250,000. CDARS has a network of banks involved in the program. Essentially, banks trade CDs with one another, so that each bank can make sure their depositors' money, up to $50 million, receives full FDIC insurance coverage. The trading process allows each bank to also receive back the full value of any deposits that they've entered into the system (by accepting CDs from other network banks). In addition to receiving complete FDIC insurance coverage, depositors also achieve streamlined administration of their deposits—one account statement summarizes the locations of all their deposits.

Think Critically Why is CDARS an appealing idea for businesses? How does this type of financial innovation benefit the economy?

In addition, the SBA operates a Small Business Investment Company (SBIC) program, consisting of about 40 for-profit corporations that raise and distribute venture capital to promising businesses. The program has been around since the 1950s but expanded greatly in the 1990s. The SBICs have SBA guidelines about how and with whom they invest, but they operate independently of the SBA on a day-to-day basis. Federal Express and Outback Steakhouse are examples of companies that received funding from SBICs.

Fraud Prevention

The SBA is very serious about making sure that SBA loans go only to businesses that truly meet the small business qualifying criteria. During a recent year, U.S. SBA Office of the Inspector General (OIG) investigations resulted in 64 indictments/informations, 51 convictions, and almost $280 million in potential recoveries, fines, assets, forfeitures, civil fraud settlements, or loans/contracts not being approved or being canceled. In that year the OIG issued 19 reports with 129 recommendations for improving the agency's operations, recovering improper payments, and reducing fraud and unnecessary losses in SBA programs. It is crucially important that all individuals and businesses involved in the loan application and approval process use due diligence to ensure that parties applying for SBA-guaranteed loans actually meet the eligibility criteria.

✔checkpoint

What general criteria must a borrower meet to obtain an SBA loan?

OSABEE/Shutterstock.com

assessment 9.3

Think Critically

1. Why does our society support small businesses?

2. Compare an SBA loan to a standard commercial loan. Why would someone choose one loan over the other?

3. Why do you think most charitable and religious groups are not eligible for SBA help?

4. Why is a well-written business plan an important factor in getting an SBA loan?

Make Academic Connections

5. **COMMUNICATION** Interview a person in your community who runs a small business. Find out how he or she obtained start-up capital, what the greatest challenges are in running a small business, and what advice or assistance this person has obtained and from what sources. Summarize your interview in a one-page report.

6. **HISTORY** Learn more about the history of the Small Business Administration. Find out how it changed from an organization intended to support business in general to one dedicated to small businesses. Write a one-page report on the history of the agency.

7. **SOCIAL STUDIES** Visit the Small Business Administration's website at www.sba.gov. Learn more about emergency relief funds for businesses affected by the September 11, 2001, attacks. Outline the details you find.

The 2008 Financial Crisis

9.4

Banking Scene

Gloria Velez has had a successful few years running her own business. She has some extra money she'd like to invest. Although traditional investments, like CDs, are comforting to consider because of the low risk and guaranteed interest rate, she'd prefer to make more money faster. Gloria's heard about a great way to make money with credit default swaps. Although they sound lucrative, she's concerned about the uncertainty associated with them. What factors should she consider before making this investment?

Learning Objectives

9.4.1 Identify the root causes of the 2008 financial crisis.

9.4.2 Discuss self-regulation and its effects.

Key Terms

- risk averse
- risk preferrer
- credit default swap (CDS)
- speculation
- synthetic financial product

9.4.1 THE PROFIT MOTIVE

Most people are interested in making money. Some people rely on traditional ways to produce income, which include working for a corporation, directly selling products or services to individuals or companies, or making investments. If someone is risk averse, he or she would prefer to invest in a product that has very little risk of failure. In exchange for the certainty of the investment, he or she is willing to accept a comparatively low rate of return on the investment. Government bonds and CDs are a few examples of investments that a risk-averse investor might select. A risk preferrer is an investor who seeks a high level of return on investments. To achieve those high returns, the risk preferrer is willing to invest in assets whose soundness or long-term performance is not predictable.

Relying on Each Other

As discussed in Chapter 4, money is a fiat system. Money works as a medium of exchange because everyone agrees on the common definition of the underlying value of the money. Swapping services can also work, as it did on page 102, when friends traded services. Refer to the figure on the next page for a summary of traded services. For the service swapping system to work, each participant must hold up his or her end of the bargain. The services swap has value because everyone has agreed upon the under-lying value of the services offered. Imagine what would happen if someone in the system allowed someone else to buy something on credit. And what

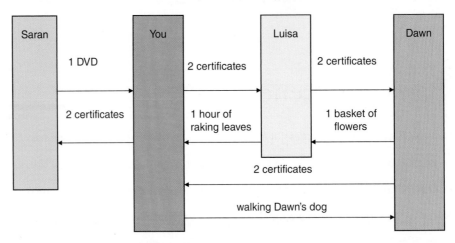

A Fiat System that Functions as an Interdependent Economy

if the person buying on credit could not pay for the product because they did not receive payment for work they did for someone else?

Suppose Dawn allowed Luisa to buy one basket of flowers on credit. Luisa raked leaves for you to earn the money to pay for the flower basket. But you decided, for whatever reason, not to pay Luisa. Income would be lost by Luisa that she could have made by providing a service for someone else. Luisa would be unable to pay Dawn because no wages were received from you. Now Dawn would be unable to pay you for walking her dog. Now multiply this scenario a million times, with payments being continually exchanged among millions of people for millions of products and services. If anyone in the chain fails to receive compensation for their service or product, then he or she will hesitate to participate in the system. The uncompensated participant may withdraw from the trading system and either hold onto his or her product and service or find a new system to participate in.

Revenue Generation from Assets of Dubious Value

A number of products were developed despite having an underlying poor asset value.

Mortgage-Backed Securities A large volume of mortgage-backed securities that pooled mortgages of various risk values were sold. These securities did not receive bond ratings that accurately reflected their level of risk. Highly rated securities lost money. Investors were shocked by these losses.

Credit Default Swaps Traditional insurance is based on the idea that a person or business that owns a specific asset, like a home or a manufacturing plant, buys an insurance policy to protect against the risk of damage. The value of the asset is clearly known. Policy owners can only be an entity with a direct stake in the asset—like a homeowner or corporation insuring their own home or business. The policy holder pays a premium to the insurance company. The insurance company can count on premium payments as a reliable income source.

A credit default swap (CDS) is like an insurance product gone awry. If a corporation wants to generate funds without getting a bank loan, then the corporation may issue bonds on the open market. These bonds are for a fixed amount of time and pay investors a fixed rate of return. Bond investors may want to protect themselves from two possible scenarios. First, they want protection from the issuing company defaulting on bond payments. Second, they want protection from tying up their money at a fixed return rate when that return rate could end up being less than return rates in the market. To protect against losses, the buyer of a bond may want to buy a CDS, which is an insurance policy to protect against losses. A third party who is neither the company issuing the bond or the buyer of the bond agrees to provide a CDS for the bond. In exchange for a regular premium, which may be based on a percentage of bond value, the CDS provides insurance against downside risks to the bond holder. In essence, the CDS seller is willing to "bet" that they understand both the financial stability of the company issuing the bond and whether market interest rates will move up or down relative to the bond. The CDS seller is happy to accept a steady income stream from the CDS investor's premium because the CDS seller does not expect to have to pay the CDS investor.

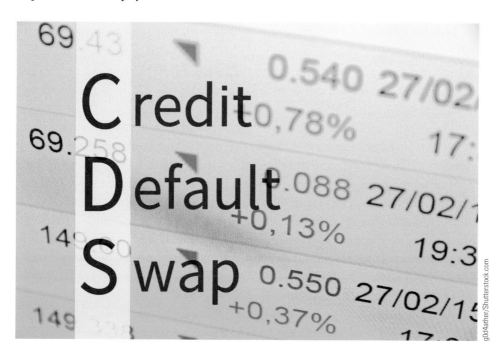

CDS Complicating Factors

There are a number of factors making CDSs more complicated than traditional insurance. Perhaps the most astounding complicating factor is that, unlike a traditional insurance policy where the person or business taking out the policy has a direct ownership stake in the asset being insured, anyone can take out a CDS on anything. For example, say you live in Arizona. Say that, due to growing concerns that global warming will wreak havoc on traditional weather patterns, you predict that hurricane-force winds will damage homes in Ohio. You decide to take out an insurance policy on a friend's home in Ohio. You have absolutely no ownership stake in the home, but you've got a feeling that your friend's home will incur damage from hurricane-force winds. With a CDS, you can, in essence, place a bet on your feelings. Speculation occurs when people make investments based on anticipated or hoped-for outcomes without having an ownership stake in the asset being insured. High risk is associated with speculation.

CDSs are financial products that have a value. To maintain that value, buyers of CDSs need to be financially stable enough to pay their premiums in a timely fashion. Sellers of CDSs need to be stable and have sufficient reserves to pay any claims that arise from their buyers' losses.

Initially developed to insure against downside interest rate risks on a tangible asset, CDSs eventually began to be used to insure against default on securitized investments. For example, once subprime mortgages were pooled into securities, portions of the securitized mortgages were sold off. The portions that had the least risk of default were sold off with the highest ratings. In exchange for the high ratings, a lower rate of return was offered for them. Likewise, portions with a higher risk rate were sold off. A higher return rate was offered on the lower-rated portions to offset the risk. CDSs were developed to insure against default on the securitized mortgages.

There were multiple layers involved. First there were the mortgages, many of which were subprime. Then there were the mortgage-backed securities. Then there were the slices of mortgage-backed securities, all sold with different ratings and returns. Then there were the CDSs. This was a pyramiding financial structure. The structure collapsed because each level of the pyramid was unsound. Each additional level that was added to the pyramid exerted more pressure on the levels beneath it. Each level added to the pyramid was more diluted in actual assets than the level below it. Companies were buying each other's investments. So when one level of the pyramid collapsed, they all came tumbling down.

Another complicating factor is that CDSs are unregulated. There is no limit to the number of people allowed to bet on the trend of someone else's assets. Unlike banks that are required to hold a certain percentage of funds in reserve to cover deposits, CDSs are not subjected to reserve requirements. Because CDSs represent a private deal between two private parties, it is hard to assign a value to the total global CDS market. Likewise, it is also difficult to assess the value of the underlying CDS assets.

Something for Nothing

Because of the potential to earn great sums of money, there are many risk-preferring people attracted to certain investment products. With an above-average understanding of financial markets and with a great drive to generate a profit, these individuals are motivated to develop profit-producing products. Sometimes, however, the hunger to develop high-yield investments clouds judgments. Sometimes people try to make a profit on synthetic financial products, which are products that lack an underlying value in their assets (such as a CDS written on a subprime mortgage-backed security).

✔checkpoint

What is a credit default swap?

9.4.2 THE INEFFECTIVENESS OF SELF-REGULATION

During the tenure of Alan Greenspan, there was an ideological belief that protecting the long-term self-interest of the companies and the industries participating in the CDS market was sufficient to keep the companies acting in a fiscally responsible way. With the realization that the CDS market players were sophisticated market participants accustomed to managing huge quantities of money, it was believed that participants had the intellectual capability to understand the long-term impact of the products they were selling and the investments they were making. Unfortunately, this ideological belief in the power of the industry to self-regulate was flawed. The sheer volume of CDSs written on pyramiding assets of dubious value, the ability of private parties to conduct CDS transactions without regulation, the increased global demand for more investment products, and the lack of a reserve requirement for CDS products proved to be overwhelming for the industry to effectively self-regulate. In addition, the complexity of the CDS process may have proven somewhat overwhelming to regulators contemplating the potential need for regulation. Failing to proactively appreciate the catastrophe looming in the future, decision makers allowed the CDS market (and related products) to grow exponentially without regulation.

Shawn Kashou/Shutterstock.com

The Aftermath

The cumulative effects of the financial crisis of 2008 are staggering. It is generally agreed that it is the worst financial crisis since the Great Depression. According to the National Bureau of Economic Research, the recession began in December 2007 and lasted 19 months, until June of 2009.

The federal government attacked the problem in several ways. It took various fiscal stimulus measures including tax rebate checks to households and the American Recovery and Reinvestment Act. It used quantitative easing by which the Federal Reserve increased the money supply through the purchase of government bonds to bring down long-term interest rates. It also established the Troubled Asset Relief Program (TARP) to inject capital into the nation's banks.

According to *The New York Times*, the purpose of government intervention in the financial markets is to resuscitate the economy and avoid a depression. By those criteria, the actions taken by government to end the 2008 financial crisis have proven to be effective.

 checkpoint

Why did industry self-regulation of the financial markets fail?

_____

_____

_____

assessment 9.4

Think Critically

1. What is a risk preferrer and how does his or her risk preference impact financial markets?

2. What is a synthetic financial product?

3. As a CDS investor, do you need to own the asset that the CDS insures?

4. What is speculation?

Make Academic Connections

5. **GOVERNMENT**   The Term Asset-backed Securities Loan Facility (TALF) provided $200 billion in government financing to lend money to private investors who purchased securities backed by small-business loans, student loans, credit card debt, and auto loans. TALF was an unprecedented government program in that the government became involved in directly helping with consumer debt financing. By purchasing consumer debt-backed securities, the intent of the TALF was to get credit in consumer markets flowing. Government purchases of debt from these markets provided lenders with revenue to make loans in these markets. Research the current status of the TALF program. How much government money has been spent on this program so far? Did the program have the intended effect? Summarize your findings in a one-page report.

chapter 9 assessment

Chapter Summary

9.1 Commercial Loans
A. Commercial lending is defined as lending to business enterprises.
B. There are numerous types of commercial loans.

9.2 Commercial Credit Analysis
A. Debt ratio, loan-to-value, and debt service coverage ratio are used in the credit analysis process.
B. To complete a credit analysis, the lender will require full access to a company's financial records.
C. Commercial lending is regulated only by the terms of the loan and some state laws.
D. The mortgage crisis affected not just the mortgage loan portfolios directly, but also the investment products that were backed by the mortgage loans.

9.3 Small Business Loan Programs
A. The SBA guarantees a lender that the loan will be paid if the borrower defaults.
B. Eligibility for an SBA loan is determined by the type of business, the size of the business, and the use of loan funds.
C. There are several SBA loan options for small businesses.

9.4 The 2008 Financial Crisis
A. Mortgage backed securities, CDSs, and a lack of regulation combined to help cause the 2008 financial crisis.
B. As self-regulation failed, the government used multiple ways to rescue the economy.

Vocabulary Builder

a. commercial lending
b. credit default swap (CDS)
c. debt ratio
d. debt service coverage ratio (DSCR)
e. factoring
f. merchandiser
g. manufacturer
h. risk averse
i. risk preferrer
j. short-term loan
k. Small Business Administration (SBA)
l. speculation
m. synthetic financial product
n. term loan

Choose the term that best fits the definition. Write the letter of the answer in the space provided. Some terms will not be used.

_____ 1. Making an investment based on a hoped-for outcome
_____ 2. Loans to business enterprises
_____ 3. Preferring to make investments with very little risk of failure
_____ 4. Comparison of net operating income to the total cost of debt
_____ 5. Financing for permanent working capital, equipment, and real estate
_____ 6. Financial products that lack an underlying value in their assets
_____ 7. Financing for a year or less
_____ 8. Agency that offers financial, technical, and management programs to help businesses
_____ 9. A form of lending that advances cash in exchange for a business's receivables
_____ 10. Total obligations compared to total income

Review Concepts

11. What is commercial lending?

12. List one purpose for commercial lending and describe how the loan might be used.

13. What is depreciation and how might it affect a loan?

14. Who is a risk-averse investor and how would he or she participate in the financial markets?

15. What is a line of credit and how would a business use it?

16. What are the costs and benefits of factoring to a business?

17. Explain the loan-to-value ratio. What do lenders consider an acceptable loan-to-value ratio?

18. What is the debt service coverage ratio (DSCR) and why does a lender prefer to see the highest possible DSCR?

19. List five things a lender will need to get from the borrower when considering a commercial loan.

_____

_____

_____

_____

_____

_____

20. How does the Small Business Administration define a small business?

_____

_____

_____

_____

21. Explain how the Small Business Administration helps businesses obtain loans.

_____

_____

_____

_____

22. Describe the SBA 7(a) loan program.

_____

_____

_____

_____

23. Why were credit default swaps (CDSs) originally developed and what was their eventual use?

_____

_____

Apply What You Learned

24. What role did CDSs play in the 2008 financial crisis?

_____

_____

_____

_____

25. Why do many businesses choose to lease equipment rather than buy it?

26. Why might a business choose to misrepresent itself as a small business?

27. Why does the government have an interest in guaranteeing loans for small businesses?

Make Academic Connections

28. **MATH** Calculate the debt service coverage ratio for a small business that has a gross income of $1,400,000, a net operating income of $800,000, and total cost of debt of $650,000.

29. **RESEARCH** Small or new businesses may need to submit a business plan to obtain financing. What is a business plan? What makes a good one? Study the information provided on the SBA website about the contents of a business plan. List the elements of a business plan here.

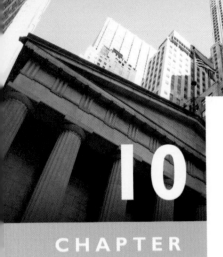

10 Specialized Bank Services

CHAPTER

10.1	International Banking
10.2	Insurance and Brokerage
10.3	Cash Management
10.4	Trusts

chainarong06/Shutterstock.com

climbing the ladder

Ike had spent the majority of his career in banking working with nondeposit products. He had joined his current employer, a regional bank, after earning a number of insurance licenses. As an associate team leader for insurance products, Ike's responsibilities included investment sales, business development, and customer service. To develop new business, he followed up on leads from bank branches. He sold investment products and services to banking customers. Sometimes he would cross-sell banking services to customers by recommending products that might be of interest to them but went beyond their original focus. He advised customers regarding investment choices. He trained branch-location personnel about products, coached them on their sales efforts, and provided support when they had questions.

Next Ike worked as a product development specialist. He was part of a team that developed product-specific strategy and pricing policies. For product maintenance or product distribution that would be outsourced, he worked on vendor agreements and information-sharing plans. When existing products were modified, he helped plan, coordinate, and communicate the changes to bank personnel. Another duty was to write or revise product-specific marketing material. He developed procedures to make sure that all product changes were reflected in product literature.

Ike took the knowledge he obtained developing products and applied it to his next position as a request for proposal (RFP) writer. When businesses need banking services, they formalize those needs by writing an RFP that outlines the required products and services. As an RFP writer, Ike prepared detailed responses to a prospective client's RFP that described the products his bank offered, the costs associated with those products, and the benefits of working with his bank. Ike helped the bank increase its business by writing accurate and informative RFPs. In some instances, such as when a city was looking for a bank to provide CDs each month, successful completion of the RFP process allowed Ike's bank to participate in the monthly bidding process that occurred for the CDs.

Leveraging his in-depth product and marketplace knowledge helped Ike obtain his current position as a product manager. In his new role, Ike conducts competitor and market research, develops new products, and creates marketing and sales plans for those new products.

Upper Rungs to Consider

Ike is thriving in his current position. Each day he comes to work with many new ideas. He enjoys keeping current on banking industry topics, anticipating what his competitors might do, and proactively developing products to grow his bank's business. Although he wants to stay on this career path, he hopes to earn a promotion to become a new product director. In that role, he would provide direction to the entire department and manage other product managers.

Preparing for the Climb

Banks sell a variety of financial services. Why is product development important? Why is it necessary to conduct research about industry changes and competitive products?

10.1

International Banking

Learning Objectives

10.1.1 Identify financial entities involved in international banking.

10.1.2 Describe international services offered by banks.

Key Terms

- foreign direct investment
- sovereign wealth fund
- edge corporations
- correspondent bank
- currency risk
- country risk
- money laundering
- letter of credit
- foreign exchange rate

Banking Scene

Amelia Lopez owns a small business. The market for the firm's major product is growing rapidly in South America, and she wants to investigate the advantages and disadvantages of selling her product there. What issues should Amelia consider? Where can she get sound advice about this possible venture?

10.1.1 INTERNATIONAL BANKING OVERVIEW

You don't need a textbook to tell you that the world of finance is increasingly an international one. The changing economy in the 1970s introduced waves of new imports to American life, and the computer and telecommunications revolution of the 1980s and 1990s eliminated national boundaries in many ways. Companies looking for new markets began selling to developing nations, and expanding economies in the Pacific Rim altered the balance of economic power. Changes in geopolitics, such as the end of the Soviet Union and the emergence of the People's Republic of China, realigned trading partnerships. New trade agreements and economic alliances such as the North American Free Trade Agreement and the European Union shifted the way the world conducted business, as did the growth of multinational corporations with branches in many countries. Middle Eastern countries flush with cash from oil revenues and newly industrialized countries generating revenues from manufacturing contributed to an increase in global cash flow.

Money flows into and out of a country from other countries in the form of **foreign direct investment (FDI)**. The U.S. government defines FDI as "the ownership or control, directly or indirectly, by one foreign person [individual, branch, partnership, association, government, etc.] of 10% or more of the voting securities of an incorporated U.S. business enterprise or an equivalent interest in an unincorporated U.S. business enterprise." At the end of 2014, total FDI by firms from other countries in the U.S. was $2.9 trillion. The top five countries investing in the U.S., in order, are the United Kingdom, Japan, the Netherlands, Canada, and Luxembourg. Inflow of FDI in 2014 was $164.8 billion. In 2015, the annual inflow decreased 7% to $153.3. Outflow of FDI by U.S. entities to other countries at the end of 2014 was $4.9 trillion. The following five countries were the top recipients of FDI from the United States: the Netherlands, the United Kingdom, Luxembourg, Canada, and Ireland.

Behind all this investment is money, and international banking is a huge and growing segment of the banking industry. With more and more U.S. companies operating abroad and involved in international trade, banks are expanding their services to provide the expertise that is needed. International banking can be a complicated business, with traders needing to understand the differences among currencies, governments, languages, laws, customs, and even computer systems that affect funds transfers. It is a vital business for the future of banking, because in the global economy, more business will have an international component. Banks that can help provide smooth, efficient, and trouble-free flow of funds and credit around the world may find a profitable and growing business.

International Lending and Other Services

Relatively few banks specialize in international lending. In a recent year, only about 750 of more than 14,000 U.S. commercial banks had international lending departments, with a smaller number having foreign branches or subsidiary corporations abroad. Although the number of these banks is small, both the scope and the size of their international business are expanding rapidly, and more banks are likely to expand into this area.

Lending is not the only international service banks provide. The number of banks that are helping companies conduct business overseas is growing. Other international services offered range from foreign exchange to collection of payments from overseas customers. Banks with knowledge of international business offer help in a complex world with which a firm may have little experience. It makes good business sense for companies to buy expertise they may not possess.

Governing Organizations

The *World Bank* is a partner in strengthening economies and expanding markets to improve the quality of life for people everywhere, especially the poorest. Unlike aid programs, the World Bank doesn't make grants but lends money to developing countries and expects the loans to be repaid. A member of the World Bank Group, the International Finance Corporation (IFC) promotes sustainable private sector investment in developing countries to reduce poverty and improve people's lives. The functions of the IFC include the following:

- Financing private sector projects located in the developing world.

- Helping private companies in the developing world mobilize financing in international financial markets.

- Providing advice and technical assistance to businesses and governments.

The *European Payments Council (EPC)* was formed in 2002 to streamline and coordinate payments for the European banking industry. The EPC developed the Single Euro Payments Area (SEPA), which provides an area for standardized euro payments either within a country's borders or across countries' borders. The SEPA is governed by the Euro Retail Payments Board (ERPB) and supported by the European Commission and the European Central Bank.

Foreign Banks

Many types of foreign-based banks, branches, agencies, subsidiaries, and holding corporations share features with U.S.-based banks doing international business, and they are supervised accordingly. Foreign bank branches and agencies may be chartered either by federal or state governments. They may offer a full range of banking services, but most of their business involves short- and long-term commercial loans. Although foreign branches can accept deposits of any size from foreigners, they can accept deposits only greater than $100,000 from U.S. citizens and residents (in order not to harm domestic banks), and deposits made after 1991 are not insured by the Federal Deposit Insurance Corporation (FDIC).

Since 1991, the responsibility for supervising the branches and agencies of foreign banks operating within the United States has belonged primarily to the Federal Reserve. It annually examines the banks' policies of **R**isk management, **O**perations, **C**ompliance, and **A**sset quality (ROCA). If an examination reveals problems with a foreign bank, the Fed has a range of actions it can take. Usually, a letter of commitment from the bank to the Fed explaining how a problem will be corrected is required. Occasionally, further legal action occurs, and in extreme cases, the activities of a foreign bank in the United States will be terminated.

U.S-Based International Banking

The *Office of the Comptroller of the Currency* (OCC) charters and supervises U.S. national banks that conduct international business. The OCC has the power to remove bank officers and directors, negotiate agreements to change banking practices, issue orders to stop certain practices, and levy financial penalties for unsound practices. The Federal Deposit Insurance Corporation, whose director

is the Comptroller, reviews the safety of international banking operations.

Sovereign Wealth Funds

When the government of a country has excess cash to manage, the government may create a sovereign wealth fund. These funds are segregated from the country's official currency reserves. Sovereign wealth funds can be used to generate profit for a country by making investments. According to the Sovereign Wealth Fund Institute, as of January 2016, sovereign wealth fund assets worldwide were valued at nearly $7.1 trillion, up from $3.4 trillion at the beginning of 2008. About $4 trillion in assets were funded with revenues from energy exports. With the drastic drop in the price of a barrel of crude oil (down to $30 a barrel from a peak of $140 in 2008), oil-rich nations are beginning to sell off assets accumulated in their sovereign wealth funds to finance government spending. In Chile, for example, the fund was $14 billion at the end of 2015, down from $15.5 billion a year earlier. Azerbaijan's fund decreased to $7.3 billion at the end of 2015, which is less than half its value of $16.5 billion in 2014.

Automation to streamline processes is a critical component of staying competitive in the banking industry. Bottomline Technologies® provides a modular platform for automating payments, including international payments. Find the Global Payments page on the Bottomline Technology® website. Review the functionalities offered. How is it helpful to have alternative currency and multilingual capabilities?

Other Types of International Operations

Edge corporations or *agreement corporations* are financial corporations that are federally chartered and allowed to engage only in international banking or other financial transactions related to international business. Edge corporations must verify that every transaction is related to international business.

A correspondent bank acts as a point of contact for other banks that do not have a branch, agency, subsidiary, or corporation in the host country. Correspondent banking is unique as highly competitive banks competing for the same businesses share services with one another for a fee. These banks are subject to the banking regulations of the host country. The Federal Reserve, as well as other international banking organizations, works to communicate and standardize international banking policies to ensure a more stable flow of funds.

Special Considerations

Think of the potential hazards of doing business globally. Different economic conditions, different currencies, different political systems, and different cultural practices add uncertainty. For bankers involved in underwriting such business, these other elements of risk must be considered.

- **Financial Risk** Financial risk may not seem all that different compared to domestic banking, and the evaluation of credit risk is similar. However, acquiring reliable information about a creditor's financial position may be considerably more difficult. The format, quality, and relative detail of financial statements around the world vary considerably. Many of these statements are unaudited, and in some cases, they are unreliable. Although international banks do share information, there are sometimes political barriers to the free flow of accurate information, especially when the potential borrower is a government itself. The task of assessing risk is considerably harder.

- **Currency Risk** The risk posed by variations in exchange rates between countries is called **currency risk**. In every transaction, the lender or borrower is at some degree of risk because of currency risk, as relative values fluctuate with economic and political conditions. The value of currencies compared to each other at the outset of the term may not be at all the same later in the term. Although many lenders minimize their risk by dealing only in U.S. dollars, some countries must convert those dollars into local currency to use them. If the exchange rate changes, more local currency may be required to repay the loan than was expected at the outset. Banks need to be able to assess this risk as accurately as possible, which is not always an easy task.

- **Country Risk** The term for the entire range of political, legal, social, and economic conditions that may put international business at risk is **country risk**. International bankers spend a lot of time trying to assess country risk. Analysts consider the likelihood of political or social changes or unrest, the economic condition and prospects of the country, whether a government might seize private assets or renounce foreign debts, and whether the government is able to ensure the stability of its currency. These analyses produce varied classifications of risk for international business. A bank's activities in a foreign country in light of the country's risk classification are part of the Fed's regulatory examination of a bank.

The political and cultural environment in other parts of the world differs from those in the United States. Bankers must be vigilant not only to protect their own interests, but also to avoid being unwitting allies of people who have illegal or harmful intent. The Bank Secrecy Act of 1970, updated again in 2000, intended to create a "paper trail" for currency so that people could not engage in **money laundering**, which refers to depositing, investing, or exchanging money in such a way as to conceal its illegal source. The Foreign Corrupt Practices Act of 1977 requires banks to follow strict accounting procedures in their international dealings and prohibits offering or accepting bribes. Commerce Department regulations prohibit exporters and banks from complying with boycotts that discriminate against U.S. citizens or companies on the basis of race, color, religion, sex, or national origin, and require reporting of them.

The financing of illegal activities came into sharp focus after the terrorist attacks in September 2001. Among its many provisions, the USA

Patriot Act of 2001 sought to make money laundering more difficult. The law prohibits establishing correspondent relations with foreign "shell" banks, banks that had no physical presence in their host country. It also requires due diligence on the part of banks to know the identity and source of transactions as well as to report suspicious transactions. Some privacy advocates whose fierce objections had led to the withdrawal of expanded "Know Your Customer" provisions in 1999, worried that the Patriot Act gave banks and government too much power. Even so, the law passed quickly and went into effect October 26, 2001, with most of its provisions in place by summer 2002.

 **checkpoint**

Name three types of risk for international banking.

10.1.2 INTERNATIONAL BANKING SERVICES

Banks offering international services help their customers negotiate, finance, ship, transfer, and collect their international accounts. Specialists in international finance and the export-import business help clients make their way through the sea of documents that are part of doing business across national boundaries.

Trade Financing

There are numerous forms of trade financing for international business. Some may take the form of simple domestic loans to be used for capital in an import or other international venture. Some may be direct loans to

Lemonpink Images/Shutterstock.com

foreign governments through government-run banks or industries. Funds may go to foreign banks in the form of deposits or other loans as a means of making an indirect loan to a foreign business. Sometimes a direct loan may be made to a foreign business or individual. Loans for complex syndications of businesses may be very complicated but are not uncommon. In all cases, banks must review international financial statements, the borrowers themselves, and any other parties involved, such as parent companies, banks, and government institutions. Bank management must estimate if it can safely extend credit based on its own financial position; the financial condition of the borrowers and other parties; the bank's own marketing objectives; and the financial risk, currency risk, and country risk involved.

Letters of Credit The most common type of trade financing involves a letter of credit. A letter of credit is an instrument given by a bank on behalf of a buyer (applicant) to pay the bank of the seller (beneficiary) a given sum in a given time provided that documents required by the letter are presented to the issuing bank. The required documents usually consist of an invoice, transportation documents (listing the cargo), insurance, and other verification that the goods have been delivered. Until those documents have been accepted by the issuing bank, the letter of credit is of no value. When the documents are accepted, the bank debits the buyer's (applicant's) account, wires the specified amount to the correspondent bank of the seller (beneficiary), and the buyer can collect the shipment. In this way, both buyer and seller have some guarantee of the performance of the other, and the bank's funds are secured by the documentation for the goods. A *standby letter of credit* assures the seller of the buyer's creditworthiness by guaranteeing the bank to pay the seller in the event of nonperformance by the buyer. Standby letters of credit are charged an origination fee, which varies based on the size of the letter and the security pledged. Typically the fees range from one to three percent of the size of the letter of credit.

Drafts and Wires Similar to a check, a draft is an order signed by one party (the *drawer*, or drafter) that is addressed to another party (the *drawee*) directing the drawee to pay someone (the *payee*) the amount indicated on the draft at sight or some specified time. Banks dealing in international banking can provide drafts in the specified currencies of many nations if necessary, so that the draft can be negotiated within that country. Banks can also provide international wire transfer. Messaging is not necessarily limited to ledger entries of funds but may also include letters of credit or any other communication or documentation necessary for international business.

International Collections Banks perform international collections services based on their relationships with correspondent banks and their knowledge of international commerce.

Foreign Currency Exchange Foreign currency exchanges are essential for international transactions. For example, before a U.S. importer can purchase commodities from Japan, it must first obtain Japanese yen to pay for them. Banks can provide this service. Banks may exchange currency through foreign exchange markets or may have correspondent relationships with banks in other countries for the trading of currency. A foreign exchange rate is the value of one currency in terms of another. Current foreign exchange quotations must be used to calculate the exchange. For example, the table below shows the recent exchange rates for select countries.

Currency	1 U.S. $	1 Yen ¥	1 Euro €	1 Can $	1 U.K. £	1 Aussi $	1 SFranc	1 MexPeso
U.S. $	1.00	0.0089	1.09	0.74	1.39	0.71	1.00	0.055
Yen ¥	0.92	1.0000	122.79	83.48	157.01	80.51	112.98	6.230
Euro €	0.92	0.0081	1.00	0.68	1.28	0.66	0.92	0.051
Can $	1.35	0.0120	1.47	1.00	1.88	0.96	1.35	0.075
U.K. £	0.72	0.0064	0.78	0.53	1.00	0.51	0.72	0.040
Aussi $	1.40	0.0120	1.52	1.04	1.95	1.00	1.40	0.077
SFranc	1.00	0.0089	1.09	0.74	1.39	0.71	1.00	0.055
MexPeso	18.12	0.1600	19.68	13.38	25.18	12.91	18.14	1.000

To calculate what $1,000 U.S. dollars would be worth in euros, use the exchange rate from the table for U.S.$ to euros: $1,000 × 1.09 = $1,090.

To calculate what 1,090 euros would be worth in U.S. dollars, use the exchange rate for euros to U.S.$: $1,090 × 0.92 = $1,000 (rounded).

Factors affecting exchange rates for the currency of a given country are interest rates, rate of inflation, trade balance (if a country's exports exceed its imports), and economic forecasts for that country. The demand for a given currency will be strong if the country is experiencing relatively high interest rates, low inflation, a positive trade balance, and a strong economic forecast.

Trade Consulting

Using their expertise, banks can help companies assess both their prospects and risks in international commerce and help companies with the paperwork associated with international transactions. The international banking consultant may also work with and/or recommend other agencies that can be of help to a business wanting to branch into international markets.

Photodisc/Getty Images

The Export-Import Bank of the United States (EXIM) Some banks work with the Export-Import Bank of the United States (EXIM) to help raise capital for companies that have the potential to produce goods or services for export but need funds to do so. EXIM offers a number of financing and credit insurance programs that cover the risks of nonpayment by foreign buyers. EXIM does not compete with commercial banks, but it assumes higher risks than commercial banks can normally accept. Its goal is to increase U.S. exports.

Overseas Private Investment Corporation The goal of the Overseas Private Investment Corporation (OPIC) goal is to assist U.S. companies in building their business in developing nations. OPIC's programs are beneficial for both the developing nations and U.S. exports. OPIC will provide loans, loan guarantees, and political risk insurance to qualifying companies. OPIC will provide this assistance for ventures seen as too risky for commercial banks. In spite of the assumed risks, OPIC has made money every year since it was created in 1971.

 **checkpoint**

What is a letter of credit?

One World

Export-Import Bank of India

Developing "brand India" is the current focus of the Export-Import (Exim) Bank of India. Founded in 1982, India's Exim Bank was created by an act of the Indian Parliament, and the government of India wholly owns it. Its purpose is to finance, facilitate, and promote India's foreign trade. Exim Bank of India has 10 offices in India, overseas offices in Singapore, Dubai, Addis Ababa, Yangon, Johannesburg, and Washington, DC, and a branch office in London. It has expanded services to include financing at competitive rates to buyers of Indian goods in foreign countries.

Think Critically Of what potential benefit is the Indian government's involvement in export-import banking? Why might a foreign buyer benefit by financing through a bank of the seller's home country?

assessment 10.1

Think Critically

1. What factors do you think contribute to the increasing globalization of economies?

2. Name two organizations that specialize in helping U.S. firms engage in foreign trade.

3. Describe two specific circumstances that might entail country risk.

4. Why might banks dealing in international services be in a good position to offer trade consulting?

Make Academic Connections

5. **COMMUNICATION**   Although English is the language of business around the globe, it helps traders immensely to know the language of their business partners. Find out the top five languages in the world, as ranked by number of speakers. List them and the number of speakers for each below.

6. **MATH**   In January 2002, eurodollars, or euros, became the currency of member nations of the European Union, a group of Western European nations banding together for economic purposes. Using the Internet, find the current value of a euro as compared to the U.S. dollar and convert the cost of U.S. goods valued at $40,000 to euros.

10.2

Insurance and Brokerage

Learning Objectives

10.2.1 Explain the effects of the Gramm-Leach-Bliley Act of 1999.

10.2.2 Identify typical insurance products available from financial institutions.

10.2.3 Discuss various brokerage services available through financial institutions.

Key Terms

- stock
- bond
- mutual funds
- annuity

Banking Scene

As a small business owner, Amelia Lopez is considering offering a health insurance plan for her employees, but she is undecided as to which type is the best. She is surprised to learn that her bank now offers insurance policies. What types of plans are available to her? What are some of the choices she must make in addition to the type of plan to offer?

10.2.1 A NEW ERA

Banks are offering more products and services than ever before. The competitive nature of today's banking business, along with the mergers and acquisitions many banks have undertaken, have placed them in a position to diversify even further. As a result of ongoing changes in financial services industries and new legislation, banks may now offer financial services that they once were prohibited from selling. This "one stop shopping" approach can offer customers a way to combine their financial planning into a single package, with products and expertise available from a single source. In addition, the door swings two ways: insurance companies can acquire banks just as banks can enter the insurance business. The new rules do more than open the door to unsupervised market chaos in the financial services industry. One sure result of the new era is that competition for consumers' financial business, whether in banking, insurance, or securities, will become even more keen.

The Old World: Glass-Steagall Act

In response to bank failures and investment losses that led to the Great Depression, Congress passed the Glass-Steagall Act of 1933. Among other provisions, the law prohibited banks from owning brokerage firms and selling stock and from affiliating or sharing offices with businesses that did. The intention of the law was to create a "firewall" between speculative businesses and banking institutions. Enacted during our nation's darkest economic period, it was part of a set of legislative actions that stabilized the banking system.

The Glass-Steagall Act kept banks from competing with other financial service providers. As the economy modernized, banks and other financial institutions suffered and occasionally were at risk because they couldn't compete. Gradually, laws such as the Bank Holding Company Acts of 1956 and 1970 allowed some side roads into other financial businesses, but they still prohibited direct affiliation and limited the regions in which banks could do business. Even as banks became deregulated in the 1980s, the prohibition of direct securities trading and insurance underwriting remained.

The New World: Gramm-Leach-Bliley Act

The Gramm-Leach-Bliley Act (GLBA) of 1999 was the most dramatic change in banking regulation since the Great Depression. After years of very limited involvement in insurance and securities businesses, banks were at last free to pursue those businesses directly. The law also required financial services companies to provide customers with a written privacy policy. Furthermore, the law allowed affiliated firms to share consumers' financial information as long as the consumer was notified. The responsibility to prohibit sharing of information with third parties, called an "opt-out," rests with the consumer. Some proponents of the law oppose the privacy-policy portion of it. They feel that requiring companies to seek permission of every consumer to share information creates an unnecessary burden of compliance. They also believe that free sharing of information among affiliates allows for quicker, more efficient, and less costly service to customers with less duplication of effort. Some privacy advocates strongly oppose this view, feeling that the law was structured to make it easier for companies to trade in private data with little restriction. They note that many of the uses of data in affiliated companies fall outside the third-party opt-out provisions.

In June 2008, HR 6312 was passed to remove the requirement that debt buyers provide an annual privacy notice to consumers. *Debt buyers* are companies that buy delinquent accounts from other companies. Debt buyers were concerned about the administrative costs of not only the initial mailing of the notices but also about the subsequent phone calls made by consumers who were confused by the notices.

Limits and Regulation

The Gramm-Leach-Bliley Act effectively supersedes state law, although it acknowledges the interest of states in "reasonable" regulation of the financial service industries. State commissions on banking, insurance, and securities still have jurisdiction on some practices, but may not discriminate in licensing against affiliated firms. Other controls come from agencies directly involved in the businesses themselves, such as the Securities and Exchange Commission and the Federal Trade Commission.

Our privacy commitment t
- Protect Customer Informati
- Inform on use of Custome
- Offer choices on the use
  Information and honor yo
- Collect, use and process
  Information respectfully

JohnKwan/Shutterstock.com

✔checkpoint

What was the major result of the Gramm-Leach-Bliley Act?

10.2.2 INSURANCE PRODUCTS

The GLBA essentially repealed the Glass-Steagall Act, sweeping away legal barriers that had separated the securities, insurance, and banking industries. Modernizing the financial services industry, the law allows for a new corporate structure, called the financial holding company (FHC), and allows banks, securities firms, and insurance companies to diversify and/or merge their businesses if they so choose. The stated purpose of the GLBA is to promote competition. Banks, therefore, can offer a complete range of insurance products for individuals and businesses.

The Workings of Insurance

The primary goal of insurance is to allocate the risks of loss from the individual to a great number of people, or to protect holders against financial disaster. Each individual pays a *premium* into a pool from which losses are paid. Whether the particular individual suffers the loss or not, the premium is not returnable. Thus, when a home is destroyed by fire, the loss is spread to the people contributing to the pool. In general, insurance companies are the safekeepers of the premiums. The government and the courts use a heavy hand in ensuring these companies are regulated and fair to the consumer.

Personal Insurance Products

Operating as full-service financial institutions, banks offer a full spectrum of insurance products.

- **Auto Insurance**   Auto insurance protects the owner from the risk of injury to people and damage to vehicles or other property in the event of an accident. It can also protect the owner against loss or damage through theft, vandalism, or natural disasters.

- **Credit Insurance**   This insurance, sometimes called *credit life,* is designed to repay the balance of a loan in the event the borrower dies before the insured loan is repaid.

- **Disability Insurance**   Disability insurance pays benefits when the holder is unable to earn a living because of illness or injury. Most disability policies pay a benefit that replaces part of the disabled holder's earned income.

- **Life Insurance**   Various types are available, as shown in the following table.

Types of Life Insurance Policies

Policy Type	Characteristics	Suitable For
Decreasing Term	Level premium, decreasing coverage, no cash value	Financial obligations that reduce with time, such as mortgages or other amortized loans
Annual Renewable Term	Increasing premium, level coverage, no cash value	Financial obligations that remain constant for a short or intermediate period, such as income during a minor's dependency
Whole Life	Level premium, level coverage, cash value that typically increases based on insurance company's general asset account portfolio performance	Long-term obligations, such as surviving spouse lifetime income needs, estate liquidity, death taxes, funding retirement needs
Universal Life	Level or adjustable premium, level or adjustable coverage, cash value that increases based on the performance of certain assets held in the company's general account	Long-term obligations, such as estate growth, estate liquidity, death taxes, funding retirement needs, and so forth
Variable Life and Variable Universal Life	Level or adjustable premium, level coverage (can be increased by positive investment performance), cash values that are directed to a choice of investment accounts (bond, stock, money market, and so forth) by the policy owner	Long-term obligations, such as estate growth, estate liquidity, and death taxes, and so forth for the more active investor
Single-Premium Whole Life	Entire premium is paid at purchase, level coverage, cash values	Asset accumulation vehicle for long-term obligations, such as surviving spouse lifetime income needs, estate liquidity, death taxes, funding retirement needs

- **Health Insurance**   The need for a comprehensive, high-quality health-care program, equitably accessible to all residents of the United States, has been the topic of national debate for years, but no national policy has been legislated. Health insurance is available through group plans that employers offer as a benefit to employees and individual plans purchased directly from insurers. Various health policies include the following.

Traditional   This type of policy allows holders to visit any doctor or hospital they want and receive coverage for any treatment covered under the policy. Premiums for traditional insurance tend to be higher than those for other plans.

HMO   A health maintenance organization (HMO) is a health-care system that organizes doctors and hospitals in a network. An HMO's two basic features are that members must choose a primary care network physician who performs basic health checkups and approves visits to other specialized physicians, and members pay a set per-person fee that gives them access to the HMO's services.

PPO   A preferred provider organization (PPO) is a collection of physicians and hospitals that agree to provide health care at reduced cost to PPO members. PPOs limit health-care costs without the restrictions of an HMO.

- **Homeowner's Insurance**   Homeowner's insurance is designed to protect against a wide range of potential disasters, such as fire, vandalism, and theft of property, as well as against lawsuits if someone is injured while on the owner's property.

- **Mortgage Disability Insurance**   Generally, if an illness or accidental injury renders an insured borrower disabled, mortgage disability insurance pays monthly home loan payments up to a specific amount.

- **Title Insurance**   This policy type compensates the owner of real estate if his or her clear ownership of property is challenged.

Business Insurance

Whether for-profit or nonprofit, businesses need certain types of insurance, such as liability insurance, which is highly recommended for property and automobiles. Workers' compensation is state-required insurance for any business with employees. The following briefly describes several types of business insurance.

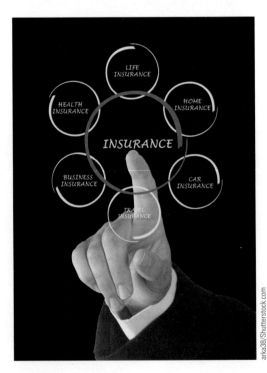

- **Commercial Liability**   Commercial liability insurance pays part or all of the damages for liability that the law applies to a business as well as the cost of defending the firm when a claim is made against it. Unprotected liability could cause financial hardship or bankruptcy.

- **Disability—Short-Term**   Regular employees working 30 hours or more a week who become disabled are provided with a level of income protection for a short period of time, such as 90 days. Coverage is generally for a percentage of normal income, often as much as 90 percent.

- **Disability—Long-Term**   This insurance is available to regular employees meeting short-term requirements but who have been disabled beyond the time limits of short-term disability benefits. Coverage is for a percentage of income less than that normally covered by short-term disability, often 60 to 70 percent.

- **Health Insurance**   Many firms allow employees to participate in group health insurance plans covering basic health care, sometimes including vision and dental care. The employer determines the plan's coverage and the portion of the cost, if any, that employees must pay for it.

- **Officers' Liability Insurance**   This insurance protects the company from losses due to the company's directors' and officers' alleged or actual breach of duty, neglect, error, misstatement, misleading statement, omission, or act.

Tech Talk

First Internet Bank of Indiana

Based in Indianapolis, Indiana, First Internet Bank of Indiana (or First IB) was one of the first state-chartered Internet banks with accounts insured by the FDIC. It was one of the first "extended value online banks" to deliver a full range of real-time Internet banking products with personalized interactive services as well as offering competitive rates. "Real-time" means that transactions are reflected in the customer's accounts immediately. First IB's business model enables customers to facilitate Internet banking in a real-time environment and to empower users to better manage their own finances.

First Internet Bank was one of the earliest banks to allow customers to conduct bank-related business from their web-enabled cell phones. First IB customers were among the first who could check their account balances online, transfer funds from one First IB account to another, view their last 10 transactions, set up new electronic bill payments, change due dates, and alter amounts or cancel planned payments from their computer or mobile device.

Think Critically   How does the success of this bank reflect on changes in our society? Why might some people be hesitant to use a bank without an advertised address for a walk-in lobby? Would you use an Internet-only bank? Why or why not?

- **Property Insurance** Like individual policies, business insurance protects the policyholder against risk. Policies can be customized to meet the special risks the specific firm faces.

- **Workers' Compensation** This insurance pays for medical care and physical rehabilitation of workers injured in the performance of their job, and it helps to replace lost wages while they are unable to work.

✔checkpoint

What is an HMO?

10.2.3 BROKERAGE SERVICES

Brokerage refers to bringing together parties interested in making a transaction, such as buying and selling shares of stock. A broker charges a fee to execute such a transaction. Banks now offer full investment services. To enhance the liquidity offered by brokers, the Securities and Exchange Commission strictly regulates them to ensure accurate disclosure of information, to prevent fraud, and to restrict trades based on insider information. *Insider information* refers to facts known by people inside an organization or to parties to a transaction but not known by the general public.

Stocks

Stock is the capital raised by a corporation through the issuance of shares entitling holders to an ownership interest, or equity, in the corporation. Stocks represent the largest single category of assets in the capital market, which is the financial market where stocks, bonds, and other types of securities are sold. *Common stock* entitles owners to regular dividends (payments of money) when they are declared. It also provides a voice, through voting rights, in how the corporation operates. *Preferred stock* owners usually receive a limited but set dividend amount and have no voting right, but their claim to the corporation's earnings and assets upon liquidation takes precedence over claims of common stock owners.

Bonds

A bond is a debt instrument issued for a period of more than one year with the purpose of raising capital through borrowing. The federal government, states, cities, corporations, and many other types of institutions sell bonds. Generally, a bond is a promise to repay the principal along with interest on a specified maturity date. As a buyer, you do not gain any ownership rights to the bond's issuer as you would with a stock. However, as a bond holder, your claim to the issuer's income is greater than that of a shareholder in the case of financial distress. Bonds are often divided into different categories based on tax status, credit quality, maturity, secured/unsecured, and issuer type. U.S. Treasury bonds are generally considered the safest unsecured bonds, because the possibility of the Treasury defaulting on payments is almost zero.

Mutual Funds

Mutual funds are investment companies that pool money from many savers who have small amounts to invest. With this money, the mutual fund purchases stocks, bonds, government securities, and short-term money market investments. These funds provide risk-sharing benefits by offering a diversified portfolio. *Diversification* refers to the distribution of assets in a portfolio among different types of securities and maturity dates instead of putting "all your eggs in one basket." Investing in mutual funds enables you to reduce your costs. You can buy into all shares in the funds with one transaction cost rather than incurring a cost on each instrument if you bought it separately.

Annuities

An annuity is a series of payments, often to a retired person, of a set amount from a capital investment. The annuity is paid at a specified frequency and for a set number of years or until the annuitant's death. Payments begin only

Photodisc/Getty Images

when the annuitant reaches a certain age. All annuities are tax-deferred, meaning that the earnings from investments in these accounts grow without being taxed until withdrawal. However, withdrawal before the specified age results in penalties and taxation.

✔checkpoint

What is a diversified portfolio?

assessment 10.2

Think Critically

1. How did the Glass-Steagall Act restrict banking services?

2. Why are banks now able to provide one-stop shopping to customers?

3. Explain how insurance works.

4. What is the difference between an HMO and a PPO?

5. What are the advantages of investing in mutual funds?

Make Academic Connections

6. **RESEARCH**   Consumers can use the Internet to do comparison pricing. Identify four different brokerage firms that offer Internet purchases. How do the firms charge for their services?

7. **SOCIAL STUDIES**   The GLBA has brought dramatic changes to the banking industry. Some people contend that these changes make sharing private data among companies too easy. How did the public communicate this concern to government officials? What has the government done to prevent banks from sharing nonpublic personal information?

Cash Management

Banking Scene

Amelia Lopez recently attended a seminar on outsourcing. Because her business recently began to sell its products in South America, the firm is growing, and its needs have changed. She thinks that outsourcing her accounting services might be a wise thing to do. How could this help Amelia manage her growing business? What advantages and disadvantages should she consider?

Learning Objectives

10.3.1 Explain why banks offer cash management services.

10.3.2 List several cash management services banks perform for businesses.

Key Terms

- outsourcing
- factoring

10.3.1 SYSTEMS IN PLACE FOR CASH MANAGEMENT • • •

Every business, no matter how large or small, needs to disburse and collect cash to complete business transactions. Banks are in a good position to provide cash management services to businesses for several reasons.

- **Experience** Banks have decades of experience in managing cash.

- **Business Knowledge** In conducting their own operations, banks have experienced the same opportunities and challenges that all businesses face, and they understand the nature and implementation of practices and policies that apply to efficient cash management for all businesses.

- **Technology** Banks have experience in applying technology to their cash management practices. Banks can afford to invest in the applicable technology and develop expertise in its use that most individual firms cannot. Banks allow other companies to tap into these efficiencies through the bank's cash management services.

- **Industry Expertise** Through their dealings with specific companies over the years, individual banks have developed expert knowledge of the practices of various industries. They can offer this expertise to other companies with similar needs.

Businesses recognize that constant changes in the financial industry and the regulatory world have increased their need to proactively manage cash, but with constant change, they find they no longer have the knowledge and experience to do so. It is not unusual for organizations that have had effective cash management systems to seek ways to improve them.

10.3 Cash Management   **319**

✔checkpoint

Why is a bank in a good position to offer cash management services?

10.3.2 CASH MANAGEMENT

Firms' focus on the "bottom line" has caused them to evaluate all activities they perform and to identify those that do not add value to the product or service they offer. For many reasons, one company can make a product or provide a service less expensively than other firms can.

Outsourcing refers to the practice of having an outside party supply a product or service that the firm had been producing or performing itself. For example, the firm can hire a business that specializes in human resources rather than hiring individuals knowledgeable in this field. Savings would include inside employees' salary packages, including paid vacation and sick days, benefits such as health insurance, and various payroll taxes. The firm can devote the savings obtained to the activities that differentiate it. For example, a greeting card company might hire a new artist. Outsourcing may be practical for firms with seasonal/fluctuating needs that make keeping some full-time employees impractical. The Sutter Consortium reports that firms outsource for the following reasons.

29% Difficulty hiring skilled professionals
20% Lack of in-house skills
14% Budget
12% Business changes
12% CIO/senior management mandate
 7% Reorganization
 2% Downsizing

Frequently outsourced accounting services include the following.

- **Payroll**   All functions related to paying wages to employees. These include calculating deductions, paying employees, filing payroll taxes, and all related recordkeeping.

- **Accounts Payable**   Short-term debt from purchases on credit that must be paid to suppliers of goods or services typically within 60 days or less. These are paid for the client at the appropriate time and the client's creditor account records are kept up to date.

- **Accounts Receivable**   Money due for services performed or merchandise sold on credit. Money is collected and records maintained.

Many businesses outsource cash management services to banks. Many banks outsource services as well. For example, Fidelity National

Information Services provides information processing management and professional consulting to many financial institutions, from community banks to megabanks and mortgage lenders to consumer finance companies.

Bank collection services enable banks to collect funds and integrate information easily and cost effectively. Various products accomplish this.

- **Deposit Services** Service that allows customers to make deposits in various ways. The bank maintains and manages deposit accounts to minimize balances in noninterest-bearing accounts and maximize balances in interest-bearing accounts.

- **Lockbox Service** Service that allows accounts receivable payments to be sent directly to the bank, accelerating the conversion of receivables into usable cash.

- **Zero-balance Accounts (ZBAs)** Accounts that start each business day at a zero balance and are related to a central account. Throughout the day, transactions are debited or credited as payments are made or received. At the end of the day they are reconciled with the central account and are returned once again to a zero balance. This type of program ensures that funds do not stand idle in multiple accounts and eliminates the need for the customer to monitor accounts and initiate account transfers.

- **Automated Clearing House (ACH) Network** This is a highly reliable and efficient nationwide batch-oriented electronic funds transfer system. It is governed by rules that provide for the interbank clearing of electronic payments for participating depository financial institutions. The American Clearing House Association, Federal Reserve, Electronic Payments Network, and Visa act as central clearing facilities through which financial institutions transmit or receive ACH entries. Banks' use of this network helps them provide cash collections and transfer services efficiently. In 2015, the ACH Network transferred 23 billion electronic payments valued at more than $40 trillion. Categories of ACH Network payments include online payments (WEB transactions), business-to-business (B2B) payments (CTX and CCD transactions), consumer-initiated payments (CIE transactions), and recurring payments (PPD transactions), such as Direct Deposit via ACH.

Information Services

The ACH Network is a part of the broader category of Electronic Data Interchange (EDI), which is generically defined as the computer-to-computer exchange of business information through standard interfaces. Today, more than 300,000 organizations are estimated to have implemented EDI. Banks can advise companies concerning this interchange and provide the services to the firms. EDI is especially useful in the financial services industry due to the growth of international trade. International financial transactions can become complex due to differences in currencies, regulations, and

accounting practices. EDI enables a fully automated international financial supply chain that allows buyers, suppliers, and financial institutions to transact seamless, accurate, and timely exchanges.

Capital Services

Businesses must often commit large sums of money (capital) to projects that will continue well into the future. Capital expenses usually involve the purchase of things that last more than a year. Examples of firms' capital purchases are large printing presses, equipment to implement environmental regulations, expansion into a new territory, and a fleet of new trucks. Many firms aren't able to perform the complex analyses necessary for making the decisions, so they turn to their bankers for help.

Capital Investments   Capital investments differ from investments in stocks and bonds in one significant way. Stocks and bonds can be sold on an organized market for cash. A capital investment requires a much longer time to convert to cash, during which time the firm might incur additional expenses, such as building or equipment maintenance. Making capital investment decisions requires the use of numerous analytical tools and techniques for evaluating if the investment will result in the desired profits. Banks have the expertise to use these techniques in advising their clients. Establishing capital budgets is also part of the service.

Financing   Once capital investment projects are decided, banks can provide advice to their clients regarding the best ways to finance while keeping the company's debt-to-equity ratios at the desired level.

Factoring   The practice of buying debt at a discount is called factoring. A firm that needs cash can sell a debt. The purchasing bank provides this service for a fee, often a percentage of the amount owed. In making its decision to provide this service, the bank evaluates the ability of the firm's customer to pay the debt. The customer pays the amount owed to the bank. Factoring dramatically improves a company's cash flow so it may meet current financial obligations.

 **checkpoint**

Explain how a zero-balance account works.

Banking Math *Connection*

A small business was able to make a large sale only by accepting a note of $8,075 plus a $925 service fee to be paid in 12 months rather than immediate payment. Shortly afterward, the business unexpectedly had to replace an expensive machine four years ahead of schedule. The business was short of cash and arranged for a local bank to purchase the debt for a factoring fee of 3 percent. How much will the business receive from the bank?

Solution

First calculate the factoring fee. The formula for calculating this is

$$(Principal + Service\ charge) \times Factoring\ fee\ percent = Factoring\ fee$$
$$(\$8,075 + \$925) \times 0.03 = \$270$$

Then subtract the fee from the total amount owed.

$$Principle + Service\ charge = Total\ amount\ owed$$
$$\$8,075 + \$925 = \$9,000$$

$$Amount\ owed - Factoring\ fee = Amount\ received\ from\ bank$$
$$\$9,000 - \$270 = \$8,730$$

assessment 10.3

Think Critically

1. Many firms now outsource activities that they once performed themselves. What are the advantages of this?

2. Name three accounting services commonly outsourced.

3. What puts banks in a position to offer cash management services?

4. What is the EDI service that banks offer?

Make Academic Connections

5. **TECHNOLOGY** Many banking functions are offered over the Internet. Choose one of the services discussed in this lesson and research its availability over the Internet. Prepare a written, oral, or computer presentation that discusses how this service is purchased on the Internet, describes the way the service is performed, and includes the fees involved.

6. **COMMUNICATION** Contact several local businesses and find out whether they outsource any of the accounting services discussed in this lesson. Determine the reason(s) they do or do not outsource. Compile your results as a class.

Trusts

10.4

Banking Scene

Now that Amelia Lopez's business is successful, she thinks it's time to start planning for her family's financial future. Her two daughters plan to go to college. She also wants to make sure that she and her husband will be comfortable during retirement. Amelia realizes that she will need to plan carefully to minimize the tax consequences on her estate when she dies. What are some of the options she should consider? Could IRAs meet her needs? What should Amelia know about estate planning?

Learning Objectives

10.4.1 Describe trust services.

10.4.2 Identify important types of trust services banks provide.

Key Terms

- trust
- donor
- beneficiary
- corpus
- IRA
- 401(k) plan
- variable annuity
- estate
- will
- probate
- executor
- living trust

10.4.1 WHAT ARE TRUST SERVICES?

The concept of trusts dates back some seven hundred years to Medieval England. At its simplest, a trust is an arrangement by which one party holds property on behalf of another party for certain defined purposes. Banks are well versed in providing trust services to their clients. Banks typically have trust departments whose members understand all types of trusts and their advantages and disadvantages and have experience in setting up and administering trusts to meet their clients' needs. Banks advise clients on the various types of trusts, which are discussed in the next section. Terminology related to trusts is somewhat specialized, and you should understand the following terms.

- **Donor** or *settlor* is the person who creates a trust.

- **Beneficiary** is the person for whose benefit the property is held.

- **Corpus** or *res* refers to the property that is held. Sometimes a distinction is made as to the *principal*, which is the property that is held in trust, and the *income* that the principal produces.

What is a trust?

10.4.2 TRUST SERVICE PRODUCTS

In addition to assisting a client in planning how to provide for financial needs during that person's employment years, banks offer advice regarding the client's retirement requirements and for passing assets upon death.

Retirement Planning

Various products are available to help individuals plan and save for their retirement. An **IRA** (individual retirement account) is a great way to save for retirement. There are two kinds of IRAs—traditional and Roth. Funds are invested in a traditional IRA on a before-tax basis, which allows the earnings on the investment to compound on a tax-deferred basis. This means that the money invested in a traditional IRA isn't taxed until it is withdrawn. There are penalties for withdrawal before age 59½. You must begin withdrawals from a traditional IRA beginning at age 70½.

Beginning January 1, 1998, the Roth IRA became available. This investment is made with after-tax dollars. As long as the assets have remained inside the account for five years, all earnings and principal can be withdrawn totally tax-free after age 59½. Unlike the traditional IRA, funds do not have to be withdrawn at age 70½. The Economic Growth and Tax Relief Reconciliation Act of 2001 made changes to the amounts that an individual can invest in either a traditional or a Roth IRA. Beginning in 2015, individuals can invest up to $5,500 a year. Individuals age 50½ or older can add another $1,000 for a maximum annual contribution of $6,500.

Employers offer another retirement plan, the **401(k) plan**, that allows employees to make tax-deferred contributions to a trust and direct their funds to be invested among a variety of choices. The employees get their money back at departure or retirement. Many companies match the employee investment, usually between 25 and 75 cents per dollar, to a defined maximum (such as 6 percent of pay).

Many people find annuities to be a good complement to tax-deferred retirement investments. A **variable annuity** combines the opportunity for tax-deferral with a choice of portfolios and the flexibility to vary annual contributions according to the investors' needs or market conditions.

Estate Planning

Estate planning is the process by which an individual or family arranges the transfer of assets in anticipation of death. An **estate** is the total property, including real estate and personal property (all other possessions, such as automobiles, jewelry, and bank accounts) that an individual owns. The cornerstone of any estate plan is a **will**, a document by which the individual gives instructions as to what is to happen upon his or her death in regard to property and remains. An estate plan seeks to preserve the maximum amount of wealth possible for the intended beneficiaries and to provide flexibility for the individual prior to death. Federal and state tax laws are major considerations in estate planning.

Probate is a court proceeding that settles an estate's final debts and formally passes legal title to property from the decedent to his or her heirs.

It is initiated in the county of the decedent's legal residence at death. Wills must undergo formal probate administration, which can last two years or more, depending on the size and complexity of the estate. Court permission is needed to buy and sell assets, and beneficiaries usually must wait until the probate is concluded to receive the bulk of their inheritance. There are measures that may be taken to avoid assets being tied up in probate, such as naming beneficiaries for retirement accounts and placing assets in a living trust.

Estate Settlement

Estate settlement generally involves the following.

- **Identifying and valuing the estate assets**   An **executor** or *fiduciary* (the person named in the will to administer the estate) must identify all assets in the estate, including securities, business interests, and retirement plans, and determine their value. The executor arranges for professional appraisals of such items as real estate, artwork, and jewelry. If there is no will, the court will appoint an executor.

- **Paying creditors, estate expenses, and taxes**   The executor must ensure that the estate has sufficient cash to pay legitimate creditors and related estate expenses, including taxes. In fulfilling this role, the executor may have to decide to sell securities or other assets.

- **Preparing and filing the necessary tax documents with federal and/or state authorities**   Recordkeeping must be exemplary to ensure that all documents are present, accurate, and complete. The executor must file all documents with the appropriate courts and other agencies in accordance with specific requirements and deadlines.

Ethics in Action

Banks have the ethical responsibility to inform customers in a clear manner on subjects such as the customers' rights and obligations as well as any and all benefits and risks of the products and services provided to them.

Think Critically

1. What are some things you believe a banker should tell a prospective customer about the risks related to retirement planning?
2. What are some things customers should do to be sure they are making informed decisions relative to retirement planning?

- **Distributing assets to beneficiaries**   The executor must make timely decisions concerning the distribution of estate assets in a prudent and efficient manner.

Testamentary Trusts

Testamentary trusts are established by a will and take effect at the donor's death. They receive the assets of the estate to hold and manage for the benefit of the heirs.

Charitable Remainder Trusts

A *charitable remainder trust (CRT)* is an irrevocable trust designed to convert the highly appreciated assets of a *trustor*—the person who sets up the trust—into a lifetime income stream without generating estate and capital gains taxes. CRTs have become very popular in recent years because they not only involve valuable tax advantages, but they also enable the trustor to provide a gift to one or more charities. A CRT can potentially

- Eliminate immediate capital gains taxes on the sale of appreciated assets.
- Reduce estate taxes that heirs might have to pay upon the trustor's death by as much as 55 percent.
- Reduce current income taxes with an income tax deduction.
- Increase the trustor's spendable income.
- Create a charitable gift.
- Avoid probate and maximize the assets the trustor's family will receive.

Living Trusts

In simple terms, a living trust is a legal document that provides an expedient way to transfer property at a person's death. Generally, living trusts are established during an individual's lifetime and can be modified or changed while that person is still alive. For this reason, a living trust is set up on a "revocable" basis. The *revocable trust provision* means that while the person lives, he or she still owns all of the property that has been transferred into the trust and can sell it, spend it, or give it away. The trust does not transfer to the beneficiary until the trustor dies. Living trusts speed up the process by which property moves to designated beneficiaries upon the trustor's death. One of the advantages of a living trust is that it avoids probate, although it may not offer the tax benefits related to CRTs.

 **checkpoint**

What are the responsibilities of an estate executor?

assessment 10.4

Think Critically

1. Why would a person want to set up a trust?

2. Why would a person want to avoid having his or her estate go through probate?

3. What information would you need to know if you were interested in setting up a living trust?

4. Why might people avoid deciding how to dispose of their assets at their death?

Make Academic Connections

5. **COMMUNICATION** Talk to adult family members or friends about the type of retirement plan(s) that they have. Discuss at least four different retirement plans. Prepare a one-page report summarizing your conversation. Mention any concerns that your friends and family members have about the plans.

6. **RESEARCH** Use the Internet to find information on the topic of estate tax repeal. List the advantages and disadvantages of this legislation.

chapter 10 assessment

Chapter Summary

10.1 International Banking

A. International banking institutions include branches of foreign banks operating within the U.S., edge corporations, U.S. banks offering international services, and correspondent banks.

B. International services help customers negotiate, finance, ship, transfer, and collect their international accounts.

10.2 Insurance and Brokerage

A. The Gramm-Leach-Bliley Act allowed banks to enter a new era in which they are able to provide financial services not previously allowed.

B. Banks offer personal and business insurance, and brokerage services.

10.3 Cash Management

A. Banks possess the expertise to provide cash management services to clients.

B. Banks assist their clients in managing their cash by providing accounting, information, credit card, and capital services.

10.4 Trusts

A. Trusts are financial planning vehicles that arrange for the transfer of property from one entity to another under specific circumstances.

B. Retirement planning, estate planning and settlement, and trust establishment and supervision are services offered by banks.

Vocabulary Builder

a. 401(k) plan
b. annuity
c. beneficiary
d. bond
e. corpus
f. correspondent banks
g. country risk
h. currency risk
i. donor
j. edge corporations
k. estate
l. executor
m. factoring
n. foreign exchange rate
o. IRA
p. letter of credit
q. living trust
r. money laundering
s. mutual funds
t. probate
u. outsourcing
v. sovereign wealth fund
w. stock
x. trust
y. variable annuity
z. will

Choose the term that best fits the definition. Write the letter of the answer in the space provided. Some terms will not be used.

____ 1. Political, legal, social, and economic conditions that affect international businesses

____ 2. Practice of depositing, investing, or exchanging money in such a way as to conceal its illegal source

____ 3. Arrangement by which one party holds property on behalf of another party

____ 4. Court proceeding that settles estates

____ 5. Refers to the property held in a trust

____ 6. The value of one currency in terms of another

____ 7. Federally chartered institutions allowed to engage only in international banking

____ 8. Person who creates a trust

____ 9. Degree of risk posed by variations in exchange rates between countries

____ 10. Excess cash of a country used to invest for a profit

____ 11. Investment companies that pool money from investors with small amounts of money to invest

____ 12. A series of fixed payments from a capital investment

Review Concepts

13. List four ways that banks seek to meet their clients' international banking needs.

14. Describe the functions of the World Bank and the International Finance Corporation.

15. How does a letter of credit work?

16. What are the differences between a stock and a bond?

17. How did the Gramm-Leach-Bliley Act change banking institutions?

18. Why might firms seek to outsource products or services that they may have been previously producing or performing within their own organizations?

19. List reasons why businesses seek expert help when making capital investment decisions.

20. Give three examples of retirement planning services.

21. What is the purpose of the probate process?

22. List four advantages that a charitable remainder trust provides.

Apply What You Learned

23. How does the USA Patriot Act of 2001 attempt to stop the financing of terrorist activities?

24. How does the term *one-stop shopping* apply to banks?

25. Why are sovereign wealth funds significant?

26. Name four types of trust services.

27. Describe factors that impact foreign exchange rates.

Make Academic Connections

28. **SOCIAL STUDIES**   Laws often result from what is happening in a society. Write a two-page report on how the Glass-Steagall Act and the Gramm-Leach-Bliley Act impacted banking. Discuss how each act was a reaction to current events of the time. Did GLBA contribute to the 2008 financial crisis? Explain your answer.

29. **ECONOMICS**   Discuss the economic environment in the twenty-first century in terms of what makes it important for banks to advise their customers in the international arena.

30. **COMMUNICATION**   Interview an executive of a local bank on the subject of a specific insurance product. Get detailed information about how the product protects the consumer. Present your findings to the class in an oral report. Jot down ideas for interview questions here.

31. **MATH**   Find the current value of a Japanese yen (¥) as compared to a Chinese yuan. What is the price, in yuan, of an item valued at 70,000¥?

32. **RESEARCH**   Using the Internet, find out more about the World Bank and the International Finance Corporation. List additional functions of both institutions.

CHAPTER 11

Security, Fraud, and Ethics

kadmy/iStockphoto.com

skills that pay dividends

Strong relationships are fundamental to successful banking. Ongoing courteous, professional relationships between customers and bank representatives help maintain customer loyalty. Fair, prompt, and proactive service helps cement the relationship between businesses and banks. How do customers form their initial and ongoing impressions of a bank? What sways customers and businesses to select one bank over another? What can bankers do to put clients' minds at ease that the bank will carefully and thoughtfully handle their money?

A professional appearance of bank personnel helps influence customers' decision making. A professional-looking bank staff helps customers feel assured that their finances will be handled carefully and thoughtfully. Components of a professional appearance include personal hygiene, clothing, and demeanor.

You need to be aware of your personal hygiene every day. Your body should be clean and hair should be neat. Fingernails should be well groomed. Remember, if you and a customer are exchanging forms or if you are counting out money to give to a customer, your hands will be quite visible. Perfume or cologne should be used moderately. Teeth should be brushed and your breath should be fresh. If you have body piercings or tattoos in nontypical, visible locations, you should consider how seeing those will influence customers' opinion of both you and your bank.

The banking industry tends to be conservative. You should select clothing that is appropriate to the industry. Trendy outfits that may make you a fashion leader in social situations may not be appropriate for the workplace. Classic, conservative styles are a better long-term wardrobe investment. You can still inject your own personal or creative style with a well-coordinated scarf or tie.

Match your clothing selection to the specific requirements of your job, your customer, and your agenda for the day. For example, if you are going to your customer's worksite to do a presentation on services your bank can offer to employees, a suit is probably most appropriate. If you are participating in a golf outing with the same customer on another day, then golf attire would be appropriate.

Your demeanor toward customers should be cheerful, respectful, and helpful. In most situations, discussing professional facts pertaining to the business situation is appropriate. Personal information should be avoided. Demonstrate a knowledge of your industry and of current events that extends beyond the particular transaction you are conducting with the customer.

Develop Your Skill

Visit three workplaces in different industries. Observe the appearance of various staff members. Take notes on how the job duties of staff members affected their appearance. Reflect on how the appearance of staff members impacted your opinion of not only the employees, but of the business. Be prepared to share your observations with the class.

11.1

Robbery Prevention and Response

Learning Objectives

11.1.1 Discuss how security measures can prevent bank robbery.

11.1.2 Describe what bank employees should do during a robbery.

Key Term

• bandit barrier

Banking Scene

Cheyenne Rainwater has read about the recent increase in bank robberies in her city and is concerned. She knows that her money is protected, but she doesn't want to be present for one of these terrible events, which have resulted in harm to bystanders from time to time. What are some things she should look for that indicate her bank is trying to prevent robberies?

11.1.1 SECURITY AS PREVENTION

When asked why he robbed banks during the 1930s and 1940s, notorious bank robber Willie Sutton simply replied, "Because that's where the money is." You might think that bank robbery in today's world is merely a plot line for television and movies, but it is a reality and actually occurs all too often. Armed robbery is an inherent risk associated with financial institutions. According to the Federal Bureau of Investigation, 3,879 bank robberies—which are federal offenses—occurred in the United States during the year 2014. Every bank is a potential temptation to would-be robbers. Despite the expensive and state-of-the-art measures banks have taken to prevent robberies, make them unprofitable, and enhance the capture and conviction of the perpetrator, robberies are a persistent problem.

Physical Security

Ensuring the security of assets, employees, and customers is a major concern for financial institutions. Physically securing the bank is an important deterrent to robbery. It's easy to picture vaults and safe deposit boxes when you think of physical security at banks. Locking devices are certainly necessary, but physical security includes other considerations sometimes less obvious.

- **Building design plays a role in physical security.** Everything from resistance to attack to placement of sprinklers is a consideration in facility design. Planning the facility for technology, control of physical access to the building, location and security of records, and even the types and placement of furniture are part of an integrated security plan. The bank should be well lit with the lights positioned so that they do not interfere with processing images of perpetrators captured on security video or film. The view of tellers by other employees should be unobstructed.

- **Surveillance and alarm technology continues to evolve.** Increasingly sophisticated devices with higher and higher resolution are appearing in banks. From closed-circuit television (CCTV) systems to monitoring software for all phases of processing operations, forms of surveillance are becoming increasingly complex. Surveillance cameras should be placed so they are seen by possible robbers and positioned to ensure a full front photograph of the robber.

- **Safety devices can be used.** Bandit barriers, which are bulletproof plastic shields, can be positioned in front of each teller's station. Popup security screens, which rise in a fraction of a second out of the counter to protect the teller, may also be used. Time-delay locks that require a PIN and allow access to the safe only during specific hours can be installed.

- **Transportation security is a part of physical security.** With the necessity of safeguarding cash and checks in transit, security measures involve screening of employees involved in transportation. Companies providing this service are liable for the actions of employees.

Best Practices Recommendations

It is wise for a bank to adopt a list of "best practices" to help deter bank robberies and to aid in the apprehension of bank bandits. Some measures prevent robberies, some protect staff and customers during a robbery, some help apprehend the criminal, and some accomplish a combination of these objectives. Training is a critical factor in carrying out the best practices.

Training is the core of preventing robbery. For this reason, banks invest a lot of resources in teaching their employees how to recognize and what to do in an emergency. These procedures both lessen the risk of harm for staff and customers and minimize financial loss to the institution.

Most banks are required by law to install surveillance cameras and alarms, and properly trained staff can aid in ensuring that security devices work accurately and are used during a robbery. Security guards, customer service representatives, or others should engage customers as they enter the bank to present a plain view of the security presence and make potential robbers aware that they could be recognized later.

Tech Talk

Using Technology to Prevent Robberies

In the early 1990s in Los Angeles, as the number of bank robberies, particularly violent ones, soared, FBI and financial institutions worked together to address this problem. Subsequently, banks deemed "robbery-prone" constructed bullet-resistant "bandit barriers" or access control units (ACUs). The clear, bullet-resistant, Plexiglas partitions completely enclose the teller and adjacent cash storage areas from the top of the counter to the ceiling or from the floor to the ceiling at the entrance. The ACUs consist of an electronically controlled, double-door entrance and adjacent exit. Customers access the inside of the bank, one at a time, by entering through the entry's outer door. When the outer door closes, a device conducts an automatic magnetometer-type search for weapons. If the search proves negative, the inner door automatically unlocks, allowing entry into the facility. If the search yields a positive result, indicating a possible weapon, the bullet-resistant second door remains locked, and the person must retreat from the entry.

Think Critically   How would you feel about doing your banking in a bank that uses "bandit barriers" and ACUs?

What activity is critical to carrying out best practices to prevent robbery?

11.1.2 ROBBERY PREPARATION • • • • • • • • • • • • • • • • • •

Just as tellers are usually the first to do business with customers, they also are the first line of defense during a robbery. It is critical that teller training include what to do and *not* to do during a holdup. Training should emphasize that physical resistance is dangerous, not helpful. Tellers should do nothing that would risk their safety or that of others on the premises. Training should also include these instructions:

- Remain calm. Knowing what to do through training eliminates the need to make decisions during the crisis.

- Obey the robber's instructions. Employees should be assured that this is bank policy.

- Trigger foot-pedal or bill-trap alarms and security cameras as soon as possible both to protect the safety of customers and employees and to help apprehend the robber. A *bill trap* is a device that sets off a security system when a bill or switch is pulled.

- Use decoy or marked money or specially prepared packs that contain an exploding device with a dye to mark the cash. Bills containing GPS tracking systems have proven to be very effective.

- Call 911 as soon as reasonably possible to provide a detailed description of the perpetrator and the direction he or she seemed to be heading after fleeing the bank.

- Keep anything, such as a demand note, when possible for fingerprint identification, and minimize contamination of evidence and the crime scene. Countertops are ideal places to look for robbers' fingerprints.

- Note the robber's physical characteristics, particularly any outstanding feature. Also, if possible, note any characteristics of the get-away vehicle, such as the make, model, color, and license plate number.

- Write a description of the robber as soon as possible because memory fades quickly, especially in crisis situations. A robbery description form, such as the one below, can be used to help authorities gather information.

ROBBERY DESCRIPTION FORM (Sample)

Sex _____ Age _____ Race _____ Height _____ Weight _____

Build _____ Complexion (light, dark, etc.) _____

Hair _____ Eye Color _____ Facial Hair Beard _____ Mustache _____ Goatee, etc. ____

CLOTHING

Hat _____

Shirt _____

Coat or jacket (length and color) _____

Trousers (color and style) _____

Tie _____

Shoes _____

Other _____

MISCELLANEOUS

Weapon _____ Type _____

Speech _____

_____

Mannerisms _____

_____

Physical characteristics _____

(limp, deformities, etc.) _____

It is not uncommon for tellers to become paralyzed with fear during a robbery, leading them to forget procedures for safety and suspect identification. To avoid this situation, some banks provide training at teller schools several times per month and at high-risk banks at least annually. Individual branches reinforce the lessons through practice drills and at staff meetings. By doing so, the tellers are more likely to remember how to react during a robbery without endangering customers or employees.

Other employees at the bank play a critically important role by being sensitive to a tellers' body language and demeanor. For example, a change in a teller's voice tone or pitch could indicate that a holdup is in process. A normally relaxed teller who tenses up or a chatty one who becomes quiet could indicate trouble. In one Seattle bank, for instance, a coworker who noticed that sounds from a normally lively teller had become stiff realized that a robbery was occurring and triggered an alarm.

Types of Bank Robberies

Although bank employees can never be fully prepared for a bank robbery, it may be helpful for them to know the different types of robberies that commonly occur to help plan the appropriate actions to take.

Morning glory robberies take place prior to opening the bank for the day. The morning glory robber could break in and wait for employees to arrive, seize the employees outside the bank as they arrive, use a ruse tactic to attempt to enter the bank, or even seize an employee en route to or from work or at the employee's home. In a *takeover* bank robbery, two or more robbers carry weapons and invade the bank. This is the least common type of robbery. The most common type of bank robbery committed involves *note passing*. In this case, the robber enters the bank and passes a note to a bank employee. The note demands money. The robber may issue a verbal demand instead of passing a note. Weapons may be displayed in all types of robberies as a means of intimidating and coercing bank employees.

The FDIC as a Safety Net

When robberies occur, it is important that consumers understand that the Federal Deposit Insurance Corporation (FDIC) insures deposits in banks and thrift institutions for up to $250,000 per depositor in the event of failure. Although it is highly unlikely that a robbery could result in bank failure, FDIC provides safety for individual accounts.

✔checkpoint

Why should bank employees not resist a robbery attempt?

assessment 11.1

Think Critically

1. How does the building facility design contribute to the physical security of a bank?

2. Closed-circuit television systems and security cameras are part of the technology that can identify suspects in bank robbery cases. What role do they play in preventing robberies?

3. Why are robbery training and preparation critical for bank employees, especially tellers?

4. In your opinion, what is the best deterrent in preventing robberies?

Make Academic Connections

5. **COMMUNICATION**   Visit a local bank to find out what types of security measures it uses and employee training/preparation for robberies it offers. Present your findings in an oral report.

6. **RESEARCH**   Internet banking presents new security challenges for financial institutions. Use the Internet to investigate what the most important issues are and how they are being resolved. Prepare a two-page report summarizing your findings.

7. **HISTORY**   Study the bank robberies during the Great Depression. Why did the Secret Service become involved instead of leaving the crimes to local law enforcement?

11.2

Ethics in Banking

Learning Objectives

11.2.1 Explain how ethics applies to financial institutions.

11.2.2 Identify ethical dilemmas that occur in banking.

Banking Scene

Recent scandals related to unethical and illegal activities have rocked the corporate world. Several banks have been involved. What can Cheyenne Rainwater do to determine whether her bank seeks to emphasize ethical behavior among its employees?

Key Terms

- ethics
- code of ethics
- conflict of interest

11.2.1 ETHICAL BEHAVIOR • • • • • • • • • • • • • • • • • •

Ethics refers to beliefs that distinguish right from wrong. An *ethical dilemma* involves a situation that is problematic and makes a person question what is the "right" or "wrong" thing to do. Ethical dilemmas make individuals think about their obligations, duties, or responsibilities. These dilemmas can be either easy to resolve or highly complex and difficult to resolve. Most people will agree, for example, that it is unacceptable to pretend that someone else's work is your own. However, complex ethical dilemmas involve less clear-cut alternatives. An example might involve uncovering a colleague's error. To whom are you obligated—your colleague or your employer?

A **code of ethics** is a statement adopted by an organization's management and board of directors to guide employees in taking appropriate actions in situations that could reflect negatively on the organization. A code can help employees answer questions about a bank's policy on matters such as receiving gifts from customers and taking outside jobs. Most banks require employees to read the code regularly and certify that they are in compliance with its provisions. KPMG, the international accounting and consulting firm, found in its 2013 Integrity Survey that the ethical behavior of top executives affects employees' perception of their companies. They found that the companies with the highest reported ethical behavior believed their executives were ethical. Companies that provided training on ethics and business practices also saw the highest scores.

Important Elements in a Code of Ethics

Most banking codes of ethics include the following.

- **Confidentiality** Banking business is confidential, so only authorized individuals can receive information.

- **Dishonesty and fraudulent behavior**   Such behavior will not be tolerated.

- **Representation of the institution**   The behavior of employees must positively reflect the bank's integrity.

- **Gifts**   Accepting gifts or money given to influence employees' performance of duties is strictly prohibited.

- **Financial management**   All employees should practice wise financial management. Customers won't trust a bank to take care of their funds if its employees can't take care of their own money.

- **Conflict of interest**   Employees must act with honesty and integrity, avoiding any personal activity, investment, or association that could appear to interfere with good judgment concerning the bank's best interests. A conflict of interest occurs when two interests are at cross-purposes. Employees are strictly prohibited from exploiting their position or relationship with the bank for personal gain.

- **Compliance with laws and regulations**   Employees are required to provide full, fair, accurate, timely, and understandable disclosure in reports and documents that the bank files. Employees must perform their duties in accordance with all applicable laws and regulations.

- **Responsibility for violations**   The conduct of employees can reinforce an ethical atmosphere and positively influence the conduct of their colleagues. Employees who are unable to stop suspected misconduct or discover it after it has occurred are required to report it immediately to the appropriate management.

When a bank develops its code of ethics, it must decide what it wants to stand for and then put appropriate information in writing (often in the company handbook or on the company website), discuss it with its employees, and then enforce it. This policy reflects the values that the bank has determined to be important.

What is the purpose of a code of ethics?

11.2.2 Ethical Issues in Banking and the Corporate World

At the beginning of the twenty-first century, a wave of corporate scandals broke out in the United States. A number of leading companies admitted that they had violated numerous regulations, including misstating their accounts, in order to project a positive impression of their status. In public companies, this type of "creative" accounting is considered to be fraud. These companies' actions were both illegal and unethical.

- PNC Financial Services Group Inc. reached a resolution with the Securities and Exchange Commission regarding charges that in violation of generally accepted accounting principles, PNC transferred from its financial statements approximately $762 million of volatile, troubled, or underperforming loans and venture capital assets. In addition, PNC issued a materially false and misleading press release that, among other things, overstated its 2001 full-year earnings per share by 52 percent.

- U.S. Bancorp settled a lawsuit brought by the Attorney General of Minnesota over the bank's sales of customer data to MemberWorks, a telemarketing company, for $4 million and a 22 percent commission on sales to those customers. The bank promised to end third-party sharing of information for marketing of nonfinancial products and provide customers the opportunity to opt out of affiliate-sharing of information for the purposes of selling additional company services.

- Citigroup Inc. agreed to pay $215 million to resolve charges that its Associates First Capital Corporation and Associates Corporation of North America had engaged in systematic and widespread deceptive practices designed to encourage borrowers to unknowingly purchase optional credit insurance products. It also participated in abusive lending practices.

rkankaro/iStockphoto.com

- Enron Corporation, the energy trading and communications company based in Houston, Texas, used fraudulent accounting techniques that, when uncovered, caused it to become one of the largest corporate failures in history. It has become the symbol of institutionalized and well-planned corporate fraud.

- Merrill Lynch & Co., Inc., an investment banking company recognized as one of the world's leading financial management and advisory companies, reached an agreement in 2003 with New York State's attorney general on charges the firm's investment advice was influenced by conflicts of interest.

- Arthur Andersen, founded in 1913 and one of the Big Five U.S. accounting firms, was forced to cease business after accounting scandals involving Waste Management, Sunbeam, and Enron. Revelations of fraud in presenting Enron's financial statements and its felony conviction for obstructing justice for shredding tons of Enron documents led to the Arthur Andersen's demise.

Sarbanes-Oxley Act of 2002

On July 30, 2002, the *Public Company Accounting Reform and Investor Protection Act of 2002* (the *Sarbanes-Oxley Act of 2002*), also called SOX, was signed into law. It established a new Public Company Accounting Oversight Board with the power to set rules, investigate suspected wrongdoing, punish violators, and conduct regular inspections of accounting firms. The act gives broad new protections to corporate whistle blowers—employees who publicly report illegal activities occurring inside their company—and makes security fraud a criminal offense. A chief executive officer or chief financial officer who certifies false financial reports could get 20 years in prison and be fined $5 million. Shredding documents could result in a 20-year sentence. This act also places restrictions on loans by corporations to their executives. These restrictions strive to eliminate the interest-free loans that became a popular form of compensation for executives.

Ethics in Action

Warren Buffett, chairman of the board and chief executive officer of Berkshire Hathaway Inc., is one of the richest men in the world. In a letter to Berkshire Hathaway shareholders, Mr. Buffett stated that "a significant and growing number of otherwise high-grade managers … have come to view that it's okay to manipulate earnings to satisfy what they believe are Wall Street's desires. Indeed, many CEOs think this kind of manipulation is not only okay, but actually their duty. They also argue that in using accounting shenanigans to get the figures they want, they are doing only what everybody else does … Berkshire has kept entirely clear of these practices: If we are to disappoint you, we would rather it be with our earnings than with our accounting."

Think Critically

What ethical responsibility do managers who manipulate earnings on financial statements owe to the company, the business community, and the public in general?

Everyday Ethical Dilemmas in Banking

The Sarbanes-Oxley Act addresses the behavior of corporate executives, but all bank employees, including tellers, accountants, loan officers, marketing directors, and customer service representatives, also face ethical dilemmas. Consider the ethical dilemmas in the following scenarios and suggest an appropriate ethical action to take in each case.

- Luisa Sillas realizes that her immediate supervisor, who orders the bank's supplies, is taking kickbacks to order from several suppliers.

- Jerry Cappocci is a teller who processed the deposit of a rather confused customer for $1,600. The customer actually gave him $1,600 in checks and $75 in cash without realizing it.

- Several years ago while working with a client, Tanisha Higgins learned confidential information about the company's research. The company is now planning to go public, and the information she learned indicates that purchase of its stock will be an excellent investment.

- Susan Issacs works for the marketing director of a large bank. She is sure that the facts of a new advertising campaign for bank loans are misleading but was told by her supervisor that things were "okay."

Ethical Behavior as the Final Decision

Because banking is essential to the efficient functioning of the financial system, all decision making should be based on ethical principles. Banks must provide safe and convenient places for customers to take care of their financial needs. In providing essential services, bankers must be dedicated to giving advice based on the particular customer's financial position and situation in general, including loan and investment choices, willingness to take risks, and ability to assess the impact of the advice provided. Bankers should ensure that sufficient information about the bank's products and services is available to customers.

Describe the powers of the Public Company Accounting Oversight Board.

assessment 11.2

Think Critically

1. Why should corporate whistle blowers receive special protection?

2. Why is confidentiality a critical element in banking?

3. Discuss the ethical implications of the ability of a bank to determine the interest rate for a loan.

4. Why did Congress and the President see the need for the Sarbanes-Oxley Act?

Make Academic Connections

5. **TECHNOLOGY**   Use the Internet to find out about ethical issues regarding online banking that are of concern to bank regulators. Present your findings to the class orally.

6. **RESEARCH**   Locate the websites of three commercial banks that have a code of ethics. List any elements not covered in this chapter.

7. **CRITICAL THINKING**   As a supervisor, you must decide what to do about a loyal, honest employee who tries really hard but can't perform up to par, forcing coworkers to pick up the slack. You know that the employee is a single parent whose child has serious medical problems. What do you do?

11.3

Fraud and Scams

Learning Objectives

11.3.1 Identify types of fraud that are committed against banks.

11.3.2 Discuss mortgage-based scams.

Key Terms

- fraud
- check kiting
- forgery
- check counterfeiting
- scam
- house flipping
- straw buyer

Banking Scene

Cheyenne Rainwater has learned from the news media that several people in her city have been victims of checking account scams. What can she do to protect herself from these crimes?

11.3.1 FRAUD RELATED TO BANKING

Although robbery is a concern for banks, far larger dollar values are lost through computer crime, vandalism, and various forms of fraud. **Fraud** is a deception deliberately practiced to secure unfair or unlawful gain. During 2014, the total amount of online fraud was estimated to be $32 billion, a 38% increase over 2013. The Federal Bureau of Investigation's Internet Crime Complaint Center (IC3) received 269,422 complaints in 2014, worth about $800 million in losses. The center has received 3,175,611 complaints since its establishment in May 2000. Only about 15% of fraud victims report their losses to law enforcement, so the actual number of victims and money involved is much higher. The sheer volume of check and credit card transactions presents many opportunities for the unscrupulous. Various forms of fraud, some simple and some sophisticated, cost banks and consumers billions of dollars a year. The banking industry must be continually vigilant in fighting and preventing these crimes.

Fraud prevention occupies more resources of the banking industry than any other activity except routine processing. Bank administration is an important part of fraud prevention. Adhering to established procedures, including technology security rules, insisting on careful record keeping, conducting audits, and investigating suspicious activities of employees or customers are all part of an overall plan for security and fraud prevention.

Employee training may be the best return on investment for fraud prevention. Detailed checklists for ways to identify questionable or counterfeit checks, identification verification procedures, and frequent updates on new types of counterfeit and fraud schemes all help combat fraud on the front lines. Tellers, operations personnel, technicians, investment counselors, loan officers, and other personnel require training.

Consumer education is an effort that banks see as increasingly worthwhile. Most frauds are crimes of opportunity. If consumers protect their checks, credit cards, identities, and account information more carefully, committing fraud becomes a more difficult task.

Counterfeit Currency

Bureau of Engraving & Printing

Counterfeiting money has been a crime throughout the history of the United States. It was a serious problem during the nineteenth century when banks issued their own currency. At the time of the Civil War, it was estimated that one-third of all currency in circulation was counterfeit. The adoption of a national currency in 1863 did not, as expected, solve the counterfeiting problem. On July 5, 1865, the United States created the Secret Service to suppress counterfeiting. In 2006, an estimated $62 million dollars was lost in the U.S. due to counterfeiting. Nearly 4,000 people were arrested for crimes relating to the counterfeiting.

To address the continuing problem, the Federal Reserve began issuing redesigned bills. To date, the $5, $10, $20, and $50 bills have been redesigned. The most noticeable difference in the new $20 notes is the use of subtle green, peach, and blue colors featured in the background. The new $20 note design retains three important security features:

- The watermark, the faint image similar to the large portrait, which is part of the paper itself and is visible from both sides when the bill is held up to the light.

- The vertical strip of plastic making up the security thread—also visible from both sides when held up to the light—is embedded in the paper. "USA TWENTY" and a small flag are visible on the thread.

- The color-shifting ink—the numeral "20" in the lower-right corner on the face of the note—changes from copper to green when the note is tilted. The color shift is more dramatic and easier to see on the new notes.

Check Fraud

Statistics indicate the seriousness of check fraud. In a recent eight-month period, postal inspectors seized more than $2 billion of fake checks. The advancement of computer technology has made it increasingly easy for criminals, either individually or in organized groups, to manipulate checks to deceive unknowing victims. Desktop publishing and copying to create or duplicate an actual financial document are responsible for a significant amount of check fraud today. In most cases, these crimes begin with the theft of a financial document, such as a blank check, taken from your home or vehicle during a burglary, a canceled or old check you threw away, or a check you just put in your mailbox. Two of the most common schemes directed at banks are check kiting and money laundering. Other check fraud includes forgery, counterfeiting or alteration, and paperhanging.

Check Kiting The fraud of check kiting requires opening accounts at two or more institutions and using the "float time" of available funds to create fraudulent balances. A person draws a check for an amount that exceeds

interesting *facts*

The National Consumers League is America's oldest non-profit consumer group. In 1996 it launched the Internet Fraud Watch program (now called Fraud.org) to prevent online and Internet fraud by helping people recognize possible scams. Common signs of fraud on the Internet are incredibly low prices, extravagant promises of profits, guarantees of credit regardless of bad credit histories, or prizes that require payment to obtain. ■

the account balance at one bank and then deposits it at another bank. Before that deposit can be processed, the individual draws a check on the second bank to deposit at the first bank. Although neither bank account has enough money to cover the checks, the person may withdraw more than the collected balance from the first account.

Check kiting has become easier in recent years due to the Expedited Funds Availability Act of 1987, which requires banks to make funds available sooner. The Check 21 Act passed in October 2003 has probably helped counteract this problem. Instead of requiring physical possession of a paper check by the issuing bank before funds are transferred, Check 21 allows the receiving bank to treat an electronic image of the check, called an Image Replacement Document (IRD), the same as the check itself. This significantly reduces the check-clearing process time and has the power to help eliminate check kiting.

Money Laundering The scheme of money laundering received its name because criminals use it to make money "clean." Criminals use the process to conceal illicitly acquired funds by converting them into seemingly legitimate income. Originally used to refer to the proceeds of organized crime, the term is now often associated with financial activities of drug dealers who seek to launder the large amounts of cash they generate from the sale of narcotics. Money laundering does not cause financial institutions a loss, but it makes large sums of money difficult to trace.

To help combat money laundering, Congress has passed several laws. The Bank Secrecy Act requires financial institutions to report suspicious transactions that may be a possible violation of law. This act creates a paper trail for currency so that money cannot be deposited, invested, or exchanged in a way that conceals its illegal source. This discourages the use of banks to hide transfers or deposits of money derived from criminal activity.

Banking Math *Connection*

Many insurance policies currently will protect for losses caused by the acceptance in good faith of counterfeit money. Most pay from $500 to $1,000 for a loss. During a garage sale, a family accepted $500 in counterfeit bills for a purchase. The family's insurance policy covered losses from counterfeit money up to $700 with a $200 deductible. Did the family experience a loss from this transaction? If so, how much?

Solution
Because the loss is less than the $700 ceiling, the formula for determining loss is

Amount of loss − Deductible = Amount covered
$$\$500 - \$200 = \$300$$

The insurance covers $300, so the actual out-of-pocket loss is $200 ($500 loss − $300).

The Patriot Act of 2001 prohibits financial relationships with banks that have no physical presence in their host county. Under this act, banks must use due diligence to determine the identity and source of transactions. The Patriot Act seeks to curtail the financing of terrorism with laundered money.

Forgery Check forgery, or counterfeiting a check or other document with the intent to defraud, is difficult to detect. Criminals steal a check, endorse it with a forged or unauthorized signature, and, using fake identification, present it for payment at a retail location or a bank.

Counterfeiting and Alteration Check counterfeiting can mean either entirely creating a check with desktop publishing equipment (personal computer, scanner, cutting-edge software, and top-grade laser printer) or simply duplicating a check with advanced color photocopiers. *Alteration* removes or modifies handwriting and information on the check with chemicals and solvents such as acetone, brake fluid, and household bleach.

Paperhanging The act of purposefully writing checks on closed accounts or reordering checks for closed accounts is *paperhanging*. It is also known as *closed account fraud*.

Signs of Counterfeit Checks

Several signs can indicate a bad check. Telling signs are lack of perforations, a low number (such as 101 through 400 on personal checks or 1001–1500 on business checks), or no address for the customer or the bank. Stains or discoloration perhaps caused by erasures or alterations are other signs. Be alert to the Magnetic Ink Character Recognition coding number printed along the bottom: if it is shiny, if it does not match the check number, or if it is missing, the check may be fraudulent.

The first and probably most important line of defense against counterfeit checks is teller training. Knowing how to verify a check and what to look for on a suspicious one is the focus of training efforts.

Consumer Tips for Preventing Check Fraud

Checks are the most common negotiable instrument and should be treated as carefully as cash. Here are some steps to prevent check fraud.

- Use checks that have built-in security features. Many of these checks have a padlock icon on them to indicate the presence of enhanced security features such as watermarking and microprinting.

- Don't have your Social Security number imprinted on checks. Your SSN is enough for a criminal to get a credit card, bank account, or fake loan.

- Don't endorse a check until just before you cash or deposit it. It is better, in fact, if you sign the check in a teller's presence.

- Don't leave spaces on checks. Draw horizontal lines to fill any blank spaces, and write words close together, especially on amount lines.

- Reconcile your account regularly. Call your bank immediately if you notice any suspicious transactions on your statement.

"communicate"

Conduct a poll of at least 10 people in your community about checking account scams. Have they experienced any attempts to obtain their checking account information that they thought were suspicious? If so, what were the circumstances?

- Shred statements, canceled checks, ATM slips, and credit card receipts, rather than just throwing them in the trash.

- Be careful on the phone, in person, and on the Web. Never give out account information or numbers to anyone you don't know or of whom you are not certain. Don't be afraid to contact authorities.

How has computer technology affected counterfeit checking scams?

11.3.2 MORTGAGE-BASED SCAMS

Scam is a slang term for something that is fraudulent or a swindle. When a scam is perpetrated, trickery is used to intentionally dupe an individual or business into a transaction for the financial benefit of the thief. Available scams are limited only by the creativity of the thief.

Illegal Mortgage Practices

The recent mortgage and financial crisis put a lot of pressure on people throughout the economy. Businesses affected ranged from those who supply the raw materials to build a house through those that provide the décor for a finished home. Increased pressure to compensate for lost income due to tightened credit and reduced home sales has made many participants in the housing industry vulnerable to illegal schemes.

According to FBI research in 2010, loan origination schemes were the most prevalent mortgage schemes. The graph provides a detailed overview of the incidents of fraud that occurred. Some of their schemes are summarized below.

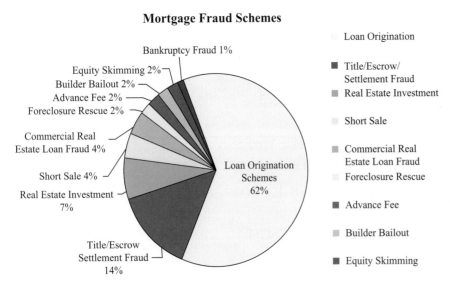

Mortgage Fraud Schemes

Source: Federal Bureau of Investigation 2010 Mortgage Fraud Report

Illegal House Flipping Buying a house for below market value and selling it at or above market value is a practice called house flipping. The buyer often sells the house for more than the purchase price either because renovations were made to the home or because a distressed seller originally sold the house at below market value. This process becomes illegal if a fraudulent appraisal, which artificially inflates the value of the house, is used to secure a loan by a second buyer. In some schemes, a straw buyer is used to help with the scheme.

One World

A slick online banking scam fooled New Zealanders into losing large sums of money. A website with a professional look claiming to be business partners with all leading New Zealand banks was customized for New Zealand readers. The scam worked by convincing people to accept deposits into their bank accounts and then to send the funds minus a transaction fee to a third party. The initial deposit is then canceled. For example, a scam "associate" might deposit $14,000 into the account of a New Zealander, who then sends $13,500 on to someone else as soon as possible on the same day. The scammer then quickly cancels the $14,000 deposit. The result: The unlucky New Zealander has lost his or her own $13,500 sent to its perpetrators.

Think Critically What can be done to protect people from scams such as this?

A straw buyer is someone who agrees to use his or her personal information to buy the home at a falsely inflated price. The straw buyer agrees to state that they intend to live in the home even though their actual intent is to flip the home. Sometimes a straw buyer knows that they are participating in a fraudulent scheme and sometimes they themselves are victims.

Profits from illegal house flipping can be obtained by intentionally defaulting on a loan. For example, Buyer A purchases a house for $30,000 and then has it fraudulently appraised for $100,000. Buyer A solicits the help of Buyer B, a straw buyer, to purchase the house for $100,000 by obtaining a bank loan for $80,000. Buyer B does not plan to move in to the house and plans to default on the loan. An illegal profit of $50,000 is available to be shared between Buyer A and Buyer B. (An $80,000 loan minus the initial $30,000 investment in the house.) The bank is then left with a loss of $50,000. This loss arises because the bank has an $80,000 mortgage on a house that has a true value of $30,000. According to the FBI, if the loan was FHA-insured, then the loss is absorbed by the government.

Other Mortgage-Based Schemes A variety of other schemes exploit the same concepts of illegally inflating the value of a house, obtaining financing to pay for the inflated value, and defaulting on loans for personal gain. Names of some of these schemes include *Builder-Bailout Schemes*, *Seller Assistance Scams*, *Short-Sale Schemes*, and *Foreclosure Rescue Scams*.

✔checkpoint

What is the necessary step in the process to ensure that an illegal house-flipping scheme achieves a profit?

assessment 11.3

Think Critically

1. How have $20 bills been redesigned to prevent counterfeit scams?

_____

_____

2. Discuss how a person could commit check fraud on your account. When are you likely to first be aware that you've been a victim of the scam?

_____

_____

3. How does mortgage fraud generate a profit for participants?

_____

_____

4. Why have mortgage-based schemes been rising over the last few years?

_____

_____

_____

_____

Make Academic Connections

5. **COMMUNICATION**   Talk to a local bank official about check fraud. Does the bank use any technological devices to identify counterfeit checks? If so, explain them in a one-page report.

6. **MATH**   If you accept counterfeit bills in payment for an antique desk you sell at a flea market for $750, what will be your actual loss if your insurance has a $900 limit and a $225 deductible?

_____

_____

_____

Identity Theft

Banking Scene

Cheyenne was puzzled and embarrassed. While pumping gas, the attendant had said, over the loud speaker where everyone could hear, that her credit card had been declined. As she paid her bill in full and on time each month, she did not know how this could have happened. When she got home, Cheyenne called her bank. She was informed that her credit card had been closed due to suspicious activity that included charges in two separate states within hours of each other. Cheyenne then regretted not checking her voice mails promptly, as the bank had left her a message to call. Apparently, someone had obtained access to Cheyenne's account information and illegally used her identity. What should she do? How could she have prevented this?

Learning Objectives

11.4.1 Explain the concept of identity theft.

11.4.2 Describe various identity theft methods.

11.4.3 Discuss identity theft prevention.

Key Terms

- spam
- phishing
- war driving
- sniffer program
- fraud alert
- credit freeze

11.4.1 AN OVERVIEW OF IDENTITY THEFT

Identity theft occurs when someone intentionally obtains your personal information to use that information for personal gain. By illegally identifying themselves as you, they engage in financial transactions that enable them to receive goods and services that are charged to your accounts. According to a Bureau of Justice Statistics (BJS) report, an estimated 7.6 million Americans were victims of identity theft in 2014. This is roughly 7% of U.S. residents age 16 or older. About 86% of the cases involved the misuse of the victims' credit card or bank account. In about 4% of the cases, the victims' personal information was stolen and used to open a new account or to perform other fraudulent activity.

Categories of Identity Theft

According to the BJS report, there are five categories of identity theft: existing credit card, existing bank account, existing other account, new account, and personal information theft. Theft from existing credit cards or bank accounts involved 16.4 million victims age 16 or older. Of these, 8.5 million victims had information from credit card accounts stolen and about 8.1 had information from bank accounts stolen. The pie chart on page 356 shows the totals for all types of theft. An additional 1.5 million people were victims of other types of existing account theft, including misuse or attempted misuse of an existing telephone, online, or insurance account. Of the 16.4 million

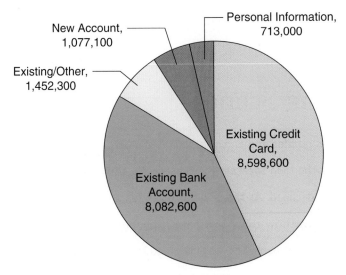

Victims of Identify Theft by Type of Theft, 2014

Personal Information, 713,000

New Account, 1,077,100

Existing/Other, 1,452,300

Existing Credit Card, 8,598,600

Existing Bank Account, 8,082,600

Source: Bureau of Labor Statistics, "Victims of Identity Theft, 2014."

victims, 45% discovered the identity theft after being contacted by a financial institution. About 18% noticed fraudulent charges on the account.

Costs of Identity Theft

When identity theft occurs, victims experience financial costs, emotional costs, and loss of productive time. They have to use their time to resolve the many issues that arise from the identity theft.

According to the BJS report, about 14% of identity theft victims experienced out-of-pocket losses of $1 or more. Of these victims, about half suffered losses of less than $100. Overall, in 2014, victims who experienced a direct and indirect financial loss of at least $1 lost an average of $1,343, with a median loss of $300.

Some victims also incur expenses in trying to straighten out their stolen accounts. Attorney fees, loss of salary, and paying for any charges attributed to the thief are among the potential costs. There are many laws designed to protect consumers from out-of-pocket losses that result from identity theft.

The feelings of identity theft victims range from vulnerability to violation of personal privacy to anger to sadness. The emotional stress caused by identity theft adds to the overall fatigue victims experience when dealing with what can be a long process to thoroughly resolve all issues stemming from the theft.

 **checkpoint**

What are the five categories of identity theft?

11.4.2 METHODS FOR STEALING IDENTITIES ● ● ● ● ● ● ● ● ●

Identity thieves use a variety of methods for stealing identities. As technology evolves and as customer payment systems change, new methods of obtaining personal information arise. Some theft methods are manual and other methods are electronic.

Manual Ways to Commit Identity Theft

Identity thieves can be fairly creative. They have found ways to steal personal information through telephone scams, by using information from employment records, through stealing mail in residential mailboxes, by going through the trash, and through observation. Once these methods are used to construct a false identity, the thief either steals the individual's funds or obtains credit in the name of the victim.

Telephone Scams   Many scams are committed using the telephone. The scam may begin with a postcard advertising easy credit approval or low credit card interest rates. When consumers call these phone numbers, someone asks for their checking account number, supposedly as part of a "verification process." Other scams involve con artists that call and claim to be from the person's bank, saying they need to verify certain information about the checking account for various reasons. Another common scam is to call people to tell them that they have won a prize. After a few minutes of pleasant chat, the thief requires the person to read the numbers off the bottom of a check to "confirm" that he or she "qualifies" for the prize. With checking account information, the con artist can issue a bank draft on the person's checking account.

Mail Theft   Some identity thieves steal mail from residential mailboxes. In 2015, 154.2 billion pieces of mail were processed and delivered. Personal information, including credit card numbers and bank account numbers, can be obtained this way. Offers addressed to the resident for new credit or new loans can also be stolen. Once the thief obtains these documents, the information can be used to illegally establish accounts, apply for a loan, or access funds in existing accounts.

The U.S. Postal Inspection Service works hard to prevent mail theft. According to their website, in a recent year:

- Forensic scientists examined more than 75,000 documents, fingerprints, controlled substances, audio, video, digital media, and other items of physical evidence, resulting in the identification of 778 criminal subjects.

- Forensic analysts responded to 130 locations to provide crime scene and search site assistance for inspectors' investigations. Two incidents involved violent crimes against postal employees, which required the mobilization of a team from the National Forensic Laboratory to process remote crime scenes within 15 hours of notification.

interesting *facts*

The Identity Theft Enforcement and Restitution Act of 2007 was developed in response to increased occurrences of identity theft and increased losses due to identity theft. The Act increased the ways in which identity theft could be prosecuted and ensured that victims are compensated by making the thieves pay restitution. ■

The Federal Trade Commission (FTC) is dedicated to helping individuals and businesses avoid becoming victims of identity theft. Go to the Federal Trade Commission website. Type "warning signs of identity theft" into the search box. What are some clues that someone has stolen your information? What steps can you take to protect yourself from identity theft?

- Forensic computer analysts recovered more than 690,000 pieces of data from mobile devices.

Trash Retrieval   Dumpster diving occurs when a thief goes through the trash of a business or individual with the specific intent of finding either personal identifying information or account information to construct a false identity.

Observation   In this day and age, it's hard to know who is watching you. Discrete image-taking devices, ranging from cell phone cameras to pocket-sized video recorders with micro button cameras, can record you discretely. Thieves can record an image of a credit card left exposed on a restaurant table or can photograph a customer entering a PIN in a retail store.

Electronic Ways to Commit Identity Theft

Just as the Internet has streamlined financial transactions, it has also streamlined identity theft. The Internet allows individuals or companies to communicate with tens of thousands of people without spending much time, effort, or money. The Securities and Exchange Commission says that spam, or junk e-mail, allows "the unscrupulous to target more potential investors than cold calling or mass mailing." Spammers can use a bulk e-mail program to send personalized messages to thousands of Internet users at a time. In addition, anyone can also reach a large audience by posting a message on an online bulletin board. Fraudsters use spam to find investors for bogus investment schemes. Electronic methods for stealing identities abound.

Phishing   Common attacks on banks through the Internet include phishing, which is the act of sending a user an e-mail falsely claiming to be a legitimate enterprise in an attempt to solicit private information. The e-mail directs the users to visit a website onto which they are to update personal information, such as passwords and credit card, Social Security, and bank account numbers. The scammer commits identity theft using this information.

Hacking   Computer hackers that gain access to records or systems pose another threat to consumers and banks. Banks should use tools such as anti-virus software and *autobots*, programs that constantly monitor all transactions looking for abnormalities. *Firewalls*, programs that monitor and limit incoming and outgoing transmissions, have become increasingly important as banks allow access to records for online banking via the Internet. Banks must safeguard the technology that makes doing business possible.

Fraudulent HELOC Accounts   A HELOC loan enables borrowers to borrow against a home equity line of credit. Withdrawals against the credit can be made by check or credit card. An identity thief can open an online

HELOC account using a false identity and then methodically withdraw funds from the account.

Fake Websites   There are multiple ways to extract personal information from fraudulent websites. One method is to develop a website that looks like an authentic business and prompt people to pay for a product or service from that website. When the victim enters identifying credit information, the thieves can use that information for their own purposes.

Another method exploits design weaknesses in the Domain Name System (D.N.S.). In the early 1980s, the D.N.S. was developed to provide Internet addresses. The system was not initially intended to safeguard transactions, such as credit transactions, that required specific identity verification. Internet-savvy thieves can exploit the D.N.S. to redirect website visitors to nonlegititmate locations where their personal account information can be collected.

Personnel Data Theft   In the age of laptops and flash drives, it is fairly easy for confidential employee information to be lost or stolen. In recent years, electronic versions of personnel data have been stolen from a diverse array of organizations including the United States Veteran Affairs, Equifax, the District of Columbia, and Google. In many instances, an employer will offer employees a one-year free subscription to an identity-theft monitoring service after a data theft occurs.

Looking for Opportunities   Some thieves seek to abuse Wi-Fi systems used by stores to transmit customer credit information. War driving refers to the criminal practice of driving around to find retailers with weaknesses in their Internet security systems. Once a weakness has been found, sniffer programs, which are electronic programs that capture account numbers and PINs, can be installed.

One particularly effective example of this was widely reported late 2013 and early 2014. In this case, an international ring of thieves exploited weaknesses in the Internet security of major retailers Target and Home Depot. Almost 1 billion debit and credit card numbers were stolen. Other corporations also struggled with security breaches, including Dairy Queen, Sally Beauty Supply, UPS, and Michaels, among others.

✔checkpoint

List six ways to steal identity information electronically.

11.43 IDENTITY THEFT PREVENTION

There are a number of ways to proactively protect your personal information to try to avoid being an identity theft victim.

Common Sense Precautions

Keep your radar up at all times regarding any suspicious activities or inquiries. If someone unfamiliar is walking around your neighborhood and looking into mailboxes, keep an eye on them. If you think they are stealing mail, contact law enforcement authorities. Never provide account access codes, Social Security numbers, or other personal identifying information over the phone or online unless you are absolutely certain of the validity of the parties with whom you are interacting. Shred all documents containing personal identifying information—including offers for new credit that arrive in the mail.

Electronic Precautions

A fraud alert is an electronic warning placed on your accounts to monitor for suspicious financial activity. According to the FTC, you are legally entitled to two free types of fraud alerts. An *initial fraud alert* is good for 90 days and could be put in place if you suspect you may soon be a victim of identity theft. (This type of alert would be helpful if your wallet was recently stolen, for example.) An *extended fraud alert* lasts for seven years. An extended alert is a good idea if you have been a victim of identity theft. A copy of the Identity Theft Report must be submitted before an extended fraud alert can be placed on your account. A credit freeze prohibits access to your credit report. These electronic protections provide a good first step, but they do not necessarily prevent all types of identity theft.

Commercially Sold Identity Protection Packages

Many private companies offer a variety of services to help combat identity theft. Some companies offer services, like fraud alerts, that are available for free. Some companies may help you resolve complications resulting from being an identity theft victim. Carefully evaluate the services and costs of such programs. Determine the true value they offer before purchasing them.

 ✔checkpoint

Distinguish between the two types of fraud alerts.

assessment 11.4

Think Critically

1. What types of costs are associated with identity theft?

2. Name four manual ways to commit identity theft.

3. How have electronic transactions and the Internet made identity thieves more efficient?

4. List some ways to prevent identity theft.

Make Academic Connections

5. **GOVERNMENT** The U.S. Postal Service is actively involved in trying to catch criminals. Go to its website and review the information on consumer awareness. List and define the types of fraud on the website that are not covered in this section. Be prepared to discuss your answers.

6. **RESEARCH**   In one year the U.S. Postal Service made 77 arrests that spanned three countries to stop the flow of 666,000 fake checks. Research other recent arrests for fraud. Summarize the nature of the crime, the amount of the damage, and the agency that caught the thieves. Be prepared to share your research with the class.

chapter 11 assessment

Chapter Summary

11.1 Robbery Prevention and Response

A. Robbery prevention involves installing security equipment and training employees how to behave during a robbery.

B. During a bank robbery, employees should be concerned with the twin goals of safety and identification.

11.2 Ethics in Banking

A. Many banks provide written codes of ethics to help their employees know how to choose the "proper" behavior in specified circumstances.

B. Making the correct ethical decision for a company has become clouded recently with the concern for the "bottom line." Banks must be especially careful to make ethical decisions.

11.3 Fraud and Scams

A. Banking fraud has always occurred, but methods of performing bank fraud have increased with technological advances.

B. Checking account scams seek to find ways to illegally obtain money from the accounts of unsuspecting victims.

11.4 Identity Theft

A. Identity thieves use your identity and accounts to buy goods and services for themselves.

B. Identity thieves use various methods for stealing identities.

C. Identity theft can be prevented.

Vocabulary Builder

a. bandit barrier
b. check counterfeiting
c. check kiting
d. code of ethics
e. conflict of interest
f. credit freeze
g. ethics
h. forgery
i. fraud
j. fraud alert
k. house flipping
l. phishing
m. scam
n. sniffer program
o. spam
p. straw buyer
q. war driving

Choose the term that best fits the definition. Write the letter of the answer in the space provided. Some terms will not be used.

____ 1. Another term for junk e-mail

____ 2. Act of sending an e-mail to a user falsely claiming to be an established legitimate enterprise to scam the user

____ 3. Refers to beliefs that distinguish right from wrong

____ 4. Situation in which two interests are at cross-purposes

____ 5. The practice of buying a house for below market value and selling it at or above market value

____ 6. Slang term for something that is fraudulent or a swindle

____ 7. Deception deliberately practiced to secure unfair or unlawful gain

____ 8. Name for bulletproof plastic shield at a teller's station

____ 9. Act of opening accounts at two or more institutions and using the "float time" of available funds to create fraudulent balances

____ 10. Statement adopted by management to guide employees in taking appropriate actions in critical situations that could reflect on the organization

Review Concepts

11. How can bank security measures function as robbery prevention?

12. Name several actions that should be part of a "best practices" list for a bank.

13. Why is training the key to preventing bank robbery?

14. Discuss some actions that tellers should take during a robbery to help identify a suspect afterward.

15. Explain how fraud related to banking may be committed.

16. How does a credit freeze help prevent identity theft?

17. Discuss the signs to look for that could identify counterfeit checks.

18. List and explain some steps to take to avoid becoming the victim of check fraud.

19. Describe what is involved in identity theft.

20. What is the relationship between war driving and sniffer programs?

21. What is the Sarbanes-Oxley Act? What behavior does it seek to prevent?

Apply What You Learned

22. Why are the services of an appraiser critical for an illegal house-flipping scheme?

23. Why do banks insist that employees not take any heroic measures during a robbery?

24. What aspects of currency design can help prevent counterfeiting?

25. How has computer technology affected bank fraud?

26. Give at least two examples of a conflict of interest or of a breach of confidentiality that could occur in banking.

27. What do you think caused the accounting scandals of the early twenty-first century?

28. Why should you be concerned about who is watching your financial transactions?

Make Academic Connections

29. **CRIMINOLOGY**   Crooks can be quite clever. Use the Internet or other research materials to learn about some specific forms of fraud that are currently problematic. Present a report to the class about how they work and how they can be prevented.

30. **CRITICAL THINKING**   As the head of the HR department in your bank, you must develop screening procedures to be used during the hiring process. Create a list detailing the background information required of prospective employees and the steps to take to verify the information.

31. **ETHICS**   Make a list of ethical dilemmas you have experienced during your daily life and describe how you handled each situation.

32. **COMMUNICATION**   Do you believe that fraud can ever be effectively eliminated from the banking system? Explain your answer.

12

Bank Marketing

goodluz/Shutterstock.com

skills that pay dividends

Understanding Consumer Motives

People have a variety of reasons for buying products and services. Some of these reasons are based on thoughts and some are based on feelings.

Banking is a basic need in modern society. Intellectually, most people understand that they need a bank to deposit a paycheck, to hold their funds, to provide various checking and savings accounts, and to provide ATM services. How a bank is chosen depends on the personality and values of the customer.

Analytical customers may do a lot of research to compare products, service levels, and costs among competing banks. If analytical customers value cost effectiveness and efficiency, they may select the bank that provides the best combination of both. These customers take a detached, objective approach to decision making.

Some customers take a more emotional approach when choosing a bank. Customers who either lived through the Great Depression or who are worried about the lasting impact of the 2008 credit crisis may place a high premium on the security of their funds. These customers may gravitate to a bank with personnel who convey a strong sense of financial knowledge and financial responsibility. During banking transactions, these customers may often seek reassurance that their funds are safe.

Customers who have a strong need either to feel like part of a community or to do business with people they know socially may place a higher premium on banking where they can develop strong personal relationships. These customers may not compare alternative banks and banking products but instead opt for a bank with a good reputation and trustworthy employees.

When interacting with customers regarding product or service selection, ask them to rank what is most important to them in their selection process. Their answers will reveal whether they are more analytical, emotional, or a combination of both. Using their responses to frame your discussion, emphasize the qualities of your products or services that are most important to them. For example, value-driven customers might be influenced to buy from you if they hear about all of the free online services offered by your bank. Socially oriented customers might like to hear about outings to pro baseball games sponsored by your bank.

Customers make post-purchase evaluations. Follow up with customers after a purchase to see if there is anything you can do to improve their satisfaction.

Develop Your Skill

In small groups, assign the role of an analytical customer, an emotional customer, and a social customer to group members. Assign the role of a bank representative, focusing on specific bank products, such as a checking account or a CD, to other group members. The bank representatives should try to sell each type of customer their product by first asking the customer to list their decision priorities and then by framing the discussion around those priorities. Reflect on how the approaches and conversations are different based on the personality type of the customer. Be prepared to share your findings with the class.

12.1

Define the Customer

Learning Objectives

12.1.1 Understand customer characteristics.

12.1.2 Apply customer characteristics to banking customers.

Key Terms

- demographics
- need
- want
- customer segmentation
- target market

Banking Scene

Yuan Liang is new to the city. He grew up in a small community where most people know each other, and he went to college in a nearby small town. Yuan needs to find a bank where he can open checking and savings accounts. He knows what he expects from a bank, but he isn't sure how to identify one that meets his needs. He wants to be a valued customer at his bank. How can Yuan find a bank that is interested in a customer who is just beginning his or her career?

12.1.1 CUSTOMERS ARE THE REASON BUSINESSES EXIST

All businesses exist to serve customers. Successfully defining current customers and accurately identifying targeted customers is critical to a business's ability to prosper.

Who Is a Customer?

Marketing theories abound on how to best define a customer. However, there are common definitions of terms that describe characteristics of customers. **Demographics** refers to the specific shared characteristics that comprise distinct groups of consumers. Income, age, gender, race, profession, and home ZIP code are examples of specific customer characteristics. Knowing the demographic composition of your customers will help you decide which financial products to offer either nationally, regionally, or locally. For example, a bank branch located in a ZIP code with high net worth residents might elect to highlight investment options at that branch.

Customers have needs and wants. A **need** is a requirement for basic survival. Basic physiological needs include air, food, clothing, and shelter. A **want** is something that you would prefer to have but that you could live without if necessary. Wants may include sports cars, iPads, and designer clothes. In modern society, citizens have a basic need for money. If they want to have written records of their transactions, buy or rent a home, pay bills online, or put their money in a safe location, then they need the services of a financial institution.

Customer Segmentation

Banks recognize that they can't be all things to all people. They are aware of **customer segmentation**, the process of organizing customers into subgroups that have specific preferences or needs. They can tailor distinctive products

Kenneth Summers/Shutterstock.com

to these needs and sell them profitably to the subgroups. As an example, all customers who need to open checking accounts are not the same but want and need different things from that account. Some want to write only a few checks a month, but others prefer the ability to write an unlimited number of checks and are willing to pay a fee for the service.

A target market is a preselected group of buyers for whom a product or service is created and to whom a marketing campaign is directed. For example, the target market for a small car that gets 60 miles to the gallon of gas won't be the same as the one for a large vehicle that gets 15 mpg.

What is demographic information?

12.1.2 IDENTIFYING A BANKING CUSTOMER •••••••••

There are multiple ways to define, group, service, and sell to banking customers. The way that a bank defines its customers will impact how it provides products and services to those customers.

Individual Customers

Many bank customers are interested in services for themselves or their households. Ongoing products and services these customers need include checking accounts, savings accounts, CDs, insurance, and online banking. Lending products they need include mortgage, car, and home-equity and

branching out

Aisling

Many banks have branches in nontraditional locations such as grocery stores. In addition to providing convenience to customers, these branches need to work to stay prominent in customers' minds. A variety of creative marketing approaches have been used by personnel at nontraditional branches. At one Ohio bank, tellers take to the supermarket aisles to interact with customers. By telling customers that they can receive $100,000 if they can identify the name of the bank located in the store, customers are prompted to recall the bank's name. If they correctly identify the name of the bank, the teller then gives them a $100,000 candy bar. Undoubtedly, receiving the candy sweetens their experience!

Think Critically   How would you react if your grocery shopping experience included an individualized marketing effort by a bank? Do you think this is an effective way to engage customers?

student loans. They may also seek credit cards, wealth management assistance, retirement planning, and trust planning. Within each of these categories of need there are multiple ways to approach the customer and multiple products from which each customer can choose.

Business Customers

Business customers have a variety of needs depending on their industry and business focus. Many banks serve a wide variety of business customers ranging from small businesses to large businesses. Businesses may vary from sole proprietorships to businesses with a few employees to multinational corporations. Industries that businesses participate in may range from house-cleaning services to consumer products companies to agricultural businesses. Nonprofit groups, ranging from Girl Scout troops through various charities, need banking services. Religious institutions also need banking services.

Various Approaches to Specific Customer Groups

There are many ways to approach individual groups that are in the targeted segment of a market.

Demographic Approach for Individuals   Some financial institutions structure their sales approach and websites to appeal directly to specific age groups. For example, one credit union offers products to the following four distinct age groups: ages 20–34, ages 35–49, ages 50–64, and ages 65 and over. Advice on financial products is tailored to each age group. Customers in the ages 20–34 age group may be advised to focus on saving for a house down payment. Customers in the ages 65 and over group may be advised to consider the ongoing income generated by their investments.

prism68/shutterstock.com

Business Approach A separate section of a bank's website may be dedicated to businesses. Categorizing products by basic business accounts, from checking accounts through loan lines, by services that will benefit employees, and by services that will help the business manage all types of routine transactions, from merchant services through payroll, is one approach.

Functionality Approach A national banking chain presents its products from a more functional standpoint. The website of a national banking chain breaks down personal banking services into the categories of earned income, loans, and savings accounts. Specific product offerings, from checking accounts through investment products, are positioned within these broad categories.

Product Approach A community bank prefers to offer product categories, from savings accounts through IRAs to loans, as direct product offerings. This is a straightforward approach that presumes that the customer has a basic understanding of products. This approach allows an educated customer to directly access specific products of interest.

 **checkpoint**

Why is identifying the age group of a customer an important consideration for a bank?

assessment 12.1

Think Critically

1. Define customer segmentation.

_____

_____

2. What is a target market?

_____

_____

3. Compare and contrast how national banking chains organize product offerings with how community banks organize their offerings.

_____

_____

_____

4. How would your interaction with a customer be different for an analytical customer versus a customer with strong social needs?

_____

_____

_____

_____

Make Academic Connections

5. **ECONOMICS**   Survey ten adults about their "wants" relative to banking services. Ask them to name at least five services they would like a bank to provide them. Make a list of each person's responses and then organize a master list based on the demographic characteristics of all your respondents. Draw conclusions about the desired bank services of each demographic segment represented.

_____

_____

6. **RESEARCH**   Have students visit three bank websites, one for a national bank, one for a community bank, and one for a credit union. Have them compare website organization relative to customer and product focus. Have them identify similarities and differences in how the banks identify and target their customers. Prepare a two-page report to share results with the class.

Develop and Maintain the Customer

Banking Scene

Yuan Liang is happy with his new bank. He looks forward to the occasional Friday when he can get a free lunch sponsored by his bank. Last summer the bank even gave him two free tickets to a professional baseball game. Yuan has taken advantage of the bank's online bill payment option and uses it to pay his regular bills. Some of his friends, who get a financial reward for referring new customers, are trying to get him to change banks. Yuan is hesitant to do so. What should he consider before changing banks?

Learning Objectives

12.2.1 Discuss a strategic approach for developing and maintaining profitable customer relationships.

12.2.2 Explain how to keep customers in the midst of a highly competitive environment.

Key Terms

- customer relationship management (CRM)
- cross-selling

12.2.1 CUSTOMER DEVELOPMENT

There's a popular business saying that says it is much less expensive to keep an existing customer than it is to obtain a new customer. Competition for banking customers is fierce. Traditional sources, like other brick-and-mortar banks, are a source of competition. Nontraditional sources that are part of the ongoing financial innovations in the industry, like automotive companies that offer financial products and online banks, also change the competitive dynamic within the industry.

Customer Relationship Management

Customer Relationship Management (CRM) captures the idea that the most profitable way to view customers is not merely in terms of the current products or services they buy from you, but in terms of the customer's present and future potential value to your business. By fully understanding the customer's financial position, financial needs, and long-term financial goals, you can cross-sell customers into more lucrative financial products. Cross-selling occurs when you apply your understanding of your customer to suggest other products from which the customer could benefit. A quantitative way to understand your customer is through a thorough analysis of past buying patterns. *Customer relationship management software* can track customers' online transactions to garner up-to-date customer behavior information.

Strategically Developing Banking Customers

Banks, like all businesses, need a distinct business focus. Once banks have determined which products and services they want to sell, they need to develop methods for attracting customers from within their target market. They may align certain products to specific demographic groups.

Unique Product Benefits   Banks need to identify the unique, value-adding benefits of the products they offer. Highlighting these benefits to customers in all marketing, sales, and service interactions will help persuade customers that buying the product would be a good investment.

Keep Existing Customers   Banks need to strive to maintain all existing customers. Providing exemplary, proactive customer service is one way to do this. Offering customers structured ways to provide feedback, and then responding to that feedback, enables customers to help the bank continuously improve.

Expand Existing Customer Relationships   By cross-selling other products to customers, by servicing their accounts, and by forming partnerships with them to provide for their evolving needs, you can maintain customers.

Letting Go of Less Profitable Customers   Although this can be controversial, if a bank's business model or product offerings change, in some cases it may make sense to provide disincentives for a customer to continue in the banking relationship. For example, if current customers no longer fit the desired customer profile, then increasing the charges on their accounts may cause them to start to look for a new financial institution.

On the other hand, there are those who would argue that banks have fixed costs and the incremental cost of maintaining a less-desirable customer is not that great. One financial institution consulting company, Peak Performance Consulting Group, states that banking is basically a fixed-cost business. Two hundred dollars per customer is an industry-accepted level of per-customer cost. However, the marginal cost of each customer is only $35–$40. In essence this means that, on average, it is relatively inexpensive to keep a less-profitable customer. This line of reasoning would further the line of thought that it is all right to keep a less-profitable customer. A bank's decisions on overall profitability and its desire to maintain a rigid business focus will influence its decisions about whether to maintain less-profitable customers.

✔checkpoint

What is customer relationship management and why is it significant to the banking industry?

12.2.2 Keeping Customers

With abundant industry-wide competition and with customers' easy access to information, you will need to find innovative and cost-effective ways to maintain your customers.

Providing Customers with Incentives to Stay

Financial institutions use a variety of customer incentive and loyalty programs. Reasons to use incentive programs may include increasing customer loyalty, elevating the bank beyond merely a business and into becoming part of a customer's social network, and encouraging the purchase of specific products. A few of the programs are listed below.

Scorecard   This incentive program provides points for merchandise purchased with a bank card. The points can be redeemed for merchandise or travel. Financial institutions participate in this reward program.

Upromise   If you sign up for the Upromise program with your bank's credit or debit card, many retailers will make a donation to your children's college savings fund after certain purchases are made. Some banks offer an additional percentage contribution for the college fund.

Fun and Lively Customer Incentives   These can run the gamut from providing free lunches at branches on a rotating basis to offering sweepstake drawings for a month's free rent or mortgage payment to offering a chance to win a $100,000 sweepstakes to a lucky bank customer.

Referral Programs   Some banks offer a financial reward to customers who recommend the bank to friends or businesses. Each new account opened as the result of a referral can yield a cash reward of $25–$50 to the customer who made the successful referral. Reward levels vary by bank.

Exclusive Social Engagements for High-Value Customers   Customers with strong financial portfolios that provide ongoing, high-value business to a bank may also be invited to exclusive social engagements for the bank's top customers. This not only rewards customers for their business, but flatters them to know they are part of an exclusive group.

The Entrenched Online Customer

Automatic payroll deposit, online bill pay, and automatic monthly payments for repetitive, fixed-price bills all provide great convenience for customers. Although it may take a bit of time to set up each of these account options, once they are established they save customers a great deal of time for routine financial transactions. However, the thought of changing all of these transactions from one bank to another can become quite a disincentive for customers to change banks. Administratively it is very time consuming to make the necessary changes to both the vendor's account and the bank account. Avoiding this administrative time can provide an incentive for online customers to maintain current banking relationships.

Competitive Threats

The best way to avoid losing customers to the competition is to not only know what the competition is currently doing, but also what they plan on doing. With a thorough knowledge of the competition, you can proactively address competitive programs and provide programs that will keep your customers with you. Below are some examples of some nontraditional competitors to the financial market.

Automotive Manufacturers Offering Car Loans, Credit Cards, and Insurance Products   Most car manufacturers offer buyers financing services as well. For example, BMW Financial Services offers customized leasing and loan options for customers. It also offers a variety of financial products. Through partnerships with Visa for credit card products and Liberty Mutual Insurance for home and auto insurance products, the company competes with banks that also offer these services. BMW offers these services to enhance the BMW customer relationship. BMW is cross-selling these products to its customers.

Peer-to-Peer Lending   New lending opportunities are available for both borrowers and prospective lenders. With Internet sites to facilitate the borrower and lender matchmaking, a variety of streamlined financing methods are available. Although specifics vary, common options include using social networks to facilitate connections, allowing lenders to participate in earning interest at low risk (by offering a relatively small contribution as part of a larger loan), and selecting borrowers to finance by their personal narrative in addition to their credit ratings.

✔checkpoint

Why might a customer with an established online banking relationship hesitate to change banks?

assessment 12.2

Think Critically

1. What is cross-selling and why is it important in banking?

2. Why would a bank decide to let go of less-profitable customers?

3. Why is peer-to-peer lending attractive to both lenders and borrowers?

4. Provide five examples of customer incentive programs. Which program would appeal to you most? Why would you prefer that program?

Make Academic Connections

5. **RESEARCH** Investigate peer-to-peer lending sites. Read the compelling narratives of potential borrowers. Do their stories move you? Would their personal stories influence your decision to lend to a prospective borrower? What factors would you weight most heavily in your lending decision making—earnestness, tough times, shared hobbies, shared political beliefs, volunteer activities, or others? How much of a competitive threat do peer-to-peer websites present to traditional banks? Summarize your thoughts and findings and be prepared to participate in a lively class discussion.

6. **MARKETING** An Ohio bank recently offered prospective customers $100 to open a new checking account. Search your local media, including newspapers, billboards, and the Internet. Are similar offers currently offered in your area? Are the customers who open such an account likely to be profitable customers to the bank? Why do banks provide customer incentives for new accounts? Summarize your findings and your thoughts. Be prepared to use the collected information to participate in a class discussion.

12.3

Public Relations

Learning Objectives

12.3.1 Discuss the process of creating a public image.

12.3.2 Name the major tools used as part of a public relations effort.

Key Terms

- public image
- public relations

Banking Scene

Yuan was surprised to learn of the philanthropic causes his bank sponsors. When he went to the local community theater production, he saw his bank helped sponsor the community theater troupe. Yuan wondered why the bank would be willing to donate money to such a cause. What do you think are some of the reasons?

12.3.1 CREATION OF A PUBLIC IMAGE • • • • • • • • • • • • •

One of the most important assets a company has can't be found on its financial statements, but it can constitute a significant percentage of the company's value. Corporate *image* and *reputation* contribute to the bottom line in many ways—from attracting customers and investors to how successfully a company can recover from a crisis. A public image is the concept the public has of a business and should reflect its mission, values, and culture. You choose the businesses you frequent and the products you buy based on your image of the company. If the image is good, you buy; if it is negative, you don't. A bank's image or prestige is a critical factor in whether it will be able to attract and retain customers, sell its products and services, support its claims, attract the best employees, and satisfy its stockholders.

Steps in Creating an Image

It is important for a bank to consider the public image it wants to project. Many banks support local activities to keep their names before the public. They sponsor home and garden shows, fireworks displays, youth clubs, teen organizations, sport teams, playing fields, and even arenas, as well as cultural events such as theater, opera, ballet, and orchestra performances.

A bank must take a number of steps to create its public image, including the following.

Step 1 Analyze the image the bank wants to present. Does the bank want to be known for the services it offers? Does it want to be known as a community supporter?

Step 2 Determine the bank's target audience.

Step 3 Determine the current image the bank has with its target market.

Step 4 Define the bank's goals in creating its image. Goals should be specific as well as measurable within a specific time period.

Step 5 Develop a plan to accomplish the goal. It should consider the way the bank will communicate or reinforce its image. Many banks engage professional public relations consultants to implement this step.

Step 6 Track the results of the public relations campaign to create or revise the bank's image. Determine whether the bank achieved its defined objectives and goals.

✔checkpoint

Why does a bank pay attention to creating a public image?

12.3.2 PUBLIC RELATIONS ACTIVITIES ● ● ● ● ● ● ● ● ● ● ● ●

An organization's reputation, profitability, and even its continued existence can depend on the degree to which its targeted "public" supports its goals and products. This support is often the result of the organization's public relations efforts. The Institute of Public Relations defines **public relations (PR)** as "the planned and sustained effort to establish and maintain goodwill and mutual understanding between an organization and its public." The term includes activities associated with areas such as customer relations, marketing, and advertising. PR work also includes keeping management aware of the attitudes and the concerns of the many individuals, groups, and organizations with which the company interacts. Effective public relations efforts are carefully planned and executed. The planning phase should address the following questions.

- What objectives does the PR program aim to accomplish?

- Is there a clear definition of the targeted audience or public? Have the methods to reach the targeted audience been clearly defined and described?

- Are employees prepared to support the activity? Will they need training?

- Do current forces, such as local, state, national, or international events, affect the message?

- What are the organization's current PR activities? Do they fit the plan?

- What does the budget allow?

- Who will implement the plan? Will outside help be needed?

In large banks, the key public relations executive, frequently a vice president, may develop the overall plans and policies with other executives. The public relations department employs specialists to write, research, and prepare materials for distribution, to maintain contacts, and to respond to

Ethics in Action

Because companies emphasize and expect immediate monetary benefits from their public relations programs, attention to ethics in this arena has increased in recent years. The Council of Public Relations Firms (PR Council) has adopted a code of professional ethics for its members.

Think Critically

Do you see any problems with activities that businesses use to establish and maintain the public's goodwill toward them? Would you expect to find ethical problems in banks' PR efforts? Why or why not?

inquiries. In a small organization, there may be either one person or a few people who deal with all aspects of the PR function.

Public Relations Tools

The PR function uses various techniques to influence and direct the attention of the general public, interest groups, and stockholders to the company and its products. Public relations can and should use any media, including radio, television, the Internet, and print advertising, to gain a competitive advantage as well as to establish and maintain goodwill and mutual understanding between the company and the public.

Public relations activities can inform the public about facts relating to a bank such as its Community Reinvestment Act projects, a new branch, and the extension of its hours of business. News or press releases keep editors and readers up to date on positive developments including business news, technological advances, promotions and new hires, and special events. A bank submits written feature articles or "leads" to local and state news media about specific projects, industry trends, and so forth that involve the bank, suggesting that it is a leader in these areas. Brochures are PR tools that inform prospective customers about some aspect of the bank, such as its history, involvement in community events or special programs, interesting facts about its building architecture, and the details of its services. Brochures can also call attention to any special recognition the bank has received. Newsletters provide a valuable, ongoing channel for delivering a bank's message to current and potential customers.

Photodisc/Getty Images

Special events, such as anniversaries of doing business or winning an award for community reinvestment activities, offer the public and the media a reason to focus on the bank. Hosting professional organizations or associations can help a bank create the impression that it is well respected in the profession. Holding business seminars for customers allows a bank to explain new banking-related developments, trends, services, and products in detail, suggesting that it has expertise in these areas.

✔checkpoint

To whom are public relations activities addressed?

assessment 12.3

Think Critically

1. Why do you think a bank needs to be cautious and careful in creating its public image?

2. List and explain the first four steps in creating the public image of a bank.

3. What public relations tools may be used?

4. In your opinion, what are the most effective public relations tools discussed in the lesson?

Make Academic Connections

5. **ETHICS**   Use the Internet to investigate ethical issues relating to public relations. Write a one-page report or prepare an oral presentation on your findings.

6. **COMMUNICATION**   Collect at least four pieces of written documents or web-based documents such as brochures, news releases, newsletters, or printouts from the Internet for a local bank. What image do you believe the bank is trying to create through them?

7. **ECONOMICS**   How do economic conditions affect the image a bank communicates?

Customer Service

Banking Scene

Yuan Liang was asked to participate in a customer service survey offered by his bank. The bank wanted to understand whether they were meeting his needs and expectations on service. Yuan reflected on the service he had received and thought about ways that service could be improved. What elements of service could he include?

Learning Objectives

12.4.1 Explain the elements of good customer service.

12.4.2 Identify behaviors that are inappropriate in dealing with customers.

Key Terms

- customer service
- empathy

12.4.1 CUSTOMER ASSISTANCE

In their classic book *In Search of Excellence,* Thomas J. Peters and Robert H. Waterman, Jr., listed eight characteristics of large, profitable companies. One was being "close to the customer." According to Peters and Waterman, profitable companies learn from the people they serve and provide unparalleled quality, service, and reliability. Customer service can be defined as the activities and programs a seller provides to make the relationship with its customers satisfying. Customer service is a concept that can be difficult to measure, but when it is good you know it, just as you do when it is bad.

Companies consider customer service to be a way they can differentiate themselves from competitors. The money that you receive from Bank A is the same as the money you receive from Banks B through Z. What distinguishes your experience in getting the money is service. In a 2016 survey reported in *Fortune*, respondents cited Apple, Google, Amazon, Berkshire Hathaway, Walt Disney, and Starbucks as the most admired corporations in the United States. Megabanks JP Morgan Chase, Goldman Sachs, and Wells Fargo ranked in the top 30. Banks have become keenly aware of the importance of customer service to their image as well as their bottom line.

Meeting Customers' Needs

Financial institutions share common needs for developing strong customer loyalty, and offering outstanding customer service is a key component of customer loyalty. Before a bank develops its customer service program, it needs to consider customer preferences. Most customers want responsive service, a competent staff, courteous treatment, consideration of their perspective, and reliable service in their dealings with a bank. They also want easy access to bank personnel and to their funds.

interesting *facts*

The U.S. government offers the Malcolm Baldrige National Quality Award to motivate American companies to improve the quality of their goods and services. ▪

Responsive Service You want your bank to be ready and willing to serve you promptly. Such responsive service makes it clear that the bank wants and values your business. You expect all bank personnel to be willing and ready to provide service, to answer your questions quickly and correctly, and to keep you informed about your accounts. To provide responsive service, bank employees must be sensitive to customer needs and help solve problems. They must also demonstrate flexibility, go "the extra mile," and follow up as needed. By proactively meeting customer needs, bank employees increase customer loyalty and good will.

Competent Staff You expect all members of the bank staff to be professional and knowledgeable. Employees should have the skills to explain the bank's products and services accurately and clearly and be able to answer your questions. When staff members can assure you that they are trustworthy and competent, it increases your confidence in the bank.

Courteous Treatment You want to hear "thank you" when you finish your business and "excuse me" if the bank employee needs to interrupt your service for any reason. You expect all bank staff to be considerate of your feelings and sensitive to your financial situation. You need assurance that you have the right bank that provides both courtesy and competence. The degree of caring and individual attention shown customers is known as empathy. A step beyond assurance, it demonstrates commitment to understanding customers' needs and finding the answer to exactly what they need. Empathetic service is caring and individualized. It is another way the bank lets you know that customer satisfaction is a top priority.

Customer Perspective Bank employees should consider the customer's perspective. As the customer, you want a bank to communicate with you in clear, concise language that doesn't use banking "jargon." You don't want to have to decipher a lot of technical terminology. Bank employees can help acquire and secure business by making certain that the customer has a clear understanding of the product or service.

Reliable Service   The concept of reliability refers to a bank's ability to provide you what it promised in a dependable and accurate manner. In addition, reliability means that the bank will provide its services with consistency, dependability, and respect. Finally, reliability means that the bank will follow through when it says it will.

Easy Access to Staff and Funds   As a customer, you want your bank to make its services available when and where you need them. You need to access services without unacceptably long waits. You expect convenient locations for branches and ATMs.

Tech Talk

Technology: Customer Service Asset or Problem?

According to a recent article in *The Dallas Morning News*, companies around the nation are beginning to recognize that technology can have both negative and positive effects on customer service.

Technology can be a huge asset for customer service. For example, Dallas-based 7-Eleven Inc. uses sophisticated software daily to identify which products sell and which don't. That way, the stores can keep what the customers want in stock. "By their purchases, we know what they want in their stores," said Margaret Chabris, a 7-Eleven spokeswoman.

Technology also can be advantageous in training. Sprint Corp. uses technology to put sales representatives through "hard-core training" with the use of simulations, according to Jed Dodd, vice president of training and development. Mad, angry customers have been filmed so that sales representatives get first-hand experience dealing with such customers. The video is a great training tool. It can be stopped as needed to discuss the best way to handle a situation.

In contrast, automated messages are prone to cause frustration for consumers. Frequently, the choices on the menus don't apply to their needs. At one point, Sprint used a computerized representative known as Claire, who was intended to help people through the interactive phone maze. But customers hated her, so the company "killed her" said Roxie Ramirez, a Sprint spokeswoman.

Think Critically
Search the Internet for examples of companies that are finding technology an asset or a problem for their customer service. Do you think the effect of technology on customer service is more positive or negative? Explain your answer.

Professional Appearance   Both the banking environment and its employees should meet your expectations of professional appearance. The bank should be clean, uncluttered, and inviting, creating an atmosphere in which you expect safety for yourself and your funds. The employees should be dressed appropriately to convey a sense of professionalism. Employees that are dressed too casually or sloppily can project an apathetic image, which many customers may find disrespectful.

✔checkpoint

How does the concept of reliability apply to customer service?

12.4.2 INAPPROPRIATE BEHAVIOR AND PROBLEMS

Sam Walton, founder of Walmart, once said, "There is only one boss, the customer. And he can fire everybody simply by spending his money elsewhere." A typical dissatisfied customer will tell 8 to 10 people about the bad experience. One person in 5 will inform 20 or more. Some behaviors are certain to annoy or anger customers. These inappropriate behaviors may seem obvious to you, but they do occur and should be avoided.

- **Don't make negative remarks on social media.** Criticizing customers or the financial institution is never a good idea.

- **Don't be rude to the customer.** Remember that you represent the bank to the customer. Remember to say "please," "thank you," and "excuse me"; make eye contact; avoid having a conversation with other employees or customers while serving the current customer; don't be abrupt; and never use rude or offensive language. Think about checkout clerks who mumble, "Have a nice day. Thank you for shopping at Blank Store" without ever looking at you and in a manner that suggests they really care nothing about you and where you shop but are required to memorize and repeat this phrase.

- **Don't argue with the customer.** Even if you are absolutely certain you are correct, arguing will insult and embarrass the customer without resolving the problem and will likely make it worse.

- **Don't ignore a customer.** Ignoring the person basically treats him or her as a nonperson.

- **Don't make excuses or use negative phrases.** Avoid the phrases "I don't know," "It's not my job," "I can't help you," or "You'll have to wait." Instead, use phrases such as "I'll get that information for you," "Rick can help you with that," or "I'll be happy to help you as soon as I finish this transaction." Be helpful in recognizing what the customer needs and quickly find an answer or solution.

- **Don't criticize, condemn, or complain.** You should never criticize the bank, any employees, or customers. Avoid condemning bank policies or complaining about anything while with a customer.

- **Don't be condescending.** Never treat a customer as if he or she is not your equal. Don't "talk down" to them, treat them as if they are incapable of understanding, or give them "pat" answers.

- **Don't leave customers on the telephone.** If talking to clients on the telephone is part of your job, be constantly aware of them when they are on hold. Check with them frequently to let them know that you are still working with them. Apologize for delays.

Responding When Things Go Wrong

Some days are simply difficult, and things will go wrong no matter how you try to prevent problems. These are some steps you can take to salvage the situation.

- **Apologize.** Start by saying you are sorry, even if you believe the customer is at fault.

- **Listen and ask questions.** Listen carefully to the customer, show empathy, and ask questions that will allow you to gain and keep control.

- **Correct the problem quickly and fairly.** Tell the customer how you are going to solve the problem.

- **Keep your promises.** Be realistic about what you can and cannot do. Don't promise something just to pacify the customer.

- **Follow up on the problem.** Check with your customer to ensure that what was wrong has been addressed and corrected.

✔checkpoint

Why should an employee not argue with a customer?

assessment 12.4

Think Critically

1. It has been said that profitable companies learn from their customers. Explain in your own words what this means.

2. Why is it important that employees convey a sense of assurance?

3. Why do you think an empathetic attitude is important in dealing with a bank's customers?

4. What do you think is wrong with using the phrases "I don't know" and "I can't help you" with a customer?

Make Academic Connections

5. **HISTORY** Investigate the Malcolm Baldrige National Quality Award. Identify the criteria for this award. Make a list of firms that have received this honor. Do you see any consistency in the service standards among these companies?

6. **CRITICAL THINKING** Inappropriate employee behavior may seem obvious to you, but customers encounter it all too often. Suggest ways that businesses can prevent this behavior.

Marketing and Advertising

12.5

Banking Scene

Yuan Liang now knows what he expects from a bank in terms of customer service. What are some ways that banks market their services to potential customers like Yuan?

Learning Objectives

12.5.1 Explain how banks create a target market.

12.5.2 Identify the way banks advertise their products and services.

Key Terms

- marketing
- social responsibility
- advertising
- cybermarketing
- search engine optimization (SEO)
- direct marketing
- viral marketing

12.5.1 MARKETING

Many people think that marketing is only about advertising or selling goods and services. However, advertising and selling are just two of many marketing activities. Marketing is the process of planning and executing the conception, pricing, promotion, and distribution of goods, services, and ideas to create exchanges that satisfy individual and organization objectives. A bank can identify the goals of its marketing plan by answering the following questions: Where is the company now? Where does it want to go? How will the company get where it wants to go? How will the company know when it gets there? Marketing objectives for a bank should be measurable, flexible, and complement its financial objectives. The marketing plan also needs to stretch the entire bank to a higher level of performance. The plan should include the "4 Ps" of marketing—*P*roduction (development), *P*ricing, *P*romotion, and *P*lacement (distribution)—which classify the controllable elements of a marketing plan.

- **The bank should have the same goals as its target market.** If the target market is teenagers, advertisements for mortgage lending would be inappropriate.

- **Its target market should be consistent with its resources.** A bank without an adequate computer system and technical support should not advertise online banking services.

- **Its target market should generate sufficient profit.** The selected market must provide profits that warrant the effort.

- **Its target market should be adequate in size.** A market in which many competitors are already present is difficult to enter. Thus, it's important that the customer base is large enough to support all participants.

Extensive research is required in identifying a target market. Banks generally hire companies that specialize in developing this information to direct the research.

Marketing Strategy

Before setting its marketing plan, a bank needs to develop a marketing strategy. This strategy pinpoints the target market and develops the marketing mix. It also establishes specific goals for the marketing effort and a statement of what makes it stand out from its competition.

In developing a marketing strategy, the bank needs to carry out a thorough analysis of the market and identify the ways the business can serve it. The marketing analysis involves gathering and analyzing information, considering alternative courses of action, and determining the responses of competitors and customers to each course of action. The analysis of a proposed strategy will allow the bank to determine whether the strategy will be effective as planned, or if not, how to modify it.

Marketing Planning

Whereas the marketing strategy describes the bank's marketing goals, the marketing plan will detail how to accomplish and then evaluate the goals. In establishing a marketing plan, the bank will need to gather information on the following:

1. The bank's performance and performance of competitors
2. Environmental changes such as changes in economic conditions, laws, or technology
3. The target markets to be served

Once the information is gathered, it should be organized in an easy-to-access marketing information system. The bank can find supplemental information from government agencies, trade associations, and research firms. In some cases, it may need to hire a marketing research firm to conduct research on a specific topic.

Based on the above information, the bank will develop a marketing plan. The marketing plan provides details on how the strategy will be executed. Once developed, the plan then needs to be shared with everyone in the organization responsible for executing the marketing strategy.

Marketing and Social Responsibility

Social responsibility is the obligation to profitably serve employees and customers in an ethical and law-abiding manner. Like other respected institutions in the community, banks are expected to take an active, socially responsible role in civic affairs. This is especially important because banks provide somewhat of a public service. Financial institutions frequently require their officers to be involved with local service organizations and give them time to do so.

✔checkpoint

What is the purpose of marketing?

_____

_____

_____

12.5.2 ADVERTISING ●

Your daily life is saturated with advertisements. One estimate suggests that the average person encounters 1,500 to 1,800 ads a day. This is an enormous number, but you have learned to "turn off" most of these ads. Advertising is the paid description or presentation of a product, service, idea, or organization to encourage individuals to buy, support, or approve of it. It is one element in a firm's marketing plan.

Organizations use a variety of media to send their messages. Ad distribution can occur via the Internet, print media, broadcast media, outdoor media, mobile media, and through direct marketing. An effective advertising campaign uses a combination of these.

Cybermarketing and Search Engine Optimization

Some estimates predict that online business will either triple or quadruple in the future. As Internet usage displaces print media, advertising on the Internet has transformed into a highly effective way to reach customers. Cybermarketing is a carefully planned and sustained effort to advertise a company, its products, and/or services through the Internet by using the most practical, effective, and up-to-date strategies. Public relations information, marketing materials, and online data transactions can all take place on the Internet.

Search engine optimization (SEO) is the most effective way to drive Internet business to your site. A *search engine* is a software program that indexes web content so that it can be referenced in Internet searches. There are complicated mathematical formulas, called *algorithms*, that are used by search engines to select relevant

Banking Math *Connection*

Financial success in a business is far more likely if the projects in which it invests provide a return on its investment. Assume that Third State Bank is considering two marketing opportunities. One is a newspaper advertising campaign budgeted at $75,000 and estimated to have a positive benefit of $11,000 in the first year. The other is a series of television commercials that will cost $200,000 in the first year with an expected return of $33,000. Using the return on investment (ROI) formula below, what return on investment from each option can the bank expect?

ROI = Average annual net benefit ÷ Initial costs

Solution

The newspaper ads will have the following return:

ROI = $11,000 ÷ $75,000 = 15%

The TV ads will have this return:

ROI = $33,000 ÷ $200,000 = 17%

These figures indicate that although it involves a considerably larger investment, Third State Bank should choose the television campaign.

---

data in response to an Internet search. The selection algorithms are being continually tweaked. There are precise methodologies available to optimize how valuable your website is relative to other websites. Developing intriguing web content that will increase web traffic to your site, either through direct hits or via links from other websites, is a bit of an art and a science. Training staff to do this or outsourcing this work to a qualified vendor will greatly improve your marketing presence online.

Print Media

Look in any Sunday newspaper, and you will find advertisements for a number of banks. The ads describe the characteristics of checking accounts, mortgage and home equity loans, free Internet banking and online bill payment, and extended lobby and drive-up hours.

Although circulation is declining, newspapers are still common in U.S. homes. By advertising in local newspapers, a bank can target a specific geographic area. Newspapers provide a quick turnaround for ad distribution for ads that highlight bank promotions. Ads that promote a bank's image can be found in other printed materials including programs at theater, orchestra, opera, and dance events.

Broadcast Media

In the early years of the twenty-first century, commercials for banks seemed to saturate television and radio advertising. Banks use these media to emphasize their low lending rates, especially those on home mortgages and home equity loans. Although broadcast media is more costly than print media, broadcast media is better at reaching the target market. For example, the bank may target a certain age group by selecting a radio station that caters to those specific age demographics. A bank may want to target young families by running television advertisements during family-oriented shows.

Outdoor Media

Many of you may have become somewhat immune to outdoor advertising, but because people now spend much more time in their vehicles than ever before, it is experiencing a resurgence. A billboard may be the most obvious form of an outdoor ad, but its style has changed in recent years. Computer technology enables the modern "billboard" to present digital images that can be changed on a daily or even hourly basis. A tri-vision billboard allows up to three advertisements to rotate at various intervals on a single billboard.

People tend to notice moving objects when they are driving. Ads printed on buses are eye-catching and unique and therefore memorable. Full-wrap and tail-wrap ads on buses and even cars are so distinctive that people often remember them after only one viewing.

Advertising at airports and subways offers a range of opportunities. It includes signage along an airport's concourses or at subway entrances and stops.

Outdoor advertising also includes large banners such as those draped around the entrance to a museum stating, "Treasures of the Orient Presented by City National Bank."

Direct Marketing

Another form of advertising, direct marketing is a promotion technique that delivers the materials individually to a target market via direct mail, telemarketing, or other direct means. Its purpose is to generate a revenue-producing response. Direct mail campaigns generally consist of printed material such as flyers, brochures, or letters that appear to be first-class mail. These documents offer low-cost checking accounts, interest rates on auto loans, and limited-time specials. In the last few years, consumers have become so bothered by telemarketers that the United States has implemented a national "do-not-call" list intended to block most phone sales pitches.

Viral Marketing

Viral marketing is intentionally using ordinary people to help spread the word about a product or service. Referral programs are one form of viral marketing. Some websites are so intriguing and entertaining that you are inclined to share them with your friends. One online bank even developed an animated website complete with games to draw people to it. Finding a specific, unique, or fun attribute associated with your product or service is another way to promote viral marketing.

Digital Signage

Some banks are using digital signs, which can resemble flat-screen TVs, to provide continually updated information to customers visiting branches. Updated information can pertain to rate changes, referral incentives, or new product offerings and can be programmed to change based on typical traffic patterns in the bank. Some digital signs have embedded radio frequency identification (RFID) technology to record what products a customer picks up from a shelf. Digital ads that are shown can be changed in response to RFID signals to reflect the interest of customers in the branch.

Advertising Budget

Banks can determine their advertising budgets in a number of ways. One way is to spend what is left over after paying the rest of its expenses. This method usually will not cover all advertising needs. Another method is to base the amount of spending on what was spent in the previous year. This method does not consider the effects of competition or market changes. The most effective way to set an advertising budget is to determine the cost of the activities necessary to achieve the bank's advertising objectives.

Several factors may affect the budget for a specific advertising campaign, including the target market for the campaign, the geographical location of the market, how long the product has been on the market, whether an advertising agency will need to be paid, and the type of media to use. The pie chart on this page shows the breakdown of advertising dollars spent by U.S. companies by media type in 2015.

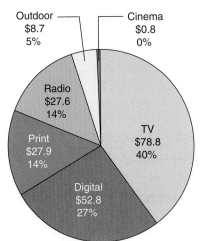

Share of U.S. Ad Spending by Media Type, 2015 (Billions)

Outdoor $8.7 5%
Cinema $0.8 0%
Radio $27.6 14%
Print $27.9 14%
TV $78.8 40%
Digital $52.8 27%

Source: Strategy Analytics Advertising Forecast, 2015

 checkpoint

What is advertising and how does it relate to marketing?

assessment 12.5

Think Critically

1. What are the "4 Ps" of marketing?

2. Why should banks engage in socially responsible activities?

3. Banks often support community cultural activities. In your opinion, what does this say about their target markets?

4. What is search engine optimization (SEO) and why is it important to banking?

Make Academic Connections

5. **MATH**   Woodstown Bank is considering investment in several advertising projects. Ads in the local orchestra's programs will cost $5,000 and have an expected return of $400 in the first year. The other is to build a playground at the local park. This project will cost $9,000 with an expected first-year return of $900. Which project will have the higher return on investment? List any nonfinancial considerations that could affect this decision.

6. **COMMUNICATION**   Work in teams to survey at least 20 people. Find out how many can recall an ad from any medium in the last month. Which medium did most people name?

chapter 12 assessment

Chapter Summary

12.1 Define the Customer

A. Demographics, customer segmentation, and target markets provide an organized method for grouping customers.

B. Customer characteristics drive product recommendations.

12.2 Develop and Maintain the Customer

A. Customer relationship management provides a methodology for viewing the long-term potential value of a customer.

B. Banks need to provide customers with incentives to maintain their existing banking relationships.

12.3 Public Relations

A. Banks need a positive public image to attract and retain customers.

B. Public relations strategies are used to create and maintain goodwill between an organization and the public.

12.4 Customer Service

A. Banks must provide exemplary customer service.

B. Banks must ensure that their employees understand the importance of customer service and avoid behaviors that are inappropriate.

12.5 Marketing and Advertising

A. The 4 Ps of marketing are producing, pricing, promoting, and placing.

B. Multiple advertising methods should be used.

Vocabulary Builder

a. advertising
b. cross-selling
c. customer relationship management (CRM)
d. customer segmentation
e. customer service
f. cybermarketing
g. demographics
h. direct marketing
i. empathy
j. marketing
k. need
l. public image
m. public relations
n. search engine optimization (SEO)
o. social responsibility
p. target market
q. viral marketing
r. want

Choose the term that best fits the definition. Write the letter of the answer in the space provided. Some terms will not be used.

____ 1. The concept the public has of a business that should reflect its mission, values, and culture

____ 2. Degree of caring and individual attention shown to customers

____ 3. Paid description or presentation of a product, service, idea, or organization

____ 4. Technique that delivers promotions directly to targeted individuals

____ 5. Preselected group of buyers who are the focus of marketing efforts

____ 6. Activities and programs a business provides its customers to satisfy them

____ 7. Company's effort to advertise through the Internet

____ 8. Planning and executing a program to create exchanges that satisfy the objectives of both an organization and individuals

____ 9. Organization of customers into subgroups

____ 10. Effort to establish goodwill with the public

____ 11. The most effective way to drive Internet traffic to your website

____ 12. Viewing customers in terms of their total present and future value to your company

Review Concepts

13. Name some ongoing bank products that individual customers need.

14. What is public relations, and how does it relate to customer service and marketing?

15. Name four components of a plan to strategically develop customers.

16. You can choose to do business with any number of banks. How does customer service affect your decision of which bank to use?

17. List five types of customer incentive programs.

18. What is empathy? Why is it an important part of customer service?

19. How can offending a customer affect a bank's public image?

20. List competitive threats to traditional banks. Why are banks concerned about the competition?

_____

_____

_____

21. What activities make up the marketing process?

_____

_____

_____

22. What is customer segmentation?

_____

_____

_____

23. Describe cybermarketing.

_____

_____

Apply What You Learned

24. Why is it important that a bank identify the audience for its public relations activities?

_____

_____

25. In what ways does corporate or public image contribute to a bank's bottom line?

_____

_____

26. Why is search engine optimization critical to the effective use of an Internet advertising budget?

_____

_____

27. What does responsive service entail?

28. Why is viral marketing important?

29. Do you think that banks should use computer pop-up ads? Why or why not?

Make Academic Connections

30. **CRITICAL THINKING**   As a bank teller, you have an obviously upset customer because the bank has returned checks to the telephone and utility companies due to nonsufficient funds in her account. The customer believes this is a bank error. She states that the bank has ruined her credit rating and that she must now pay late fees plus "excessive" bank fees for the returned checks. Write a one-page paper discussing how to appease this customer.

31. **MATH**   Use the Internet to find the financial statement of a bank that shows its marketing budget. This information may be listed under various headings such as advertising and promotion, marketing, and so on. Calculate the percentage of sales/revenue this amount represents. (*Hint:* Divide advertising/marketing expense by net sales/revenue.)

32. **COMMUNICATION**   Use the Internet to investigate one of the companies that *Fortune* listed in its 2016 survey of most admired companies. Describe the characteristics of the customer service policies of one of these businesses.

33. **RESEARCH**   In 2013, the U.S. Department of Justice (DOJ) accused the London-based bank HSBC of allowing billions of pounds in unlawful money transfers through its U.S. division. According to the DOJ, the bank had neglected to notice $670 billion in wire transfers and $9.4 billion in cash transactions from its branch in Mexico. Using the Internet, research other instances of banks being prosecuted for unlawful money transfers. Find out the outcomes of the cases and what the banks did, if anything, to protect their image and customers.

13 Employment Opportunities

CHAPTER

monkeybusinessimages/iStockphoto.com

climbing the ladder

From Teller to District Manager

After her first morning of college classes, Beth went to work her shift as a part-time teller. As she had demonstrated a solid understanding of the job and a good work ethic while working at the bank during the summer, the bank had agreed to schedule her for about 20 hours a week. This flexibility enabled her to schedule her classes efficiently.

As a part-time customer service representative/teller (CSR), Beth's responsibilities ran the gamut from processing routine customer transactions, maintaining consistent balances at her station, and developing a strong customer rapport, to helping the branch achieve its sales goals by promoting banking products.

After her first four quarters of college, Beth enrolled in the college's internship program. By alternating a quarter of classes with a quarter of full-time professional work, Beth was able to expand her responsibilities at the bank.

For her first two internships, Beth worked as a lead customer service representative (LCSR). She was responsible for assisting with opening new accounts and safe deposit boxes, training new tellers, delegating daily projects, and finding solutions to customer issues. To address the fears customers had after the credit and mortgage crises, Beth provided customers with information on the bank's overall stability.

Upon graduation, Beth accepted a position at her bank as an assistant branch manager. In support of the branch manager, her duties included helping the branch staff meet and exceed sales goals, selling to individual customers, meeting compliance requirements, and assuming operational responsibility for the branch in the manager's absence.

After a few years, Beth accepted a cross-town transfer to become a branch manager. Her new duties included achieving financial goals for the branch; expanding her involvement in the community to develop relationships that would bring new business to the branch; managing sales, service, and operations for the branch; and protecting the branch's assets and the assets of its customers.

Beth enjoyed working as a branch manager but believed she had the talent to perform similar functions on a larger scale. Consequently, she applied for and obtained a position as a district manager. Rather than focusing on a specific branch, her new duties focused on a specific territory. Beth was now responsible for overseeing the sales, service, expenses, operations, and credit controls for her district. With an eye on future business, she was also responsible for community leadership, human resources planning, and developing short- and long-term business objectives for her area.

Upper Rungs to Consider

Although Beth's role as a district manager was challenging, gratifying, and lucrative, she decided to develop a tentative series of new jobs to target. Positions included on that list are private banking relationship manager, senior relationship manager, or a senior sales and leadership coach. Each of the targeted jobs would enable her to make broad-based contributions that would help improve the bottom line of the bank.

Preparing for the Climb

As promotions occur, a broader overview of the business is required. How would obtaining a broad range of experience including assignments dealing with automotive lending, credit card services, retail lending and commercial lending help a candidate prepare for higher-level jobs?

13.1

Organizational Structure

Learning Objectives

13.1.1 Explain how banks organize their business by department.

13.1.2 Identify jobs that provide operational support at banks.

Key Terms

- operations
- departmentalization
- customer service representative (CSR)
- integrity
- teller

Banking Scene

Nathaniel Bryant has just graduated from high school and is looking for a job. He isn't interested in just any job. He wants something that will provide an entry-level position leading to a career. His aunt suggested that he apply at one of the local banks. He wonders what skills are needed for bank jobs. What research should Nathaniel conduct on job opportunities in banking?

13.1.1 DEPARTMENTS IN A BANK

Commercial banks experienced many changes in the last decades of the twentieth century. Some became huge entities operating throughout the country and offering a complete line of financial services. Others remained small, serving only one community and offering highly personalized services. Information and communications technologies created new strategic possibilities. Today's commercial banks are more diverse, although they continue to provide the three traditional deposit-gathering, loan, and trust functions. The deposit-gathering functions establish checking and savings accounts. The deposit and loan functions are closely linked because the deposits provide the funds to lend. The trust area's funds come specifically from the fees it charges customers. Each of these areas may have marketing and operations components. Operations provides support services such as bookkeeping and human resources.

No matter how big or small the bank or how many services it offers, it must have some type of organizational structure. This departmentalization, or organization of the bank into departments, can vary as widely as the products and services the bank offers.

Functional Departments

Banks can have many different departments that make up the traditional business of banking. These departments work to meet consumer and business needs. Smaller banks may not have as many departments or offer as many services as larger banks.

Individual or Personal Banking The name of the personal banking department varies from bank to bank. Personal banking, consumer banking, and personal services are some names of the departments that meet the needs of individual customers. In this department, new account personnel or customer service representatives (CSRs) help customers open checking and savings accounts, obtain debit and credit cards, and learn the various options available for interacting with the bank, such as in person, through an ATM, by phone, or online. CSRs may also direct customers to departments that offer other services.

Small Business and Consumer Lending   Consumer loan specialists, loan officers, financial services representatives, and underwriters explain products to customers interested in starting a small business, buying a new car, buying a home, or financing college tuition. These departments are also called business banking, business services, and small business lending. Some banks have departments dedicated to serving specific market segments, including women and minority businesspeople.

Trusts   In the trust department, sometimes known as wealth management, the trust officer, personal trust administrator, or trust account officer manages assets placed in trust with the bank according to clients' wishes. The assets vary greatly from real estate to money to securities to artwork.

Brokerage   Brokers, investment assistants, and financial planners are just a few of the titles of employees who provide financial and investment services to individuals and institutional customers.

Photodisc/Getty Images

Insurance   Some banks offer a full-service, independent insurance agency dedicated to serving the needs of their customers. Agents advise personal and business clients about various services and policies to meet their insurance needs.

Operational Departments

Other departments in a bank provide "behind the scenes" operational support for the basic functional departments. In small banks, one or two individuals may provide the operational support. Large banks have entire departments dedicated to various operational activities.

Accounting/Finance   Accountants, auditors, and controllers provide critical support. They prepare financial reports and budgets. They also write, analyze, and verify financial reports containing current financial information and check that the records are accurate.

Human Resources   The recruiters, job analysts, benefit coordinators, compensation specialists, and trainers in this support area are responsible for hiring and training employees. They also design compensation/benefit programs and maintain personnel records. The responsibility for firing employees, when necessary, also falls to this department.

Operations   Proof operators, bookkeepers, wire transfer specialists, account research and reconcilement specialists, and statement processors provide "back office," or operations, support. These employees provide assistance to other employees as needed to help manage customer accounts.

Treasury Management   Financial experts in this department manage the bank's monetary assets/liabilities and financial risks. They manage the bank's cash and funds in reserves on deposit at the Federal Reserve and in interbank loans to minimize interest expense and maximize interest income. This department is also responsible for placing and liquidating investments and managing foreign exchange and interest rate exposures.

Public Relations/Marketing   Marketing coordinators, public relations representatives, and marketing specialists now work at banks to sell the various products and services. They perform market research, set marketing strategy, create advertising and promotions, and inform the public of the bank's policies, activities, and accomplishments.

Technical   Computer operators, programmers, analysts, and support specialists provide critical technological support for the products and services the bank offers. The employees program and service the computers that allow banks to store and manipulate the vast amount of information the bank processes.

4X6/iStockphoto.com

Maintenance, Purchasing, and Security   These departments provide the support you would expect. Engineers, custodians, plumbers, and so on provide the day-to-day upkeep of the building. Purchasing agents monitor the supplies, from office furniture and computer monitors to paperclips, and purchase them as needed. Security guards or officers patrol and inspect property to protect against fire, theft, vandalism, and illegal activity.

Bank Officers   Although these positions don't really represent a specific department in banks, officers fulfill the necessary management/oversight function. Large banks may have officers known as president, chief executive officer, chief financial officer, chief operating officer, controller, and vice presidents. Smaller banks have fewer of these positions.

 **checkpoint**

What is the difference between functional and operational departments?

13.1.2 JOB POSITIONS WITHIN A BANK'S DEPARTMENTS • •

There are several job positions within a bank's many departments. While the tasks and responsibilities that come with these positions may vary, all bank employees are held to the highest employment standards. Honesty and integrity are two characteristics that are especially important for bank employees. Integrity is the steadfast adherence to a strict moral or ethical code. An important factor for all bank employees to remember is that banking revolves around people. Thus, good people skills are a must. Detailed below are a few of the more common positions available at banks.

Bank Teller

The teller position is the most common one at banks. Tellers are likely to have the most contact with customers. They perform the following duties:

- Balance the cash drawer daily by adding deposits and subtracting withdrawals from the opening cash funds

- Process customer transactions (checking and savings deposits, check cashing, and savings withdrawals)

Banking Math *Connection*

Bank tellers accept credit card deposits from local merchants. Some merchants submit charges to customers' credit cards electronically. The credit card companies automatically deposit funds from the sale into the seller's bank account. This service isn't free. Credit card companies charge vendors a percentage of the sales for providing this convenience.

On Valentine's Day, Noble's Flowers and Gifts electronically charged $2,200 of sales transactions. The card companies charge Noble's a 5 percent service fee. How much was deposited in Noble's account from these credit card sales?

Solution

The formula for finding the amount is

$$\text{Amount deposited} = \text{Amount of sales} - (\text{Amount of sales} \times \text{Fee rate})$$
$$= \$2,200 - (\$2,200 \times 0.05)$$
$$= \$2,200 - \$110$$
$$= \$2,090$$

In this example, the 5 percent fee amounts to $110. This amount is subtracted from the $2,200 total sales charged to arrive at a total of $2,090 deposited in Noble's account.

- Sell money orders, travelers' checks, and savings bonds

- Accept credit card, mortgage, loan, and utility payments from individuals and bank card deposits from merchants

- Prepare currency and coin for retail customers

- Balance automated teller machines, replenish their cash, and process deposits and withdrawals made through them

- Promote banking services and answer customer inquiries

Other Bank Positions

The banking industry provides a great number of jobs in performing its functions and operations. The following are brief descriptions of other common bank positions.

- **Customer service representatives (CSRs)** work directly with customers. CSRs open deposit accounts, interview clients to obtain financial information, explain available services, and help clients solve account problems.

- **Credit analysts** evaluate the financial condition of individuals and businesses seeking credit or a loan. Analysts research the applicant's credit record to gauge whether or not to approve the loan.

- **Trust officers** manage billions of dollars in assets placed in trust with the bank according to clients' wishes. Officers direct trust disbursements according to the terms of the trust or the beneficiary's needs, invest surpluses as the trust directs, and negotiate with public agencies, such as the Social Security Administration, to combine all eligible assets into a trust.

branching out

Nontraditional Branches

Many banks have expanded their retail presence by establishing branches in nontraditional locations. Some banks put branches in hospitals, for example. Providing convenience of services to hospital staff as well as families of patients is a benefit of these branches. From servicing high net worth individuals, including hospital staff who may earn large salaries, to providing loans to families who may need money to help with medical expenses, these branches can offer the same services as traditional branches. Some hospitals feature the branch information on their website. This has the dual benefit of reassuring incoming families that they can access financial information during their stay and provides good publicity for the bank.

Think Critically   Why would a bank choose to place a branch in a hospital? How do you think hospital staff feels about having a branch in the hospital? How do you think the patients' families feel about this?

- **Auditors** maintain and examine the bank's financial records to verify their accuracy. They also look for areas of waste, mismanagement, or fraud. For example, the auditor might check tellers' cash boxes to determine whether their transactions and records are accurate.

- **Job analysts** perform the human resources role of investigating the duties performed in the various banking positions in order to write an accurate, detailed job description. Information in the description details the skills and training required for the job.

- **Accounting clerks** provide operational support to the bank by keeping its financial records, either in books called *ledgers* or in computer documents. They also prepare financial statements that report its assets and liabilities, which summarize how much the bank earns and spends.

- **Public relations specialists** publicize information about the bank, such as an award it received, a new service it provides, or an educational program it sponsors. They also prepare visual presentations for meetings.

- **Computer operators** install, modify, clean, and repair computer hardware and software, and they monitor equipment operation. These troubleshooters analyze and fix problems. They also may train employees to use computer hardware and software.

- **Chief financial officers (CFOs)** are the top financial officers who direct all of a bank's accounting and financial activities. The CFO makes financial plans, such as examining the impact of proposed new functions on the bank's earnings, sets policies, and brings together other managers to develop creative solutions to problems.

✔ checkpoint

What does "balancing a cash drawer" mean?

assessment 13.1

Think Critically

1. What do you think is the reason for departmentalization in banks?

2. What are some characteristics that bank customer service representatives must have?

3. Why do banks need the services of public relations specialists?

4. Which bank jobs described in this lesson do you think may require college degrees?

Make Academic Connections

5. **MATH** Happy Trails is a backpacking adventures outfit that accepts credit cards for only those credit card companies that have waived the service fee. In the past year, Happy Trails has noticed that quite a few of its customers have wanted to use a certain credit card that Happy Trails doesn't accept. Happy Trails is reconsidering its policy and making an exception for this card company, which charges a 3 percent fee on sales. Assuming sales for the year charged under this new credit card are estimated to be $5,600, what is the additional expense that Happy Trails would incur by accepting this card and how much would actually be deposited in its bank account?

6. **MEDIA** Collect classified ads for banking jobs in the Sunday edition of a local newspaper and on the Internet. List all of the skills required. Make a poster that graphically illustrates various categories of skills.

Human Resources

Banking Scene

Nathaniel Bryant sees a newspaper ad about an opening for a bank teller at Farmers Bank. He applies and lands an interview. How can he use the information in the job description from the newspaper ad to prepare for the interview? What skills should he emphasize in discussing his qualifications for the position? What else should he do to prepare? How should he dress?

Learning Objectives

13.2.1 Identify the steps that a human resources department takes to hire new bank personnel.

13.2.2 List the information that an employee's record should include.

Key Terms

- job description
- benefit
- telecommuting
- merit-based employment
- job fair
- orientation

13.2.1 THE HUMAN RESOURCES DEPARTMENT ● ● ● ● ● ● ●

The heart of any organization is its employees. Employees "put a face on a bank" by answering the questions, accepting the deposits, investing the money, and recording the numerous transactions processed. With today's emphasis on providing quality customer service, banks seek to hire people who have both technical expertise and the ability to work well with customers at all levels. Most banks seek to fill entry-level positions with people who have good basic math and communication skills, enjoy public contact, and feel comfortable handling large amounts of money. The human resources (HR) department, sometimes called the *personnel department,* establishes the bank's policies and procedures for hiring, training, and evaluating employees, as well as compensation and benefits. In doing so, HR must be in compliance with government rules and regulations pertaining to hiring and employment practices.

Job Analysis and Description

The HR department analyzes each job in the bank. The analysis involves reviewing the position's responsibilities, the skills required to perform it, its supervisory relationships, and how it fits in the bank's organizational structure. Using this information, HR then prepares the job description, the formal document that factually and concisely identifies the job, responsibilities, work involved, and education required. The multipurpose job description is used in advertising openings, interviewing applicants, orienting new hires, evaluating employee performance, and making promotions. As an example, a loan officer job description might read as shown on the next page.

Commercial Loan Officer

General Responsibilities: Generating and servicing a wide variety of commercial loans; aggressively seeking and obtaining quality new business through client and prospect calls, referrals, and cross-selling efforts; building and maintaining relationships with a high degree of customer satisfaction.

Job Requirements: Skills and experience in applicant interviewing and perceptive character judgment, loan structuring, credit analysis, and monitoring credit performance; a bachelor's degree and four to five years of credit-associated lending.

Salary: $52,000–$68,000

Benefit Establishment

Banks offer competitive benefits. Human resources sets the policies for benefits as instructed by the bank's board of directors. Benefits involve matters such as hours of employment and time off for vacation, illness, holidays, and jury duty. Benefits cover health insurance policies, including dental and vision coverage, disability and unemployment insurance, and retirement plans. To become competitive in attracting high-quality employees, large banks have recently offered benefits such as child and elder care, wellness and fitness programs, and flexible benefits plans. Other new benefits include telecommuting, which lets employees do some work from their homes via computer. HR managers must be knowledgeable about changing government regulations and legislation that affect the benefits the bank offers.

Compensation Determination

The human resources department sets and maintains policy to ensure that employees receive fair and equitable pay rates. Setting the rates could involve conducting surveys to see how the bank's rates compare with those of other banks. HR also conducts research to ensure that the bank's pay scale complies with changing laws and regulations. In addition, the department oversees the performance evaluation system, and it may design reward policies such as pay-for-performance plans. The Bureau of Labor Statistics reported the following median pay for these banking occupations in 2014.

Occupation	Hourly Pay	Annual Pay
Top Executives	$49.40	$102,750
Financial Managers	55.44	115,320
Loan Officers	30.11	62,620
Administrative Services Managers	40.28	83,790
Secretaries and Administrative Assistants	17.30	35,970
Financial Clerks	17.44	36,260
Customer Service Representatives	15.00	31,200
Office Clerks, general	13.78	28,670
Tellers	12.39	25,760

Source: *Occupational Outlook Handbook*, 2014, Bureau of Labor Statistics

The Hiring Process

The human resources department is in charge of hiring new employees for the bank. It sets policy for merit-based employment, that is, selecting the person with the best qualifications for a specific position. The hiring process is somewhat detailed and, depending on the size of the bank and its need, can be long. It begins when an opening is identified.

Advertising   The first step in hiring is to advertise the position, both inside and outside the bank. Depending on the specific job, banks may advertise in newspapers, professional publications, or on the Internet. Information about the job in the ad is based on the job description. Some banks hold job fairs, which are public employment events at which they can present employment opportunities, requirements, and personnel benefits to a large number of people at one time. Interested fair attendees can apply for a position during the fair or at a later time.

Reviewing Applications   After the *closing date*, which is the last day applications are accepted, they are reviewed and screened. Candidates who are most qualified are identified and invited to interview for the position.

Interviewing   Depending on the individual bank's practice, the interview may be conducted by a human resources representative, the manager of the department

Accountant/Bookkeeper

Center City Bank, a leader in banking in the state, has an opening for an accountant/bookkeeper, 8 AM–5 PM, M–F. Accounts payable, accounts receivable, general ledger, and Excel experience required. Competitive salary matched to experience. Apply by March 25. Send resume to Center City Bank, 1504 Riverside Drive, Center City, Attn: Human Resources
An equal opportunity employer

Many human resource departments face ethical issues concerning their personnel files. Space constraints create the need to dispose of them after employees leave the firm. Also, many companies now require any documents relating to an employee's medical history be removed from the personnel file.

Think Critically

What are the ethical concerns regarding the disposal of personnel files, which are confidential? Why do you think medical-related documents should not be in the personnel file?

in which the job is located, or both. The interview focuses on the elements in the job description, which include the position's responsibilities, requirements, reporting relationships, salary, benefits, and advancement opportunities. Only job-related questions that help assess the candidate's experience, skill, and training may be asked. The applicant discusses his or her qualifications for the position and any related experience. Persons applying for the position should be prepared to ask specific questions about the bank, working conditions, special training required, and so on.

Conducting Preemployment Testing Banks may require applicants for certain jobs to take tests as part of the process of determining job suitability. Some tests determine a candidate's current level of skills, and others evaluate the person's aptitude or potential ability to perform the duties required. The test should be carefully prepared to ensure that it focuses on the skills and knowledge required to perform the job. For example, tellers might be tested on their mathematical ability. Results of such tests help the employer make unbiased decisions and distinguish between similarly qualified applicants.

Verifying Application Information and Checking Backgrounds Before making hiring decisions regarding employment at any level in the bank, the human resources department will check an applicant's references. The inquiries are made in a professional manner and may request only factually verifiable and job-related information. As technology has advanced, it is fairly common for the hiring process to include browsing personal information in publicly available online formats. Be prudent in online information that you post. Before posting any online personal information ask yourself "how would a prospective employer regard this information?"

sturti/iStockphoto.com

Orienting New Hires   The next step in the hiring process is orientation, which welcomes new employees to the bank and helps them understand its policies and how it operates. The orientation will reflect the individual bank's personality. A general session covers the bank's philosophy, a detailed explanation of the various benefits it offers its employees, and the bank's expectations of its employees. At this time, a bank that has a written employee handbook may distribute copies to the employees. The presentation of its expectations should include these topics:

- Importance of customer service and other areas that the bank emphasizes

- Rules concerning attendance and punctuality

- Standards of performance

- Performance review process, including the frequency with which an employee's performance is evaluated

- Training opportunities

- Promotion

- Salary increases

- Safety and security measures

Training   New employees learn the procedures, rules, and regulations that apply to their jobs through a combination of formal instruction and on-the-job training. They are often paired with an experienced employee who instructs them in the steps and processes required in the position. More formal instruction is provided through workshops, seminars, and training sessions, which can be held on-site or off-site.

Banks in general encourage employees to advance their careers by developing their job skills and learning new ones by taking approved courses. Some banks offer their own programs, such as those that lead to *teller certification*. Many banks provide opportunities for employees to take courses through the Center for Financial Training (CFT), a nationally recognized training group. CFT offers a wide selection of courses from webinars to three credit courses that carry college credit recommendation through the American Council on Education (ACE). Courses that carry ACE credit recommendation are likely to be accepted at colleges and universities towards a degree program.

checkpoint

Why is checking an applicant's job and educational background important?

interesting *facts*

The Wall Street Journal reported the results of a survey of 358 high-level personnel in various industries that revealed at least seven instances where executives had misrepresented their academic credentials. Irregularities were found in firms ranging from HerbaLife, to MIT, to RadioSchack, to the U.S. Olympic Committee. In most instances, when the inaccuracies surfaced, the executives either resigned or were dismissed.

13.2.2 MAINTAINING EMPLOYEE RECORDS • • • • • • • • • •

Keeping proper records is a requirement for employers. It makes good business sense to have accurate and organized information when needed. In addition, federal and state governments require certain employee data to be kept on record. The human resources department fulfills a critical organizational and legal function by keeping a personnel file for each employee. The file is updated as needed. The file typically includes the original or a copy of these items:

- Personal information including employee's full name, address, telephone number, Social Security number, and name of person to contact for emergency purposes

- Application information (resumes, references, and so on)

- Wage or salary information, including the basis on which wages are calculated (hourly or weekly, for example), the pay rate, pay record by pay period including overtime earnings if applicable, and all additions to or deductions from the employee's wages

- Job description of original and any new position as well as any changes in responsibilities

- Education information (transcripts, certificates, credentials, training)

- Federal/state documents (forms W-4 for tax withholding, I-9 regarding immigration and naturalization), and any later changes

- Performance evaluations, including the required documentation signed by the employee and supervisor

- Benefits forms

Human resources specialists must understand all legal regulations governing today's workplace. They must know, for example, the types of questions they can and cannot ask during an interview, the privacy issues concerning the employee personnel folder, and the appropriate uses of the information in the folder.

✔ checkpoint

Why would HR want to include education information in an employee's personnel folder?

assessment 13.2

Think Critically

1. From an employer's perspective, what are some advantages of allowing employees to telecommute?

2. What is the importance of merit-based hiring in the employment process?

3. What are the problems that could result from "beefing up" or exaggerating duties of a job when the company advertises it? What would the company hope to gain by this practice?

4. Why is the process of setting employee pay rates a crucial activity?

Make Academic Connections

5. **CRITICAL THINKING**   Working in groups, list the characteristics that you believe a human resources specialist in a bank should have. Then design a form to be used during an interview to help uncover an applicant's strength in those areas.

6. **MARKETING**   On the Internet, find at least three banks that offer call-center services. What do these centers do? What department would supervise the call center? Summarize your findings.

13.3 Employee Evaluation

Learning Objectives

13.3.1 State the objectives of employee performance evaluations.

13.3.2 Describe the employee discipline process.

Key Terms

- performance standard
- evaluation form

Banking Scene

Nathaniel Bryant has been hired as a teller at Farmers Bank. All new employees are hired on a probationary period and are evaluated six months after their hire date. How might Nathaniel prepare for the performance evaluation process?

13.3.1 EMPLOYEE PERFORMANCE EVALUATION • • • • • • • • •

One way to ensure that employees are meeting the bank's goals is to make sure that they understand their responsibilities and are performing at an expected level. Banks, like other businesses, periodically conduct formal employee reviews. These reviews should come at regularly scheduled intervals, such as every six months or every year, or at the end of the probationary period if the employee is on probation. Of course, effective supervisors bring obvious problems to an employee's attention as they occur rather than waiting for a formal assessment.

Employment performance evaluation can be a sensitive area. Although both the evaluator and the employee might feel awkward or uncomfortable, the review is a crucial part of the employment process. It is only fair for supervisors to let employees know how they are performing and what they need to do to improve.

Objectives

In general, employee performance evaluations have these objectives:

- To assess actual performance and accomplishments against the duties, responsibilities, and standards of the employee's position as stated in the job description

- To identify the employee's potential and interests and assist her or him in setting goals for job improvement and professional growth

- To provide a written record of employee performance to support future personnel decisions related to salary, promotion, increased responsibility, reassignment, transfer, reemployment, or disciplinary action

- To provide a communication tool through which to recognize the employee's special talents, capabilities, and achievements and identify any areas of job performance that need to be improved

Performance Standards

To ensure that evaluations are fair and objective, standards must be established related to job duties and responsibilities. Performance standards define for both supervisors and employees the expectations for completing a job's essential functions and tasks. For example, bank tellers may be evaluated on their ability to count money, keep the cash drawer in balance, and process customer transactions accurately. An understanding of the standards provides the basis for ongoing feedback and performance counseling between assessments as well as for formal evaluation.

Numerous methods can be used to develop standards. Traditionally, the human resources department identifies the standards in consultation with management. A collaborative approach involves both supervisors or HR personnel and employees. Employees bring valuable insight about their jobs to the process, and they are more likely to support the final standards that they helped define. Specific standards focus the discussion on specific elements of the employee's performance.

Evaluation Forms

In an effort to make their performance evaluations fair and objective, many banks use a standardized form, called an evaluation form, on which to record employee assessments. It is probably best for a bank to develop its own form so that it reflects that bank's standards, but many different versions are available for sale. An effective form includes the following:

- Employee's name and job title

- Name and position of person making the evaluation

- Scale used for evaluation, such as outstanding, very good, satisfactory, development needed, or a scale of 1 to 10

Tech Talk

Virtual Tellers

In 2008, IBM introduced interactive bank kiosks. The kiosks allow tellers at brick-and-mortar banks to remotely service customers with the help of webcams. With technology conveying the voice and image of both the teller at his or her workstation and the customer at a kiosk, the majority of customer-to-teller services are performed via the virtual teller. Cash transactions cannot be handled through the virtual teller, however. These virtual tellers provide an additional service option for customers, but they are not expected to replace live tellers.

Think Critically   What type of customer is mostly likely to seek the use of a virtual teller? How will bank personnel react to this new technology?

Monkey Business Images/Shutterstock.com

- List of performance standards for the job title

- A section allowing space for listing suggested steps to take for improving performance

A sample performance appraisal is shown on the next page. At the end of the review, both the employee and the supervisor should sign the form, indicating their agreement with the information it contains. Employees who disagree with anything in the review should have a specific procedure through which to appeal the process.

Appeal Process

Banks should establish standard procedures by which employees can appeal some or all of their performance evaluation. These procedures are generally detailed in the bank's employee handbook. Appeals may be made verbally or in writing, although it is generally preferred to have a written statement. A written appeal states the reason for which the employee is contesting the evaluation and any supporting information or documentation. The appeal advances through the established channels until it is resolved.

 **checkpoint**

Why do you think it is better to appeal a job evaluation in writing?

13.3.2 EMPLOYEE DISCIPLINE

Most employers are careful to provide employees detailed descriptions of their job duties and responsibilities and the proper way to perform them. Banks are no exception. Many of them provide handbooks or other written documents that explain the behavior and performance expected of their employees. These documents also explain disciplinary procedures and reasons for termination. Discipline can include informal warnings, formal written warnings, suspension without pay, and termination if the employee does not solve the problem.

Informal Warning

Minor problems, such as tardiness, failure to cooperate with employees, or forgetting to sign documents, can result in a verbal warning after the supervisor has discussed the problem with the employee. Although this is considered informal, it is recorded in the employee's personnel file.

Performance Appraisal—Teller I

Employee's Name _____

Supervisor's Name _____

Performance Review Date_____

Rating   Performance Level

7   **Outstanding:** Outstanding total performance. Consistently completes duties in an outstanding manner.

6   **Exceptional:** Very good performance; exceeds standards generally and expectations continuously.

5   **Very good:** Performance above standard at times.

4   **Satisfactory:** Overall satisfactory performance meeting the job's requirements.

3   **Borderline:** Performance unacceptable at times and requires improvement.

2   **Poor:** Performance often below expectations; inconsistent and unacceptable in many areas.

1   **Unsatisfactory:** Consistently unacceptable performance.

Standards

____ Demonstrates understanding of job requirements and implements that knowledge in performing duties

____ Balances the cash drawer daily

____ Is able to process customer transactions (checking and savings deposits, check cashing, and savings withdrawals)

____ Sells money orders, travelers' checks, and savings bonds

____ Accepts credit card, mortgage, loan, and utility payments from individuals and bank card deposits from merchants

____ Prepares currency and coin for retail customers

____ Balances automated teller machines, replenishes their cash, and processes deposits and withdrawals made through them

____ Promotes banking services and answers customer inquiries

____ Demonstrates customer-service orientation in working with customers

For areas rated 1–3, these specific actions should be taken to improve performance _____

_____

Improvement required by (date) _____

Employee Signature_____ Supervisor Signature_____

Formal Warning

When an employee commits a serious breach of the bank's policy or fails to show improvement after an informal warning, the supervisor discusses the problem with the employee, citing specific occurrences. The employee may explain any special circumstances regarding the violation. The supervisor considers the facts and may decide that a formal warning is warranted. The supervisor explains the reason for the decision, describes in detail the performance changes necessary to correct the situation, sets a timeframe in which the performance must change, and advises of any consequences if the employee does not meet the expectations, including dismissal. A copy of the formal warning is placed in the employee's personnel file.

Suspension or Dismissal

An employee who does not improve his or her performance or repeats the offensive action within the specified time may be suspended or dismissed. A hearing including members of the management team, the personnel department, and the immediate supervisor is generally held. All special circumstances are considered. If the decision is to suspend the employee, employment will be discontinued for a time specified by the bank's policy. The written notice is added to the employee's file.

If the decision is made to dismiss the employee, he or she is given the reasons. This decision is confirmed in writing, and the employee is given a termination notice. Some misconduct is so serious that the required disciplinary action is immediate dismissal. This gross misconduct includes:

- Refusal to comply with an instruction
- Failure to follow safety rule(s)
- Theft, fraud, or deliberate damage to bank property
- Alcohol or drug intoxication on bank property
- Violent behavior or threats to coworkers, management, or customers

Appeal

Disciplinary procedures must be followed to protect the employer from charges that its actions are either unfounded or performed improperly.

Procedures also serve to protect the employee from having unjustified action taken against him or her. An employee who has been given a formal warning, a suspension, or a termination notice has the right to appeal the decision according to the policies that the bank has established.

 checkpoint

Why is a standardized process needed for disciplining and dismissing employees?

assessment 13.3

Think Critically

1. Why is it unwise for a supervisor who is aware of an employee's performance problem to wait to bring it to the worker's attention until the formal job review?

2. In what way does an employee evaluation act as a communication tool?

3. Why is it important for job descriptions to be updated regularly?

4. What is the purpose of using suspension without pay as a disciplinary measure?

Make Academic Connections

5. **RESEARCH**   The Bureau of Labor Statistics is an excellent source of information about the banking industry. Access the BLS website, type "banking industry" into the search engine, and click on a link to one of the articles. Then prepare a summary of the information in the article you chose.

6. **ECONOMICS**   Analyze the impact of the use of online services on the banking industry.

chapter 13 **assessment**

Chapter Summary

13.1 Organizational Structure and Employees

A. Banks are organized by departments. Titles of departments vary. A typical bank is structured around the deposit-gathering, loan, and trust functions. Other departments support these functions.

B. Many different positions provide the services that banks offer. A wide range of skills and responsibilities is involved.

13.2 Human Resources

A. Human resources departments at banks establish the policies and procedures related to hiring, training, evaluation, compensation, and benefits.

B. The HR department maintains confidential employee records according to legal requirements and bank guidelines.

13.3 Employee Evaluation

A. To ensure that employees understand their responsibilities, perform them as required, and have a gauge as to their performance level, banks conduct periodic employee assessments.

B. From time to time, a bank must discipline and even dismiss an employee. In doing so, it must follow specific steps and perform certain procedures aimed at protecting the employer and the employee.

Vocabulary Builder

Choose the term that best fits the definition. Write the letter of the answer in the space provided.

a. benefit
b. customer service representative (CSR)
c. departmentalization
d. evaluation form
e. integrity
f. job description
g. job fair
h. merit-based employment
i. operations
j. orientation
k. performance standard
l. telecommuting
m. teller

_____ 1. The most common position at banks
_____ 2. Provides support to all functional departments
_____ 3. A form on which to record employee assessments
_____ 4. An event at which banks present information about employment to a large group of people
_____ 5. Involves policies concerning hours of work, time off, and insurance and retirement plans
_____ 6. The adherence to a strict moral or ethical code
_____ 7. States a job's duties and the skills and education required to perform those duties
_____ 8. Creates an organizational structure for a bank by dividing it into departments
_____ 9. Defines the expectations for completing a job's essential functions and tasks
_____ 10. Allows an employee to work from home via computer
_____ 11. Process that occurs at the beginning of employment that welcomes new employees and helps them understand a bank's policies
_____ 12. Selecting the most qualified candidate for a specific position
_____ 13. Account personnel that help customers open a variety of new accounts

Review Concepts

14. List three primary activities or functions of a bank.

15. What is the difference between the functional and operations areas of banks?

16. What is a financial statement?

17. List the various uses of a job description.

18. What is a job fair?

19. What is the reason for preemployment testing?

20. List the documents that a personnel file typically includes.

21. What are the objectives of employee evaluation?

22. What is the purpose of performance standards?

23. What are the stages in employee discipline?

24. List three actions for which an employee could be dismissed immediately.

Apply What You Learned

25. Why is integrity an essential characteristic for all bank employees?

26. Why must all bank employees have good "people" skills?

27. Why is it improper for an interviewer to ask a job applicant about his or her child-care arrangements?

28. Why should the personnel file be kept confidential?

29. What do you think is the purpose of having an employee sign the employee evaluation form?

30. What should employees do if they believe their performance evaluation contains inaccurate information?

31. Give examples of what employee issues would prompt an informal warning and then what problems would necessitate a formal warning.

Make Academic Connections

32. **RESEARCH** Choose one of the job positions discussed in Lesson 13.1. Investigate the job tasks, salary, and job outlook. Write a two-page report on what you learn.

33. **MATH** At the beginning of the work day, a teller's cash drawer has a total of $5 in loose change, 50 one-dollar bills, 50 tens, 30 twenties, 10 fifties, and 10 hundreds. During the day, the teller had deposit transactions totaling $3,150 and withdrawals of $4,300. At the end of the day, the drawer contains $1,060. Is the drawer in balance?

34. **COMMUNICATION** Use the Internet to find samples of resumes. Compile a resume that you can use when applying for banking jobs.

35. **CAREERS** Interview a bank employee about the position's responsibilities. Learn about the person's daily business activities and recent technological advances that have affected the job. Present your findings to the class in an oral report.

Brief Summary of the Dodd-Frank Wall Street Reform and Consumer Protection Act

Create a Sound Economic Foundation to Grow Jobs, Protect Consumers, Rein in Wall Street and Big Bonuses, End Bailouts and Too Big to Fail, Prevent Another Financial Crisis

Years without accountability for Wall Street and big banks brought us the worst financial crisis since the Great Depression, the loss of 8 million jobs, failed businesses, a drop in housing prices, and wiped out personal savings.

The failures that led to this crisis require bold action. We must restore responsibility and accountability in our financial system to give Americans confidence that there is a system in place that works for and protects them. We must create a sound foundation to grow the economy and create jobs.

Highlights of the Legislation

Consumer Protections with Authority and Independence: Creates a new independent watchdog, housed at the Federal Reserve, with the authority to ensure American consumers get the clear, accurate information they need to shop for mortgages, credit cards, and other financial products, and protect them from hidden fees, abusive terms, and deceptive practices.

Ends Too Big to Fail Bailouts: Ends the possibility that taxpayers will be asked to write a check to bail out financial firms that threaten the economy by: creating a safe way to liquidate failed financial firms; imposing tough new capital and leverage requirements that make it undesirable to get too big; updating the Fed's authority to allow system-wide support but no longer prop up individual firms; and establishing rigorous standards and supervision to protect the economy and American consumers, investors and businesses.

Advance Warning System: Creates a council to identify and address systemic risks posed by large, complex companies, products, and activities before they threaten the stability of the economy.

Transparency & Accountability for Exotic Instruments: Eliminates loopholes that allow risky and abusive practices to go on unnoticed and unregulated – including loopholes for over-the-counter derivatives, asset-backed securities, hedge funds, mortgage brokers and payday lenders.

Executive Compensation and Corporate Governance: Provides shareholders with a say on pay and corporate affairs with a non-binding vote on executive compensation and golden parachutes.

Protects Investors: Provides tough new rules for transparency and accountability for credit rating agencies to protect investors and businesses.

Enforces Regulations on the Books: Strengthens oversight and empowers regulators to aggressively pursue financial fraud, conflicts of interest and manipulation of the system that benefits special interests at the expense of American families and businesses.

Strong Consumer Financial Protection Watchdog

The Consumer Financial Protection Bureau

- **Independent Head:** Led by an independent director appointed by the President and confirmed by the Senate.

- **Independent Budget:** Dedicated budget paid by the Federal Reserve system.

- **Independent Rule Writing:** Able to autonomously write rules for consumer protections governing all financial institutions – banks and non-banks – offering consumer financial services or products.

- **Examination and Enforcement:** Authority to examine and enforce regulations for banks and credit unions with assets of over $10 billion and all mortgage-related businesses (lenders, servicers, mortgage brokers, and foreclosure scam operators), payday lenders, and student lenders as well as other nonbank financial companies that are large, such as debt collectors and consumer reporting agencies. Banks and Credit Unions with assets of $10 billion or less will be examined for consumer complaints by the appropriate regulator.

- **Consumer Protections:** Consolidates and strengthens consumer protection responsibilities currently handled by the Office of the Comptroller of the Currency, Office of Thrift Supervision, Federal Deposit Insurance Corporation, Federal Reserve, National Credit Union Administration, the Department of Housing and Urban Development, and Federal Trade Commission. Will also oversee the enforcement of federal laws intended to ensure the fair, equitable and nondiscriminatory access to credit for individuals and communities.

- **Able to Act Fast:** With this Bureau on the lookout for bad deals and schemes, consumers won't have to wait for Congress to pass a law to be protected from bad business practices.

- **Educates:** Creates a new Office of Financial Literacy.

- **Consumer Hotline:** Creates a national consumer complaint hotline so consumers will have, for the first time, a single toll-free number to report problems with financial products and services.

- **Accountability:** Makes one office accountable for consumer protections. With many agencies sharing responsibility, it's hard to know who is responsible for what, and easy for emerging problems that haven't historically fallen under anyone's purview, to fall through the cracks.

- **Works with Bank Regulators:** Coordinates with other regulators when examining banks to prevent undue regulatory burden. Consults with regulators before a proposal is issued and regulators could appeal regulations they believe would put the safety and soundness of the banking system or the stability of the financial system at risk.

- **Clearly Defined Oversight:** Protects small business from unintentionally being regulated by the CFPB, excluding businesses that meet certain standards.

Looking Out for the Next Big Problem: Addressing Systemic Risks

The Financial Stability Oversight Council

- **Expert Members:** Made up of 10 federal financial regulators and an independent member and 5 nonvoting members, the Financial Stability Oversight Council will be charged with identifying and responding to emerging risks throughout the financial system. The Council will be chaired by the Treasury Secretary and include the Federal Reserve Board, SEC, CFTC, OCC, FDIC, FHFA, NCUA, the new Consumer Financial Protection Bureau, and an independent appointee with insurance expertise. The 5 nonvoting members include OFR, FIO, and state banking, insurance, and securities regulators.

- **Tough to Get Too Big:** Makes recommendations to the Federal Reserve for increasingly strict rules for capital, leverage, liquidity, risk management and other requirements as companies grow in size and complexity, with significant requirements on companies that pose risks to the financial system.

- **Regulates Nonbank Financial Companies:** Authorized to require, with a 2/3 vote and vote of the chair, that a nonbank financial company be regulated by the Federal Reserve if the council believes there would be negative effects on the financial system if the company failed or its activities would pose a risk to the financial stability of the United States.

- **Break Up Large, Complex Companies:** Able to approve, with a 2/3 vote and vote of the chair, a Federal Reserve decision to require a large, complex company to divest some of its holdings if it poses a grave threat to the financial stability of the United States – but only as a last resort.

- **Technical Expertise:** Creates a new Office of Financial Research within Treasury to be staffed with a highly sophisticated staff of economists, accountants, lawyers, former supervisors, and other specialists to support the council's work by collecting financial data and conducting economic analysis.

- **Make Risks Transparent:** Through the Office of Financial Research and member agencies the council will collect and analyze data to identify and monitor emerging risks to the economy and make this information public in periodic reports and testimony to Congress every year.

- **No Evasion:** Large bank holding companies that have received TARP funds will not be able to avoid Federal Reserve supervision by simply dropping their banks (the "Hotel California" provision).

- **Capital Standards:** Establishes a floor for capital that cannot be lower than the standards in effect today and authorizes the Council to impose a 15–1 leverage

requirement at a company if necessary to mitigate a grave threat to the financial system.

Ending Too Big to Fail Bailouts

Limiting Large, Complex Financial Companies and Preventing Future Bailouts

- **No Taxpayer Funded Bailouts:** Clearly states taxpayers will not be on the hook to save a failing financial company or to cover the cost of its liquidation.

- **Discourage Excessive Growth & Complexity:** The Financial Stability Oversight Council will monitor systemic risk and make recommendations to the Federal Reserve for increasingly strict rules for capital, leverage, liquidity, risk management and other requirements as companies grow in size and complexity, with significant requirements on companies that pose risks to the financial system.

- **Volcker Rule:** Requires regulators to implement regulations for banks, their affiliates and holding companies; to prohibit proprietary trading, investment in and sponsorship of hedge funds and private equity funds; and to limit relationships with hedge funds and private equity funds. Nonbank financial institutions supervised by the Fed also have restrictions on proprietary trading and hedge fund and private equity investments. The Council will study and make recommendations on implementation to aid regulators.

- **Extends Regulation:** The Council will have the ability to require nonbank financial companies that pose a risk to the financial stability of the United States to submit to supervision by the Federal Reserve.

- **Payment, Clearing, and Settlement Regulation:** Provides a specific framework for promoting uniform risk-management standards for systemically important financial market utilities and systemically important payment, clearing, and settlement activities conducted by financial institutions.

- **Funeral Plans:** Requires large, complex financial companies to periodically submit plans for their rapid and orderly shutdown should the company go under. Companies will be hit with higher capital requirements and restrictions on growth and activity, as well as divestment, if they fail to submit acceptable plans. Plans will help regulators understand the structure of the companies they oversee and serve as a roadmap for shutting them down if the company fails. Significant costs for failing to produce a credible plan create incentives for firms to rationalize structures or operations that cannot be unwound easily.

- **Liquidation:** Creates an orderly liquidation mechanism for FDIC to unwind failing systemically significant financial companies. Shareholders and unsecured creditors bear losses and management and culpable directors will be removed.

- **Liquidation Procedure:** Requires that Treasury, FDIC and the Federal Reserve all agree to put a company into the orderly liquidation process to mitigate serious adverse effects on financial stability, with an up front judicial review.

- **Costs to Financial Firms, Not Taxpayers:** Taxpayers will bear no cost for liquidating large, interconnected financial companies. FDIC can borrow only the amount of funds to liquidate a company that it expects to be repaid from the assets of the company being liquidated. The government will be first in line for repayment. Funds not repaid from the sale of the company's assets will be repaid first through the claw back of any payments to creditors that exceeded liquidation value and then assessments on large financial companies, with the riskiest paying more based on considerations included in a risk matrix

- **Federal Reserve Emergency Lending:** Significantly alters the Federal Reserve's 13(3) emergency lending authority to prohibit bailing out an individual company. Secretary of the Treasury must approve any lending program, and such programs must be broad based and not aid a failing financial company. Collateral must be sufficient to protect taxpayers from losses.

- **Bankruptcy:** Most large financial companies that fail are expected to be resolved through the bankruptcy process.

- **Limits on Debt Guarantees:** To prevent bank runs, the FDIC can guarantee debt of solvent insured banks, but only after meeting serious requirements: 2/3 majority of the Board and the FDIC board must determine there is a threat to financial stability; the Treasury Secretary approves terms and conditions and sets a cap on overall guarantee amounts; the President activates an expedited process for Congressional approval.

Reforming the Federal Reserve

- **Federal Reserve Emergency Lending:** Limits the Federal Reserve's 13(3) emergency lending authority by prohibiting emergency lending to an individual entity. Secretary of the Treasury must approve any lending program, programs must be broad based, and loans cannot be made to insolvent firms. Collateral must be sufficient to protect taxpayers from losses.

- **Audit of the Federal Reserve:** GAO will conduct a one-time audit of all Federal Reserve 13(3) emergency lending that took place during the financial crisis. Details on all lending will be published on the Federal Reserve website by December 1, 2010. In the future GAO will have on-going authority to audit 13(3), emergency lending, and discount window lending, and open market transactions.

- **Transparency – Disclosure:** Requires the Federal Reserve to disclose counterparties and information about amounts, terms and conditions of 13(3) emergency lending and discount window lending, and open market transactions on an on-going basis, with specified time delays.

- **Supervisory Accountability:** Creates a Vice Chairman for Supervision, a member of the Board of Governors of the Federal Reserve designated by the President, who will develop policy recommendations regarding supervision and regulation for the Board, and will report to Congress semi-annually on Board supervision and regulation efforts.

- **Federal Reserve Bank Governance:** GAO will conduct a study of the current system for appointing Federal Reserve Bank directors, to examine whether the current system effectively represents the public, and whether there are actual or

potential conflicts of interest. It will also examine the establishment and operation of emergency lending facilities during the crisis and the Federal Reserve banks involved therein. The GAO will identify measures that would improve reserve bank governance.

- **Election of Federal Reserve Bank Presidents:** Presidents of the Federal Reserve Banks will be elected by class B directors – elected by district member banks to represent the public – and class C directors – appointed by the Board of Governors to represent the public. Class A directors – elected by member banks to represent member banks – will no longer vote for presidents of the Federal Reserve Banks.

- **Limits on Debt Guarantees:** To prevent bank runs, the FDIC can guarantee debt of solvent insured banks, but only after meeting serious requirements: 2/3 majority of the Federal Reserve Board and the FDIC board determine there is a threat to financial stability; the Treasury Secretary approves terms and conditions and sets a cap on overall guarantee amounts; the President initiates an expedited process for Congressional approval.

Creating Transparency and Accountability for Derivatives

Bringing Transparency and Accountability to the Derivatives Market

- **Closes Regulatory Gaps:** Provides the SEC and CFTC with authority to regulate over-the-counter derivatives so that irresponsible practices and excessive risk-taking can no longer escape regulatory oversight.

- **Central Clearing and Exchange Trading:** Requires central clearing and exchange trading for derivatives that can be cleared and provides a role for both regulators and clearing houses to determine which contracts should be cleared.

- **Market Transparency:** Requires data collection and publication through clearing houses or swap repositories to improve market transparency and provide regulators important tools for monitoring and responding to risks.

- **Financial Safeguards:** Adds safeguards to system by ensuring dealers and major swap participants have adequate financial resources to meet responsibilities. Provides regulators the authority to impose capital and margin requirements on swap dealers and major swap participants, not end users.

- **Higher Standard of Conduct:** Establishes a code of conduct for all registered swap dealers and major swap participants when advising a swap entity. When acting as counterparties to a pension fund, endowment fund, or state or local government, dealers are to have a reasonable basis to believe that the fund or governmental entity has an independent representative advising them.

New Offices of Minority and Women Inclusion

- At federal banking and securities regulatory agencies, the bill establishes an Office of Minority and Women Inclusion that will, among other things, address employment and contracting diversity matters. The offices will coordinate technical

assistance to minority-owned and women-owned businesses and seek diversity in the workforce of the regulators.

Mortgage Reform

- **Require Lenders Ensure a Borrower's Ability to Repay:** Establishes a simple federal standard for all home loans: institutions must ensure that borrowers can repay the loans they are sold.

- **Prohibit Unfair Lending Practices:** Prohibits the financial incentives for subprime loans that encourage lenders to steer borrowers into more costly loans, including the bonuses known as "yield spread premiums" that lenders pay to brokers to inflate the cost of loans. Prohibits pre-payment penalties that trapped so many borrowers into unaffordable loans.

- **Establishes Penalties for Irresponsible Lending:** Lenders and mortgage brokers who don't comply with new standards will be held accountable by consumers for as high as three-years of interest payments and damages plus attorney's fees (if any). Protects borrowers against foreclosure for violations of these standards.

- **Expands Consumer Protections for High-Cost Mortgages:** Expands the protections available under federal rules on high-cost loans – lowering the interest rate and the points and fee triggers that define high cost loans.

- **Requires Additional Disclosures for Consumers on Mortgages:** Lenders must disclose the maximum a consumer could pay on a variable rate mortgage, with a warning that payments will vary based on interest rate changes.

- **Housing Counseling:** Establishes an Office of Housing Counseling within HUD to boost homeownership and rental housing counseling.

Hedge Funds

Raising Standards and Regulating Hedge Funds

- **Fills Regulatory Gaps:** Ends the "shadow" financial system by requiring hedge funds and private equity advisors to register with the SEC as investment advisors and provide information about their trades and portfolios necessary to assess systemic risk. This data will be shared with the systemic risk regulator and the SEC will report to Congress annually on how it uses this data to protect investors and market integrity.

- **Greater State Supervision:** Raises the assets threshold for federal regulation of investment advisors from $30 million to $100 million, a move expected to significantly increase the number of advisors under state supervision. States have proven to be strong regulators in this area and subjecting more entities to state supervision will allow the SEC to focus its resources on newly registered hedge funds.

Credit Rating Agencies

New Requirements and Oversight of Credit Rating Agencies

- **New Office, New Focus at SEC:** Creates an Office of Credit Ratings at the SEC with expertise and its own compliance staff and the authority to fine agencies. The SEC is required to examine Nationally Recognized Statistical Ratings Organizations at least once a year and make key findings public.

- **Disclosure:** Requires Nationally Recognized Statistical Ratings Organizations to disclose their methodologies, their use of third parties for due diligence efforts, and their ratings track record.

- **Independent Information:** Requires agencies to consider information in their ratings that comes to their attention from a source other than the organizations being rated if they find it credible.

- **Conflicts of Interest:** Prohibits compliance officers from working on ratings, methodologies, or sales; installs a new requirement for NRSROs to conduct a one-year look-back review when an NRSRO employee goes to work for an obligor or underwriter of a security or money market instrument subject to a rating by that NRSRO; and mandates that a report to the SEC when certain employees of the NRSRO go to work for an entity that the NRSRO has rated in the previous twelve months.

- **Liability:** Investors can bring private rights of action against ratings agencies for a knowing or reckless failure to conduct a reasonable investigation of the facts or to obtain analysis from an independent source. NRSROs will now be subject to "expert liability" with the nullification of Rule 436(g) which provides an exemption for credit ratings provided by NRSROs from being considered a part of the registration statement.

- **Right to Deregister:** Gives the SEC the authority to deregister an agency for providing bad ratings over time.

- **Education:** Requires ratings analysts to pass qualifying exams and have continuing education.

- **Eliminates Many Statutory and Regulatory Requirements to Use NRSRO Ratings:** Reduces over-reliance on ratings and encourages investors to conduct their own analysis.

- **Independent Boards:** Requires at least half the members of NRSRO boards to be independent, with no financial stake in credit ratings.

- **Ends Shopping for Ratings:** The SEC shall create a new mechanism to prevent issuers of asset-backed securities from picking the agency they think will give the highest rating, after conducting a study and after submission of the report to Congress.

Executive Compensation and Corporate Governance

Gives Shareholders a Say on Pay and Creating Greater Accountability

- **Vote on Executive Pay and Golden Parachutes:** Gives shareholders a say on pay with the right to a non-binding vote on executive pay and golden parachutes. This gives shareholders a powerful opportunity to hold accountable executives of the companies they own, and a chance to disapprove where they see the kind of misguided incentive schemes that threatened individual companies and in turn the broader economy.

- **Nominating Directors:** Gives the SEC authority to grant shareholders proxy access to nominate directors. These requirements can help shift management's focus from short-term profits to long-term growth and stability.

- **Independent Compensation Committees:** Standards for listing on an exchange will require that compensation committees include only independent directors and have authority to hire compensation consultants in order to strengthen their independence from the executives they are rewarding or punishing.

- **No Compensation for Lies:** Requires that public companies set policies to take back executive compensation if it was based on inaccurate financial statements that don't comply with accounting standards.

- **SEC Review:** Directs the SEC to clarify disclosures relating to compensation, including requiring companies to provide charts that compare their executive compensation with stock performance over a five-year period.

- **Enhanced Compensation Oversight for Financial Industry:** Requires federal financial regulators to issue and enforce joint compensation rules specifically applicable to financial institutions with a federal regulator.

Improvements to Bank and Thrift Regulations

- **Volcker Rule:** Implements a strengthened version of the Volcker rule by not allowing a study of the issue to undermine the prohibition on proprietary trading and investing a banking entity's own money in hedge funds, with a *de minimis* exception for funds where the investors require some "skin in the game" by the investment advisor – up to 3% of tier 1 capital in the aggregate

- **Abolishes the Office of Thrift Supervision:** Shuts down this dysfunctional regulator and transfers authorities mainly to the Office of the Comptroller of the Currency, but preserves the thrift charter.

- **Stronger Lending Limits:** Adds credit exposure from derivative transactions to banks' lending limits.

- **Improves Supervision of Holding Company Subsidiaries:** Requires the Federal Reserve to examine nonbank subsidiaries that are engaged in activities that the subsidiary bank can do (e.g., mortgage lending) on the same schedule and in the same manner as bank exams. Provides the primary federal bank regulator backup authority if that does not occur.

- **Intermediate Holding Companies:** Allows use of intermediate holding companies by commercial firms that control grandfathered unitary thrift holding companies to better regulate the financial activities, but not the commercial activities.

- **Interest on Business Checking:** Repeals the prohibition on banks paying interest on demand deposits.

- **Charter Conversions:** Removes a regulatory arbitrage opportunity by prohibiting a bank from converting its charter (unless both the old regulator and new regulator do not object) in order to get out from under an enforcement action.

- **Establishes New Offices of Minority and Women Inclusion at the Federal Financial Agencies**

Insurance

- **Federal Insurance Office:** Creates the first ever office in the federal government focused on insurance. The Office, as established in the Treasury, will gather information about the insurance industry, including access to affordable insurance products by minorities, low- and moderate-income persons and underserved communities. The Office will also monitor the insurance industry for systemic risk purposes.

- **International Presence:** The Office will serve as a uniform, national voice on insurance matters for the United States on the international stage.

- **Streamlines** regulation of surplus lines insurance and reinsurance through state-based reforms.

Interchange Fees

- **Protects Small Businesses from Unreasonable Fees:** Requires Federal Reserve to issue rules to ensure that fees charged to merchants by credit card companies for debit card transactions are reasonable and proportional to the cost of processing those transactions.

Credit Score Protection

- **Monitor Personal Financial Rating:** Allows consumers free access to their credit score if their score negatively affects them in a financial transaction or a hiring decision. Gives consumers access to credit score disclosures as part of an adverse action and risk-based pricing notice.

Sec and Improving Investor Protections

- **Fiduciary Duty:** Gives SEC the authority to impose a fiduciary duty on brokers who give investment advice – the advice must be in the best interest of their customers.

- **Encouraging Whistleblowers:** Creates a program within the SEC to encourage people to report securities violations, creating rewards of up to 30% of funds recovered for information provided.

- **SEC Management Reform:** Mandates a comprehensive outside consultant study of the SEC, an annual assessment of the SEC's internal supervisory controls and GAO review of SEC management.

- **New Advocates for Investors:** Creates the Investment Advisory Committee, a committee of investors to advise the SEC on its regulatory priorities and practices; the Office of Investor Advocate in the SEC, to identify areas where investors have significant problems dealing with the SEC and provide them assistance; and an ombudsman to handle investor complaints.

- **SEC Funding:** Provides more resources to the chronically underfunded agency to carry out its new duties.

Securitization

Reducing Risks Posed by Securities

- **Skin in the Game:** Requires companies that sell products like mortgage-backed securities to retain at least 5% of the credit risk, unless the underlying loans meet standards that reduce riskiness. That way if the investment doesn't pan out, the company that packaged and sold the investment would lose out right along with the people they sold it to.

- **Better Disclosure:** Requires issuers to disclose more information about the underlying assets and to analyze the quality of the underlying assets.

Municipal Securities

Better Oversight of Municipal Securities Industry

- **Registers Municipal Advisors:** Requires registration of municipal advisors and subjects them to rules written by the MSRB and enforced by the SEC.

- **Puts Investors First on the MSRB Board:** Ensures that at all times, the MSRB must have a majority of independent members, to ensure that the public interest is better protected in the regulation of municipal securities.

- **Fiduciary Duty:** Imposes a fiduciary duty on advisors to ensure that they adhere to the highest standard of care when advising municipal issuers.

Tackling the Effects of the Mortgage Crisis

- **Neighborhood Stabilization Program:** Provides $1 billion to states and localities to combat the ugly impact on neighborhood of the foreclosure crisis – such as falling property values and increased crime – by rehabilitating, redeveloping, and reusing abandoned and foreclosed properties.

- **Emergency Mortgage Relief:** Building on a successful Pennsylvania program, provides $1 billion for bridge loans to qualified unemployed homeowners with reasonable prospects for reemployment to help cover mortgage payments until they are reemployed.

- **Foreclosure Legal Assistance:** Authorizes a HUD administered program for making grants to provide foreclosure legal assistance to low- and moderate-income homeowners and tenants related to home ownership preservation, home foreclosure prevention, and tenancy associated with home foreclosure.

Transparency for Extraction Industry

- **Public Disclosure**: Requires public disclosure to the SEC of payments made to the U.S. and foreign governments relating to the commercial development of oil, natural gas, and minerals.

- **SEC Filing Disclosure:** The SEC must require those engaged in the commercial development of oil, natural gas, or minerals to include information about payments they or their subsidiaries, partners or affiliates have made to the U.S. or a foreign government for such development in an annual report and post this information online.

Congo Conflict Minerals

- **Manufacturers Disclosure:** Requires those who file with the SEC and use minerals originating in the Democratic Republic of Congo in manufacturing to disclose measures taken to exercise due diligence on the source and chain of custody of the materials and the products manufactured.

- **Illicit Minerals Trade Strategy:** Requires the State Department to submit a strategy to address the illicit minerals trade in the region and a map to address links between conflict minerals and armed groups and establish a baseline against which to judge effectiveness.

- **Deposit Insurance Reforms:** Permanent increase in deposit insurance for banks, thrifts and credit unions to $250,000, retroactive to January 1, 2008.

- **Restricts U.S. Funds for Foreign Governments:** Requires the Administration to evaluate proposed loans by the IMF to a middle-income country if that country's public debt exceeds its annual Gross Domestic Product, and oppose loans unlikely to be repaid.

A

Adjustable rate mortgages (ARMs) mortgages in which the interest rate and payments are fixed for a period of time at the outset but then change according to an index value (p. 228)

Adjusted-balance method payments made are subtracted during the billing cycle, however new purchases are not included (p. 209)

Adverse feedback loop occurs when financial disruptions cause investment and consumer spending to decline (p. 72)

Adverse selection concept that the borrowers who are most willing to accept a high interest rate are the same borrowers who are most likely to default on their loans (p. 188)

Advertising paid description or presentation of a product, service, idea, or organization to encourage individuals to buy, support, or approve of it (p. 391)

Aggregate measures the collective components of the money supply that are used to estimate its size (p. 100)

Annual percentage rate (APR) nominal rate on which interest is calculated per year (p. 132)

Annual percentage yield (APY) represents the effect of compounding (p. 132)

Annuity series of payments, often to a retired person, of a set amount from a capital investment; it is paid at a specified frequency and for a set number of years or until the annuitant's death (p. 317)

Asset anything of value (p. 19)

Asset transformation the use of deposits to generate revenue by putting them to work via loans (p. 187)

Average-daily-balance method credit card balances for each day of the billing cycle are added and then divided by the number of days in the billing cycle to yield an average figure on which the finance charge is calculated (p. 210)

B

Balance of payments record of all the exchanges of goods and services that occur between two countries for a specified time period (p. 88)

Balloon mortgage mortgage in which the interest rate and payment stay fixed, but at some specified point, perhaps five years, the entire remaining balance of the loan is due in one single "balloon" payment (p. 228)

Bandit barriers bulletproof plastic shields placed between tellers and the public (p. 337)

Bank run occurs when many people try to withdraw their money at once (p. 49)

Bearer instrument instrument which is payable to whomever holds it (p. 154)

Beneficiary in a trust, the person for whose benefit the property is held (p. 325)

Benefits involve matters such as hours of employment and time off for vacation, illness, holidays, and jury duty, as well as health insurance policies, including dental and vision coverage, disability and unemployment insurance, and retirement plan (p. 410)

Bill of exchange negotiable and unconditional written order, such as a check, draft, or trade agreement, addressed by one party to another (p. 155)

Blank endorsement on a check, simply the signature of the holder; the least secure, but most negotiable, of the four main types of endorsement (p. 160)

Bond debt instrument issued for a period of more than one year with the purpose of raising capital through borrowing (p. 316)

Buy-down mortgage mortgage in which the borrower buys down, or prepays, part of the interest in order to get a lower rate (p. 230)

C

Call Report quarterly report of income and financial condition that all U.S. commercial banks are required to file with their federal and state regulatory agencies (p. 82)

CAMELS rating system examiners use to evaluate six criteria of safety and soundness of banks. Each letter stands for one of the criteria: capital adequacy, asset adequacy, management, earnings, liquidity, and sensitivity to risk (p. 83)

Captive borrower consumer with a weak credit history and limited options for securing a loan (p. 189)

Cash card commonly used at an automated teller machine (ATM) to withdraw cash, make transfers and deposits, or perform almost any other banking function at the machine by inserting the card and entering a personal identification number (PIN) (p. 172)

Central banks government banks that manage, regulate, and protect both the money supply and the banks (p. 6)

Certificates of deposit (CDs) certificates issued by banks that guarantee the payment of a fixed interest rate until a specified date in the future (p. 127)

Charge card card that specifies that consumers must pay the account in full at the end of the month (p. 171)

Charter legal approval to operate a business as a bank (p. 82)

Check 21 federal legislation that allows banks to process check information electronically (p. 123)

Check counterfeiting creating a check with desktop publishing equipment or duplicating a check with advanced color photocopiers (p. 351)

Check kiting act of opening accounts at two or more institutions and using the "float time" of available funds to create fraudulent balances (p. 349)

Code of ethics a statement adopted by an organization's management and board of directors to guide employees in taking appropriate actions in situations that could reflect negatively on the organization (p. 342)

Collateral item that secures a loan (p. 194)

Commercial banks institutions commonly thought of as banks (p. 6); banks owned by stockholders who expect a profit on their investments (p. 26)

Commercial lending lending to business enterprises (p. 264)

Commodity money money based on some item of value—for example, gold or precious stones (p. 102)

Compound interest practice of adding interest to the principal and charging interest on the new total (p. 131)

Conflict of interest occurs when two interests are at cross-purposes (p. 343)

Consumer Financial Protection Bureau (CFPB) established by the Dodd-Frank Act; sets and enforces clear rules for financial firms (p. 76)

Consumer reporting agency (CRA) company that compiles and keeps records on consumer payment habits and sells these reports to banks and other companies to use for evaluating creditworthiness (p. 202)

Corpus in a trust, property that is held (p. 325)

Correspondent bank a point of contact for other banks that do not have a branch, agency, subsidiary, or corporation in the host country (p. 303)

Country risk entire range of political, legal, social, and economic conditions that may put international business at risk (p. 304)

Credit card card that allows consumers to pay all or part of their bills each month and finance the unpaid balance (p. 172)

Credit default swap (CDS) arrangement to transfer the credit exposure of fixed income products between parties (p. 289)

Credit freeze prohibits access to your credit report (p. 360)

Credit rationing occurs when banks refuse to provide a loan, or when they lend less than the customer requested (p. 189)

Credit risk a bank's estimate of the probability that the borrower can and will repay a loan with interest as scheduled (p. 216)

Creditworthy describes a customer with a good credit rating, sufficient collateral for loans, and ongoing income (p. 14)

Cross-selling the application of a salesperson's understanding of their customer to suggest other products from which the customer could benefit (p. 373)

Currency all media of exchange circulating in a country (p. 38)

Currency risk risk posed by variations in exchange rates between countries (p. 304)

Customer Relationship Management (CRM) an approach that emphasizes the profitability of viewing customers in terms of both their present and future potential value to the business (p. 373)

Customer segmentation process of dividing customers into subgroups that have specific preferences or needs in order to tailor distinctive products to these needs and sell them profitably to the subgroups (p. 369)

Customer service the activities and programs a seller provides to make the relationship with its customers satisfying (p. 383)

Customer service representative (CSR) helps customers open checking and savings accounts, obtain debit and credit cards, and learn the various options available, such as how to bank, whether in person, through an ATM, by phone, or online; directs customers to departments that offer other services (p. 403)

Cybermarketing carefully planned and sustained effort to advertise a company, its products, and/or services through the Internet by using the most practical, effective, and up-to-date strategies (p. 391)

D

Debit card transfers money from a person's designated account to the account of the retailer (p. 172)

Debt ratio total obligations compared to total income (p. 272)

Debt service coverage ratio (DSCR) compares net operating income to the total cost of debt (p. 273)

Demand deposit type of transaction account that is payable on demand whenever the depositor chooses (p. 122)

Demographics specific shared characteristics that comprise distinct groups of consumers (p. 368)

Departmentalization organization of a bank into departments (p. 402)

Depositor a person who puts money into a bank (p. 17)

Depository intermediaries financial institutions that get funds from the public and use them to finance their business (p. 26)

Deregulation loosening of government control (p. 21)

Direct marketing promotion technique that delivers materials individually to a target market via direct mail, telemarketing, or other direct means (p. 393)

Discount rate interest rate that the Federal Reserve sets and charges for loans to member banks (p. 113)

District Reserve Banks twelve regional banks in the Federal Reserve System that carry out banking functions for government offices in their area, examine member banks in the district, decide whether to loan banks funds, recommend interest rates, and implement policy decisions of the Board of Governors (p. 61)

Dodd-Frank Act legislation resulting from the financial crash of 2008 that created the Consumer Financial Protection Bureau, ended "too big to fail" bailouts, tightened regulations, and expanded shareholders' rights (p. 76)

Donor person who creates a trust (p. 325)

Draft order signed by one party (the drawer, or drafter) that is addressed to another party (the drawee) directing the drawee to pay to someone (the payee) the amount indicated on the draft (p. 155)

E

Edge corporation financial corporations that are federally chartered and allowed to engage only in international banking or other financial transactions related to international business (p. 303)

Elements of negotiability a written, signed, unconditional promise or order to pay a fixed amount on demand or at a defined time (p. 158)

Empathy degree of caring and individual attention shown to customers (p. 384)

Equal Credit Opportunity Act (ECOA) prohibits creditors from discriminating against applicants on the basis of race, color, religion, national origin, sex, marital status, and age (pp. 75, 239)

Equity represents net assets, or total assets, minus total liabilities (p. 20); the difference between the market value of an item and what is owed on it (p. 231)

Escrow amount of money lenders require to be paid to them in advance, from which they pay the real estate taxes (p. 235)

Estate total property, including real estate and personal property, that an individual owns (p. 326)

Ethics beliefs that help people distinguish right from wrong (p. 342)

Evaluation form standardized form on which employee assessments are recorded (p. 417)

Excess reserves reserves held by a bank beyond its reserve requirement (p. 106)

Executor person named in a will to administer the estate who must identify and determine the value of all assets in the estate including securities, business interests, and retirement plans (p. 327)

F

Factoring form of asset-based lending which advances cash to a business in exchange for its receivables (p. 268); practice of buying debt at a discount (p. 323)

Fair Credit Reporting Act (FCRA) promotes accuracy, fairness, and privacy of information in the files of consumer reporting agencies (pp. 75, 239)

Fair Debt Collection Practices Act (FDCPA) protects consumers from unfair collection techniques (p. 76); prohibits abusive practices by debt collectors (p. 239)

Fannie Mae Federal National Mortgage Association (FNMA) was created during the Great Depression in 1938 to help lenders find funds to make available for mortgages (p. 247)

Federal Deposit Insurance Corporation (FDIC) guarantees deposits against bank failures up to $250,000 per depositor, per bank, and sometimes even more for special kinds of accounts or ownership categories (p. 49)

Federal funds rate amount of interest charged for short-time interbank loans (pp. 67, 113)

Federal Open Market Committee (FOMC) makes discount rate decisions (p. 68)

Federal Reserve Act created a system to stabilize the banking system in 1913 (pp. 45, 165)

Federal Reserve System Open Market Account (SOMA) account in which the Fed maintains international reserves (p. 89)

Fiat money money that is deemed legal tender by the government and it is not based on or convertible into a commodity (p. 102)

FICO score three-digit number that credit granters can use in making a loan approval decision (p. 204)

Financial intermediary institution, firm, or individual who mediates between two or more parties in a financial context (p. 5)

Fiscal policy congressional and presidential adjustment of budgetary deficits or surpluses to achieve desired economic goals (p. 70)

Fixed exchange rate occurs when the monetary valuation of one country's currency is tied to the valuation of another country's currency (p. 88)

Fixed rate mortgages loans with a fixed interest rate for the life of the loan (p. 227)

Flexible exchange rate enables currencies to fluctuate based on market conditions (p. 88)

Float funds that are on deposit at two institutions at the same time due to inefficiencies in the collection system, which allows a person or firm to earn extra income because the two institutions are paying interest on the same funds (p. 167)

Foreclosure occurs when a mortgage is not paid and the creditor seeks a court-ordered sale of the property (p. 227)

Foreign direct investment (FDI) the means through which money flows into and out of a country from other countries (p. 300)

Foreign exchange rate value of one currency in terms of another (p. 306)

Forgery counterfeiting a check or other document with the intent to defraud (p. 351)

401(k) plan allows employees to make tax-deferred contributions to a trust and direct their funds to be invested among a variety of choices; funds are redeemable upon departure or retirement (p. 326)

Fractional-reserve system (FRS) monetary policy in which only a percentage of assets must be on reserve for withdrawal; the basis of the modern banking system (p. 103)

Fraud deception deliberately practiced to secure unfair or unlawful gain (p. 348)

Fraud alert electronic warning placed on an individual's accounts to monitor for suspicious financial activity (p. 360)

Freddie Mac Federal Home Loan Mortgage Corporation buys home mortgages from banks and other lending institutions and combines them into large groups, selling interest in the groups to investors (p. 248)

Full endorsement transfers a check to another specified party (p. 161)

G

Ginnie Mae Government National Mortgage Association is part of the Department of Housing and Urban Development (HUD); it backs securities issued by holders of pools of mortgages (p. 249)

Governing documents formal set of documents that outline customer rights, the policies and rules of a bank, and how customers can expect their bank to operate (p. 141)

Government Accountability Office (GAO) the auditing arm of Congress that helps ensure that federal laws and policies are implemented properly (p. 79)

Grace period amount of time a consumer has to pay a credit card bill in full and avoid any finance charges (p. 197)

Great Depression the worst and longest economic crisis of Western industrialized nations during the twentieth century; it began in 1929 and extended worldwide until about 1939 (p. 48)

H

Holder in due course person or financial institution that acquires a check or promissory note received in good faith as payment and is entitled to payment by the drawer of the check or note (p. 158)

House flipping the practice of buying a house for below-market value and selling it at or above-market value (p. 352)

I

Identity theft occurs when someone intentionally obtains another person's personal information to use that information for personal gain (pp. 11, 355)

Inflation occurs when rising prices decrease the value of money (pp. 50, 70)

Installment loan loan for which the amount of the payments, the rate of interest, and the number of payments (or length of term) are fixed and are repaid on a periodic basis (p. 193)

Integrity steadfast adherence to a strict moral or ethical code (p. 405)

Interbank transactions transactions that occur when banks make or receive deposits from each other or from the Fed (p. 136)

Interest price paid for the use of money (pp. 17, 130)

IRA individual retirement account in which funds are invested on a before-tax basis, which allows the earnings on the investment to compound (p. 326)

J

Job description formal document that factually and concisely identifies the job, responsibilities, work involved, and education required to perform a job (p. 409)

Job fair public employment events at which employers can present employment opportunities, requirements, and personnel benefits to a large number of people at one time (p. 411)

L

Letter of credit instrument given by a bank on behalf of a buyer (applicant) to pay the bank of the seller (beneficiary) a given sum in a given time provided that documents required by the letter are presented to the issuing bank (p. 306)

Liability a cash obligation (p. 19)

Lien legal claim to the property to secure a debt (p. 194)

Liquid asset anything that can readily be exchanged, such as cash (p. 19)

Liquidity measure of how quickly things may be converted to something of value like cash; liquidity is variable, depending on the nature of the asset or liability (p. 99)

Liquidity risk risk that a bank will have to sell its assets at a loss to meet its cash demands (p. 216)

Living trust legal document that provides an expedient way to transfer property upon a person's death (p. 328)

Loan-to-value (LTV) value of the loan compared to the value of the asset (p. 236) ; the principal amount of the loan divided by the value of the securing property is the LTV ratio (p. 273)

M

Manufacturer business engaged in manufacturing some product (p. 269)

Margin stock bought for a fraction of its price and resold at a profit without the full purchase price of the stock ever having been paid (p. 48)

Marketing process of planning and executing the conception, pricing, promotion, and distribution of goods, services, and ideas to create exchanges that satisfy individual and organization objectives (p. 389)

Market risk risk that an investment will decrease in price as market conditions change (p. 216)

Medium of exchange an agreed-upon system for measuring the value of goods and services (pp. 4, 38)

Member bank any bank that is part of the Federal Reserve System (p. 61)

Merchandiser business engaged in retail trade (p. 269)

Merit-based employment selecting the person with the best qualifications for a specific position (p. 411)

Modern portfolio theory (MPT) states that within any portfolio of investments, diversification should be used to spread out risk (p. 187)

Monetary policy the Federal Reserve's goals, which include maintaining economic growth, stabilizing prices, and keeping international payments flowing smoothly (p. 67)

Money laundering depositing, investing, or exchanging money in such a way as to conceal its illegal source (p. 304)

Money market deposit accounts (MMDAs) time deposits that offer a higher rate of interest than regular savings accounts and usually require a higher initial deposit to open (p. 127)

Money supply liquid assets held by banks and individuals (p. 98)

Moral hazard occurs when borrowers take greater risks if they think the harm they will incur from those risks will somehow be minimized (p. 189)

Mortgage a (typically long-term) note secured by real property that places a lien on the property and is not released until the debt is paid (p. 227)

Mortgage-backed securities businesses that pool individual loans and sell them as a group to other investors; any risk associated with a specific loan becomes part of the collective risk of the pool of loans (p. 254)

Mortgage origination new mortgages (p. 226)

Multiplier effect expansion of the money supply that results from a Federal Reserve System member bank's ability to lend significantly in excess of its reserves (p. 106)

Mutual funds investment companies that pool money from many savers who have small amounts to invest (p. 317)

N

Need requirement for basic survival; basic physiological needs include air, food, clothing, and shelter (p. 368)

Negative equity occurs when the amount owed on a home is more than the current value of the home (p. 256)

Negotiable instrument written order or promise to pay a sum of money, either to a specified party or to the person who holds it (p. 152)

Niche market a specific customer base in a defined location that wants particular services (p. 21)

Nondepository intermediaries financial institutions that do not take or hold deposits (p. 26)

O

Open-end loan loan that is flexible, as is the term; the longer the loan is used, the more will be paid (p. 197)

Operations provides banking support services such as bookkeeping (p. 402)

Orientation employer-sponsored event which welcomes new employees to their new workplace and helps them understand its policies and how it operates (p. 412)

Outsourcing practice of having an outside party supply a product or service that the firm had been producing or performing itself (p. 320)

Overdrawn when an account has insufficient funds to meet its obligations (p. 142)

P

Performance standard defines the expectations for completing a job's essential functions and tasks for both supervisors and employees (p. 417)

Person-to-person (P2P) online payments from consumers to other consumers; facilitated by business platforms that generate revenue by charging a fee for serving as the payment intermediary (p. 173)

Phishing act of sending a user an e-mail falsely claiming to be a legitimate enterprise in an attempt to solicit private information (p. 358)

PITI acronym for principal, interest, taxes, and insurance, the four components of a typical mortgage payment (p. 234)

Point a value equal to 1 percent of a loan's principal (p. 230)

Post-dated check check which is dated later than when it was written (p. 143)

Predatory lending occurs when lenders create problems for consumers by making credit too easily available without regard to the borrower's ability to pay (p. 211)

Previous-balance method the amount owed at the beginning of the billing cycle with calculated interest on that figure, regardless of payments or charges (p. 209)

Primary reserves a bank's cash on hand as well as the required percentage amounts it has on deposit in the Federal Reserve District Bank (p. 105)

Prime rate interest rate that banks charge their best and most reliable customers (p. 113)

Probate court proceeding that settles an estate's final debts and formally passes legal title to property from the decedent to their heirs (p. 326)

Profit what is left of revenue after costs are deducted (p. 18)

Promissory note written promise to pay at a fixed or determinable future time a sum of money to a specified individual (p. 155)

Public image concept the public has of a business; should reflect the business's mission, values, and culture (p. 378)

Public relations (PR) planned and sustained effort to establish and maintain goodwill and mutual understanding between an organization and its public (p. 379)

Q

Qualified endorsement attempt to limit the liability of the endorser without limiting an instrument's further negotiability (p. 162)

R

Radio frequency identification (RFID) uses a transponder to convey identifying information including the account holder's account or balance information and the fees being assessed to the account by the business for products or services (p. 174)

Recession occurs when there is a decline in total production lasting a minimum of two consecutive quarters (at least six months) (p. 51)

Redlining illegal banking practice in which banks refuse to lend to residents of certain neighborhoods (pp. 113, 240)

Reserve liquidity ways to convert reserves readily to cash (p. 47)

Restrictive endorsement limits the use of the instrument to a means specified by the endorser (p. 161)

Retail banks thrift institutions such as mutual savings banks, savings and loans, and credit unions, developed to help individuals who are not served by commercial banks (p. 6)

Returned check check written on an account that does not have adequate funds to cover it and which is returned unpaid to the person who deposited it (p. 169)

Return on assets (ROA) the ratio of net income to total assets (p. 20)

Return on equity (ROE) measures how well a bank is using its equity (p. 20)

Revolving credit line of credit with a maximum limit that can be used on an ongoing basis until the limit is reached (p. 207)

Risk averse describes an investor who would prefer to invest in products that have a low risk of failure (p. 287)

Risk preferrer investor who seeks a high level of return on investments (p. 287)

ROCA score composite score of foreign bank performance in four distinct areas: risk management, operational controls, compliance, and asset quality (p. 87)

S

Scam fraudulent scheme or swindle (p. 352)

Search engine optimization (SEO) the practice of maximizing the number of visitors to a website by ensuring that the site appears near the top of the list of search engine results (p. 391)

Secondary reserves bank reserves that include securities the bank purchases from the federal government and deposits that are due from other banks (p. 105)

Secured loan loan in which some item of value backs the loan in case the borrower defaults on it (p. 194)

Shared appreciation mortgage mortgage which can lower interest rates for borrowers who agree to share profits with the lender when the house is sold (p. 230)

Short-term loan loan, usually for a year or less, used by businesses to finance expenses for seasonal or cyclical business costs, such as increasing inventory or maintaining the business until predictable receivables arrive (p. 266)

Small Business Administration (SBA) federal entity that offers a number of financial, technical, and management programs to help businesses (p. 279)

Smart card credit, debit, or other type of card that has an embedded microchip (pp. 23, 172)

Sniffer programs electronic programs that capture account numbers and PINs; they can be installed on computers via spyware (p. 359)

Social responsibility obligation to profitably serve employees and customers in an ethical and law-abiding manner (p. 390)

Sovereign wealth fund government program where excess cash is segregated from a country's official currency reserves and can be used to generate profit for the country by making investments (p. 303)

Spam junk e-mail (p. 358)

Speculation the act of making investments based on anticipated or hoped-for outcomes; speculators do not have an ownership stake in the asset being insured (p. 290)

Spread difference between what a bank pays in interest and what it receives in interest (p. 17)

Stagflation condition of a high rate of inflation, a slow rate of economic growth, and a high rate of unemployment (p. 51)

Stale check check which is dated six months or more before it is presented for payment or deposit (p. 143)

Statement savings account provides a monthly or quarterly computerized statement detailing all account activity, including interest credited and fees charged (p. 126)

Stock capital raised by a corporation through the issuance of shares entitling holders to an ownership interest in the corporation (p. 316)

Straw buyer someone who agrees to use their personal information to buy a home at a falsely inflated price (p. 352)

Strength of Support Assessment (SOSA) reflects how well a foreign bank is able to provide appropriate guidance, oversight, and financial backing to its U.S. offices (p. 87)

Subprime rates rates that are higher than normal to offset the increased risk represented by a less-than-perfect borrower (p. 201)

Sum-of-digits method method of calculating finance charges that takes the total finance charge, divides it by the number of months in the loan term, and assigns a higher ratio of interest to the early payments (p. 208)

Synthetic financial products products that lack an underlying value in their assets (p. 291)

System to Estimate Examinations Ratings (SEER) automated system that analyzes and compares historical supervisory ratings of banks with their Call Report data and provides an additional method of capturing changes in financial performance that may require supervisory intervention (p. 83)

T

Target market preselected group of buyers for whom a product or service is created and to whom a marketing campaign is directed (p. 369)

Taylor rule provides ideas for how to use short-term interest rates to achieve the goals of a central bank, including keeping the economy stable and controlling inflation (p. 69)

Telecommuting allows employees to work from home via computer (p. 410)

Teller bank position responsible for processing customer transactions and balancing the cash drawer daily by adding deposits and subtracting withdrawals from the opening cash funds (p. 405)

Term loan finances permanent working capital, equipment, real estate, business expansion, or acquisition of another business; terms and rates vary with the asset securing the loan or the expected life of the asset (p. 266)

Time deposits deposits including savings accounts, money market deposit accounts, certificates of deposit (CDs), and various bonds that are held for or mature at a specified time (p. 126)

Transaction account account that allows transactions to occur without restrictions on the frequency or the volume of transactions (p. 122)

Transit number nine-digit number that identifies the bank that holds the checking account and is responsible for payment (p. 168)

Trust arrangement by which one party holds property on behalf of another party for certain defined purposes (p. 325)

Truth in Lending Act (TILA) Title I of the Consumer Credit Protection Act of 1968; landmark legislation guaranteeing that all information about cost of a loan is provided in writing to consumers (p. 74); promotes informed use of consumer credit by requiring disclosures about its terms and costs (p. 239)

U

Underwriting process of reviewing a loan for soundness (p. 200)

Unsecured loan loan backed only by the reputation and creditworthiness of the borrower (p. 195)

U.S. Treasury Exchange Stabilization Fund (ESF) account in which the Treasury maintains international reserves (p. 89)

V

Variable annuity combines the opportunity for tax-deferral with a choice of portfolios and the flexibility to vary annual contributions according to the investors' needs or market conditions (p. 326)

Viral marketing using ordinary people to help spread the word about a product or service (p. 393)

W

Want something that an individual would prefer to have but could live without if necessary (p. 368)

War driving criminal practice of driving around to find retailers with weaknesses in their Internet security systems (p. 359)

Wholesale banks commercial banks that specialize only in business banking (p. 26)

Will document by which an individual gives instructions as to what is to happen upon their death in regard to property and remains (p. 326)

INDEX

regulations that facilitate private
stability of, 81–83
trust and, 83–84
Basic checking accounts, 123–124
Beneficiary, 325, 328
Benefits, 410
Bill payment services, 173
Bills of exchange, 155
Biometrics, 174–175
Blank endorsement, 160–162
BMW Financial Services, 376
Board of Governors (Fed), 6, 60–62, 68
Bonds, 316–317
Brick and mortar banking model, 8
Bridge loans, 268
Broadcast media, 392–393
Brochures, 381
Broker, 29
Brokerage services, 29, 310, 316–317, 403
Buffet, Warren, 345
Builder-bailout mortgage schemes, 353
Bump-ups, 127
Business
interest rates and, 111–113
types of, 269–270
Business customers, 370
Business insurance, 314–316
Business plan, 274
Buy-down mortgage, 230

C

Call report, 82,
Callable CD, 127–128,
CAMELS rating system, 83–84
Capacity, 201, 237
Capital investments, 322
Capital services, 322–323
CAPLines loan program (SBA), 284
Captive borrower, 189,
Car loans, 193–194
Careers in banking. See Climbing the Ladder feature; Employment opportunities; and specific job titles
Cash back transaction, 160
Cash cards, 172
Cash flow, loan decision and, 218
Cash management, 319–324
Catalog of Federal Domestic Assistance, 250
CDS. See Credit default swap

Center for Financial Services Innovation (CFSI), 218
Center for Financial Training, 413
Central bank, 6
Certificates of deposit (CDs), 127–128
Charge cards, 171
Charitable remainder trust (CRT), 328
Charter, 82
Chartered financial analyst (CFA), 121
Check(s), 154–155
alteration of, 351
presenting for payment, 158–164
Check 21 Act, 52, 123, 166, 177–178, 350
Check fraud, 349–351
Checking account, 122–126, 169
Check kiting, 349–350
Check processing, 165–170
Chief financial officer (CFO), 407
Circulation of money, 107–108
Citigroup Inc., 344
Clay, Henry, 44
Clearing House Interbank Payment System (CHIPS), 177
Climbing the Ladder feature
Associate Team Leader to Product Manager, 299
Commercial Banking Associate to Portfolio Manager, 263
Human Resources Assistant to Specialist, 3
Loan Service Clerk to Credit Card Risk Specialist, 185
Teller to District Manager, 401
Trust Associate to Trust Department Director, 121
Web Content Consultant to Documentation Manager, 37
Closed account fraud, 351,
Closed-circuit television (CCTV), 337,
Closing, loan, 201, 237
Code of ethics, 342–343
Coins, 39–40, 102
Collateral, 194–195, 201, 215, 218, 237
Colonial currency, 39–40
Commercial bank, 6, 26, 81
Commercial credit analysis, 272–276
Commercial lending, 264, 275–276
Commercial liability insurance, 314–315
Commercial loan(s), 262–297

credit analysis for, 272–276
nature of, 264–266
purposes of, 65
types of, 266–268
Commercial loan officer, 410
Commercial paper, 156
Commodity Futures Trading Commission (CFTC), 65, 79
Commodity money, 102
Common stock, 316
Community Advantage 7(a) Loans, 284
Community Reinvestment Act (CRA) projects, 217–218, 240–241, 381
Competition in banking, 8
Compound interest, 131–132
Comptroller of Currency, 45, 47, 49, 82
Computer operator, 407
Confidentiality, 342
Conflict of interest, 343
Congress, fiscal policy and, 70
Consumer Credit Protection Act, 74–75
Consumer Financial Protection Bureau (CFPB), 12, 29, 76, 79, 82, 243
Consumer loan(s), 193–196. See also Loans
Consumer loan theory, 186–192
Consumer payments, 171–176
Consumer protection, 64, 74–80, 83
Consumer protection legislation, 239–240
Consumer reporting agency, 202–203
Contract financing, 268
Conventional mortgage, 227–228
Corporate world, ethics and, 344–345
Corpus, 325
Correspondent bank, 167, 303
Cost of credit, 208–211
Council of Economic Advisors, 68
Council of Public Relations Firms, 380
Counterfeit currency, 349
Counterfeiting, check, 351
Country risk, 304
Coverdell Education Savings Account (CESA), 326
Credit
analyzing, 202–205
commercial, 272–276
cost of. See Cost of credit